Fabric for Fashion
The Complete Guide

Natural and man-made fibres

Clive Hallett and Amanda Johnston

Photo editing and commissioned photography by Myka Baum

Laurence King Publishing

Introduction

Section 1:
Animal fibres

Section 2:
Plant fibres

Section 3:
Man-made fibres

Useful information

Introduction   8

Fibres to fabrics   12

Introducing colour   44

Wool   62

Luxury animal fibres   86

Silk   104

Linen   128

Cotton   142

Alternative plant fibres   166

Synthetic fibres   184

Artificial fibres   212

Fabric and the fashion industry   236

Resources/Glossary   248

Index/Credits/Acknowledgements   262

Introduction

Fashion design and textile knowledge are often taught as separate disciplines, and knowledge of the raw materials and processes that make up a fabric are not usually integrated into fashion studies.

A confident understanding of fabrics, and the fibres they are composed of, is fundamental to the design process, allowing one to make informed choices rather than arbitrary decisions based upon surface appeal.

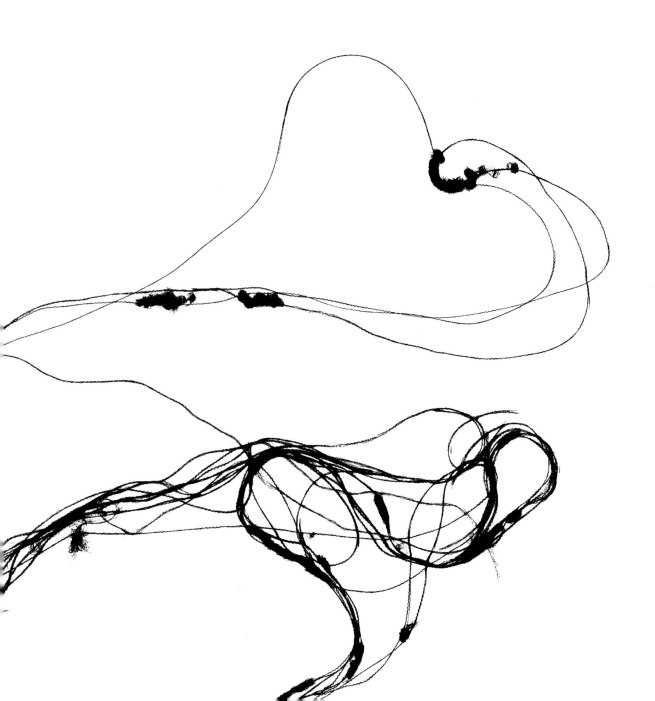

This book is intended as an easily navigable fabric lexicon that explores the relationship between fashion and textiles and encourages an awareness of fibres and fabrics in a broader fashion context. It is designed to inform the reader of the endless possibilities that fabrics offer to the design process. It is not intended as an exhaustive technical manual, but rather as a tool to inform, inspire and encourage the creative use of fabrics. The content of the book is intended to support an essential knowledge base, which is fundamental to developing a range of fashion products.

Focusing in turn on animal, plant and man-made fibres, each of three sections considers the origins of specific fibres within these classifications, their history, provenance and the processing journey to finished fabric. Additionally, it explores the socio-economic factors that may have influenced the importance of a specific fibre, in order to create an awareness of how one's choice of material may impact upon ecological, sustainable and ethical issues.

Each section provides an extensive database of terminology, to encourage informed and effective communication with industry professionals. This is underpinned with information about processes generic to all fibres regardless of origin. The importance of colour is explored within a separate section and the final chapter contextualizes the interrelationship of all the components that make up the fashion industry.

'The bond between fashion and textiles is one of mutual dependency and reciprocal influence; a shared destiny based upon our need for clothing.'
Fashion and Textiles: An Overview
Colin Gale and Jasbir Kaur (Berg Publishers, 2004)

Our relationship with fibres and fabrics is intimate and all-encompassing; we are surrounded by, sleep in and are clothed by them. Historically textiles have been valued not only for their practical and aesthetic properties, but also as incredibly powerful cultural indicators. Textiles display the artistry and ingenuity of a civilization, the most precious examples of which even help to denote status within society. In contemporary life an ever-more sophisticated and growing range of fabrics expresses the complex language of fashion.

The textile industry may be simplistically viewed as the supplier of the raw materials for the fashion industry, whereas in reality the two industries are inextricably linked. Developments in the textile industry invariably impact upon the fashion industry, and vice versa. Fabrics are also incredibly powerful as a strong visual indicator of a brand, often defining aspects of a brand identity.

The fashion designer's relationship with fabric is at the heart of the creative process. The right choice of fabric is fundamental to good design and is instrumental to its success. The better the understanding of the material, the more effective is the symbiosis between the design and fabric.

'The future of fashion lies in fabrics. Everything comes from fabrics.'
Donna Karan

(opposite page) Stunning creation composed of layers of different fabrics, encrusted with beadwork and embroidery over lace and tulle, by Japanese designer Tamae Hirokawa for Somarta.

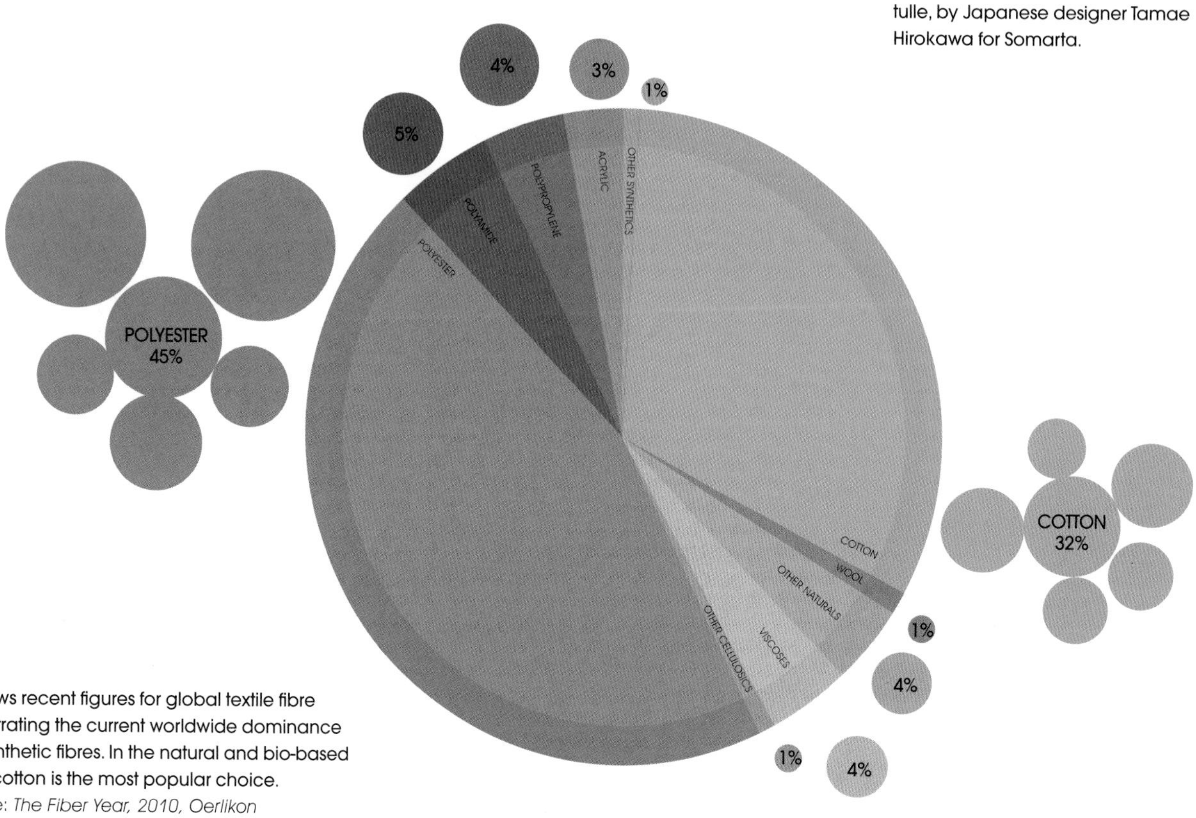

4%   3%   1%

5%

POLYESTER

POLYAMIDE

POLYPROPYLENE

ACRYLIC

OTHER SYNTHETICS

POLYESTER
45%

COTTON
32%

COTTON

WOOL

OTHER NATURALS

OTHER CELLULOSICS

VISCOSE

1%

4%

1%   4%

This chart shows recent figures for global textile fibre demand, illustrating the current worldwide dominance of low-cost synthetic fibres. In the natural and bio-based fibre sectors, cotton is the most popular choice.
Statistic source: *The Fiber Year, 2010, Oerlikon*

Fabrics: the raw material of fashion

Throughout history people have clothed themselves with natural fabrics made from animal or plant fibres. Man's ingenuity in developing and processing these raw materials has become more sophisticated over time.

The twentieth century heralded the invention of synthetic fabrics, originally developed to mimic the attributes of natural fibres, and provide inexpensive alternatives with a low-maintenance appeal. Brand names such as Dacron, Terylene, Orlon, Acrlian and Crimplene are examples of materials that were made from the main generic synthetics group that includes polyamide, nylon, polyester, acetate and acrylic. These fibres and filaments are primarily derived from coal and oil-based raw materials. The cotton and wool trade organizations have invested in fibre development technology and proactive marketing campaigns to regain the market share initially lost to the man-made materials.

Recent decades have seen a growing appreciation of natural fibres at accessible price points. Today, exciting potential is offered by leaps in technology with natural fibres, man-made artificial regenerates and refined synthetics. They offer exciting options for an increasingly complex range of consumer demands. Sophisticated developments in man-made textiles offer a look quite different to traditional, natural materials, and do not work against them but alongside them instead. Combinations of microfibres (the new generation of ultra-fine synthetics), with regenerated yarns, silks, cottons and linens provide new looks and performance potential. The emphasis placed on recycling in our everyday life has influenced current research into the development of biodegradable synthetics.

'Fashion designers are alert to the recent developments in fibres and fabrics and the importance of the right choice for their collections.'
Sarah E. Braddock Clark and Marie Mahoney, *Techno Textiles 2*

The future of fabrics

As well as aesthetic considerations, there are many issues to take into account when working with fabrics. This showpiece from the exhibition 'Wonderland' (opposite page) explores alternative approaches informed by factors such as biodegradability and the lifespan of a product.

'Wonderland' is the result of a dynamic collaborative project between Professor Tony Ryan from Sheffield University and designer Helen Storey, incorporating the work of textile designer Trish Belford. The project brings together the worlds of art, fashion and science in an engaging installation first opened as an exhibition at the London College of Fashion in January 2008.

'Wonderland' was conceived as a series of disappearing dresses made from textiles that slowly dissolve in water to create a visually arresting metaphor for the central themes of the project. Each dress behaves differently as it enters the water, resulting in vibrant underwater fireworks that express the beauty of biodegradability.

The disappearing dresses provoke inquiry into the environmental sustainability of our current fashion industry and how we deal with waste. The original focus of the collaboration was the problem of plastic bottle waste and the concept of 'intelligent' packaging. This has resulted in the development of a material that dissolves in hot water to form a gel in which seeds can be sown, with the potential to revolutionize the packaging industry.

Introduction

Fibres to fabrics

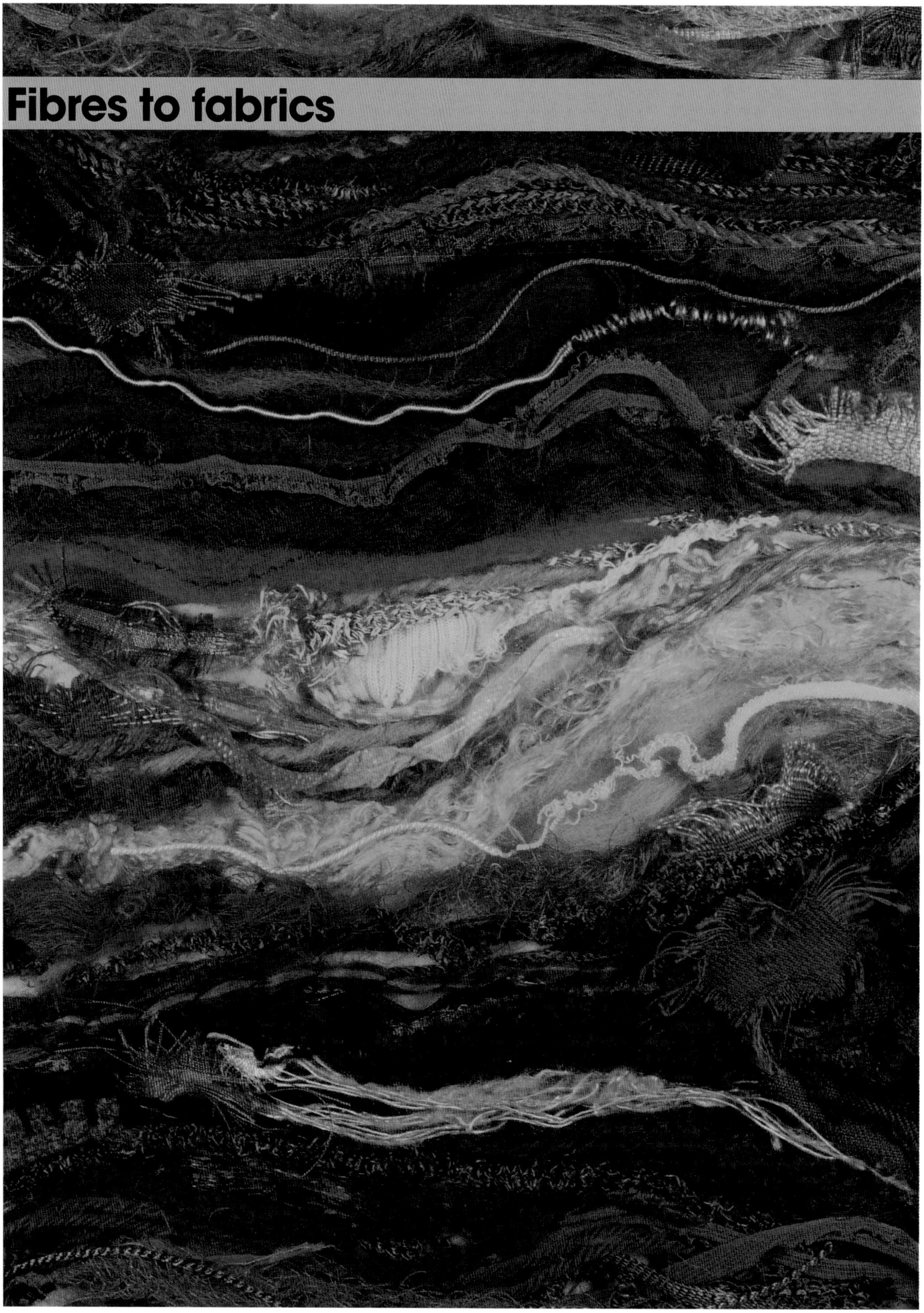

As an introduction to the world of natural fabrics, this chapter examines the processes involved in the manufacturing of textiles, from the raw fibre through to the finished material, ready to use. It is a generic account irrespective of fibre category, whether derived from animal or vegetable sources. Each fibre type will be examined in detail in its respective chapter.

Fibre to yarn

All natural fabrics begin life as **fibres**. These natural fibres, whether animal or plant in origin, are spun into **yarn**, which in turn is constructed into fabric.

Fibre

The term fibre can be applied to animal, vegetable or mineral substances, and describes a long, thin, flexible structure. Fibres exist in a natural or **synthetic** form and can be processed into yarns.

Yarn

Yarns, or threads, are fibres that have been spun together to create a continuous length of interlocked fibres. They are usually knitted or woven together to make fabric, and may be dyed before or after this process.

Carding

Carding is the process of brushing raw or washed fibres to prepare them for spinning. A large variety of fibres can be carded, including all animal hairs, wool and cotton. **Flax** is not carded, but is threshed, a process of beating cereal plants in order to separate the grain from the straw. Carding can also be used to create mixes of different fibres or of different colours.

Hand carding uses two brushes that look a little like dog brushes. The fibres are brushed between them until they all align, more or less, in the same direction. The fibres are then rolled off the brushes and evenly distributed into a **rolag**, a loose roll of fibres, ready for spinning.

The machine-carding device is called a drum carder and can vary in size from tabletop to room size. The fibres are fed into a series of rollers that straighten and align them. When the fibres are removed from the roller drums they form a flat orderly mass known as a **bat**.

Combing

Combing is usually an additional operation after carding, and gives a better, smoother finish to the fibres and to the eventual fabric. Combs are used to remove the short fibres, known as **noils**, and arrange the remaining fibres in a flat bundle, all facing in the same direction.

(opposite page) Yarns or threads, visible in these frayed fabric edges, can be made of both natural and man-made fibres. Colour can be applied to either finished fabric or the yarn, which is then knitted or woven together to make the fabric.

Wool fibre dyed in a range of glowing autumnal shades in preparation for the spinning process. This image captures the characteristic springy ringlets of wool fibre.

Hand carding and blending fibres. Association of Weavers, Spinners and Dyers.

Blending fibres of different characteristics together creates innovative new yarns that can embody the best aspects of each fibre. The mixture of alpaca and silk in this example creates a mélange of both texture and colour; the alpaca lends warmth and softness while the silk sharpens the texture by lending it lustre.

Spinning

Twisting fibres together by **spinning** binds them into a stronger, longer yarn. Originally fibres were twisted by hand, then a hand-held 'stick', or spindle, made the process a little more comfortable. The invention of the spinning wheel allowed for continuous, faster spinning. Used in a domestic environment, spinning wheels were hand or foot operated. Water-driven spinning machines were followed by steam-driven machinery, which took domestic spinning out of the home and into the factory. The invention of electricity made the spinning process much more sophisticated and, with the exception of handicraft spinning, made it a full-time commercial enterprise.

Twist and ply

The direction in which the yarn is spun is called **twist**. A 'Z' twist shows a right-hand angle, while an 'S' twist has a left-hand angle. The tightness of the twist is measured in TPI (twists per inch).

Two or more spun yarns may be twisted together to make a **ply**, a thicker yarn, or as a way of introducing an alternative yarn to create a **mélange** effect.

(above) Hand spinning – in this case llama wool in Peru – is a labour-intensive process that is today only practised for specialist craft purposes. The yarn is spun by means of a hand-held wooden spindle, using methods that remain fundamentally unchanged since early spinning techniques that predate the spinning wheel.

Useful terminology

Blend A yarn containing two or more different fibres.

Bouclé yarns Curled or looped yarns.

Cellulose fibres Natural and man-made fibres regenerated from plants.

Chenille yarn Woven fabric is cut into warp strips and used as yarn, which has a velvet-like, 'caterpillar' appearance.

Cotton system Spinning system for cotton and similar fibres.

Crêpe yarn Highly twisted yarn with a granular texture.

Crimp Natural or artificial wave to the fibre or yarn.

Elastane Generic name for stretch yarn.

Filament A single, continuous strand of fibre. Any man-made yarn of one or more strands running the entire length of the yarn.

Hank Unsupported coil of yarn. The two ends are tied together to maintain the shape. Also called a skein.

Marl yarns Two different-coloured yarns twisted together.

Metallic yarns Yarns containing metal threads or metallic elements.

Roving A long narrow bundle of fibre with a slight twist to hold it together.

Scouring Removal of natural fats, oils and dirt from a yarn.

Skein Coiled yarn with tied ends to keep the shape.

Tow Mass of man-made filaments without twist.

Yarn count Numerical expression for size of yarn, denoting a certain length of yarn for a fixed weight. The higher the count, the finer the yarn.

(left) Sophisticated modern spinning in a pristine industrial environment.

(above and right) Spinning frames processing single-ply and two-ply yarn at Lightfoot Farm in Maine, USA.

Outfit in double-faced 100 per cent wool jersey. The face of the cloth is a marl, or mélange, jersey and the reverse is a looped fleece, which resembles the fabric more usually associated with casual cotton sportswear. Designer Julien David has fashioned a luxurious take on the ubiquitous grey marl in this version of the sports-luxe trend.

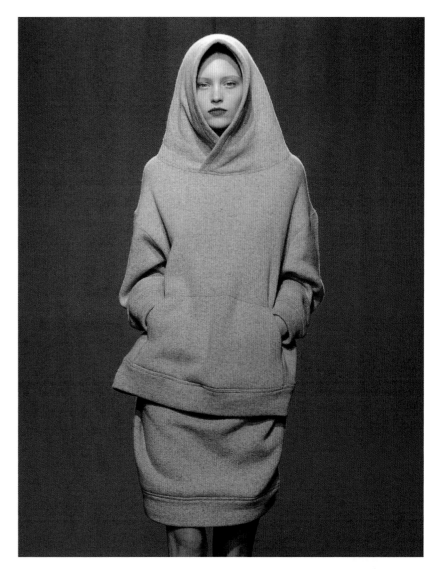

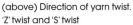

(above) Direction of yarn twist. 'Z' twist and 'S' twist

(right) Plying yarn. Simple 'S' twist with two single yarns, 'S' twist with three single yarns and 'Z' twist with two two-ply yarns

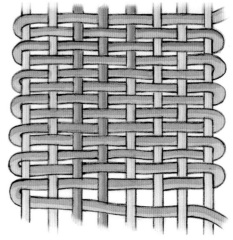

Warp and weft threads. Warp threads run along the length of the fabric. Weft threads run across the width of the fabric from selvedge to selvedge. Weaving can be described as the incorporation of the weft threads, which are sometimes referred to as picks or filling yarns.

Fabric construction

Fabric is a flexible material comprised of natural or artificial fibres that have been spun into threads or yarns. Textile fabric can be manufactured in several ways. The primary techniques are **weaving** or **knitting**, although yarns can also be knotted or interlaced, for example by **crocheting**, **lace** making or **macramé**. **Felting**, the process of pressing together and matting fibres so that they interlock, is another alternative.

Weaving

Weaving is the process of interweaving two sets of threads, the **warps** (vertical) and the **wefts** (horizontal), on a weaving loom. Three basic weave types, **plain**, **twill** and **satin**, form the majority of woven fabrics. There are also several alternative weaving techniques that create more complex fabrics.

Plain weave

Plain weave is the most basic and possibly the oldest type of weave construction. The warps and wefts criss-cross each other at right angles, with each weft thread passing over one warp thread then under the next warp thread. Plain weaves are sometimes referred to as **taffeta** weaves.

A plain weave can be coarse or smooth in texture, dependent on the fineness or coarseness of the **thread count** used to weave the fabric.

Basket weave is a variation on plain weave, where two or more threads are bundled together and woven as one in the warp and weft directions, resulting in a more pronounced 'basket' construction.

Types of plain-woven fabrics include chiffon, organza, taffeta and canvas.

Twill weave

Twill weave has a visual diagonal line or rib effect, caused when the weft yarn crosses over and under two or more warp yarns. The diagonal line may also be referred to as a **wale**. The visual effect is most obvious on a heavyweight cotton fabric. By contrast, on a lightweight shirting cotton the diagonal rib will be hardly visible.

Unlike plain weaves, twill-weave fabrics have a different appearance from the **face** (right side) to the reverse or back, the face side having the more pronounced wale. Twill weaves are harder wearing than plain weaves of the same yarn and count, and are therefore particularly suited to utility wear. **Denim** is possibly the most famous of all the workwear fabrics, and true denim is of twill-weave construction.

Any fibre type can be woven in this way, however the term is generically used to describe cotton fabrics.

Twill fabrics are more pliable and have a better **drape** than similar plain-weave fabrics, and they also tend to recover better from wrinkles. Higher/finer yarn counts can be used for twill weaving and can be packed much closer together, therefore producing higher-count fabrics that are more durable and **water-resistant**. An example is the traditional Burberry trench coat, which was designed and made for army officers and worn in the trenches of World War I.

Types of twill-woven fabrics include serge, flannel, denim, gabardine, cavalry twill and chino. Traditional iconic herringbone and hound's-tooth design fabrics, as well as Scottish tartans, are all of twill-weave construction.

(above) Weaving frame.

(right and far right) Twill weaves. Weft threads pass over and then under two warp threads (2x2 twill) and are staggered by one thread per row creating the visible diagonal construction. If the wefts pass over three and under one (warps) it would be referred to as 1x3 twill.

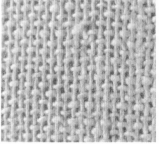
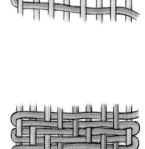

(above and right) Plain weaves. Weft threads pass under and over alternative warp threads forming a criss-cross construction.

This striking rescaled hound's-tooth abandons its tailoring connotations when expressed in oversized sequins. This A-line shift with cut-out shoulders references 1960s op art aesthetics. Autumn/Winter 2008 collection by Ashish.

An updated classic hound's-tooth fabric from Linton Tweeds.

Designer Derek Lam sculpts and feminizes the appeal of this traditional wool herringbone, a fabric that is usually associated with men's outerwear.

The alternating diagonal ribs of this traditional woollen tweed fabric, with a twill-weave construction, are executed in two colours, creating a classic herringbone design. The scale of design and the contrasting colours have almost limitless possibilities.

Up-cycling

This term describes the reappropriation of fabric that has already had one life for one purpose, and reworking, reassigning or reinventing it to give it a new life serving a different purpose or aesthetic. Here, cotton twill is glamorized through this process. This conceptual evening dress from Gary Harvey Creative was constructed to showcase the concept of up-cycling. Vintage Burberry trench coats are used to model the skirt. Raincoats were originally made from a tightly-woven fine yarn-count twill weave to provide a drapable and water-resistant fabric.

Satin and sateen weaves

The most visible aspect of a satin weave is its high sheen and the way it reflects light. Sateen, in contrast, has a dull sheen and does not shimmer. Both, however, have a very smooth surface, due to similarities in the way they are woven. One has a predominance of warp threads to the face or right side of the fabric, while the other has a predominance of weft threads; this prevalence of threads running in a single direction accounts for the smoothness of the resulting fabric.

The construction also contributes to level of sheen in the fabric, although the deciding factor is the choice of fibre. Historically, silk yarns were used to weave satin fabrics while cotton was used for sateen. Today, high-quality satin is still made from silk while less expensive alternatives utilize man-made fibres. Cotton or cotton-rich yarns are used for sateen.

Pile weaving

When **pile weaving**, the warps that will eventually create the pile are woven over rods or wires that have been inserted into the gaps or 'loops' of the raised alternative yarns. These then lie in loops over the rods. When the rods are removed the loops can be cut to create a **pile fabric**, or left intact to create a **loop-back fabric**. Velvet and corduroy are examples of pile woven fabric.

This sample of sateen jacquard weave is a cotton-and-viscose blend. Viscose is a less expensive alternative to traditional silk that offers similar visual characteristics. The sheen is achieved by a combination of the sateen weave and the viscose fibre; the cotton component of the design has a more matte finish.

A magnified image of cotton sateen showing a predominance of weft threads to the face of the fabric. In this example, each weft loops over four warps. It is this predominance of wefts to the face side of the fabric that gives sateen its smooth finish and helps reflect the light that gives it its characteristic sheen.

Corduroy

Corduroy is described using the term wales; these refer to the raised ridges or ribs that run vertically down the fabric parallel to the **selvedge**. The wider the wales, the lower the numerical expression, and vice versa. The number of wales that fit into one inch (2.5 cm) is the wale count. 21-wale corduroy implies there are 21 wales per inch. Counts vary from 1.5 to 21. 16 and smaller can be referred to as pin cord, while 3 and under is sometimes referred to as elephant or jumbo cord. Corduroy was originally made from cotton. Bedford cord has a flatter surface with a minimal raised wale, originally made from cotton or wool.

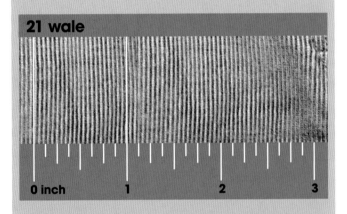

21 wale

0 inch   1   2   3

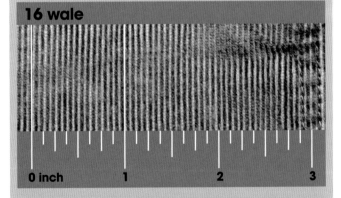

16 wale

0 inch   1   2   3

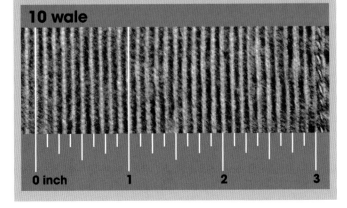

10 wale

0 inch   1   2   3

Double-cloth weaving

Double-cloth weaving creates a fabric that has two face or right sides (**double face**) and no wrong or reverse side. The fabric is constructed by using several sets of warps and wefts, interconnected to form a cloth of two layers held together by additional binding wefts.

Examples of double-cloth weaving date back to pre-Columbian Peru, where cotton and **alpaca** yarns were woven to create a warm alpaca outer layer and a comfortable cotton under layer, all as a single fabric.

Double-cloth weaves make up well into self-lined or double-faced coats and jackets, closed off with quasi-invisible hand stitching that eliminates the need for facings or bindings to finish off the raw edges.

Examples of double-cloth weave include **brocade** fabric, blankets and satin ribbons.

Men's silk velvet quilted baseball-influenced jacket and multi-coloured straight weave trousers by Ioannis Dimitrousis. The sporty styling lends this traditionally luxe woven pile fabric a casual appeal.

Gloverall double-faced check-back cloth. The cloth is woven and held together with draw threads. After being woven the cloth is teasled up to create a face pile, then it is cropped/brushed and finally finished off. The little torn threads on the edge of the solid red face side of the fabric are the draw threads that hold the two sides together.

Jacquard weaving

The **jacquard loom** enables the automatic production of an unlimited variety of designs. Prior to the jacquard process the warp ends had to be manually selected and lifted by a second operator apart from the weaver. This was a slow and labour-intensive process that limited the complexity of the design. With the jacquard loom selected warps are programmed to lift independently of each other, thus creating far greater versatility of design.

This form of weaving was developed and perfected by French inventor Joseph Jacquard (1752–1834), at the advent of the nineteenth century. The mechanism allowed for the production of sophisticated patterns without lengthy, repetitive manual processing. The original machines were mechanical, with the fabric design punched onto cards that were joined to form a chain that would direct the machine. In the early 1980s, Italian manufacturers introduced the first electronic jacquard machines.

The term **jacquard** is not specific to any loom, but indicative of the added control mechanism that automates the design. It refers to a type of weaving process and is also descriptive of a type of fabric. The term can be applied to both woven and knitted fabrics, as well as some **fully-fashioned** knitwear.

Tapestry weaving

Considered an art form, **tapestry weaving** is done on a vertical loom. It is sometimes called weft-faced weaving because all the warps are hidden, unlike fabric weaving where both the warps and the wefts may be visible. By only having the wefts visible it is possible to create more precise designs. Historically the imagery was usually pictorial and very often allegorical.

Kilims and Navajo blankets and rugs are all forms of tapestry weaving.

(left) Jacquard loom showing the production of a complex double-layer jacquard weave. Image provided by CELC Masters of Linen (Confédération Européenne du Lin et du Chanvre).

(above) The floral pattern created by a jacquard loom is apparent in the light-reflective satin weave and contrasting plain weave in this Alexander McQueen oyster silk jacquard dress with tulle underskirt.

Ikat weaving

Before weaving, the warps or wefts are dyed different colours at predetermined intervals along their length, using a form of **resist** or **tie-dyeing** process. Double **ikat** implies that both wefts and warps have been dyed.

If the dyed threads are warps the pattern is visible to the weaver, who can adjust them to line up to each other. In some cultures the patterns will be aligned to perfection, while in others misalignment is preferred. Weaving with dyed wefts makes it much harder to control the design, therefore this technique is used when precision is not the objective. Double ikats are the most difficult to produce. The most precise forms of ikat weaving are the Japanese **oshima** and **kasuri**.

There is evidence of ikat weaving in pre-Columbian Central and South America as well as many regions of South and East Asia. However, the name ikat has its origins in the Malay language. Today, through extensive common use, the word describes both the weaving technique and the fabric itself.

Ikat weave silk skirt featuring the characteristic 'blurred' edge of the woven motif by Tamerlane's Daughters, launched in 2004 by Karina Deubner. The designer's own European and Asian background influences the signature aesthetic of cultural fusion that her unique pieces embody. The label pays homage to traditional crafts and vanishing cultures by creating one-off pieces incorporating nineteenth-century textiles from Central Asia and Europe.

Useful terminology

Bias Fabric cut at 45 degrees to warp and weft. This cut exploits the natural stretch of the fabric so that it drapes well over the curves of the body.

Cut pile Cut loops of yarn that form a pile, as with velvet and corduroy.

Drape The behaviour of the fabric, how it falls and hangs, affected by the yarn, weave construction, weight and finishing processes.

Grain The straight of the fabric or warp.

Handle The touch of the fabric, warm, cool, smooth, granular, fluffy, etc.

Left-hand twill Diagonal ribs run up from bottom right to top left on face.

Loop pile Uncut pile fabric, such as towelling.

Nap Raised surface of fabric.

Piece A complete length of fabric as purchased from a mill or wholesaler.

Reversible Fabric that can be used either side up.

Right-hand twill Diagonal ribs run up from bottom left to top right on face.

Selvedge The firm side edges of the fabric running parallel to the warp.

Union fabric Fabric with wefts and warps of different fibres, for example a cotton warp and wool weft.

Knitting

Knitting can refer to two areas of clothing. Sweater-knits are garments that are partially or totally constructed on a knitting machine or by hand knitting. **Jerseywear** is a range of various garments, including T-shirts and polo shirts, that are cut and made from fabric that has been knitted. Integral knitting using advanced technology is also known as jerseywear, and is used for seamless men's underwear and women's brassieres.

The term knitwear refers to any fabric that has been knitted, regardless of how fine it is.

Knitted fabrics

Knitted fabric is constructed from yarn by means of a series of interlinked loops. This can be achieved by hand using individual needles, by using hand-operated machines, known as hand-frame knitting, or by power machine, simply called machine knitting. The introduction of machine knitting turned hand knitting into a craft that has gone into and out of fashion depending on social moods of the time.

The size of the **stitch**, whether hand or machine knitted, dictates the fineness or chunkiness of the fabric, and is dependent on the size of the needles and the thickness of the yarn. In hand knitting the needles are described by a number, while in machine knitting the term **gauge** is used, but is also reflective of the needle size. In both cases the higher the numerical expression the finer the knitting. Standard gauges in commercial knitting are: 2.5 for chunky outdoor sweaters; 7 and 15 gauges are mid-weights; 18 and 21 gauges for fine knitwear; 28 gauge is interlock, used for rugby shirts and heavier-weight loop-back fabrics; 30 is classified as superfine; 32 gauge is jerseywear.

Units of measurement for fine knits

In the UK and the US very fine knitting, as used for hosiery, is described using the term **denier**, which defines opaqueness. It is a unit of measurement for the linear mass density of fibres composed of filaments, and is defined as the mass in grams per 9,000 metres.

1 denier = 1 g per 9,000 m
= 0.05 g per 450 m (1/20th of above)

DPF, denier per filament, refers to one single filament of fibre. Several filaments together are referred to as total denier. A fibre is generally considered a microfibre if it is 1 denier or less.

Tex is the international system and is more prevalent in Canada and Europe. Tex is a unit of measure for the linear mass density of fibres and is defined as the mass in grams per 1,000 metres.

Fully fashioned knitwear

All hand knitting is fully fashioned. This means that the garment is made by increasing and decreasing the number of stitches in a row to create the desired shape.

Machine knitting, irrespective of gauge, is further divided into fully fashioned or cut and sewn. With fully-fashioned machine knitting, as with hand knitting, the garment is shaped by the increment and decrement of stitches. The amount of fashioning used depends on the quality of the product and machinery. Fully fashioned is more viable with expensive yarns such as **cashmere**, and yarn usage and labour is decreased when garments are fully fashioned. A really good piece of knitwear will be totally fully fashioned, while a mass-market product may be only fashioned at the armhole, to eliminate wastage.

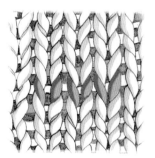

(above and right) The face side of jersey knitting is referred to as plain stitch.

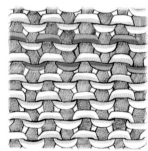

(above and right) The reverse side of jersey knitting is referred to as purl stitch.

This pale grey sweater by SANS explores the differing needle sizes or gauges possible in knitwear, and alternates plain and purl knits to create the three-dimensional 'striping'. The armhole is fully fashioned.

An installation artwork by Alfreda McHale showing extremely large-scale knitting, exhibited at the Stitching and Knitting Fair, Alexandra Palace, London, 2008.

Iconic knitting styles

Traditional Fair Isle intarsia knit designs inspired this hooded sweater in neutral tones by Hildigunnur Sigurdardottirs.

Fair Isle

This traditional technique originates from **Fair Isle**, a small island between the Orkney and Shetland Islands in the very north of Scotland. Originally, these sweaters were knitted using Shetland wool by fishermen's wives, and were worn at sea. They traditionally use five to seven colours to create complex horizontal patterns, with each sweater featuring a different pattern and **colour-way**. Fair-Isle knitting is notorious for its many floats of yarn, meaning that on the reverse of the fabric the yarn 'floats' across several needles. The floats need to remain short to avoid snagging. Fair-Isle patterns can now be replicated on a jacquard system without the floats, however these are intrinsic to the authenticity of the product.

Ashish glamorizes the traditional Argyle pattern by rescaling the motif and playing with texture.

Argyle (also Argyll)

The **Argyle** pattern, believed to derive from the tartan of the Campbell clan in western Scotland, is made up of diamond blocks of colour laid out as a diagonal chequerboard, overlaid with a further 'diamond' line called a **raker**. This particular design uses the **intarsia** technique, a single flat knit with several colours in one row of knitting. The pattern is formed by stopping one colour and twisting in a new colour over the needles each time there is a colour change. This was traditionally done by hand-frame machine or by hand knitting, but now can be done by computerized flatbed machines.

Argyle knitwear has seen a renaissance in popularity, thanks to its use by Pringle of Scotland.

Cream giant trellis knit oversized jumper in 100% merino wool. From the menswear collection 'Modern Medieval Soldiers' by James Long.

Aran

Aran is a style of Gaelic knitwear originating from the Aran Islands off the west coast of Ireland. This style of knitting is believed to originate from the early 1900s, although the three-dimensional motifs used for the stitch formation have ancient megalith origins. The knitwear was first shown in British Vogue in the 1940s, and became an instant success in the United States.

Traditionally, authentic Aran is hand knitted with undyed cream wool, and occasionally natural black wool, both of which still contain natural sheep **lanolin**, which provides an intrinsic water-resistance.

Cut and sew

Cut-and-sew knitwear is fabric that has been knitted and is then cut and sewn in a similar way to woven fabric styles. Cut-and-sew knitwear is mainly used for styling inexpensive yarns due to the wastage incurred.

Generally shirt and sweatshirt styles are cut and sew. To fully fashion very fine 30-gauge garments would require the use of very expensive yarn, and the process would be time consuming, therefore manufacturing production runs would have to be very long.

The majority of T-shirts are either of **single jersey** or interlock fabric construction. Rib fabrics can be used for close body-fitting styles.

Useful knitting terminology

Cable knitting Three-dimensional twisting effects that mimic ropes, braids and plaits, made by crossing over stitches.

Circular knitting Mainly for T-shirt fabrics, knitted on a circular machine resulting in tubular fabric. Garments tend to **spiral** after washing unless opened up and stented – the process of passing the fabric through a hot-air cabinet, which stabilizes it.

Course The row of loops that runs along the width of the fabric, equivalent to the weft in a woven fabric.

Double jersey All needle rib knitted fabric where both the face and reverse side are the same.

Jacquard Intricate design where every colour of yarn used is knitted into the back of the fabric when not in use.

Jersey Generically used to describe many types of knitted fabric. Single jersey is plain knit on one side and purl on the reverse and is used for tops. Double jersey is plain on both sides and can be double in weight. It does not unravel when cut so is fine for cutting and sewing more complicated styles.

Inlaid yarn Yarn that is held in place by the loops of the knitting rather than being knitted in. This is a rigid fabric with no stretch.

Plain knit The face side of basic jersey knitting, the reverse side is known as purl.

Plated A double face knitted fabric. This technique uses two different types or colours of yarn. One is thrown to the face side and the other to the reverse side .The fabric is knitted using a plating device fixed to the bed of the machine.

Purl The reverse side of basic jersey knitting, the face side is known as plain knit.

Single jersey Another term for plain knit.

Tuck stitch In knitwear, a held stitch giving a raised effect.

Welt A form of edge finishing on knitwear, usually knitted as a separate piece e.g. pocket.

Alexander McQueen knitted wool jacquard style poncho with horizontal-banded design referencing traditional ethnic motifs and weave techniques.

Felting

Felt is a non-woven cloth produced by matting, condensing and pressing fibres together to form the structure of the fabric. **Felted** fabrics are the oldest known to mankind and today may be soft and supple or tough enough for industry use. The technique of felting is still practised by nomadic tribes of Central Asia, while in the Western world felting is seen as an expression of art in textiles with strong eco-credentials.

Wet felting is the traditional process whereby the natural fibres are stimulated by friction and lubricated with water and alkaline, usually soap. This causes the fibres to interlock and matt together.

In industry, felting is done by a chemical process or by using felting needles. A felting effect can be achieved using a hot cycle on a domestic washing machine. Felting should not to be confused with **fulling**, which is a felting-like process, carried out after the fabric has been constructed, similar to washing a sweater in a washing machine at a high temperature.

Inexpensive felt is usually made with artificial fibres, although a minimum of 30 per cent wool is necessary for the fabric to hold together adequately.

Loden fabric, from the Alpine regions, was originally a felted fabric, however today lodens are usually woven, the name referring to the feeling of the fabric rather than its true definition.

(above) Traditional felted wool boots from Russia are known as valenki. These boots express a pure aesthetic due to the practical and comforting moulding of the felt around the foot to achieve effective and seamless insulation. The result is a perfect meeting of form and function that transcends fashion.

(above) Wet felting. The merino wool fibres are layered at 90 degrees and hot soapy water and friction cause the wool's natural scales to interlock and felt.

(right) Hand-operated needle felting. Needle felting is the alternative to wet or chemical felting. Industrial needle felting involves machines with hundreds of tiny barbed needles, which push up and down punching and entangling the fibres together. Many non-woven fabrics are made by needle felting or needle punching.

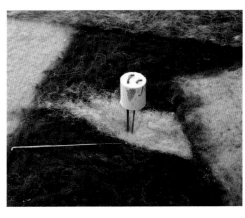

(left and below) Dress and waistcoat from Ravensbourne graduate Sue Pei Ho's collection. The pieces feature wisps of wool fibres fused onto silk – a technique originally developed by textile artists Polly Blakney Sirling and Sachiko Kotaka.

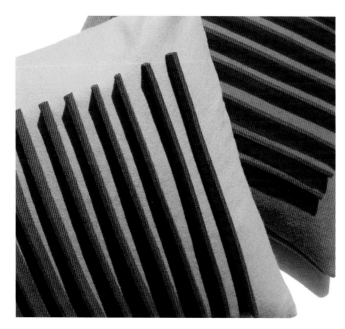

(left) Anne Kyyrö Quinn expresses the exceptional sculptural qualities of felt in this cut-edge three-dimensional application on felt cushion.

Crocheting

Crocheting is the process of creating fabric from yarn or thread using a hooked needle to pull loops of yarn through other loops.

Although scholars theorize that crochet has Arabic origins, there is no real evidence of it being practised before the eighteenth century in Europe. Ireland and northern France were centres of crochet making, much of it done to support poor communities whose livelihoods had been compromised, and hence it was often considered a domestic craft. However, crocheted items sold well to the new emerging middle classes. Crochet experienced a revival of interest in the mid-1960s with the new-wave hippy movements and their embracing of rural cultures.

(above) Unique crocheted wearable sculptures by Polish artist Agata Olek highlight the surreal aspect of creating 'moulded' clothing (such as crochet or knit). Amateur knitters often find that their work 'grows' and takes on a life of its own. Premiered in New York at the Williamsburg Arts and Historical Society Surrealist Fashion Show in 2003.

(left) Agata Olek has extended her exploration of the craft of crochet to footwear with this whimsical, historically inspired crocheted shoe.

Lace making

Lace is a lightweight fabric patterned with open holes and can be hand or machine made. The holes may be created by removing threads of previously woven cloth, however more often the holes are created as part of the lace-making process, where thread is looped, twisted or braided to other threads independently from any backing fabric. Lace was first used by priests for religious rituals, then popularized in the sixteenth century when it was highly valued as a symbol of wealth and status.

Originally linen, silk, gold or silver threads were preferred, however today cotton is also used, as are synthetic yarns for machine-made lace.

Vintage inspired slip dress in linen by designer Marina Shlosberg. Linen is the ideal fabric to showcase the Venetian-style drawn thread openwork embroidery shown on the front of the dress.

(above) Up-cycled dress featuring a bodice that incorporates different types of reclaimed and vintage cotton lace with a silk dupion skirt designed by London College of Fashion graduate Rachael Cassar. Her designs aim to use 90% recycled materials in their composition, and to challenge preconceptions of the term 'recycling'.

(left) Hand-worked lace border showing a section in process. Dozens of colour-coded bobbins show the complexity of this craft technique. Myriad overlapped and twisted threads form the intricate patterns that are indicated by the designs marked out on the card underneath. Pins are used to hold the threads in place while the patterns are formed.

Modernizing lace, Rae III, 2002, features cotton lace and elastane and is from a photographic series by Georgina McNamara that explores the relationship between the body and the imagination. The traditional associations of lace, clothing and how they work with the human form are inverted in this super-structured realization.

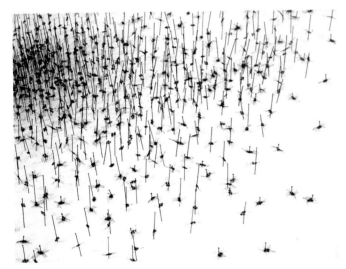

Types of lace

Some of the popular types of lace include:

Needle lace Made using a needle and thread, and the most flexible of the lace-making techniques. It can be very time consuming and is regarded as the purist form of lace art. Today it is impossible to reproduce some of the fine antique lace. Types of needle lace include punto in Aria, point de Venise, point de France, Alençon, Argentan, Armenian, Limerick and hollie point.

Cutwork lace Constructed by the removal of threads from a woven background fabric. The remaining threads are then worked on with embroidery. Types of cutwork lace include Battenberg, broderie Anglaise and Carrickmacross.

Bobbin lace Made using bobbins and a pillow. The bobbins hold the threads, which are laced together and held down onto the pillow by pins. Types of bobbin lace include Antwerp, Flanders, Bayeux, Chantilly, Genoese, Venetian, Maltese, Bruges, Brussels and Milanese.

Lace knitting Technically knitting with many 'holes' in the design work that create the lace effect. It is considered the highest form of knitting and was especially popular in the nineteenth century when Queen Victoria practised it. In parts of Russia lace knits form part of the wedding dowry, the finest of which can be pulled through a wedding ring.

Machine-made lace Any type of lace made by mechanical methods rather than by hand.

Tatting A type of lace construction first introduced in the early nineteenth century to imitate needle-lace work. It is created by a series of chain knots and loops, mainly used as lace edging, collars and doilies.

As a physical material, black lace has diverse cultural implications in relation to sexuality, death and gender. In these artworks by Anne Wilson the webs and networks of found black lace are deconstructed to create large horizontal topographies or 'physical drawings' that are both complicated and delicate. The structural characteristics of lace are understood by unravelling threads; mesh structures are also reconstructed through crochet and netting. Lace fragments are also scanned, filtered and printed out as paper images. These computer-mediated digital prints are then re-materialized by hand stitching and are placed in relationship to the found and re-made lace in the topography.

Macramé

Macramé is created by the interlinking of knots. It is believed to have Arabic origins, and was used to decorate the excess lengths of yarn along the edge of hand-loom textiles. It was taken to Spain with the Moorish conquest and eventually spread to the rest of Europe, reaching England by the late seventeenth century. It may also classify as a form of lace making.

Macramé was a popular pastime among British and American sailors all through the nineteenth century; the preference was for substantial square knots, which they used to make hammocks and belts.

As well as cotton and hemp, leather is often used. Most friendship bracelets are a form of macramé.

James Long subverts the craft connotations of macramé in this outfit that features the intricate knotting technique worn over a silk tulle T-shirt for his menswear collection 'Arabian stallions'.

Dyeing

Dyeing is the process of transferring **colourant** to fibres, yarns, fabrics or ready-made garments. Colourants take the form of **dyes**, which are in liquid form, or **pigments**, which are in fine powder form.

Until the mid-nineteenth century the primary source of colour dye and pigment was animal, plant or mineral; the plant kingdom being the most prolific provider in the form of berries, roots, bark and leaves. These natural colourants were used with very little, if any, processing. The first synthetic dye, a **mauvine** or aniline purple, was invented by accident in a failed medical experiment in 1856.

The Industrial Revolution was the catalyst for the mass development of the textile industry, and in turn the development of synthetic dyes. This resulted in a larger range of colours with a higher level of colour consistency. In addition to this the colours were more stable under continuous washing and wearing. Today, different classes of dyes are used for different generic fabric types, and also for different stages of textile production.

Yarn dyeing

Yarn is dyed to a colour of choice before it is either woven or knitted into a fabric. The two most common ways to **yarn dye** are at package form for cotton yarns and at hank form for wool and **acrylic** yarns.

Yarn-dyed fabrics tend to give a much better level of **colourfast**ness in wearing and washing than **fabric-dyed** items. Any fabric with a stripe, check or other type of design woven into it will be yarn dyed. Good-quality suiting fabrics and shirting fabrics are almost always yarn dyed, even if they are of a solid/plain colour.

Yarn-dyed fabrics are almost always more expensive than their fabric-dyed equivalents. The process of yarn dyeing takes longer and the minimum quantities to be ordered are always far greater than with fabric-dyed orders. Within the design process the selection of colours for yarn dyeing also has to be done much earlier in the season, because the mill **lead times**, to weave and then finish the fabric, are far greater.

Before a larger sample batch of yarn is dyed – known as a **dye lot** – small pieces of yarn windings are sample dyed to colours for approval. These samples are known as **lab dips**, and designers and merchandisers, as well as **technologists**, may all be involved in the approval process.

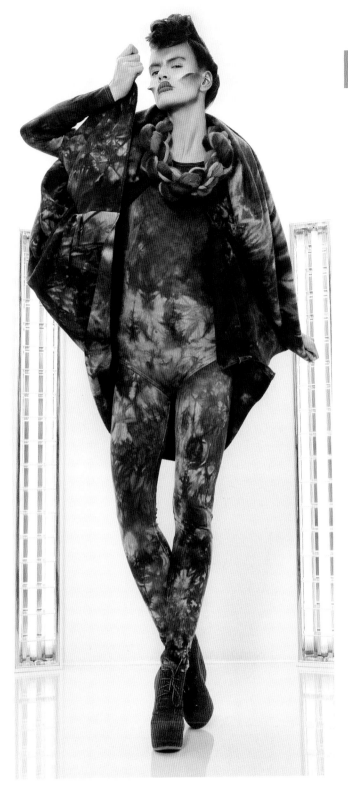

Crushed-effect random dye technique from the Ta-ste label designed by Tanja Steuer. The bodysuit and jacket are made from differing weights of cotton jersey and are soaked in water before being placed in a dye bath. They are then pressed together to form folds and creases, which inhibit the absorption of the dye, resulting in random concentrations of colour.

Fabric dyeing

Fabric dyeing is also referred to as **piece dyeing**, and in this instance the fabric is dyed after it has been woven. The advantage of fabric dyeing is that you are able to buy much smaller quantities than is necessary for yarn-dyed equivalents, making it much easier and far less expensive to carry an extensive colour palette of fabric in stock. Furthermore, the lead time involved is far shorter. For the fabric supplier or **converter** there is less of a risk, because the fabric can remain in its **greige** – undyed – state indefinitely.

Piece-dyed fabric is perfect for solid colour, woven cotton goods, as well as knitted cotton fabrics such as lightweight **jersey** and interlock fabric, heavier interlocks (sweatshirts) and fleece loop-back fabric. Plain coloured swimwear and underwear fabrics are often piece dyed. Woollen fabrics for heavy outerwear, if of a solid (plain) colour, are usually also piece dyed.

Before a final dye is agreed, lab dips are made by dyeing **pieces** of fabric in a small vessel or beaker. Three shades of the requested colour are submitted for designer approval before dyeing the sample lengths, which are usually done in 50-m **vats**. Bulk production dyeing would follow after an approved sales order.

(above) Hand dyeing fabric in a traditional dye shop in India. This form of hand dyeing is today only used for small dye lots and specialist fabrics. Constant immersion in the liquid dye has permanently discoloured the dyer's hands.

(right) Dip-dyed fabric lengths hung up to dry in an Indian workshop. In the developing world, piece-dyed fabrics and special dye treatments such as tie-dye are often processed in small lengths in a similar environment.

(top) Piece-dyed fabrics on drying racks. For solid colour fabrics piece dyeing is far less expensive and also less time-consuming than the alternative yarn-dyeing process.

(above) Before placing a bulk order for either fabric or yarn, a colour lab dip must be approved. Several variants of the hue are presented to the client for colour matching and approval. Once the selection has been made, both the factory and the client keep a sample swatch, which is used to quality check against the bulk production.

Garment dyeing

Garment dyeing, the dyeing of a ready-made garment, is the least colourfast method of dyeing, but it does give a very specific visual look. This technique also gives the manufacturer greater product colour flexibility, because ready-made garments can be made and kept in stock, then dyed to specific colours. The most common product in this category is likely to be low-cost shirts and tops.

Garment-dyed products tend to have a residue of dye sitting along the raised seam edges, and if the sewing threads used to assemble the garment are of a different colour and composition they will resist the dye, resulting in contrast **top-stitching**.

Resist dyeing

Resist dyeing refers to various methods of patterning fabric by preventing dye reaching certain parts of it. Common methods include the application of wax or paste and stitching areas together. An alternative method is to use a chemical agent within a dye that will repel a second colour when applied.

Wax and rice paste

Wax or rice paste is painted or applied to the fabric, forming a design, prior to dyeing. Once the resisting agent has dried it is removed by ironing to reveal the colour underneath. This can be repeated numerous times to build up a complex design of several overlaying colours.

Several variations of this method can be found among different cultures around the world, for example **batik** from Indonesia, Malaysia and India; and roketsuzome, katazome, yuzen and tsutsugaki from Japan.

(above) This crisp retro-futuristic sunray-pleated Metropolis dress features a shocking-pink dip-dyed hem designed by Kamila Gawrońska-Kasperska. From a collection inspired by Art Deco style and the film *Metropolis* by the director Fritz Lang. The dress is made from hand-pleated and hand-dyed silk organza.

(left) Batik, a type of resist dyeing, is an ancient craft and can be an intricate and labour-intensive process. It involves the use of molten wax or rice paste, which is applied directly onto the fabric and allowed to dry. This prevents the dye from reaching the treated part of the fabric. Intricate multidimensional effects can be built up by repeating the processes.

Multicoloured batik silk design by textile artist Isabella Whitworth. Here, the batik wax resist technique is expressed in a painterly and free-form approach showing the characteristic 'crackle' that occurs when dye seeps into cracks in the cooled wax.

Stitching and tying

Fabrics can be stitched or tied in specific areas to shield them from dye. Variations of these techniques from different cultures include ikat from Indonesia and Malaysia; **tie-dye** from India; and adire from Africa.

Chemical resist

A resisting agent is added to the first dye colour that is applied. When the second colour is applied it will be repelled where it crosses the first colour. This is a common method used in T-shirt printing.

Mordants

A **mordant** is used after some dyes as a method of **fixing** the colour to the fabric. Historically mordants were used as a means of altering the colour and intensity of natural dyes, as well as to improve their colourfastness. Environmental concerns have now restricted the use of some types of mordants, in which case they have been replaced with **reactive** and metal complex dyes that do not require a mordant.

Reversing the dyeing effect

To remove unwanted dye a process called **stripping** destroys the dye by the use of a powerful reducing agent, which may damage the substructure of the fibre; the alternative is to **over-dye** to a darker colour, such as navy or black.

Twist-dyed silk scarf by Isabella Whitworth. The silk fabric is tightly twisted in one direction and tied, stretched, folded in half, twisted in the counter direction and tied. Dye is applied and allowed to absorb through the layers. When dry the fabric is untied to reveal the final design.

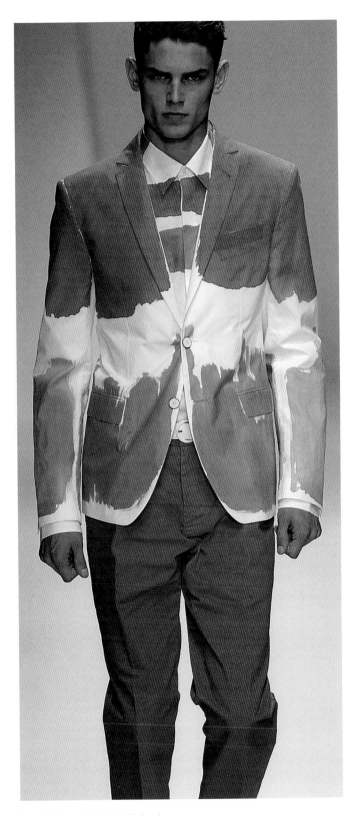

The discipline of classic tailoring is given an edgy, painterly appeal in this summer jacket, trousers and shirt made of cotton by Salvatore Ferragamo. The hand-painted dye treatment is applied directly to the finished garment in graduated shades of red and coral.

Useful dyeing terminology

Acid dye Class of dye used on protein fibres such as silk and wool.

Alum Mordant for natural dyes.

Aniline dye The first synthetic dye, made from alcohol and coal-tar derivatives.

Azo or azoic dye Petroleum-based dye typically used on cellulose fibres.

Basic dye Class of dye used on some synthetic fibres.

Batch dyeing A large batch of yarn is dyed in the same vat. The batch is called a dye lot.

Bleeding Loss or transfer of colour.

Changeant An effect whereby the colour appears to 'change' depending on the angle it is viewed from. Also called two-tone or shot effect.

Chrome dye Class of dye used on wool.

Continuous dyeing Processing fabric in sequence through all dyeing stages to give continuous output.

Direct dye Class of dye used on cellulose fibres.

Disperse dye Class of dye used on some synthetics, such as polyester and acetate.

Fugitive Colour that washes out or 'bleeds', ie not colourfast.

Hank dyed Dyed as yarn in hank format.

Indigo Possibly the only natural plant dye still in mass use.

Match Two samples in which the colour match is commercially acceptable.

Mordant dye Alternative to chrome dye.

Off-shade Not an acceptable match.

Ombre Graduated colour from light to dark.

Reactive dyes Class of dyes used on cellulose and protein fibres.

Shading Defective dyed fabric featuring lighter and darker shades.

Shot A fabric that appears to change colour when viewed from different directions, an effect of cross dyeing yarn.

Strike-off Preliminary small sample for approval of colour and print.

Tendering Adverse reaction of dye to light.

Vat A dyeing vessel.

Vat dyes Common cotton dyes.

Surface decoration

This generic term refers to any form of decoration applied to a ready-made fabric to embellish it with texture and/or colour. The two most important methods of surface decorating are printing and **embroidery**.

Printing

Printing is the process of creating a design on fabric by the application of colour.

Hand-block printing
The blocks are engraved with the design, which is used to transfer the dye onto the fabric. The registration of each repeat design is carefully positioned by hand.

Silk-screen printing
This is the original hand-printing technique and is based on stencilling. A fine woven mesh (originally silk) is stretched over a frame and an impermeable stencil is applied to it. The surface to be printed is then placed underneath and ink or dye is drawn across it and thereby forced through the areas of open mesh circumscribed by the stencil. A series of such screens can be used for successive layers of colour.

(top) Indonesian hand-block printing.

(above) Batik treated fabric overprinted using copper blocks.

(above) Giant T-shirt photographic silk-screen print on an oversized 100 per cent cotton jersey dress by Undercover.

(left) Trompe l'œil enlarged 'bias weave' silk-screen print by Ioannis Dimitrousis.

Rotary-screen printing

Rotary-screen printing is less expensive to produce than roller printing and suitable for large repeats and complex designs with more than five colours. It is also good for printing on knitted fabrics.

Roller printing

A fast technique suitable for large **print runs**. Set-up costs include engraving the copper rollers – one per colour. Pigment prints are referred to as **dry prints** because the fabric is **cured** by heat, while fabrics printed with dyes are referred to as **wet prints**.

Heat-transfer printing

Fabric and pre-printed paper are passed between heated rollers, transferring the dye from the paper to the fabric. This is a low-cost technique suitable for short print runs.

A film positive is used to expose and harden light-sensitive emulsion to create the stencil design.

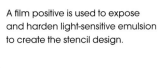

Print House Inc. is a state-of-the-art manufacturing facility providing full-service product development for screen-printed clothing.

(top) Traditional hand silk-screen printing.

(above) Mechanized silk-screen printing for lengths of fabric.

(left) Mechanized silk-screen printing for individual garments, most commonly T-shirts.

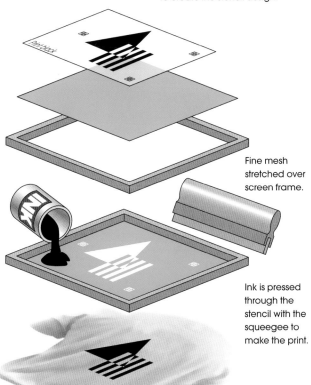

Fine mesh stretched over screen frame.

Ink is pressed through the stencil with the squeegee to make the print.

Mordant printing

A mordant – dye fixative – is pre-printed as a pattern prior to dyeing the fabric. The colour only adheres where the mordant has been printed.

Resist dyeing

A resist substance such as wax is printed onto the fabric, which is then dyed. The waxed areas will not take the dye, leaving uncoloured patterns against a coloured **ground**.

Discharge printing

A bleaching agent is printed onto previously dyed fabrics to remove some or all of the colour.

Digital printing

Digital printing has reduced the cost and time required to produce samples, allowing more experimentation. In digital printing, there is no limit to the number of colours possible in a single print and no issue with the scale of the **design repeat,** so photographic quality is the norm. Specialist software allows accurate colour-matching directly from the monitor, eliminating manual colour-matching.

Digital printing is perfect for **JIT (just-in-time)** production. Lead times are short with, usually, no minimum print run. This enables companies to produce new designs frequently, as they are not tied to **stock fabric**. Most digital printers can print on any fabric by using appropriate ink. Fabric passes through the printer on rollers, and the ink is applied in the form of thousands of tiny droplets, then set by heat or steam. In some cases the fabric is also washed and dried.

Water consumption is reduced by as much as 50 per cent, there are no screens or rollers to wash, there is little ink wastage and discharge into drains is reduced.

Useful printing terminology

Devore A fabric containing two or more fibre types is printed with a substance that burns out or destroys one or more of the fibres. The result is usually a fabric that is partly sheer.

Flock print An adhesive agent is printed onto the fabric and flock particles are applied.

Glitter print An adhesive agent is first printed, followed by glitter particles.

Ground colour The base colour of the fabric, or predominant colour of the print.

Half tone Colour graduation within an area of a single colour.

Metallic print Printing with metallic pigment.

Over-print A design motif printed over an existing all-over print.

Pigment print A print made from pigment and binder rather than dyes. Tends to sit on the fabric rather than being absorbed.

Placement print An image printed in a designated position on a garment.

Repeat One complete unit of a design. A small repeat has an all-over effect, while large-scale repeats need to be carefully considered for positioning before cutting the fabric.

Run Complete length of printed fabric.

Transfer print The colour image is transferred from one material, or paper, onto the garment or fabric, usually by heat.

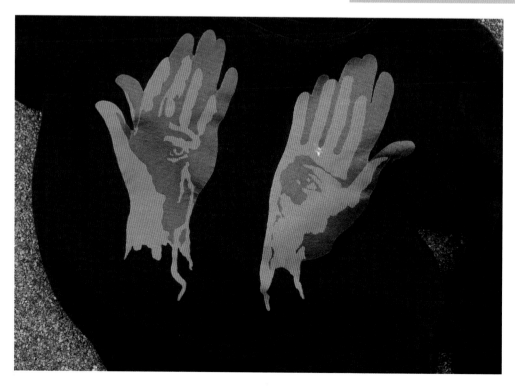

Hallucinations from the 'State of Mind' series by Myka Baum. Vinyl placement print on 100 per cent cotton sweatshirt.

Devoré

The technique of devoré (from the French *dévorer* 'to devour') is also known as 'burn out'. It describes the effect achieved when part of a fabric composition is eaten away by the application of a corrosive paste to produce a design. The acidic dévorant paste will eat away the areas of the fabric that are cellulosic (viscose, rayon, cotton or linen for example). The base weave (silk or synthetic) will remain. The technique is particularly effective with pile fabrics, such as a silk/rayon velvet, where the contrast between the sheer silk ground and the texture of the pile is pronounced.

Laser cutting and engraving

Laser cutting and engraving offers exclusivity to small-scale designers, which would be impossible if buying stock fabrics. Fabrics can be cut or engraved to very intricate designs with the guarantee of a precise copy of the shape or design, as often as required. Most fabrics can be laser cut. The high temperature of the laser beam seals as it cuts, thus eliminating fraying, design work can be achieved on both rolls of fabric and individual panels, and there is no limit to the complexity of cutting or engraving that can be achieved.

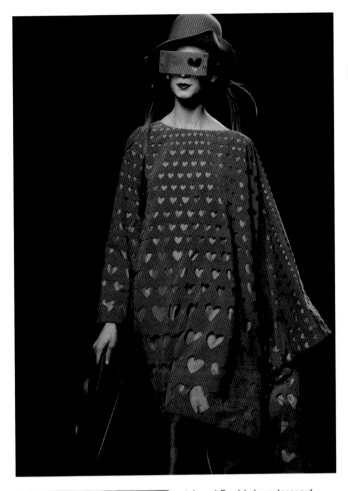

(above) Original devoré design on a silk velvet fabric by Hayley Cheal.

(above) Structured digitally printed dress by innovative London-based designer Mary Katrantzou. A complex series of digital prints in one garment creates arresting visual effects and emphasizes different parts of the body.

(right) This Dragonfly dress from the 'Mimesis' collection by Polish designer Kamila Gawrońska-Kasperska showcases the precision of digital printing. The delicate dragonfly wing motif is digitally printed onto silk organza. The lower part of the dress is constructed from more than 100 pieces of printed cut-edge fabric.

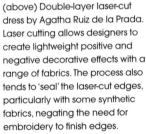

(above) Double-layer laser-cut dress by Agatha Ruiz de la Prada. Laser cutting allows designers to create lightweight positive and negative decorative effects with a range of fabrics. The process also tends to 'seal' the laser-cut edges, particularly with some synthetic fabrics, negating the need for embroidery to finish edges.

Embroidery

Embroidery is a form of surface decoration made using threads and yarns in various stitches and combinations of stitches. The process may also include the addition of beads and sequins, as well as other applied decorative **trimmings**.

There are many roots to the origins of embroidery, and similarly many differing styles reflecting various cultures and geographic regions.

Embroidery is classified depending on its under-fabric, or according to the relationship of the stitches' placement to the fabric. Further divisions indicate whether the stitching is on top of the fabric or through it.

Freehand embroidery
The designs are applied without regard for the weave structure of the base fabric; it is also a form of surface embroidery. **Crewel-work** and traditional Chinese embroidery are two examples of freehand embroidery.

(above) Thickly worked wool yarn embroidery applied on wool crêpe creates a customized textile in this dress by Ashish. The dress features a shaped bodice top and full skirt reinforced with a silk tulle underskirt.

(right) Emerald green folklore-inspired jacket by Colette Vermeulen. The highly textured fabric is constructed using a large-scale jacquard technique, and is woven from mohair and viscose raffia skeins. The embroidery is applied to the jacquard after weaving, and is executed by hand using ripped strips of pre-washed silk.

Counted-thread embroidery

The warp and weft threads of the base fabric are pre-counted by the embroiderer before inserting the needle and embroidering thread. Designs tend to be symmetrical. **Needlepoint** embroidery and **cross stitch** are two examples of this style of embroidery.

Canvas work

Threads are stitched through canvas to create a dense pattern and completely cover the under-fabric. **Canvas work** requires the use of an embroidery hoop or frame to stretch the fabric. Needlepoint, **petit point** and **bergello** are examples of canvas work.

Smocking

Smocking is an embroidery technique used to gather fabric, developed in England in the Middle Ages. The gathered fabric is held in place with decorative stitch-work. It derived its name from the tunic or smock worn by the farm labourers who favoured this technique. Before the use of elastic, smocking was used for cuffs and necklines in place of buttons, and gave the garment a degree of stretch.

(above) Embroidered brocade coat by Josep Font. The encrusted 'freefall' sprinkle of beads and sequins highlights the collar and shoulder area.

(left) Fine grey wool tunic by Carta e Costura showcasing a modern interpretation of the craft of smocking. The fabric is contoured and moulded to the body by graduated elastic shirring, which causes tiny gathers and bubbles in the fabric and lends it great stretch.

Up-cycled dress composed of reclaimed Indian cotton crochet lace encrusted with beaded embroidery on a nylon–Lycra blend base by Rachael Cassar. The designer's aim is to produce one-off pieces that comprise 90 per cent recycled materials and to challenge the preconception that luxury and sustainability are mutually exclusive.

Machine embroidery

Embroidery designs can be stitched with automated machines. Today logo badges on T-shirts, sweatshirts and polo shirts make the greatest use of **machine embroidery**.

Appliqué

This needlework technique uses pieces of fabric stitched or embroidered onto a base cloth to create a design. The technique is French in origin but extensively used in North America for traditional quilts. West Africa and parts of India and Pakistan are also famous for **appliqué quilting**.

Quilting

The technique of stitching through two or more layers of fabric with a layer of **wadding** in between to produce an insulative and decorative three-dimensional effect.

(above) Nude organza dress with hand-stitched raw-edged appliqués, cut from woven silk-striped fabric. From Vivienne Westwood's Spring/Summer 2009 'Do it Yourself' collection.

(right) Pewter dress by French-born designer Julien David, who trained in New York and is now based in Tokyo. Made from a silk and polyester circular metallic voile, the garment's sculptured, bell-shaped silhouette is supported by wadding inside the quilted fabric.

(above) Fine worsted wool suit by Ichiro Suzuki. The London College of Fashion and Royal College of Art graduate plays with the optical graphic effects of the traditional pinstripe and subverts the expectations of classic tailoring by creating three-dimensional stiffened patchwork structures across the shoulders.

Finishing processes

There are many processes that can be applied to fabrics after they have been made, from traditional operations such as **brushing** the surface to make it feel warmer and to compact the weave, to chemical impregnation, making the fabric **water-repellent**, or even adding **fire-retardant** properties. Most of these treatments are for woven fabrics, but also include knitted fabrics, and are executed at the manufacturing **mill**, although some specialist finishes may require the fabric to be sent out to a specific finishing plant.

Waterproofing treatments

These treatments are applied to the fabric to enhance its rain- and general weather-proofing properties. It is important to understand the difference between the terms 'proof' and 'repellent'. Water- or rain-proof implies there will be no ingress of water; this term applies to both the fabric and the manufacturing process of the garment. The manufacturing process that makes a garment waterproof requires either seam-taping to stop water ingress through the stitching holes or, alternatively, the inclusion of a membrane fabric. This is a middle layer referred to as a drop liner, which sits between the outer fabric or shell and the inner lining.

Oiling and **waxing** wear away with time and will need to be reapplied.

Enhancing treatments

There are many treatments that change the basic appearance of the fabric.

Milling and washing are generic terms for numerous specific variations all of which will give quite different effects. These treatments are often an inexpensive way to give added design value to base fabrics. Denim is a fabric that benefits from experimental washing treatments.

Brushing will raise the surface of the fabric and give a softer colour bend; **calendering** and **mercerizing** will add lustre to a fabric.

Additive treatments

These are treatments that enhance the performance or endurance of a fabric or yarn. Some treatments will make a fabric easier to care for; other treatments will inhibit the fabric's natural tendency to crease. Fire-retardant treatments are often required on children's nightwear and on display fabrics.

Examples include antibacterial, anti-soiling, easy-care and crease-resisting fabrics.

Useful finishing terminology

Antibacterial Inhibits bacterial growth.

Anti-soiling Makes stain removal easier.

Blowing Steam is blown through the cloth to remove creases, and gives a specific look to the fabric.

Bonding Two layers of fabric are attached or fused together, with or without a middle layer, for depth and warmth, for example foam sandwiched between two layers to provide structure and insulation.

Brightening agent Increases whiteness or brightness of fabric.

Calendering Process of adding lustre and smoothness to fabric by passing it through heated steel rotary cylinders.

Chemical finishes Any number of treatments applied to give a specialist finish.

Crease-resistant A treatment that improves fabric recovery.

Easy-care Minimal ironing needed to finished garment.

Emerized Emery-covered rollers produce a suede-like finish to fabric.

Enzymes Naturally occurring proteins that catalyse chemical reactions.

Milling A process that blends colours, obscures weave and makes the fabric more compact.

Mill washing Any of a number of washing treatments that softens and ages fabric.

Oiling (cloth) Water-repelling treatment applied to fabric.

Pre-shrunk Fabric that has been shrunk at the weaving mill and should not shrink further.

Scouring Process of removing the grease and natural fats from yarn, giving fullness to the fibre and bulking up the fabric.

Shower-proofing Any number of applications to proof fabric against water.

Waxing Impregnating fabric with wax to make it shower-proof.

Introducing colour

Colour is a powerful communicator, as complex as language or music.

Colour is fundamental to the way we experience the world; it is central to our visual and emotional sense of our surroundings. Colour is the first thing we notice, usually perceived before shape and detail, and as children we are primarily stimulated and most responsive to high-**contrast** combinations of colour. Colour can provoke strong emotive associations and reactions, even making things feel warm or cool, exciting and stimulating or soothing and tranquil. Colour has the suggestive power to affect mood and enhance our experiences. It enriches our sense of the world and how we perceive it by helping us to interpret our visual language. It may camouflage us in times of danger, and is an effective tool, a code that may alert us to hazardous situations and steer us to safety, even if only subliminally.

Colour theory

The ancient Greek philosopher Empedocles (492–431 BC) was the first person to formulate a colour theory. It was his hypothesis that colour is not the property of the object, but that it exists in the eye of the observer. This seemingly philosophical leap of understanding was proven centuries later. The science of colour is also known as **chromatics**, which takes in the perception of colour by the human eye and brain, the origin of colour in materials, colour theory in art and the physics of electromagnetic radiation in the visible range – or what we commonly refer to as light.

Colour and light

Colour from the viewer's perspective may be referred to as a 'sensation', but it is technically contained within light. The individual's perception of colour is synthesized in the mind. The concept of colour is a reaction to the sensation of light, which is transmitted to the brain through the eye. Light is made up of waves of energy, which travel at different wavelengths; the brain interprets these into the complex nuances of colour and processes these minute differences in wavelengths.

Pigment is pure colour, but even the colour of a pigment is essentially the colour of the light it reflects. Whenever we look at a colour we are viewing coloured light, because pigments have a special ability to absorb specific wavelengths from the light that falls on them, and to reflect others to the eye.

A white surface will reflect all light rays that strike it, while a black surface will absorb them. A coloured surface, such as red, will reflect the red light, but absorb all the other light rays. It could be said that white is pure light, while black is the total lack of light, and both are not actually colours.

Physicist and mathematician Sir Isaac Newton (1642–1727) pioneered the study of light in laboratory conditions and formulated a logical framework for understanding colour. The proof of Newton's theory, that sunlight is composed of the colours of the spectrum, is apparent each time a rainbow is formed, or when the sun's rays are dispersed on the skin of a bubble, or by a film of oil on a puddle.

Visible spectrum

When a ray of light enters a prism, the array of colours that is refracted through the prism appears in the following order:
Red
Orange
Yellow
Green
Blue
Blue-violet
Violet

(opposite page) Room sized installation, 'Tribute', by Alain Guerra and Neraldo de La Paz, constructed from a rainbow-hued heap of discarded clothing.

(right) Design duo Basso and Brooke create an extravagant explosion of sunset colours by using analogous hues from the 'warm' section of the spectrum in this multi-layered evening gown.

These constituents of light are known as the visible spectrum. Each colour has a different wavelength. When light strikes a surface certain wavelengths are absorbed, and others are reflected by its pigments or colouring. Most light sources emit light at many different wavelengths, a process that gives a surface its colour.

In 1860, Scottish physicist James Clerk Maxwell (1831–1879) showed that light was a form of electromagnetic energy. The eye is able to receive light waves between 400 and 800 million cycles per second, and we perceive these cycles as colour. Violet is the shortest and red the longest.

Hue

The first dimension of colour is **hue**. A hue is the name or type of a colour. When we refer to a colour by its name we are referring to its hue. A pure hue is one which has no other colour mixed in.

Certain hue combinations conform to standard categorizations.

Monochromatic: Of a single hue.

Analogous hues: Colours that are adjacent to each other in the spectrum.

Complementary hues: A pair of opposite colours as viewed on a **colour wheel**. Mixing complementary colours lowers the **saturation**, or richness, and **value**, or **luminosity** of the resulting colour, in other words it has a darkening effect.

Triadic hues: Any three equidistant colours on the colour spectrum when it is configured as a circle of hues. Red, yellow and blue form the **primary triad**. When the full spectrum of colour is presented as a wheel the relative positions of red, yellow and blue conform to a perfect equilateral triangle.

Colour groupings and systems

The various terms used within the colour-wheel models.

Primary colours
The term **primary** refers to a colour that cannot be made from other colours. Red, yellow and blue form the primary triad.

Secondary colours
Secondary colours are the result of mixing two primary colours, for example blue and yellow mixed to produce green. The secondary triad consists of green, orange and violet.

Tertiary colours
Tertiary colours result when a primary and an adjacent secondary colour are mixed together.

Subtractive colour system
The **subtractive** method of creating colours is based upon pigments or dyes, and explains the way these colours mix by absorbing some wavelengths of light and reflecting others.

Additive colour system
This is the process of mixing coloured light, as in theatrical or retail applications. An **additive system** begins with no light – black – and light is added to make colour.

Partitive colour system
The **partitive** colour model is based on the viewer's reaction to colours when they are placed next to each other.

Ensembles of garments in monochromatic colours.

Colour wheels

The colour spectrum can be organized into wheels to help rationalize and predict colour interactions. Colour wheels are the first basic tools used in the analysis and discussion of colour. There are many variations on the visual organization of colour, some are simple in format and others highly complex, but their principles are all linked.

Pigment colours

In subtractive, or pigment, mixtures, the primaries are traditionally said to be red, yellow and blue. If two primaries are mixed, they theoretically produce the secondaries orange, green and purple. If all three are mixed, they theoretically produce black.

The pigment and process wheels

On the conventional 12-colour wheel of pigment hues, the primaries are red, blue and yellow; the secondaries are orange, green and purple; and the tertiaries are mixtures of adjoining primaries and secondaries. If colours are mixed with their complement (the hue lying opposite on the wheel), a neutral grey should be created, as indicated in the centre. The 12-step **pigment wheel** is the basis for working with subtractive colour; textile artists will use a subtractive wheel to create colours of yarn and textiles by dyeing.

The 12-step **process wheel** also deals with subtractive colour but the three basic primaries are purer – yellow, magenta and cyan – that upon mixing also result in purer hues. This arrangement is the standard employed in colour printing and photography, as well as pigment manufacture.

The Itten wheel

Devised by Swiss teacher and artist Johannes Itten (1888–1967), the **Itten wheel** shows a logical and easily remembered format for working with colour pigments. Itten was captivated by colour from both a scientific and a spiritual point of view, and taught at the influential Bauhaus School in Germany in the 1920s. He observed that colours can be classified as warm or cool shades, and how the two combined can affect each other. Theoretical elements, including the Itten colour wheel, generated from the Bauhaus teachings still inform art instruction around the world today.

The Itten colour wheel organizes the basic theory of the interrelationship between the primary, secondary and tertiary colours in a practical graphic format. The triangle in the centre shows the three primary colours, yellow, blue and red, which cannot be created by mixing any of the other pigments. Surrounding them are the three secondary colours, which are produced by mixing the primaries. The wheel that encircles the primaries and secondaries is divided into 12 sectors. Six of these are primaries and secondaries, and between each of these is another colour. Itten referred to these as tertiary colours. A tertiary colour is the result of mixing a primary and a secondary colour.

(above) The Itten colour wheel organizes the basic theory of the interrelationship between the primary, secondary and tertiary colours.

(left) The 12-colour pigment wheel.

The Munsell wheel

Albert Munsell (1858–1918) developed a partitive colour system (below) based on five primary hues, or as he referred to them, principal colours of yellow, red, green, blue and purple. These primaries are based on **after-image** perceptions – when the brain supplies the opposite colour after staring at a particular hue – that derive from hues we see in nature.

Light colours

These colours are additive rather than subtractive (like pigments). If primary-coloured lights – red-orange, green and blue-violet – are projected in overlapping circles, they mix to form the light secondaries yellow, magenta and cyan. In additive mixtures, the secondaries are paler than the primaries. Where all three primaries overlap, they produce white. This system is used for lighting and also forms the basis for video and computer graphics.

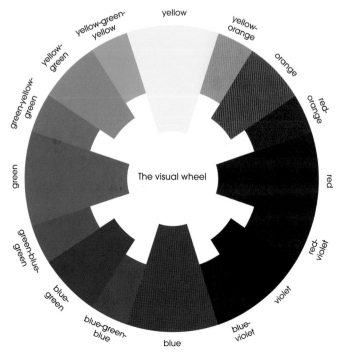

The visual wheel

The 16-step **visual wheel** (below) was arranged by the Italian artist Leonardo da Vinci (1452–1519), whose understanding of complementary colours greatly influenced Renaissance painting. It is a partitive and subtractive colour wheel.

Light colours are additive (above), and react differently to pigment colours, which are subtractive (below).

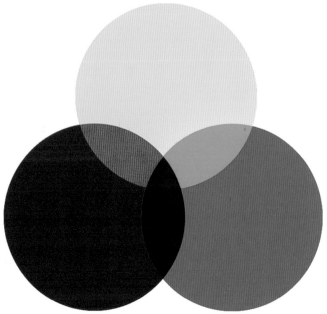

Perception of colour

Our perception of colour is fundamental to our ability to define our world and our emotions. Experience teaches us to connect certain colours with cool or warm sensations. Colour can help us identify freshness and levels of ripeness or decay, can be an indicator of potential illness, and help us recognize fear, anger or embarrassment.

Mind and matter

Three elements are needed to appreciate colour: a light source, a subject and a viewer. The brain interprets as colour the waves of light that are received by the lens of the eye. The information received by the eye is conveyed to the brain, so the perception of colour is therefore a mental, psychological and physical phenomenon. Our perception of colour is affected by the context it exists in: what surrounds it, what other colours are next to it and the lighting conditions under which it is seen. It is the human eye in conjunction with the brain's ability to synthesize that informs how we distinguish the type of colour seen.

Our ability to perceive texture, distance and three-dimensionality is affected by colour: generally darker colours appear to recede, or make things look smaller, while lighter colours tend to have the opposite effect.

Yellows and greens tend to be seen before other hues, while reds and violets are the most difficult to perceive.

Cultural reference

The meaning or emotional impact a colour imparts will vary across different cultures and can fluctuate over time, acquiring both positive and negative connotations throughout the ages. Fashion also exerts a significant influence on the associations we make with various colours. Anyone involved in the use of colour for the development of fashion products needs to be conversant with the 'codes' that different colours can communicate.

Symbolic colour associations rely on an audience that shares the same cultural experiences. The idea that blue, green and violet are 'cool' in temperature, and red, orange and yellow are 'warm' colours is shared by many cultures worldwide. This association is rooted in our shared physical experience with water, shadow and icy climates, or fire, sun and deserts. The meaning of colour seems to be generated from a psychological reaction to a physical experience.

A men's coat by Japanese designer Ichiro Suzuki uses a stiff white cotton drill as a base for digitally printed op art forms inspired by the work of artists including Bridget Riley and M.C. Escher. Parts of the body of the coat are patchworked and others use cotton printed with an all-over check pattern.

Chromatic Convergence by
Myka Baum illustrates the principle
of simultaneous contrast.

Colour communication: the vocabulary of colour

The human eye can differentiate between several million colours of varying hue, saturation and **tone**, and we recognize that colour has more than one visible quality by the adjectives we use.

The vocabulary used to describe colour is often imprecise. We say red, but red can be yellow or bluish in cast, shockingly intense, cloyingly dark or tender and bordering on pink. Differences in colours are not adequately communicated by a broad colour name alone. Therefore, colour names, such as red, are often coupled with evocative adjectives that enhance the communication of the colour 'feeling', for example hellfire red, cherry red or blood red.

Cultural necessities

Thinking about colours as moods and feelings inspires evocative or emotive language and descriptive adjectives that can provoke recognition of very specific colours.

Many thousands of colours have been apportioned names, but these are generally limited. The basic colour vocabulary of even the richest language is surprisingly small, often fewer than a dozen words. All other colour terms are arrived at by qualifying a basic word with the addition of 'light' or 'dark', or by illustrating the colour by referencing it to an object or material, such as ivory, lemon, coffee or mahogany.

No one knows exactly how precise colour terms developed in different languages, but there seems to be a correlation between the importance of a particular commodity, or the need to describe environmental factors, and the complexity of descriptive colour terms. Where precision is found in colour language it is often influenced by a society's environment, for example, desert tribes have a large range of terms for yellows and browns, conversely Eskimos possess a wide vocabulary that enables them to differentiate the colours and variations of snow and ice. The Maoris have over 100 words in their vocabulary for what we would call 'red'. Many African tribes have extensive colour vocabularies for their most significant possessions, cattle. Old Germanic people's reliance on their horses is reflected in their many horse adjectives, a tradition that has passed into English, which also boasts a large variety of descriptive words for the colouring of horses, including roan, bay, chestnut, piebald and skewbald. In most cultures human hair and skin colour are also descriptors that can reflect quite complex shade variations to establish a person's heritage or caste.

Colour trends

The consumer's first response is to colour. Selecting colours and forming a defined colour palette is one of the first considerations when planning a range or collection.

Many industries depend heavily on our constantly changing taste in colour. The prediction of colour trends involves an ongoing assessment of all the subtle factors that influence consumer tastes.

Crazes in colours can be associated with a certain lifestyle. A group of colours can express a cultural attitude or inspirational lifestyle fantasies such as 'sporty', 'classic' or 'ethnic'. The most enduring colour trend of the twentieth century began in the late 1980s. Inspired by the stark aesthetic of a new wave of Japanese designers, black relentlessly encompassed all levels of fashion, and became no longer a colour to be associated with mourning or glamour, but the ultimate expressive 'non-colour' for all aspects of contemporary urban life.

Simultaneous contrast

The effect produced by placing colours of the same intensity together is known as simultaneous contrast (see opposite page). Colours that oppose each other in the spectrum can create striking optical effects, appearing to flicker, shimmer or even undulate depending on the proportion and sequence they are used in. This effect will only be fully apparent if both hues have the same intensity. The value of each colour can appear to change in relation to the colour it is placed next to. In prints or stripes this can cause an optical 'flicker'.

Colour forecasting

The textile industries collaborate with a range of experts for guidance on trend direction. Part of the symbiotic relationship between fashion and textiles is rooted in trends, and these influence the preliminary stages of the development of colour palettes.

For the first view of the new season's trends, the fabric fair **Premier Vision** is held twice-yearly in Paris. Here consultations with industry professionals serve to predict and formulate future trends in colours and fabrics. The principal colour organisations are renowned for their precise and accurate colour predictions. They are made up of international expert colourists that assure a global perspective on colour forecasting. The principal colour consultants are the **Colour Group of Great Britain**, the **International Colour Authority (ICA)**, the **Color Association of the United States (CAUS)** and the **Colour Marketing Group (CMG)**. Colour forecasters analyse and interpret the underlying social, cultural and consumer preferences for colour 'moods' or families and make projections for the future. They do not impose colour selections upon markets, but are adept at analyzing and interpreting underlying trends that indicate the moods and preferences of consumers. Most predicted colour palettes are ready to be distributed to the textile and fashion industries at least one or two years in advance of the retail selling period.

Matching colour

The designer, product developer, merchandiser and retailer need to be aware of the role that light plays in the perception of colour. Every colour we view is modified and defined by its surroundings and by the type of light that illuminates it. Different types of light can radically alter the way a colour looks. A fabric that looks greyish green under a fluorescent light in a retail environment can look bluish green under a domestic light, in context with other colours. The lighting in a retail environment can affect the way a colour is seen, therefore colour matching for this purpose needs to be well considered in order to avert potential merchandising disasters.

Artificial light is also known as reduced spectrum lighting because it is deficient in some colour frequencies. Incandescent bulbs give a warm light that favours the yellow, orange and red frequencies. Warm colours will therefore look more vivid when viewed with this light. Fluorescent light conversely favours the cool frequencies of blue and green colours; this light source will make the colours appear livelier. Light naturally behaves in a random and chaotic manner. Sunlight or electric light, for example, can scatter a mixture of wavelengths in all directions. If various components of product ranges are manufactured in different countries and the colour matching is done under light sources that differ from those of the retail environment, the resulting colours can appear dramatically different.

Colour matching. Artist Isabella Whitworth has experimented with natural dyes to complement the ethically-farmed semi-wild Eri silk. Her swatchbook documents the recipe as 4 cups of onion-skin, 2 parts water and 2 tablespoons of white vinegar, boiled for 15–20 minutes and allowed to stand for a further 30 minutes.

Eco considerations

Consumers are becoming increasingly aware of the impact that their purchasing habits may have on the environment. Colour forecasters identified this attitude in the 1990s and it informed the trend for 'natural state' fabrics: undyed, unbleached textiles and a feel for softer, more 'real' colours.

The environmental and social impact of producing and finishing coloured textiles can be immense and there is no doubt that certain chemicals, dyestuffs and finishing processes have a negative impact on the environment. The toxins discharged by chemical dyes and the waste of natural resources involved in processing are a major consideration when sourcing textiles. Recent years have seen non-governmental organizations (NGOs) driving legislative change that resulted in 22 carcinogenic **azo dyes** being banned in Europe. Informed choices by consumers and commitment by developers of products can help protect the environment.

The surface of the material that a light source falls upon can also affect the way we perceive the colour of that material. Corduroy, velvet, satin and **bouclé** tweeds all have very different surface textures that will affect our visual perception of colour due to the level of absorption or reflection of light upon the fabrics' textures. If a surface is rough or porous, it will absorb a greater proportion of light waves hitting it, and the colour will look darker, while a shiny surface will reflect more of the light and will therefore appear lighter.

Commision Internationale de L'Eclairage (CIE) is an organization that was founded in 1931 at the International Commission on Illumination, following the exploration of the need for a standardization of colour. This system was based on lights. A colourimeter was used to measure three variables of any colour, the luminance (intensity of light given off), the hue and the saturation. Together these values determine the 'chromacity' of a colour. The advantage of the CIE system is that it provides the industry with the means of accurately and consistently matching colours of barely perceptible differences. This objective standard eliminates differences in human interpretation. The **SCOTDIC (Standard Color of Textile Dictionnaire Internationale de la Couleur)** and the **Pantone Professional System** are also widely used in the fashion and textiles industry.

Combining colour

Colours are rarely seen or used in isolation. When working with colour try to transcend the received wisdom of which colours should and should not be seen together. Fashion constantly demands a new perspective on colour and needs to express new ideas. When colours share similar visual qualities we perceive them as harmonious or unified. Colours when juxtaposed can play tricks with our perception of them; they can appear to alter in cast, tone or even size.

A colour moodboard compiled to develop an autumnal palette.

Creating a colour palette

Selecting colours and formulating a colour palette is one of the first considerations in the design and planning of a fashion range. A colour palette (or gamme) is a grouping of colours that show the colour offering of a fashion range. Some of the colours in the palette will take precedence and be used as base colours – these may be the darker shades or neutrals – while others will be used more sparingly as highlight colours or within prints. It is important to be aware of the effect that certain colours can have against skin tones and how the strategic use of colour can create optical effects on the shape of the body.

Inspiration for a fresh approach to colours and forming palettes can be found in the most unlikely sources.

Compiling a colour library involves drawing from diverse inspirational sources such as paintings, photographic imagery, paint samples, coloured yarn, found objects and myriad textures and materials.

Colour resourcing requires the collection of examples of colours. The direction the palette will take is often derived from a combination of the inspirational material gathered while researching a collection, coupled with trend information.

Connecting colour choices to an inspirational mood or 'feeling' helps to define the character of the individual colours and how they relate to each other in a collection. For example, the mood may be for a grimy, urban, degraded-looking neutral palette contrasted with accents of acidic neons. Colour selections can be refined by comparing shades from an archive and matching to professional colour systems. Awareness of the minute differences between shades helps create sophistication within tones.

Fashion demands novelty, and colours we think we have seen before need to be revisited; their tone, cast and intensity reinvented and placed in fresh combinations.

(opposite page) Monochrome shadows form subtle variations of grey. The palest can be clean, pearly, luminous and discreet. Faded and gentle tones have a dusty, ashy and powdery feel. Mid tones are flinty, mature, refined and serious. Cast with other hues grey can take on a deceptive mercurial liveliness.

Useful colour terminology

Achromatic No hue present, without chroma.

Chroma The saturation or brightness of a colour. This term can also define the purity or strength of a colour.

Chromatic Having a hue.

Chromotherapy The use of colour for healing purposes.

CMYK system The four-colour screen system used to reproduce colour photographs: cyan, magenta, yellow, black.

Colour harmony Colour relationships, colours in proportion to each other.

Contrast The visual difference between colours. For example black and white are high-contrast colours.

Co-primary triad The result of the primary triad when split into three pairs consisting of cool and warm versions of each hue.

Muted colour A subdued version of a hue.

Neutral Colours based on the tertiary hues.

Pastel A colour tinted with white to produce a pale version of a hue.

Secondary triad In subtractive colours: orange, green and violet. They are referred to as secondary, because combining two primaries can make them.

Shade The colour resulting from adding black to a hue.

Tint The colour resulting from adding white to a hue, or a colour appearing to weakly modify another, for example 'grey with a green tint'.

Tone A 'greyed' colour.

Colour communication: the vocabulary of colour

White exudes ethereal purity and ultimate light. Modern whites are shimmering, reflective and tinged with dilute blue and ultra violet. Naturally sun-bleached, starchy and chalky hues have a transient brightness. A creamy or misty cast is evident in antique whites.

Introducing colour

The startling, almost chemical, astringency of citrus yellows and acidic chartreuse are tempered and softened by gilded flaxen tones and orange-tinged saffron which convey egg yolk, custard and sun-baked days.

Naturally fresh and verdant chlorophyllic greens can possess an intensely invigorating effect that, when deepened, can verge on poisonous. Verdigris and saturated glowing emerald denote sophistication, and cast with blue become elegant jade. Ripened, muddied and mouldy tones appear in olive, khaki and lichen.

Pale, insouciant diluted pinks are flirtatious, powdery and intimate. Flushed with pigment they become florid and hyper real. Lurid pinks can appear to pulsate with a searing flamboyant appeal akin to red. Tinted with violet, pink can be saccharine and cloying. Tinted with yellow, pink becomes fleshy, limpid and tender. Ripe, reddened tones of orange convey a juicy fruitfulness with an intense glowing warmth. Tinted with browns they mature into earthy, autumnal, rusted and bronzed tones.

Full-spectrum saturated scarlet raises the pulse in its most fierce and fiery shades. Intense ruby and vermillion deepen to become rich crimson and claret.

Blued reds develop into maroons and border on purple. Reds sullied with browns and violets take on a rustic appeal, developing complex shades such as puce.

Icy or salt-bleached tints of blue convey a languid ozonic clarity. Pale, liquid and patinated hues are almost reflective. Intensely saturated blue can be electric and invigorating. Shades with a violet cast inject warmth, and iconic indigo denim spans shades from the merest tint through to the deepest, blackened navy.

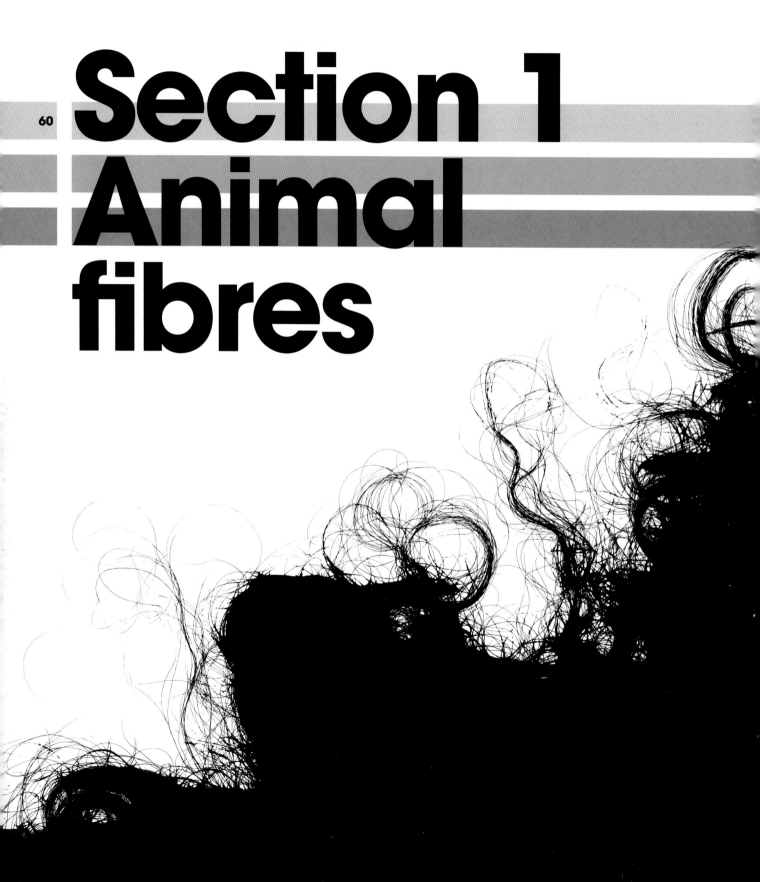

Section 1
Animal
fibres

Wool

62

Wool is the ultimate natural chameleon fibre, embodying many diverse aspects.

Wool can be satisfyingly soft, warm, cosy and sensuous, or rugged, tough and functional, while its inherent drapability allows its finest fibres to appear lustrous, sleek and elegant.

The history of wool

Our relationship with this historic fibre is almost as old as civilization itself, and wool's unique thermally responsive and insulating qualities remain as relevant today as at any time in history.

Early history

The use of felted wool for clothing can be traced back tens of thousands of years. Taking inspiration from the matting of the fleece that occurs naturally on the animal's back, primitive cultures worldwide developed processes of wetting, massaging and pressing the wool to produce a dense, matted felt 'blanket' that could be cut or manipulated into varying thicknesses, or moulded into shape. Felted wool was commonplace in China and Egypt long before the technologies for spinning and weaving were developed.

However, wool was the first animal fibre to be woven, and by Roman times wool, together with linen and leather, clothed Europe. Cotton was seen as a mere curiosity, while silk was an extravagant luxury. It is believed that the Romans invented the carding process to brush, tease and comb the fibres into alignment to facilitate the smoother spinning and weaving of the yarn. It is also believed that the Romans started the selective breeding of sheep to provide better and finer qualities of wool.

(right) A contemporary expression of a historic process, this red merino wool 'boxing' dress is hand felted by US-based German artist Angelika Werth. The boxing dress was one of a series of twelve 'Madeleines' conceived by the artist to express specific personalities. Her interpretation of a baroque-inspired dress exploits the sculptural nature and robust qualities of traditionally felted fine merino wool.

(opposite page) These wool ringlets show the natural curl and lustrous aspect of the fibre in this scoured, washed and dyed wool from a Wensleydale sheep.

Pre-industry

By the beginning of the medieval period the wool trade was the economic engine of both the Low Countries and central Italy, and relied on English wool exports for cloth production. Wool was, at this time, England's primary and most valuable export commodity. Pre-Renaissance Florence's wealth was similarly built on the textile industry, which guided the banking policies that made Florence the hub of the Renaissance.

By the time of the English Restoration, in the mid-seventeenth century, English woollens had begun to compete with silks in the international market. To help protect this lucrative trade the Crown forbade its new American colonies to trade wool with anybody other than the 'mother' country.

Spain's economy was similarly reliant on this valuable export, to such an extent that the export of **merino** lambs was only permitted by royal consent. Spanish merino sheep, with their finer quality fleece, became the most desirable breed. A great majority of today's Australian merino sheep originated from here, via a circuitous route as part of a gift to the Governor of the Dutch Cape, and then onto Australia, where the vast areas of dry pastures perfectly suit fine-wool sheep breeds. The Spanish also introduced sheep to Argentina and Uruguay, where the climate and pastures were favourable for their growth and expansion, and today they represent a sizeable percentage of the two countries' export revenue.

Modern times

By the mid-nineteenth century the Industrial Revolution had turned Bradford in Yorkshire into the centre of the industrialized world's spinning and weaving industry. Bradford's insatiable appetite for fine woollen fibres is said to have built and maintained Australia's colonial economy. By the beginning of the twentieth century Australian sheep rearing and its wool trade had usurped Europe's industry, and to this day Australia remains the most important global producer of wool.

The end of World War II was a catalyst for many socio-economic and political changes. Man-made materials were in tune with the modern world of working women, busy lifestyles and greater social mobility. New sporting and leisure pursuits encouraged the use of easy-care fabrics. The synthetics first developed between the 1930s and 1940s were in general use throughout the 1950s and 1960s, and were considered sophisticated and in tune with postwar values.

Acrylic was developed as a substitute for knitted wool, while **polyester**, or **Terylene** as it was known in tailoring, was the perfect medium for drip-dry, non-iron, easy-care lifestyles.

By contrast, by the mid-1960s new socio-political movements were emerging in North America and Western Europe; the flower-power movement questioned Western values and especially materialism. In the search for a new world order many alternative lifestyles and cultures were embraced. One outward sign of this was in a revival of traditional crafts. Wool and cotton, both natural and traditional fibres, were favoured, preferably if **homespun** and ideally with an organic pedigree. It may be said that the hippy movement was instrumental in jump-starting the wool revival.

The hippy movement of the 1960s questioned Western values and was instrumental in jump-starting the revival of fortune for natural fibres. Fabrics with an organic pedigree became *de rigueur*, an irony lost in this advertisement of the period using hippy imagery to promote synthetic fabrics.

Looking to the future

While wool's heritage and association with reliability and quality may be one of its defining strengths as a commodity, contemporary consumers are now increasingly more sophisticated and demanding, with myriad lifestyle issues that fabrics and fashion must strive to address. In the drive to be responsive to contemporary needs and also remain relevant, scientists and textile designers are researching and developing new technological solutions to extend the existing attributes of this important, traditional fibre. Technological advances in textiles can provide natural fibres with adaptive aspects, which give an already desirable raw material specific enhancements and new benefits, allowing it to remain competitive and aspirational. Current research aims to develop innovative treatments that will enhance, extend and manipulate wool's properties in order to respond to the increasingly shifting requirements of the twenty-first-century consumer.

New-generation wool technology is no longer cost driven, but is about adding alternative fibres, be they synthetic or high-tech, as visual, tactile or practical enhancements to give an alternative aspect to wool. In the two decades after World War II synthetics and natural fibres had no shared common goals, and there was a cultural class divide between the selection of one over the other. Today, natural fibres and synthetics can blend harmoniously, both from a fibre and social viewpoint. Adding 2 per cent **LYCRA**® will give fine-wool suiting a 'memory', while **LUREX**™, for example, can liven up a flat worsted suit fabric; the options are endless.

Modern interpretations of wool can provide the designer with a broad, tactile vocabulary that can express a wide range of design requirements, from classic, traditional and authentic themes, through to the most challenging futuristic explorations in performance fabrics.

Once upon a time wool care, for the consumer, meant careful hand washing, a dedicated cleaning agent and towel drying. Today's consumer is able to enjoy the beauty of woollen products while caring for them in much the same way as they would many other fibres.

The chameleon qualities of this versatile fibre can express and respond to myriad fashion personalities, from urbane, contemporary modern luxury to functional and technologically advanced sportswear.

Classifying wool

Fine
under 24.5 microns

Medium
24.5 to 31.4 microns

Fine cross bred
31.5 to 35.4 microns

Coarse cross bred
35.5 microns plus

Wool ready for grading classification and carding at Coldharbour Mill, Devon, England.

Wool fibre

The natural properties of wool make it flexible, resilient, insulative, absorbent, hygienic and mouldable.

Wool is an organic compound composed of **keratin**, an animal protein that is also found in hair, nails, feathers and horn. As distinct from hair or fur, wool has many tiny overlapping scales, all of which point in the same direction.

The predominant natural colour of wool is a creamy white, although some sheep breeds produce other natural colours, such as brown, black and silver, as well as some random mixes.

Wool fibres, while still on the animal, are coated in a grease that contains lanolin, a slightly yellowish substance. The lanolin is removed and collected during the washing process of raw wool, and used in products such as cosmetics, skin ointment and waterproofing wax. On occasion the wool may be processed without the removal of its natural oil, in which case it retains excellent water-repellent qualities. Traditional **Aran wool** does not have its lanolin removed and was originally used by Scottish and Irish fishermen because it offered excellent protection from the elements.

Crimp

Wool fibres have a **crimp**, a natural wave that allows air to be trapped within the structure, giving wool its natural insulating quality. Fine merino wool may have as many as 100 crimps per inch, while a coarser **karakul** may have as few as one or two crimps per inch. In the spinning process the crimps of the fibre wrap around each other, increasing wool's already excellent tensile strength, which can be stretched from 25 to 35 per cent of its length before reaching breaking point. The springiness of the crimp gives wool its inbuilt recovery, or 'memory', enabling woollen clothes to maintain their shape. Hanging a creased suit in a damp or steamy environment will allow the creases to drop out in very little time without any need to press or iron.

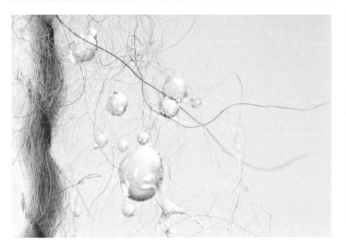

(above left) The three-dimensional stitch work of this traditional Aran sweater helps to trap the air for added warmth. Aran wool has not had its natural lanolin removed.

(left) Wool fibres have an outer layer composed of tiny overlapping scales, which are hydrophobic (having a tendency to repel water). The interior of the fibre is hygroscopic (having a tendency to attract water), allowing garments made from wool to maintain their natural insulating properties even when wet.

(above) This deconstructed Aran wool knit by Natalie Jacobs modernizes the traditional knit technique by displacing the direction of the knit and dispensing with formed sleeves.

Resilience

The exterior of the wool fibre is hydrophobic and tends to repel water, while the interior of the fibre is hydroscopic and attracts water, which means it can absorb up to 30 per cent of its bulk weight in moisture vapour without feeling wet. This gives wool its comfort factor, because it can still feel warm while wet, which is one of the reasons nomads, herdsmen and fishermen living and working in harsh intemperate climates use it.

Wool has natural flame-resistant properties so needs high temperatures before igniting, and does not disintegrate until about 90°C.

Wool that has been felted and treated with lanolin is water-resistant and air-permeable, as well as being slightly antibacterial, which helps the wicking away of odour; airing a woollen product will remove much of the build-up of odour, eliminating the need for constant laundering.

Sheep

Sheep are universally domesticated animals that produce a unique fibre. They can be separated into two principal types: **hair sheep** and **wool sheep**. Wool sheep are then subdivided into three further types.

Hair sheep
Hair sheep are the ancestors of today's domesticated sheep. These originally had coarse hair and a downy or woolly undercoat. Through years of selective breeding the hair disappeared and the woolly undercoat developed to became the outer fleece we recognize today. It is estimated that today only about 10 per cent of the world's sheep population are hair sheep, the majority of which are to be found in Africa. Hair sheep are used for meat consumption and the manufacturing of leather. Sheep leather is referred to as sheep **napa** (or nappa) and lamb is referred to as lamb napa.

Wool sheep
Wool sheep are subdivided into three main categories:

the down breeds or short wools, which prefer warmer, drier climates;

the long wools, which thrive in the wetter regions, with their richer pastures;

the mountain breeds that exist comfortably on exposed hills. The land and pastures that feed the sheep influence the properties of their fleeces. Wool sheep are bred for wool production and also for meat.

Merino Perform™ Advantage Fabric

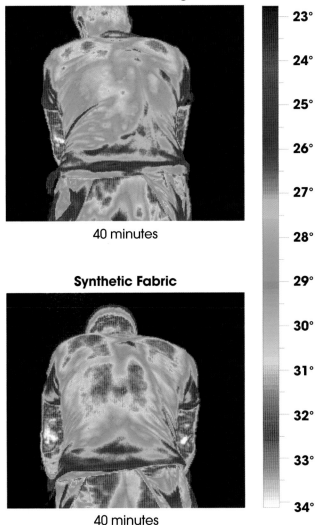

40 minutes

Synthetic Fabric

40 minutes

23°
24°
25°
26°
27°
28°
29°
30°
31°
32°
33°
34°

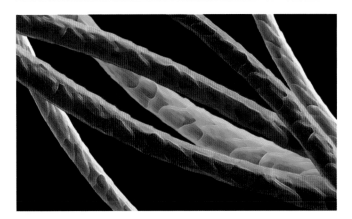

(left) A Sportswool™ garment viewed under a thermal imaging camera shows the natural thermally responsive regulating aspects of the fibre. It helps to raise the body's temperature when in a cool climate, and cools the body when the ambient temperature rises.

(above) Wool fibre under magnification, showing the many tiny overlapping scales all pointing in the same direction. The natural wave or crimp allows air to be trapped within the structure and lends the fibre its natural insulating quality.

Wool production

Over 60 per cent of global production is destined for the clothing industry. Australia is by far the largest producer of wool, of which the majority is from merino breeds. New Zealand is the second largest producer, mainly from cross-bred varieties. Organic wool is becoming popular but represents a very small percentage of global production.

Sixty per cent of all global wool production is destined for the clothing market.

Shearing

The fleece of a sheep is carefully shorn and removed in one piece. **Shearing** represents the single greatest expense of the entire wool-production cycle, constituting approximately 20 per cent of the total cost. The best lambswool is obtained from the first shearing, taken at about six months of age when the fleece is at its softest and finest. Thereafter sheep are shorn at yearly intervals.

An alternative to shearing with hand blades or electric clippers is the protein injection. A retaining net is fitted over the sheep before injecting a protein substance that forms a natural break in the wool fibre. After a week the net is removed and the wool fleece pulled off by hand.

After shearing the fleeces are thrown clean-side down onto rotating tables in the shearing sheds, where impurities and any foreign matter are removed.

Wool classes

Prior to spinning, wool is separated and graded into different quality classification categories known as **wool classes**. The diameter of the fibre is measured in **microns** and is the principal component in determining the classification category. Generally, anything under 25 microns is used for light clothing, while medium grades are used for heavy outerwear and coarse grades for rugs. Finesse, crimp, fibre length, cleanliness and colour are other key ingredients for consideration; grading is also dependent on the breed of sheep and the end purpose of the wool. At this stage, and until the wool has been **scoured** and cleaned, it is referred to as **grease-wool**, or wool-in-the-grease. Finally the wool fibres are compressed into bales ready for packaging and transportation to the mills that will carry out the next round of processes.

Wool scouring

Scouring is an essential cleaning process that removes both the grease and debris from the wool prior to spinning. Scoured wool is usually about 70 per cent of the weight of pre-scoured or grease-wool.

(left) Drafting with view of pin feed at Lightfoot Farm, Maine, USA.

(below) Bobbins of rovings ready for final spinning into yarn. The wool is from a breed of domestic Dorset Down sheep and is in its natural colour. Coldharbour Mill, Devon, England.

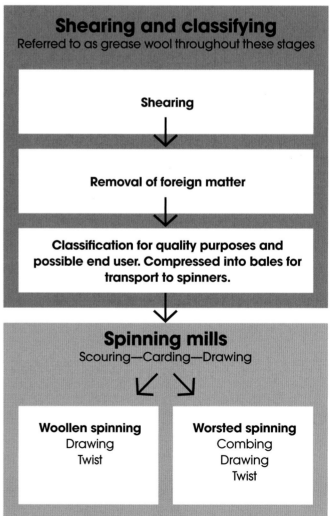

Shearing and classifying
Referred to as grease wool throughout these stages

Shearing

↓

Removal of foreign matter

↓

Classification for quality purposes and possible end user. Compressed into bales for transport to spinners.

↓

Spinning mills
Scouring—Carding—Drawing

↙   ↘

Woollen spinning
Drawing
Twist

Worsted spinning
Combing
Drawing
Twist

Carding, combing and drawing

Carding, combing (see page 13), and drawing are three independent processes that together form part of what is termed the **spinning process** – which also includes spinning itself. All of these processes are carried out in a spinning mill, which may be simply referred to as the 'spinners'.

Drawing and finisher drawing

The two processes of **drawing and finisher drawing** may be applied to both woollens and worsteds to further improve the evenness and regularity of the yarn, prior to final spinning. Woollen spun yarn will also need to go through **condensers** to separate the **web** or **batt** (multiple sheets of fibres) into predetermined weight strands. Each technique gives a uniquely different character, in both appearance and feel, to the fabric and end product. The choice of selecting one over the other is purely a creative decision.

Wool yarn count

Yarns are bought and sold by weight, not by length. Because of this, sizes (numbers or count) are used to express a relationship between the weight of yarn and its length. This relationship also reflects the diameter or thickness of the yarn.

Wool count refers to the number of hanks of yarn (each 560 yards or 512 m in length) that it is possible to spin from one pound of clean wool. The finer the count the more wool it is possible to obtain from one pound. The number of hanks produced gives the wool its count.

In tailoring-fabric terms, the prefix super refers to fabric that has been woven from yarns counted as 100 or more. Therefore a super 120s fabric has been woven from finer yarns than a super 110s fabric. The finer the wool count the softer the fabric is to the touch.

Spinning

The final stage of the spinning process is the application of twist to the yarn, giving it greater tensile strength and added flexibility in preparation for the subsequent knitting or weaving processes. Adding twist can also be a way of achieving myriad different visual effects. Twisting several shades of a colour together will produce a tone-on-tone mélange effect, while twisting together complementary colours can result in innovative colour solutions. Alternatively, different types of yarn can be twisted together to achieve more complex textures. Twisting a LUREX™ yarn with a traditional woollen yarn gives an element of shimmer that takes a traditional woollen or worsted fabric into another dimension. Yarns spun of differing thicknesses will, when woven, give interesting and complex textural surfaces.

A classic 1964 Chanel jacket believed to be cut from Linton tweed. Chanel loved the heritage and practicality of British tweeds and collaborated with mills to modernize them with lighter yarns and unexpected colour.

Twisting yarns of differing natural fibre sources is an interesting proposition from both a fabric and fashion perspective, as well as being a potential marketing lever for a brand. Twisting silk and wool together offers interesting retail marketing possibilities, expounding the contrasting but complementary qualities of both fibres. By contrast, a brand that is at a price-competitive level of the market could use a cashmere and wool mixture and market the luxury aspect of the product while not dramatically increasing the price.

In the search for something new to offer the designer, and ultimately the end consumer, traditional woollen yarns have been twisted with everything from cellophane to **metallic yarns** in the quest for creativity and to promote the use of traditional fibres with added technology.

Woollen spun yarn

Yarn that has gone through the carding and drawing processes is referred to as **woollen spun yarn**. As a result of these processes the fibres tend to lie in all directions, giving a fuzzy, textured appearance. Woollen spun yarns are perfect for knitwear of almost any machine gauge, producing sweaters that are soft, supple and comforting, while woollen spun fabrics tend to have a coarser **handle** with a less visible fabric structure than worsteds (see below). The fibres used are thicker and less even in length, making woollen spun fabrics a perfect medium for textured surfaces with high tactile fabric interest, such as tweed.

(above) Grey cropped coat with contrast sleeves in wool flannel by New York designer Michael Angel. The bold graphic appeal of the chunky proportions is emphasized by the colour blocking of the charcoal and dove grey worn with a beige marl-effect box-pleated skirt in a wool and silk blend.

(right) Sleek, androgynous styling exemplifies a take on the modern urban uniform, here in a fine wool and polyester mix suit by Kostas Murkudis.

(right) Softly draped balloon-skirted dress in a salt-and-pepper tweed blended with a subtle highlight of gold metallic yarn by Korean designer Son Jung Wan. It is worn with a charcoal grey wool turtle-neck cropped wool sweater.

Worsted spun yarn

Yarn that is carded, drawn and in addition then also combed is referred to as **worsted spun yarn**. The fibres lie almost parallel to each other, so worsted spun fabrics tend to have a flatter, smoother finish and a much more visible fabric structure, and could be described as having a cleaner-cut appearance than their woollen spun equivalents. They are used for fine tailoring and dressweight fabrics, as well as some specialist knitwear, where a flatter, less 'woolly' texture is desired. The fibres used are finer and more even in length, making worsteds a perfect vehicle for fine tailoring.

Worsted wool

Worsted wool is the ultimate cloth for expressing precise and urbane classic tailoring. New wool blends lend contemporary deconstructed tailoring a drapeable and supple elegance that moulds to the body and is supremely comfortable.

Traditional wool tweeds can provide an authentic rugged durability or a soft and comfortable sporty feel in softer yarns. New fibre technologies have enhanced the natural thermal properties of wool and make it an ideal choice for performance and fashion sportswear.

(above) This oatmeal layered outfit by designer Nicholas K plays with volume and texture provided by different qualities of woven and knitted fabrics. The draped cape-shouldered jacket is made from plain weave wool, and the fine-knit asymmetric cardigan from a merino blend.

(left) Worsted suit by Edward Sexton, 2008 collection. In the late 1960s Edward Sexton and Tommy Nutter rejuvenated the once stuffy Savile Row with the spirit and verve of swinging London, and attracted a new wave of rock and pop celebrities.

(left) A fine grey worsted wool suit by Kris Van Assche highlights the natural drape of this classic tailoring fabric, conveying ease and elegance.

Producing fabric: weaving and knitting

Once the yarns have been spun they are ready to be either knitted or woven into fabric. Specialist knitting factories and weaving mills will use selected yarns to produce the woollens, worsted fabrics or knitwear. Bi-annual yarn **trade fairs** will showcase their latest developments and new fashion colours. These trade fairs are ideally suited to knitwear and fabric designers, much more so than fashion designers. Each season's trade fairs are really the start of a new season's collection.

Textured traditional

These textured, historic fabrics, with a hand-loom provenance, express an authentic, robust, coarse, rugged aspect.

Tweed Generically describes coarse-textured woollen spun fabrics from Scotland, Ireland and Yorkshire, although Scottish in origin. Today they have been made lighter in weight and are available in all fashion colours. Tweeds are often prefixed with the town or area from whence they originated.

Harris tweed Originally hand-loomed tweed using vegetable dyes, from the Scottish Hebrides.

Donegal tweed Originally hand-spun, with coloured slubs woven into the fabric. Now a generic term for any similar fabric.

Cheviots Traditionally twill-woven outerwear fabrics made from Cheviot or cross-bred wool varieties.

Smooth and compact

These woollen fabrics have a lightly pronounced surface structure, a clean-cut touch and firm handle.

Barathea May be of woollen or worsted construction. Very flat in appearance with a very slightly raised surface.

Cavalry twill Twill weave with a more pronounced double twill.

Gabardine Twill weave with clear surface and fine diagonal rib effect.

Serge Even-sided twill weave. Although originally an Italian silk weave, it is now almost exclusively worsted and used for tailoring.

Venetian Firm touch sateen close weave with a slight matt sheen.

Wool fabrics

The fabrics listed here represent the most popular woollens and worsteds in use, and would give the designer or merchandiser an extensive selection for designing a range or building a collection. The list, however, is not exhaustive. The fabrics are all primarily made from woollen yarns, though some names are shared with other natural and/or synthetic yarns.

(above) Irish designer Paul Costelloe employs the russet tones in the weave of this large-scale checked Harris tweed to enhance the form of the body in a dress inspired by the silhouette of dancer's costumes.

(left) Herringbone is a classic two-colour design. Reversing the twill weave at regular intervals produces its distinctive 'zig zag' effect.

(right) Prince of Wales is a traditional Scottish Glen Urquhart check, usually woven in black and white and featuring a characteristic coloured windowpane overcheck. The design was popularized by the Prince of Wales in the early twentieth century.

(left) This yellow tweed suit by London College of Fashion graduate Mary Binding is made from pure wool Harris tweed. The unexpectedly fresh palette of yellow, orange and cream shades lends the classic Donegal weave a contemporary personality.

(right) This traditional wool tartan men's suit by New York brand Rag & Bone represents a contemporary take on the influence of traditional British tailoring and iconic heritage fabrics. The use of this Royal Stewart tartan communicates an instantly recognizable connection to its Scottish provenance, lending the outfit a classic appeal.

73

Raised surface

Hopsack Plain weave with a pronounced surface resembling the sacking after which it is named.

Panama Lightweight plain weave with a very lightly pronounced cross effect.

(right) Two colours are used in a twill weave construction creating a 'star' effect known as dogtooth or hound's-tooth. The same effect on a smaller scale is referred to as puppy tooth.

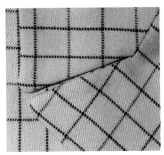

(left) Tattersall check, a traditional equestrian fabric, derives its name from an eighteenth-century racehorse auctioneers at London's Hyde Park Corner, long before it became London's premier address. Today the term Tattersall applies to fabrics of any fibre and checks of any scale, as long as they maintain the equestrian feel of the original fabric.

Iconic fabric designs

The historic fabric designs shown on pages 72–73 originated in the woollen textile industries of Scotland and England. They have been reinterpreted in other fibres, both natural and synthetic. They are constantly revisited by designers and have become instantly recognizable, even when their traditional status is subverted by re-proportioning and reinterpreting the designs in print, knit and even embroidery.

Shown here are:

Hound's-tooth

Prince of Wales

Glen Urquhart check

Tattersall

Herringbone

Tartans/plaids

Producing fabric: weaving and knitting

(below) This elegant oatmeal wool ensemble by Korean designer Son Jung Wan features a raw-edged, waterfall-ruffled blouse in fine wool crêpe, with contrasting chunky hand-knitted wool caped sleeves. It is worn with wool mélange 'sweatshirt' fabric slouchy fit trousers.

(right) A whimsical, draped and folded emerald green loden (felted wool) dress by Viennese brand Femme Maison playfully references folk-tale imagery. Loden was originally produced as a loosely woven cloth, which underwent a lengthy process of shrinking, brushing and clipping to form a thick water-resistant fabric with a short pile.

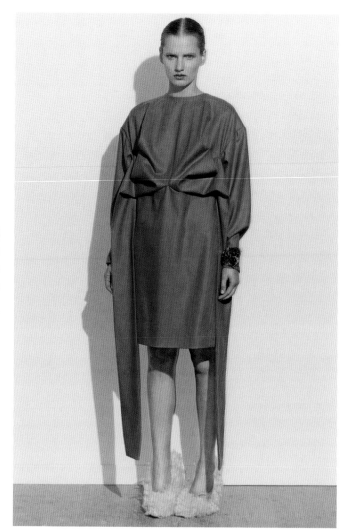

Loopy

Fluffy, airy or granular in texture.

Bouclé The French word for 'curly', the fabric may be woven or knitted. The term is applied to a yarn or finished fabric with a curled surface.

Crêpe An all-over granular effect with a very dry touch.

Moroccan Heavy crêpe effect.

Insulative

Warm and brushed with a cosy, tactile surface.

Flannel Used generically for many worsted spun fabrics. May be of plain or twill weave with napped surface to one or both sides.

Loden Brushed, raised surface, coating weight, originally from Tyrol. The name also implies a specific shade of green that camouflaged well into the local landscape.

Melton Thick, diagonal-weave fabric with a raised surface. Quite firm to the touch and used for outerwear.

Sensual

Glamorous, light and fluid with expressive drape.

Challis Very lightweight plain weave with a soft touch.

Georgette Lightweight plain weave with a very fine crêpe effect.

Mousseline Generic term for very fine, semi-opaque fabric.

(above) The bias cut and oversized blouson styling of this coat by Alexander McQueen emphasize the inherent drape and almost weightless character of this brushed wool and mohair fabric.

(right) This outfit by Colombian designer Haider Ackermann skilfully layers a spicy palette of different qualities of wool in varying weights, including melton, flannel and tweed, to create an urbane and elegant ensemble.

Luxury wool and lambswool

Luxury wools are considered to have special and more desirable attributes than standard wool varieties. Luxury wool fibres will usually be supplied with specialist labelling, a logo and appropriate brand advertising. This is a shorthand code to communicate the desirability of the product to the consumer. It also gives the confidence and knowledge of the product's key benefits.

Lambswool

Lambswool is taken from the first shearing, when the lamb is about six months old, and is especially fine and soft. It is ideal for extra-fine knitwear, especially when fully fashioned, and for superfine suiting fabrics. In the designing and production of a collection the use of lambswool should carry its own dedicated label.

Merino

Merino wool is a statement of luxury. It is soft and supple with year-round comfort.

The wool from the merino sheep is most prized, and considered the ultimate in wool luxury. The lightness, softness and springiness of its crimp make merino yarn a perfect vehicle for fine-quality luxurious clothing.

Superfine merino is one of the finest and softest fleeces of all, while ultra-fine merino wool is often used for blending with prestigious fibres such as silk, cashmere and alpaca.

An important characteristic of merino wool is the tightness and spring of its crimp, as well as the length of its **staple**, which varies from 6 to 10 cm in length. Each sheep produces between 3 and 6 kg of wool per year. Over time merino breeds have been genetically engineered to produce improved qualities of wool and, more recently, following fashion demand, lighter and finer counts of wool.

Merino sheep are valued for their fine wool. The finer the micron count, the more valuable the product.

Classifying merino

Ultra fine
under 17.5 microns

Super fine
up to 18.5 microns

Fine
under 19.5 microns

Fine medium
up to 20.5 microns

Medium
up to 22.5 microns

Strong
over 22.6 microns

The merino was originally indigenous to Asia Minor, then introduced into Spain via North Africa by the Romans, where the breed developed and became an integral part of the economy. The sheep were so important to the Iberian economy that from the fifteenth to the seventeenth centuries they could only be exported with royal consent. Merino sheep also flourished in parts of England, France and Saxony, now southeast Germany.

In the 1790s a small flock of Spanish merino sheep was given as a prized gift to the governor of the Dutch Cape (South Africa). Eventually some of these were sold on and in turn transported to Australia, landing in Botany Bay. The temperate climate and lush pastures were perfect for the breed to thrive and prosper. Sheep rearing became so important an economic factor that it was a fundamental influence in Australia's key role within the British Commonwealth, with much of its economy linked to the breeding of merino sheep and the export of their wool.

Merino sheep are now successfully reared in New Zealand, South Africa, Argentina, Uruguay and in the west of the United States; however it is Australia that is the most important producer and exporter of merino wool.

The term merino was originally only used for Spanish-bred merino sheep, but the superior quality of the Australian, and later the New Zealand, strains means that the name is now used to describe merinos irrespective of country of origin.

Woollen underwear

In the late nineteenth century Dr Gustave Jaeger (1832–1917) pioneered 'the scientific theory of hygienic dress', which maintained that wool was the ideal fibre to wear next to the skin. He promoted the wearing of woollen undergarments for optimum health, based on the theories of wool's antibacterial properties. This practice was upheld in many countries, to some extent, through to the middle of the twentieth century.

Retro proportioned knitted hand-framed bodysuit by Finnish art brand IVANAhelsinki, whose ethos and production philosophy are based on ethical and ecological choices.

Australia's merino

Australia has four basic strains of merino.

Pepin: Considered to be the most important strain, thriving in drier inland regions, however its fleece falls into the mid-range of merino wool quality.

Saxon: Prefers cooler wetter regions; it is physically the smallest strain but produces the finest, most prized and most expensive quality of wool.

South Australian: Thrives in the most temperate climate and is physically the largest of the strains. The wool produced falls into the coarsest of the categories.

Spanish: The smallest in numbers and shares similar attributes to the pepin.

And wool is also marketed under the name **Botany wool** to denote wool originating from Botany Bay. The term is suggestive of very fine woollen knitwear and carries its own dedicated specialist labelling.

Merino clothing is made from the very best yarns, however in knitwear the term mainly refers to garments made from worsted spun yarns.

Sumptuous hand-knitted heather grey oversized sweater in 100 per cent merino wool by New York designer Michael Angel. The giant scale of the knit makes an exaggerated statement, emphasizing the cosiness and luxury of the merino yarn.

Rambouillet or French merino

The **Rambouillet** breed is believed to have originated around 1786, when Louis XVI either received or purchased a flock of Spanish merinos from the king of Spain. The sheep were crossed with English long-wool breeds on a royal farm at Rambouillet near Paris, producing a well-defined breed that differed in several important points from the original Spanish merino. They were now of a far greater size, with larger wool **clips** and a longer wool length.

In 1889 the Rambouillet Association was formed in the United States with the aim of preserving the breed. Today about half of the sheep on the western ranges of the United States are of this strain. Rambouillet studs have also been of great importance in the development of the Australian merino industry.

Shetland wool

Shetland sheep are the smallest of all the breeds in the British Isles. They are of Scandinavian origin and believed to have been brought over by the Vikings.

From the cold climate of the Shetland Islands, Shetland fleece has a distinctive fine fibre quality in a range of natural shades, from off-whites to reddish brown, grey, dark brown and through to black, colours that traditional Shetland patterns are based on; furthermore the many natural colours of Shetland are in tune with current market demands for ecological yarns that have not been chemically dyed.

Traditionally, Shetland fleece was hand plucked from the sheep at the time when they would naturally shed their seasonal fleece, resulting in fine and soft wool.

Shetland wool conjures up romantic notions of traditional country tweeds and knitwear, often in **muted colours** that camouflage so well with the countryside. Warm, comforting and with a slightly wiry texture, Shetland wool fabric remains popular to this day.

Extravagant Mongolian sheep-wool coat by Huwaida Ahmed. The exceptionally long and curly corkscrew locks are characteristic of Mongolian sheep wool.

Shetland colours

The different strains of Shetland sheep still carry the Old Norse names, which are also often used to describe the shades or colours.

Bleget Whitish grey.

Emsket Dusky blue to grey.

Eesit Shades of ash.

Moget Light brown, dark belly.

Shaela Shaded wool from dark to light.

Skeget Striped sides.

Skjuret Mixed brown and grey.

Under London label Colenimo, Japanese designer Aya Nakagawa, for the Autumn/Winter 2008 capsule collection, references the attitude of 1950s teddy boys and girls, and plays with feminizing masculine silhouettes and revisiting robust traditional fabrics. Here, a vintage 100 per cent Shetland wool conveys its rugged appeal and shows a contemporary take on the use of authentic fabrics.

(right) Undyed Shetland wool fibre from Hand Weavers Studios. This distinctive fibre comes in a natural colour palette ranging from off-white through to reddish brown, mid- to dark brown, grey and black. In addition to the traditionally crafted iconic country tweeds and knitwear, Shetland wool fabric has now become the perennial favourite of designers, attracted by the romance attached to the heritage surrounding the fibre.

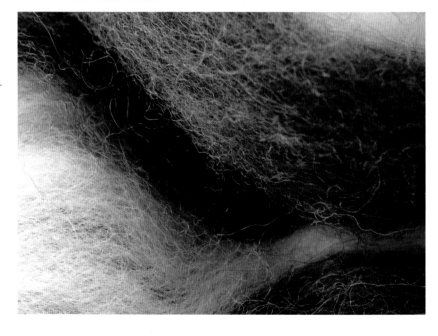

Icelandic wool

In the late ninth century the Vikings brought sheep to Iceland. Over 1,000 years of isolation from contact with other breeds has maintained the purity of their gene pool, resulting in one of the purest and rarest breeds in the world. The sheep are reared in the high mountains where they produce fleeces considered to be among the rarest in the world, their rarity compounded by the fact that their numbers are diminishing annually.

Icelandic wool fleece is double layered, made up of a fine, soft, insulating inner fibre and long, glossy, coarser outer fibre. The inner fibre is as soft as cashmere and classified as fine wool, while the outer fibre is classified as medium wool. The structure of the outer fibre allows water to run down and not penetrate and its irregularity traps air, giving warmth.

Icelandic wool is lighter than most other wool types, and its minimal crimp makes it perfect for worsted spinning, the resulting yarn being **lofty** in appearance. The two fibres may be spun separately to create yarns of different weights that are suitable for different end uses, or spun together for a yarn that when knitted or woven would give maximum protection from the elements.

The Icelandic sheep has the largest natural colour shade range of any breed, from white to grey to a large selection of browns and black. Some sheep have a differing shade of inner fleece to their outer fleece. Left unshorn the fleece would grow to about 45 cm in a year, and therefore tends to be shorn twice a year.

Karakul wool

Karakul, or Persian lamb as it is often known, is from Central Asia, and is considered to be one of the first domesticated breeds, associated with the felted fabric that predated knitted or woven fabric. Today a large percentage of South African wool is from Karakul sheep. The wool has a tight curly pattern and tends to be in shades of grey to black. As a woollen yarn it is much sought after for expensive millinery, however it is most prized for its pelts.

Useful wool terminology

100% virgin wool or 100% pure new wool The product has been produced from fibres that have not been previously processed.

100% wool The product is all wool, but possibly recycled or re-processed.

Mungo Fibrous woollen material generated from waste fabric.

Wool blends A mixture of different wools and/or other fibres.

This geometrically draped dress by Haider Ackermann is made from a deluxe wool-silk blend, creating a fabric that fuses the glamour of silk (which provides the satin face of the cloth) with the insulating softness of wool. The resulting textile expresses a contemporary glamour and ease.

Wool market

Australia is singularly the largest wool producer, supplying around 25 per cent of the world's consumption, most of which is exported to make yarn for the weaving and knitting industries. The greater majority of Australian wool is from merino sheep breeds.

New Zealand is the second largest exporter of fine wool, but is however the world's largest producer and exporter of cross-bred wool. The majority of the cross-bred wool (31.5 microns plus) goes to China to supplement its domestic production.

China produces both fine wools and cross-bred varieties. However, due to its importance as a global manufacturing hub it consumes the majority of its domestic production for its own manufacturing industries; the eventual end use is finished clothing for export. It is also a major importer of all wool qualities, which it uses to manufacture end products for export.

Uruguay is the third largest wool producing–exporting country in the world; however it is the second largest producer of clothing-weight wool. Around 10 per cent of its wool production is kept for domestic fabric consumption, which is ultimately also for export.

Argentina and South Africa are also key exporters of wool, followed by Turkey and Iran. Great Britain and Sudan produce around 2 per cent each. The United States – notably Texas, New Mexico and Colorado – produces around 1 per cent of the world's output.

The principal consumers of the good quality merino are Italy, France, Germany, Great Britain and Japan of which Italy and Japan use the very best for their sophisticated fully-fashioned knitwear industries.

Marketing wool

The marketing and promotion of wool is an important issue, which has been addressed nationally by the formation of various wool boards or associations that represent the wool growers of their respective countries. Collectively these offer a guaranteed standard of quality of the raw material that goes to the spinners and in turn to the fabric manufacturers. This quality standard is a selling and promotional tool for the design company, and in turn to the end consumer.

Australia: Woolmark

Woolmark is a registered mark used for branding different types of Australian wool, and is used as a means of guaranteeing a standard of quality. The Woolmark brands and sub-brands are designed to give the consumer confidence and knowledge of the product, as well as communicating the key benefits and promoting an awareness and understanding of the product's full potential. This is essential information for the designer because the choice of fabric, with the appropriate level of brand recognition, may give added value and increase the sales potential of the collection over that of a competitor.

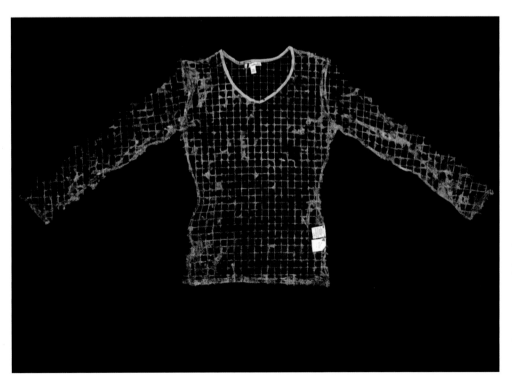

This sweater was buried by the New Zealand Merino Company in order to compare the biodegradation behaviour of its merino wool fibres with that of synthetics. After nine months the sweater had lost 99 per cent of its mass. By contrast, during the same time frame a polyester garment showed no signs of degradation.

WOOLMARK

The Woolmark trademark logo.

WOOLMARK
BLEND

The Woolmark blend trademark logo.

WOOL BLEND

Wool blend logo products are high tech new wool mixes of 30–49% new wool that maintains the natural qualities of wool combined with offering comfort and performance.

WOOLMARK
merino
extrafine

Pure Merino Wool is premium quality wool. Naturally fine and silky, it is super-soft, lightweight and comfortable to wear.

83

WOOLMARK
COOL
WOOL

Logo for new generation of lightweight fabrics and knitwear.

wool
plus
LYCRA

Wool plus LYCRA® is a dynamic mix of new wool and LYCRA®.

WOOLMARK
Natural
Stretch

Logo for pure new wool with enhanced natural stretch. Through a special selection of fibers, this wool gives woven fabrics extra ease of movement, comfort and the elasticity to recover from daily wear.

light
wool

Light wool is super lightweight wool that is truly cross-seasonal. Its ultra fine yarns make for the sheerest knitted and tailored clothing.

wool
COTTON

WOOLMARK
BLEND

Wool and cotton logo.

wool
LINEN

A special blend of yarns providing all the performance benefits of natural fibres.

GOLD
WOOLMARK

The Gold Woolmark denotes an exciting new standard, differentiating luxurious garments made of the finest quality superfine Australian wool.

I.W.T.O.

IWTO (International Wool Textile Organization) is an International organization covering all aspects of marketing wool for all major producers.

The Woolmark logo is a registered trade mark of The Woolmark Company that is owned by Australian Wool Innovation and indicates high quality of woollen products. The Woolmark is an assurance by the manufacturer that a product is made of pure new wool. End products carrying these symbols have been quality tested by The Woolmark Company for compliance with its performance and fibre content specifications (Woolmark indicates 100 per cent). The Woolmark is one of the most recognized symbols globally and represents the world's largest fibre quality assurance scheme.

Ecological and ethical considerations

Wool is, or fundamentally should be, an ecologically sound product, but the increase of production and desire for consistency of quality, together with the concern for maximum return on investment, will mean that some aspects are not as ecologically or ethically sound as today's informed and aware consumer might wish.

The designer or company manufacturing the designs needs to have its target customers in mind when selecting the source of its fabrics. This is not always straightforward, because the supply chain from sheep rearing to fabric manufacturing has many stages that could have ecological and/or ethical implications. How deeply these issues are considered is really dependent on the brand's ethos and the target customer's expectations.

A fabric manufacturer or spinner that uses yarns from ethical and ecologically sound sources will place emphasis on these virtues, especially since the fabrics will tend to be more expensive. The eco-factor may be the **USP** (unique selling point) to justify the price differential. Similarly, sheep farmers that practise a more humane form of animal husbandry as well as sounder ecological grazing methods will also promote these aspects.

Ecological criteria

The International Wool Textile Organization (IWTO) has categorized eco-wool and organic wool for clarification at retail and consumer level. The three categories for classifying eco-wool are: eco-wool; eco-wool products; and eco-wool containing products. The three categories for classifying organic wool are: organically grown wool; organic wool product; and organic wool containing product.

The guiding criteria for ecologically sound wool should consider the following points.

Correct grazing for the flocks Appropriate field rotation minimizes soil erosion and reduces the chance of the sheep incurring internal parasites. Often sheep are crowded onto land, resulting in over-grazing, and thus destroying the vegetation. When a field becomes barren the grower brings in dry feed that can add additional veggie-matter to the fleece, which needs to be destroyed by means of harsh acids that can leave wool dry and over-crimped.

Clean water Unpolluted drinking sources.

A predator friendly environment Using well-trained sheep dogs.

Healthy veterinary practices Using only certain types of medications and supplements.

Soil chemical control Not using herbicides and pesticides on fields that sheep graze on.

Livestock chemical control Sheep are bathed in chemicals to ward off pests and insects, which may leave a residue and contaminate the ground water if used improperly. After shearing, harsh toxic chemicals are often used to clean the wool, as well as bleaching agents to whiten the wool during and after scouring.

Carbon footprint The distance of travel from primary source to final destination.

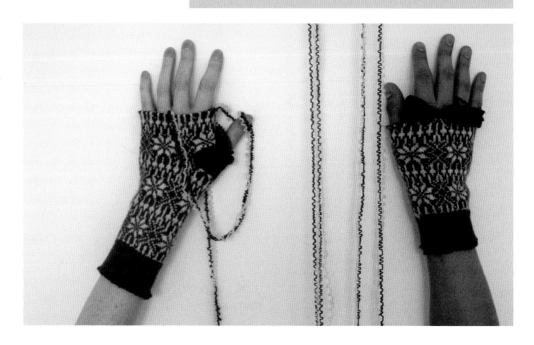

Hanging On, an exercise in deconstructed Fair Isle knit socks by Myka Baum, from the series 'A Load of Rubbish', inspired by San Franciscan performance artist Michael Swaine.

Recycling wool

The recycling of wool has always been part of the industry's production cycle. Old wool can be mixed with raw wool and wool noil, or alternatively with other fibres such as cotton. This is done to increase the average length of the recycled fibre, because the tearing process involved in its recovery tends to result in shorter fibres, making re-spinning and weaving difficult. Recycled wool is often used as weft yarns on products with cotton warps.

Fibre reclamation mills grade incoming materials into types and colours. The colour sorting means that little, if any, re-dyeing will be necessary, thus saving on energy and pollutants. The textiles are then shredded into **shoddy,** wool that is of inferior quality to the original wool product, made by tearing apart existing wool fabric and re-spinning it. Fibres are blended with other selected fibres, depending on their intended end use. The blended mixture is carded to clean the fibres and mix them together before being spun. Alternatively, the fibres can be compressed for mattress production or shredded to make filling material for car insulation, roofing felts, loudspeaker cones or other similar products.

A buyer or designer will need to check the fabric content label to ascertain the full composition of the fabric. Although it is a requirement that all fibres are disclosed, occasionally a content label may state 2 or 3 per cent marked as 'other fibres'. This is because it is not always possible to know the content of merchandise that may have already been previously recycled.

Recycling has long been part of the industry's production cycle. Fibre reclamation mills grade incoming materials into types and colours, thus saving energy on unnecessary reprocessing before shredding into shoddy.

The wool shredder is an important part of the recycling process.

Make do and mend

The 'make do and mend' ethos popularized during the First and Second World Wars gradually became obsolete as clothing became cheaper. Now, the choice to make, fix or customize our clothing is an emotionally-driven decision. The act of repairing our most cherished clothing is a statement in itself, not only as an expression of frugality and a desire to be less wasteful, but also because it speaks of our relationship with our clothes and the memories they hold.

Contemporary casual clothing brands have long embraced the artfully 'worn' aesthetic. Much research and development is invested in ripping, fading, degrading and patching techniques, particularly in the jeans market. These brands seek to replicate the wear and tear of workwear and its desirable visual appeal. These 'worn' products are perceived as authentic and steeped in an honest history, even though that history does not always reflect the life experiences of the wearer.

The 'Door to door darning' concept by San Franciscan performance artist Michael Swaine. He started the mobile 'free mending library' fixing clothes, telling stories and provoking the interrogation of our throwaway society.

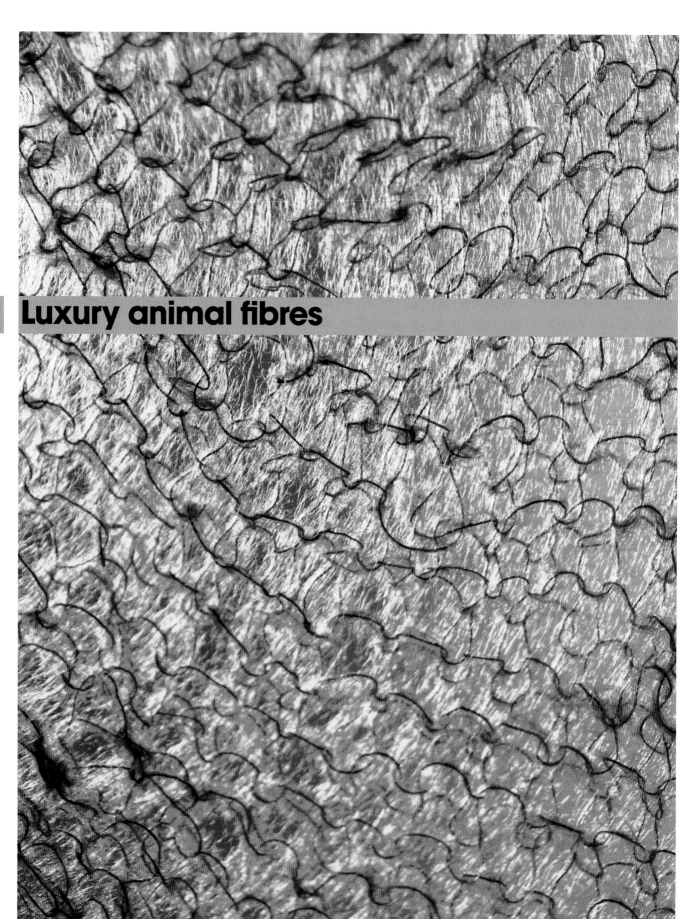

Luxury animal fibres

86

The allure of these precious 'golden fleeces' is rooted in their exotic and romantic past. Their rarity is inextricably linked with a superlative level of quality and luxury that no man-made substitute can ever match.

The fibres that make up this luxury segment of the market are derived from several different groups of animals. The enduring appeal of these noble fibres is that despite amazing developments in textile technology, their classic luxury status remains unchallenged.

The creatures that produce these fibres have evolved coats of supremely soft and warm material, uniquely adapted to cope with inhospitable extremes of heat and cold. The coats contain the finest of hairs and an all-important under-fleece that is almost heavenly to the touch. Fabrics made from these fibres possess an inbuilt elegance that expresses refinement and the ultimate in luxury.

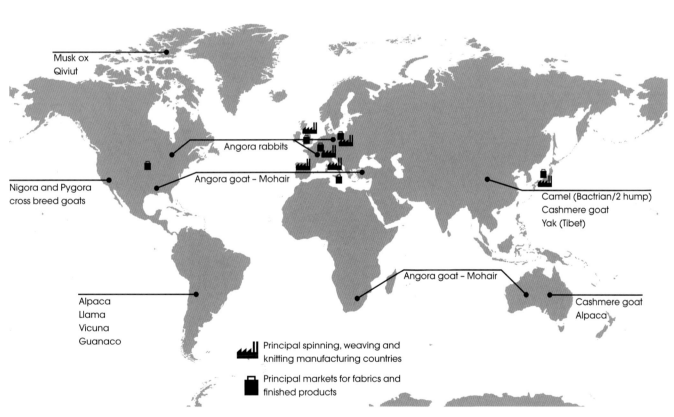

Musk ox
Qiviut

Angora rabbits

Nigora and Pygora
cross breed goats

Angora goat – Mohair

Camel (Bactrian/2 hump)
Cashmere goat
Yak (Tibet)

Alpaca
Llama
Vicuna
Guanaco

Angora goat – Mohair

Cashmere goat
Alpaca

Principal spinning, weaving and knitting manufacturing countries

Principal markets for fabrics and finished products

The animals that provide some of our most valued and luxurious raw materials inhabit a diverse range of climates. Each of the animals shown on this map have coats that possess complex and unique properties that have evolved in response to the climatic challenges presented by different geographical locations, whether in natural or cultivated habitats.

(opposite page) Referred to as 'golden fleeces', in acknowledgement of their rarity and desirability, the luxury animal fibres have whisper-light properties that lend them an ephemeral delicacy and exceptional thermal properties.

Luxury animal fibres

Camelids

A number of luxury fibres are harvested from a group of animals biologically known as the South American *Camelidae* family, which consists of four types of llama.

Alpaca

Alpaca yarn is ideal for loose spinning to produce a hard-wearing and very light garment, with great insulating properties.

The **alpaca** (*Vicugna pacos*) is a South American mountain animal; however, prehistoric remains have also been found in both the Rocky Mountains of North America and the Sierra Madre mountains of Central America. Principally found in Peru and Ecuador, smaller numbers are also found in the northern parts of Bolivia and Chile.

Superficially resembling a small llama, alpacas were domesticated by the Moche and Inca peoples of Peru, thousands of years before the Spanish conquest of South America. They were a crucial and treasured component of ancient life, used as beasts of burden and for their meat and wool. Now the alpaca is the principal South American fibre-producing animal.

The history of alpaca

In the early 1800s Spain 'rediscovered' the beauty of the alpaca's fleece, and imported the fibre, sending it to France and Germany for spinning.

Alpaca was first spun in England in the early nineteenth century, but was considered to be unworkable. This was in part due to the type of fabric being woven. By 1836, in Bradford, the centre of the English woollen textile trade, alpaca's true potential was realized when it was woven using cotton warps.

The trade in alpaca remained at a domestic level until the early 1950s, when proactive marketing of the processed fibre began.

The United States and Canada first imported alpacas in the early 1980s, followed by Australia and New Zealand later in the decade. The more sophisticated animal husbandry practised in these countries has proven successful as the alpacas are fast multiplying, and through selective breeding are now producing heavier fleeces and finer fibres.

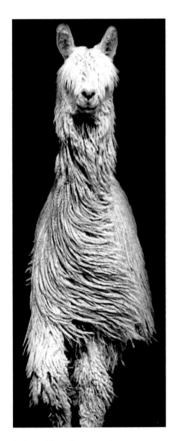

(above) Sam the suri alpaca, courtesy of Marsha Hobert at Suri Network.

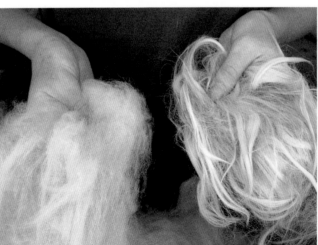

(above) An evocative image of alpaca fibre sorting in Peru. Sorting fibres into colours and qualities is a skilled operation requiring a discerning eye and dexterity of hand.

(left) Contrasting fleeces from the suri and huacaya alpaca. Sorting through the fleece is skilled specialized work, which is done by hand.

Alpaca fibre

There are two types of alpaca. The **huacaya** (pronounced wua'ki'ya) produce a dense, soft sheep-like fibre with a uniform crimp. They are the most common in both their natural South American habitat and in the countries that have since imported them. The **suri** (pronounced soo'ree) have silky, pencil-fine, mop-like locks. Suris make up the remaining 20 per cent of the population and are prized for their finer, longer fibres. Both types are highly valued and regarded to be just below that of vicuña (see page 91) in quality. An alpaca–llama cross breed, **huarizo**, is also valued for its fine fleece.

Fibre from the huacayas is marketed as **alpaca fleece**, while the fibre from suris is marketed as **alpaca suri**.

In textile terms 'alpaca' refers primarily to **Peruvian alpaca**, which is marketed with a dedicated symbol of authenticity. However, the term is also used, more broadly, to describe a genre of fabric. Sometimes Icelandic wool is referred to as alpaca because of its similar visual appearance. Alpaca fleece does have some similarities to sheep's wool but it appears much lighter in weight, silkier to the touch, warmer and less prickly. It has minimal lanolin, making it nearly hypoallergenic. It is also impermeable, thermally responsive and has a low flammability point.

Alpaca production

Alpaca farming is of low impact to the environment and therefore an interesting alternative for some sheep farmers. The animals are sheared annually, producing a fleece grossing about 7kg; after removal of the **guard hairs** the net weight is about 3kg. In their native Andean habitat alpacas are generally sheared once every two years.

Alpaca fibres are processed in a similar way to sheep wool fibres (see pages 69–70).

Colour range

Alpacas naturally range in colour from jet black through warm browns, fawns and cool greys to creamy whites at the lightest end of the spectrum. The large range of colours and shades is a special characteristic of the breed and hence colour sorting is highly skilled work carried out by hand and eye: the most important part of the business. Depending on country of classification, fleeces can range from between 12 to 52 natural colours and shades: Peru classifies 52; the United States 22; and Australia 12.

Fashion demands have made white the commercially most desirable colour, and therefore the most expensive. This has led to selective breeding, resulting in the darker colours being almost bred out of the species. There is now a revival in the demand for the darker shades, which breeders are trying to reintroduce, however the quality is not quite as fine as that of white.

Alpaca's illusion

Alpaca is an enigmatic fibre, prized for its fine, soft and silky-like characteristics. The impression of fineness in alpaca is generated by the low scale height of the cuticle cells, which allows the hand to slide easily over the surface of the fibre.

The second part of alpaca's illusion is the apparent softness of the fibre. Technically it is not soft; in fact the resistance to abrasion of the cuticle cells is more than twice that of wool, a very hard surface. The 'softness' stems from its springiness and resistance to compression: resisting forming into a solid mass under compression gives the impression of lightness of weight. In wool production this is only achieved by scouring.

The enigma of alpaca lies in that it appears fine but is not, appears soft but is actually hard and strong. It has excellent thermal properties with apparent lightness of weight; it is durable and silky in texture.

(right) Oversized chunky alpaca and leather crochet coat worn with gunmetal metallic high-waisted knitted trousers by Julia Neil.

(far right) Heirloom inspired alpaca, leather and crystal sweater dress worn with violet cashmere vest and leggings by Julia Neill. Victorian chandelier crystals are integrated into the knit in crocheted frameworks.

Llama

The llama (*Lama glama*) is the largest of the South American *Camelidae* family, believed to have originated in the mountains of North America 40 million years ago and to have migrated south around three million years ago. They became essential pack animals as well as a source of protein for the indigenous Indian peoples of the Andes. The Spanish conquistadors used thousands of llamas as a means of transporting the spoils of warfare.

At present there is only a very small commercial market for llama fibre, and it tends to be favoured by hand spinners for organic and craft clothing.

Llama fibre

The four types of llama are the **curaca** and **ccara**, or classic 'light wool' llamas, and the **tapada** and **lanuda**, or 'heavy wool' llamas. Nearly 70 per cent of the world's llamas live in Bolivia, with a smaller number in Peru. However, because the first llamas imported into Europe were from Peru, it is the Peruvian terminology that is in common use today. Of the Bolivian llamas nearly 80 per cent are of the heavy, woolly-coated type, which have fleeces suitable for making yarn.

Technically **llama fibre** is not wool because it is hollow and has a structure of diagonal 'walls'; however, it is referred to as llama wool. The fibre is strong and light and has good insulation properties. It is thicker and coarser than alpaca fibre, with a diameter ranging from 20 to 40 microns. If the micron count is under 28 it may also be described as alpaca. By way of comparison, merino wool is between 12 and 20 microns.

Llama production

Llamas are low-maintenance animals with little impact on the environment.

They are efficient and adaptable frugal foragers and adjust well to free-choice feeding or once-a-day feeding schedules based on owner convenience. Llamas are shorn either once a year or once every two years. Their fleece comes in four main colours, ranging from white through grey, brown and black, and is grease free.

A llama in its indigenous Andean habitat, dressed in locally handcrafted adornments.

Vicuña

Inca legend states that the **vicuña** (*Vicugna vicugna*) is an incarnation of a beautiful maiden courted by an ugly old king. She would only concede to his advances if given a coat of pure gold. The vicuña's fleece is still referred to as the 'golden fleece', an accolade that is reflected in the stratospheric prices paid for the fabric.

The vicuña was the first of the *Camelidae* family to be domesticated by ancient Andean tribes of Peru. The Incas raised the vicuña for their wool and protected them by law, under penalty of death. The esteem in which these animals were held ensured their mystique, and only Inca kings and the royal court were permitted to wear garments made from vicuña wool.

Endangered and reinvigorated

The huge commercial demand for vicuña fibre and unrestricted hunting in the nineteenth and twentieth centuries resulted in the species becoming almost extinct. In 1960 there were only an estimated 6,000 vicuña left in the wild; it was declared an endangered species in the mid 1970s, and trade of the vicuña fibre was prohibited.

Anti-poaching efforts in Peru, Argentina and Chile, and to a lesser extent in Bolivia, led to a dramatic comeback, and now there are an estimated 130,000 in the wilds of Peru, 30,000 in Argentina and possibly 30,000 between Chile and Bolivia. All four countries relaxed the laws in 1993, and commercial harvesting is now being practised. Vicuña is now a **cash crop** that can benefit some very poor communities.

Peru has taken the lead in vicuña conservation. It has introduced a labelling system that shows that a garment has been created through a government-sanctioned **chacu**, an Incan tradition that guarantees that the animals are captured, sheared and released back into the wild; furthermore they will not be sheared again for another two years. The programme ensures that a large percentage of the profit goes back into village communities and to fund further research into the animals' protection.

Poaching, however, still persists, and 25,000 kg of fibre is still annually exported illegally. The animal is difficult to shear, so it is likely in this instance that they are killed for their fleece. To help prevent this illegal export, some countries have introduced a blanket ban on all vicuña fibres and fabrics.

Paco vicuña

The vicuña is the smallest of the wild South American camelids, and lives in the plains, grasslands and mountain regions of the Andes. DNA tests show that alpacas have vicuña ancestry, possibly due to selective breeding 6,000 years ago. Today 80 per cent of vicuña have llama DNA.

More recently, vicuñas have been cross-bred with alpacas, resulting in offspring called **paco vicuña**. Introducing vicuña into alpaca genetics has created a fibre that is as fine as that of the alpaca (14 to 16 microns) but with a fleece longer than that of the vicuña, making it easier to shear. It can also be shorn annually rather than only once every three years. All the other characteristics of the fibre are the same as that of the vicuña, making it just as desirable.

Vicuña fibre

Vicuñas have the finest of all animal fibres, with a diameter of between 6 and 14 microns. The outer guard hairs are about 25 microns, and are easily removed with sticks from the shorn fleece. The wool is very sensitive to chemical treatments, so it is always left in its natural colour, which is a rich, golden honey.

Vicuña fibres are extremely warm, due to the structure of tiny scales that surround the hollow, air-filled fibres, which lock together and trap insulating air.

The fleece yield of a vicuña is approximately 500 g per year, in comparison to the 7 kg of the alpaca.

Vicuña production

A vicuña fleece weighs about 220 grams; it can take one person a week to **de-hair**. After washing, the remaining fibre will be about 100 grams.

Vicuña market

Peru is the principal exporter of vicuña, and garments and fabrics are registered with the Peruvian government authority, the only international body recognized for the task; it also assures quality and purity of fibre.

Current prices for vicuña fabric are from $1,800 to $3,000 per metre. Yarn is priced at around $500 per kilogram, and is the most valuable natural fibre. Italy is the primary global importer of vicuña cloth, while Germany is the primary global importer of vicuña clothing.

Guanaco

A larger cousin of the vicuña, the **guanaco** (*Lama guanicoe*) is found in the high plains of the Andes from the north of Peru to the south of Chile, Bolivia and Argentina. It is fast, wild and of a rich cinnamon honey colour. At the time of the Spanish invasion they numbered approximately half a billion, today they number a few hundred thousand.

The guanaco is double coated with coarse guard hairs and a soft undercoat similar to the alpaca, and is second only to the vicuña in quality. The guanaco is a protected species that needs a permit for hunting, to ensure that the fibre has been obtained from an approved source.

Camel hair

Camel-hair fibre

Camel hair has thermostatic properties that keep the wearer warm in winter and cool in summer, and is believed to contain anti-rheumatic and anti-arthritic properties.

Bactrian and **dromedary** are two species of camel, both Afro-Asiatic relatives of the South American family of camelids. The dromedary *(Camelus dromedarius)* is the one-humped desert-dwelling Arabian camel, which was the first of the two to be domesticated. The bactrian *(Camelus bactrianus)* has two humps and was first domesticated some 2,500 years ago in what are today the regions of northern Iran, Afghanistan, northern Pakistan and Turkistan, where temperatures are at hot and cold extremes between summer and winter. Apart from some wild bactrian camels in the Gobi Desert, and feral dromedary camels in Australia, camels are now completely domesticated.

Camel hair for commercial consumption is obtained only from the bactrian camel. The bactrian camels with the best-quality hair live in the extreme climatic conditions of Inner Mongolia (northern China) and Outer Mongolia. Camel hair also comes from Afghanistan, Iran, Russia and Tibet. Camels are not native to New Zealand or Australia but have been introduced to supplement their domestic fibre selection.

The fibres of the camel's down undercoat are between 2 and 10 cm in length, and do not felt easily. The outer coat has coarse long hairs that are used for carpets and bedding. Among the indigenous peoples of the area, the guard hairs are used to weave waterproof fabric for clothing, to withstand extreme weather conditions.

The mane of the camel is used for **interlinings** for good-quality tailoring. For clothing only the softer undercoat is used, either as pure camel hair or blended with lambswool. If it has been **tri-blended** with wool and a synthetic, then the camel hair is likely to be of an inferior quality, or possibly even recycled.

The very best camel hair is from the underside of a Mongolian baby camel. The fibres are approximately 25 to 60 mm long and 16 to 21 microns in diameter. At this standard it is almost comparable to cashmere (see page 94), and is the result of years of selective breeding. By comparison, adult camel hair has a diameter of approximately 21 to 25 microns.

Camel hair is traditionally used in its natural colour, golden tan with varying tones of red. Contemporary developments in dyeing technology allow it to respond to dye equally as successfully as wool; however, if dyed, it is often preferred in a range of faux natural colours, from blond to brown.

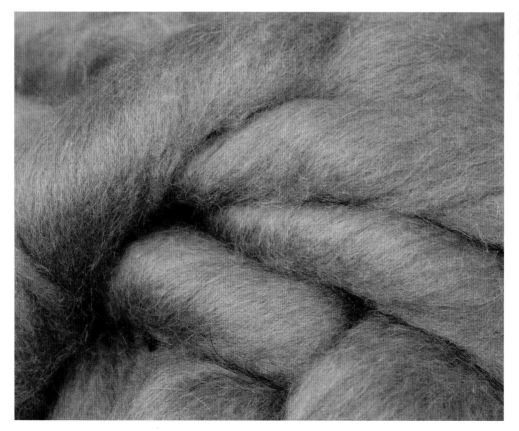

Fine fibre from the Asiatic bactrian camel, processed, cleaned and ready for spinning. As a fibre with a traditional appeal, camel hair is prized for its natural colour of golden tan with varying red highlights.

Camel-hair production

The production of camel hair is a five-step process of collecting, sorting, de-hairing, spinning and finally weaving or knitting.

Camel hair can be collected by combing or shearing, or gathered by hand when it sheds during the moulting season, which lasts for about six to eight weeks during late spring. The camel sheds its un-needed winter coat in clumps of outer hair and inner down, which grows back in the autumn.

The hair is sorted by separating the coarse hairs from the fine, soft hairs, then washed to remove all dirt and debris. The de-hairing stage is a mechanical process that removes the balance of the coarse hairs, dandruff and any vegetable matter, before sending the raw fibre to be spun, prior to weaving or knitting.

Camel-hair market

Italy is the principal destination for camel-hair fibre; the superfine baby camel-hair fibre goes to **Biella**, northwest of Milan, a centre for spinning and weaving fine woollen and worsted fabrics. The remainder goes to **Prato** near Florence, which is another important centre for Italian fabrics. The principal final destination of camel-hair clothing is the United States: no other global market has developed the same appreciation for camel-hair clothes, especially within the menswear sector.

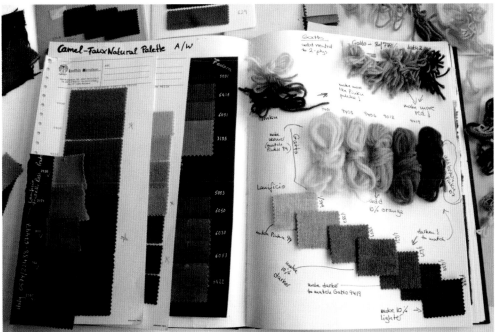

(above) Baby camel-hair jacket by Timothy Everest.

(left) The distinctive red-cast golden tones of camel hair convey enduring associations with classic luxury outerwear. The natural colour palette of camel hair can span pale, sandy blonds and tans through to quite vibrant or deep ginger tones. The fibre itself responds well to modern dye technology but it is usually dyed in a range of faux natural colours to enhance or deepen the natural warm golden tones that make camel hair so desirable.

Goat fibre

Goats are from the *Caprinae* subfamily of the *Bovidae* family of animals, and are relatives of sheep. The domesticated goat is a subspecies of the wild goats of southwest Asia and eastern Europe, and is among the oldest domesticated species, dating back over 10,000 years.

Most goats have the capability to yield fibre; however, the most important fibre-producing goats are the cashmere and **angora goats**. Additionally, within the last few decades three hybrid goats have been developed that also produce commercial quantities of fine fibre.

The proud and elegant cashmere goat shows off its fine and valuable coat. In Mongolia and parts of China the age-old method of hand combing the fleece is preferred to shearing, which is a faster process but results in a coarser hair content and a lower pure-down yield.

Cashmere

Cashmere goats originated high up in the plateau regions of the Himalayan mountains. The local Kashmiri population would spin the fibre from the goat's downy undercoat, weave it into fine fabric and make it into shawls known as **pashmina** – a term derived from the Persian word *pasham*, meaning 'goat wool'. The pashmina shawls were highly valued by the colonial British who ruled Kashmir during the eighteenth and nineteenth centuries, and were exported all over Europe. The fabric from which they were made was referred to as cashmere, named after the province of Kashmir from where they originated.

In India and Pakistan the fibre is still referred to as *pasham*, while the rest of the world knows it as cashmere, a name synonymous with luxury. Unfortunately, by association with inferior man-made copies, pashmina now commonly refers to a style of shawl, as opposed to the rare fibre itself. A genuine pashmina shawl is still hand-spun and made of pashmina wool – cashmere.

Cashmere fibre

Cashmere is not a breed of goat, but a description of a goat that has been carefully bred to produce a fine downy undercoat, the cashmere fibre. Many different breeds can produce cashmere to some degree; however, it is the **Himalayan mountain goat** *(Capra hircus laniger)* that is popularly known as the cashmere goat.

For goat fibre to be considered natural cashmere it must be under 18.5 microns in diameter. No more than 3 per cent of the down may be over 30 microns. The ratio of fine down to coarse guard hair needs to be above 30 per cent. The fibre should measure at least 3.175 cm long, be low in lustre and have a good crimp. Cashmere from Outer Mongolia and the Inner Mongolian parts of China is of the best quality. Much of this is due to the extreme climate of this sub-Siberian land, which seems to encourage the goats to grow a finer, denser under-hair.

Through years of selective breeding, Chinese goats now yield the most amount of fibre, producing over 1 kg of raw fibre per goat, of which the under-fleece (the cashmere) is about 500 g. The 50:50 ratio of cashmere down to guard hairs represents an excellent yield; in some countries the goats yield approximately 500 g of raw fibre of which only 150 g is the all-important under-down. This 30 per cent ratio of guard hair to under-down is the minimum allowed for classification as cashmere.

It is a misconception that the best cashmere down comes from the neck and belly; these are, in fact, the dirtiest parts, because they tend to collect debris. The best fibre comes from the saddle of the goat, from the sides and back and from the shoulders to the rump. The fleece has long coarse outer hairs and extremely fine, soft and silky under-hairs that are 25 to 80 mm long with a diameter of 12 to 19 microns. The natural colours of cashmere range from light fawn to brown; however white is the most sought-after colour.

The fibres are very adaptable and can be spun into either fine or thick yarns, and similarly be woven into light or heavyweight fabrics. The guard hairs are almost worthless because they cannot be spun or dyed. They are used for brushes and interlining canvas. Like wool, cashmere has a high moisture content that allows the insulating properties to change with the relative humidity in the air. It is, weight for weight, warmer than wool.

(right) Quirky British retro styling and a sophisticated colour palette showcase the contemporary appeal and premium quality of Johnstons of Elgin products. Johnstons are the only remaining vertical mill in the UK, which transforms cashmere and other luxury fibres from the raw fibre through to the finished garment.

In this design by Markus Lupfer for Armand Basi modern understated luxury meets contemporary styling. The top is 100 per cent cashmere and the trousers 100 per cent wool.

Practical luxury

Classic men's underwear styling reinterpreted in a superfine cashmere knit by Casa de Cashmere. Contrary to popular belief, cashmere fibre is relatively robust and responds well to either hand or delicate machine washing. Weight-for-weight, cashmere is warmer than wool, and its ultrafine fibres naturally possess a high moisture content, allowing its insulating properties to respond to changes in the humidity of the air.

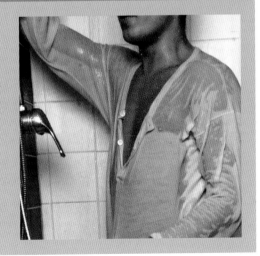

Cashmere production

Although an important and profitable fibre, global cashmere production is believed to be around 1 per cent of the total textile market, putting into perspective the uniqueness of this luxurious fibre.

The traditional method of harvesting cashmere is hand combing, which remains the preferred technique in Mongolia and parts of China. In Iran, Afghanistan, Australia and New Zealand the cashmere fibre is removed by shearing, which is a faster method but does result in a higher coarse-hair content and a lower pure-down yield. Combing is carried out using a coarse comb, which is pulled through the goat's fleece to remove the loose tufts. This usually happens in spring, when the animal is naturally shedding its winter coat. Hand combing can take between one and two weeks to complete, but does result in a far better yield, as well as finer and softer fibres for future harvesting.

The fibre is collected from the farmers and sorted by hand and eye in factories within the same regions as the goats are herded. Efficient sorting is crucial to the production of cashmere, and the fibres need to be graded by quality and colour: it is essential that no dark fibres be mixed with white fibres. Once sorted, the fibres are washed to remove coarse hairs, dirt and vegetable matter.

The de-hairing stage removes the coarse outer guard hairs from the soft under-down, which is the all-important component then used for spinning. The technology for de-hairing cashmere was developed in the nineteenth century in Bradford, Yorkshire, then the centre of the British woollen textile industry. Its pioneer, Joseph Dawson, guarded the secret of this complex process, which ensured exclusive production. The technology has since spread, breaking the monopoly of a few specialist cashmere spinners. Investment, as well as European and Japanese technical expertise, has now brought Chinese de-hairing to a high enough standard of quality for the cashmere knitters of both Scotland and Italy.

The fibres are then traded internationally. The majority are sold to Italy, Japan and Scotland, the three principal countries renowned for sophisticated and innovative cashmere spinning, knitting and weaving. **Johnstons of Elgin** of Scotland is the oldest cashmere mill still in operation.

Cashmere market

The annual global yield of pre-cleaned fibre is approximately 10,000 tons; after cleaning the remaining pure cashmere is approximately 6,500 tons. Today about 60 per cent of the world's raw cashmere production comes from China. Outer Mongolia contributes about 20 per cent and is the second largest global producer. Iran, Afghanistan, India, Pakistan and a few Central Asian republics produce the remainder.

Mohair

Mohair, from angora goats, is a luxury fibre that is desired all over the world. It is admired for its lustre, its softness and its strength, and may be one of the oldest animal fibres still in use.

The history of mohair

Angoras are an ancient breed of goat, and the first records of them being used for fibre purposes date back to the fourteenth century BC. Some believe they were native to the Anatolian plateau region of what is now modern Turkey, while others believe their true origin is the Himalayan plateau, the regions around Tibet and Mongolia. Legends tell of the goats trekking westward to Anatolia in great nomadic caravans with Suleiman Shaa when fleeing the advances of Genghis Khan and his Mongol armies around 1240 to 1245. They finally settled in the region of Ertena or Angora, now part of modern-day Ankara and its surrounding land. The sultans of the Ottoman Empire banned the export of the raw fleeces to try to keep the precious fibre exclusive.

The Holy Roman Emperor, Charles V, came across the angora goats in the 1550s at the time of his ongoing conflicts with the Ottomans. He tried to introduce the goats into Europe but the attempts were not successful as the breed is neither hardy nor prolific, and has high nutritional requirements.

Until 1847 the Ottoman province of Ankara was the only producer of angora goats and fibre. They were then imported into the United States and South Africa. Some were later bred on Navajo Indian Reservations, where the purity of the stock was compromised through interbreeding, resulting in angoras with fleeces of different colours. It is believed that current **coloured angoras** originate from these mid-nineteenth-century hybrids. In the twentieth century the goats were imported into Australia, but only reached Great Britain in the early 1980s.

The fleece of the angora goat is known as mohair. The desirable and valuable mohair fibre is protected firstly by a coarse outer kemp fibre and secondly by an intermediate medullated fibre.

Mohair fibre

Mohair fibre is white, smooth and lustrous with a high tensile strength. It is composed of keratin, a protein substance. A cross section of mohair will be slightly elliptical compared to wool, which is rounder. The scales on the fibre are larger but lie flatter, making the fibre smoother and therefore more light reflective, hence the lustre.

There are three levels of fibre to an angora fleece. The **kemps**, which are coarse, hollow, stiff and opaque, are often pigmented and undesirable because they are scratchy. The **medulated fibres** are less coarse than the kemps but coarser than the true mohair fibres, and have an interrupted or partially hollow core. They are often as long as the true mohair fibres, but still less desirable. Finally there are the true mohair fibres, from the fine under-down.

Good mohair fleece is made up of locks or ringlets of fibre held in place by their natural curl. It has a light oil-like sheen and a good staple length. The fleece has natural grease called **yolk**, its purpose to protect the fibre from the sun, rain and dust, and help hold the locks in place. Too much grease is difficult to wash out, while too little makes the fleece look dull. Goat grease is not the same as lanolin from sheep.

Kids are usually born in the spring with a coat of kemp hairs, which shed and are replaced with fine mohair ready for the first clip in the autumn. It is this first clipping that produces the finest fibre, although this only represents about 15 per cent of the total yield. The second clipping is in the spring when the kid is about one year old; this also produces a good fibre, ranging between 20 and 24 microns in diameter. Thereafter, each clipping is at six-monthly intervals, with the fibre getting progressively coarser, increasing in diameter as the animal ages. Fibre from older animals tends to be used for carpets and upholstery fabric.

The mohair fleece of a well-nourished angora goat will grow at a rate of 25 mm per month. The fleece of bucks (males) becomes coarser faster, but they produce more fleece than does (females). An average buck will yield approximately 6 kg of **skirted** (stain removed) fibre per annum, while a doe will produce about 2 kg less. Castrated males (wethers) produce excellent fibre; it does not coarsen as fast as that of bucks, but is heavier than that of does.

The ideal fibre is long in staple length with a minimum of kemp. It is durable, resilient and has moisture-wicking properties, as well as being flame- and **crease-resistant**.

Mohair production

Angoras are not as hardy as cashmere goats. They have very exacting demands, require dry climates and can perish from pneumonia if wet or cold. They have high nutritional requirements, which are needed to supplement their fast-growing fleece. They like a variety of shrubs and need an active life. If an angora's social and nutritional needs are well met, then it will yield a good-quality and substantial fleece.

The goats need to be brushed and groomed regularly to ensure the best possible coat at shearing. A clip (shearing) needs to be done in a clean environment to ensure there is no contamination. Goats are separated into age bands and clipping starts with the youngest, to prevent the coarser older hairs being mixed with the more valuable finer ones. Ideally a single cut will produce better results than second cuts. The micron count is based on the age of the animal.

In some climatic conditions, an unshorn strip, called a cape, is left along the spine to protect the goat from catching a chill after shearing.

Mohair fibre is made up of locks or ringlets held in place by natural curl. It has a high tensile strength and moisture-wicking properties.

The coarse kemps need to be removed after shearing, and the fleeces are graded into four categories according to their quality, taking into consideration micron count, colour, lustre, smoothness and general cleanliness.

The fleeces are processed to remove vegetable matter and natural grease. Mohair should be washed before spinning, and it can withstand very hot water without damaging. The use of detergent aids the removal of the grease, and final rinsing in vinegar or denatured alcohol will bring out the natural shine and lustre of the fibre.

Mohair market

South Africa and Lesotho produce over 50 per cent of the total output of mohair, followed by the United States (Texas), where the breeders are subsidized by the government. Turkey and Argentina also produce mohair fibre, as do Australia and New Zealand; their combined yield is about 6 per cent.

Cape (South Africa) mohair is the most sought-after because the animals have been genetically selected to produce minimal amounts of kemp fibres.

France, Italy, Germany, Portugal and Great Britain are all producers of mohair fabric and garments. France and Italy also specialize in mohair yarn for knitting. Japan is considered to be the largest importer of mohair fabric, especially for tailoring, because it makes ideal trans-seasonal clothing.

Total global production of mohair represents only about 1 per cent of the global natural fibre production.

Coloured mohair

The predominant fleece colour is white, while coloured fleeces are rare but becoming more popular. Coloured angoras are a hardier variety with less grease, and their fleece would be described as wavy. There are three colour groups: those that range from brown to black; those that range from tan through apricot to red; and those from silver to blue roan. The diversity of colour is not easily duplicated with artificial dyestuffs. They are, however, sometimes over-dyed to produce a deeper intensity of colour. Naturally coloured mohair fleeces are popular with hand spinners.

New York designers Rodarte playfully reinterpret the iconographic punk mohair sweater for the twenty-first century with this luxury destroyed-chic mohair cobweb-knit dress with matching stockings.

Pygora

A **pygora** is a purposeful cross between an angora goat and cashmere-producing pygmy goat, introduced in the late 1980s on a Navajo Indian Reserve in the North American state of Oregon. Pygoras come in a range of colours from light to dark caramel, greys, browns, blacks and cream. They produce three distinct types of fleece.

Type A fleece: Mohair-like fleece with fibres of 16 cm long – or longer – that drape in ringlets. It usually has a single coat or, if with guard hairs, they are very few and silky-fine. The micron count is 28 or under.

Type B fleece: Combination of cashmere and mohair qualities. The fibres are 8 to 16 cm with very few guard hairs and a micron count of approximately 24.

Type C fleece: The most cashmere-like. Very fine with fibres of between 2.5 and 8 cm long and a micron count of less than 18.5.

Although the fibre is used for clothing purposes, it is much favoured by fibre artists for tapestry and other similar work. The harvesting process is similar to that of other goats, although it is preferable that the fleece be washed while it is still on the sheep, as opposed to after harvesting.

Nigora

The **nigora** is a purposeful cross between an angora goat and cashmere-producing Nigerian dwarf goat. Those that are predominantly angora are classified as 'heavy nigora' because of their larger size and larger fleece. Those that are predominantly Nigerian dwarf are classified as 'light nigora' for their smaller size and fleece. Nigoras produce three distinct fibre types.

Type A fibre: Most closely resembles mohair. It is a lustrous fibre, cool to the touch, that hangs in long curly locks of approximately 150 mm. The fleece should be a **single coat** free of guard hairs. The goat needs to be shorn between once and twice a year.

Type B fibre: The most prevalent, referred to as **cashgora**. A good blend between cashmere and mohair, a cross between types A and C. It is a lofty, fluffy fibre between 70 and 150 mm long. Cashgora is a fleece made up of three fibre components: outer coarse guard hairs; fine crimped down, or the 'cash' component; and the intermediate, or the 'gora' component, which is longer, straighter and shiny. It can be shorn once a year or combed or plucked, or allowed to shed naturally.

Type C fibre: Often commercially acceptable as cashmere. The fibres are fine, from 25 to 75 mm long, without lustre but warm to the touch. Harvested similarly to cashgora.

Australian cashmere goat

The **Australian cashmere goat** is a hybrid and a different breed from the 'standard' Himalayan goats that produce the bulk of the world's cashmere.

Goats were introduced to Australia by the Dutch and Portuguese long before it became a British settlement. In the nineteenth century there was a movement to develop cashmere and angora farming and selective breeds were imported from India and China. However, the industry was never developed and the goats were allowed to become feral.

Cashmere was 'rediscovered' in the early 1970s when two researchers identified the down on some feral, or 'bush' goats. With a further 25 years of selective breeding the goat has now evolved into a distinct breed far removed from its bush parentage.

Australian cashmere is hardy with an excellent dense, even fleece and with a good differentiation between guard hairs and down.

A conceptual image for Timothy Everest showing mohair suiting and hair canvas interfacing. Mohair comes in many guises; it is especially favoured for fine tailoring as the structure of the fibre lends itself to enduring form. Any crease in fine mohair tailoring will just drop out when given the lightest amount of steam thus making it perfect for executive travel.

Alternative animal fibres

Luxury fibres are also harvested from **yaks**, **qiviuts** and angora rabbits.

Yak hair

Yaks *(Bos grunniens)* were domesticated in the first millennium BC in what is now Tibet. They inhabit the steppe regions around the Himalayan plateau, living above the snow levels during warmer summer months and descending to lower levels in the colder winter months. The majority of yaks are domesticated, however there is a dwindling number of vulnerable wild yaks remaining.

In the Tibetan language *yak* refers only to the male, but in English it refers to both the male and female animal.

Yaks are an essential aspect of the Himalayan mountain community, being used as beasts of burden and for their meat, milk, fibre and skin. The majority are to be found in China, however all the Himalayan regions have a yak population.

There are several species of yak. The **henduan** from the alpine regions of Tibet produces the best yield, while the **jiulong** from the plateau regions has the best fibre.

Yak-hair fibre
Yak fibre is structurally different to sheep fibre: the angle between the scales and the hair shaft on the external surface of the fibre is smaller than that of wool, so the scales stick to the shaft and feel smoother. It also has greater tensile strength than sheep's wool.

The hair is made up of three components, the coarse outer guard hairs, which are layered in several different lengths, a woolly centre part and the fine down undercoat. The percentage of each varies with age, sex and geographic location, as well as which part of the body the fibre has been taken from. Good animals produce a ratio of about 50 per cent down to 50 per cent hair.

The guard hairs exceed 52 microns in diameter and are only used for making rugs and rope. The mid-hair is between 25 and 50 microns with fewer large crimps. The desirable soft down, which grows before the onset of winter and sheds in the late spring, is under 25 microns in diameter with irregular crimps and a soft lustre. Fibre length after cleaning and de-hairing is between 3 and 4 cm long with a micron count of about 18.5.

Yak fibre tends to be quite even in thickness, has a cashmere-like feel and is very lofty. A one-year-old yak produces fine fibre of between 15 and 17 microns with a length of 4 to 5 cm. Wild yak hair is usually black, while domesticated animals range from black through brown and shades of grey. White underbelly hair is the most rare and thus the most valuable.

Since the 1970s the fibre has been seen as an alternative to fine yarns such as cashmere. However, currently the fibre is of little economic value compared to other yak by-products, and therefore it has not been fully exploited. There are now considerations to develop strains that have a better fibre for production.

Yak-hair production
Yak hair is either combed or pulled in the late spring when the animal sheds its winter coat naturally. On average an animal produces approximately 100 g of fibre annually. The fibre of yaks imported into North America is often spun with silk or lambswool for a unique selling feature. Yak wool is not a commercially viable mass-consumption fibre, but is an interesting alternative favoured by craft spinners, knitters and weavers.

Yaks live on the high steppe regions of the Himalayan plateau and are essential to the local community for their hair, milk, meat, and for carrying loads. Their dung is even burned as fuel.

Qiviut

Qiviut (pronounced kiv-ee-yut) is the under-wool of a musk ox (*Ovibos moschatus*) from the Arctic regions of Canada, Alaska and Greenland. The animals live in the wet riverbeds in the summer and ascend to higher elevations in the winter months. Qiviut, an Inuit word, has long been used to make warm clothing for the local inhabitants; however, since the 1960s cooperatives have been established to encourage the commercial production of qiviut wool from domesticated animals in Alaska and the Arctic regions of Canada, with the revenue used for local communities.

Qiviut fibre

Qiviut is stronger and eight times warmer than wool. It is also softer than cashmere and vicuña, with a micron count of 18. The animals are never shorn, instead the wool is always plucked during the spring moult, which leaves in place the guard hairs, which do not moult.

Qiviut is not a highly commercial fibre, but it does make interestingly fine knitwear.

Qiviut production

An adult musk ox can produce up to seven pounds of qiviut a year. In the spring the qiviut loosens from the animal's skin as it starts to moult. At this stage the undercoat is short but a fairly uniform distance from the skin, and lends itself to being combed from the animal in a single large sheet.

(above) Raw qiviut ready to be processed for spinning. The protective guard hairs and intermediate fibres are first removed before the fine fibre can be spun.

(right) The under-wool, or qiviut, of the musk ox is obtained by hand combing, a process that takes several hours. The animal is never sheared, because it needs its outer hair for protection against the elements.

Tibetan antelope

Although classified in the *Antilopinae* subfamily of the *Bovidae* family, the Tibetan antelope *(Pantholopas hodgsonii)* is now considered to be a closer relative of the *Caprinae* subfamily, or goat. This migratory animal moves around the Tibetan plateau regions of Mongolia, Tibet, India, Nepal and Xìzàng (China), and is traditionally followed by nomads. The animal sheds its down once, nearing the milder regions of the Tibetan plateau, which the nomads would gather and trade with the people of the Kashmir valley. The highly skilled local spinners and weavers made this finest of fibres into shawls called **shatoosh**.

The fibre measures between 9 and 10 microns and is grey to reddish brown in colour, although white from the underbelly is also used. When woven the fabric is so fine that it is almost translucent; it is possible to pull an average-sized shawl through a wedding ring.

The ruling British, during the period of the Raj, were so enamoured with this wonderful product that they exported it to Europe, where its luxury status made it so desirable that the animal became almost extinct. It was hunted down and killed, because this was quicker than waiting for it to moult naturally. Today it is still a rare and endangered species. Through the Convention of International Trade in Endangered Species it has been made illegal to trade or own a shatoosh shawl, but illegal hunting is still a problem in Tibet and the fibre is still traded on the black market.

Angora rabbit

The angora rabbit is believed to be one of the oldest breeds of domesticated rabbit, and is bred for its fine, long silky hair. It was a popular pet with the French nobility in the mid-seventeenth century, from where its popularity spread to other European courts. It first appeared in the United States in the early twentieth century.

Within Europe, France and Germany are important producers, however China dominates global production at over 80 per cent of the total yield. Chile is also important to angora production.

Angora fibre

Angora hair falls into two categories: French type, with more guard hairs and a spikier appearance; and German type, which is almost free of guard hairs and is softer.

The average fibres are between 11 and 13 microns in diameter and 36 mm in length, although the lengths vary. Super-grade angora has a fibre length of 70 mm, although China, the world's largest producer, specifies a minimum of 38 mm.

The principal fibre-producing breeds are:

French: One of the oldest breeds with more guard hairs and a woolly undercoat.

German: This breed tends to produce a higher fibre ratio to weight of animal. They have also been cross-bred with other breeds and produce a variety of colours.

Giant: The largest breed, bred for an abundant yield on small food rations. It has three types of hair, under-wool, awn fluff and awn hair. Awn hairs are the intermediate hairs, which are shorter than guard hairs but longer than the down.

Satin: Cross breed with the softest and finest fibre, said to be the strongest for spinning.

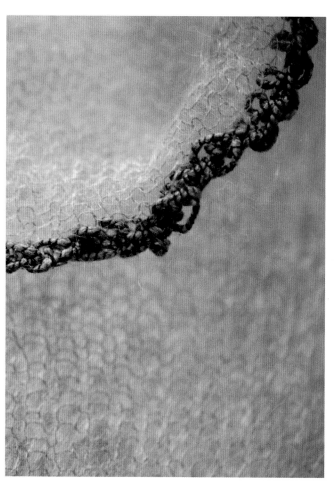

(left) Fine hand-knitted mohair yarn by Habu Textiles.

(above) Angora rabbits thrive on careful grooming and feeding, the reward of which is a fine, soft fibre. Knitted angora garments radiate an almost halo effect.

Angora production

Angora rabbits are albinos and therefore kept in semi-darkness. For a superior, large fibre yield it is important that the animals are well fed and well groomed. Their long hair needs to be combed at least once every two days in order to prevent it from matting and felting.

The fleece can either be shorn or plucked. French Angora production usually involves plucking following a depilatory-inducing injection. This method will produce finer fibres, but does leave the animal in a state of shock. The alternative popular method is to shear. Due to their fast hair growth they are shorn three to four times each year, producing an annual yield of up to 1 kg of fine hair per rabbit. The guard hairs that are then removed represent about 2 per cent of the yield.

After spinning, angora may be used for knitting or weaving. It is however more popular in knitwear, where its **halo effect** is much admired. It is also used to create novelty effects in woven fabrics. As it has no elasticity it should be blended with wool, an 80 per cent angora to 20 per cent merino ratio will still retain the halo effect.

(left) Jean Paul Gaultier subverts the traditional craft of Aran knit, glamorizing its practical provenance by interpreting it in a fluffy, luxurious yarn and creating open lattices between the traditional cable designs.

(below) Knitted angora hat clearly showing the 'halo' that this ultra-fine fibre has when it traps the light, producing an angelic downy effect.

(above) The clean, minimal styling of this wool coat by designer Elise Kim recalls the future-forward aesthetic of the 1960s. The style features a fluffy sleeve detail in a mohair and angora blend that showcases the angelic 'halo' of light trapped by the super-light downy fibres.

Silk is such a seductive, luxurious and desirable fibre that its price has, at times, exceeded that of gold.

Silk possesses a magnificent, shimmering richness that can express a lush, sumptuous personality when woven into precious satins, jacquards and brocades. It is also capable of a sensuous, supple, liquid drape that will be forever associated with the ultimate in luxurious lingerie and glamorous eveningwear.

Silk is widely perceived to be the most beautiful and elegant of all the natural fibres, and even after more than a century of attempting to provide a man-made substitute, no single synthetic fibre has come close to replicating either the magical, myriad properties of silk or the breadth of applications that it can embrace.

Natural fabrics have been the fashion designer's frequent choice, but silk has remained the designer's dream.

The history of silk

Contributing significantly to silk's mystique is its long history, laden with evocative tales of legendary romance and adventure. Silk is one of only a handful of commodities that has shaped world history.

China

The ancient Chinese developed the art of cultivating the delicate **silk moth** and produced threads of incredible quality. The ruling dynasties were acutely aware of their precious commodity, and managed to possessively guard the complex secrets of **sericulture** from the rest of the world, therefore becoming the sole cultivator and producer of silk for many centuries.

An enduring ancient Chinese legend reveres the Lady Hsi-Ling, favoured and chief wife of the Emperor Huang Ti (2677–2597 BC), as the 'lady of the **silkworms**'. Her serendipitous discovery reputedly came when a **cocoon** dropped from a mulberry tree into her cup of hot tea. She then wound the resulting thread around her finger, thus supposedly accidentally discovering the principle of **reeling** silk. Contemporary archaeological excavations, however, suggest that sericulture had long been established in China by this date.

(left) Graphic shift dress in red and black 'changeant' silk, featuring an oriental silkscreen print by Manish Arora.

(opposite page) This beautiful shot-silk pleated scarf by textile artist Karren K Brito uses the traditional Japanese technique of shibori.

The earliest examples of cultivated silk date back to around 3000 BC, and evidence of cocoons goes back to 5000 BC. There is also evidence of small quantities of **wild silk** being produced in the Mediterranean area, India and the Middle East by the time the superior quality and stronger cultivated silk from China began to be exported. The original wild ancestor of the *Bombyx mori* is believed to be *Bombyx mandarina* **moore**, a silk moth particular to China, and which lived on the white mulberry tree. This uniquely superior moth was the key to China's domination of the cultivation, production and artistry of this natural resource.

Initially, the development of this luxury fibre was seen as frivolous, and sericulture was restricted to women. The allure of the fabric quickly provoked a craze and it rapidly became so completely fundamental to Chinese life that out of the 5,000 most-used characters in Mandarin Chinese, 230 incorporate the symbol for silk. The imperial family decreed strict regulation on its use and for 1,000 years the right to wear silk was restricted to the emperor, the imperial family and the highest dignitaries. Later, other members of society were permitted its use. Peasants did not have the right to wear silk until the time of the Qing Dynasty (1644–1911).

Silk's use was confined to China until the **Silk Road** opened up trade around the second century BC. Silk fabrics and products were exported in large quantities all over the known world, to as far away as Rome. However, the mystery and intricacies of sericulture remained a secret that the Chinese guarded carefully.

China's virtual monopoly on production of silk was maintained for another 1,000 years, enforced by an imperial decree condemning to death anyone attempting to export silkworms or their eggs. Sericulture was eventually taken outside of China in the second century AD. Legend tells of a Chinese princess who was to be married to a prince of Khotan (now Hotan in Xinjiang Province) concealing the silk cocoons in her elaborate coiffure and smuggling them to her adopted country. The introduction of sericulture made Khotan, positioned at the southern end of the Silk Road, very prosperous.

The Silk Road

The Silk Road, or Silk Route, is an interconnected series of ancient trade routes, through various regions of the Asian continent, that connected China with Asia Minor and then the Mediterranean. It extends over 8,000 km across land and sea. The routes linked Antioch and the coasts of the Mediterranean to Beijing, with a journey time of about one year. In the south a second route went via Yemen, Burma and India.

The trade that took place on these routes played a significant role in the development of the great civilizations of China, Egypt, Mesopotamia, Persia, the Indian subcontinent and Rome, and helped establish the foundations of the modern world.

Europe

The earliest record of the cultivation of silk in Europe was made by Greek philosopher Aristotle, who described the metamorphosis of the silkworm, and suggested that the produce of the cocoons was wound onto bobbins for the purpose of being woven. The very origin of the term sericulture is derived from the Greek word *ser*, meaning 'silk'. **Raw silk** was brought from the interior of Asia and manufactured in Cos as early as the fourth century BC. First the Greeks, then the Romans began to speak of the *seres*, or 'people of silk', a term used to describe the inhabitants of the far-off kingdom of China.

Roman poets writing at the time of Augustus allude to the desirability of these remarkably thin, elegantly textured fine textiles. China had jealously guarded the secret of sericulture so

(right) A collaboration between Paul Smith and Gainsborough Silk has produced a collection of sophisticated upholstery fabrics. Gainsborough Silk, founded in 1903, are specialists in jacquard weaving.

(far right) Historically-inspired silk stripe taffeta layered pannier skirt with selvedges, worn with a corseted bodice. By Vivienne Westwood from the Spring/Summer 2009 'Do it Yourself' collection.

effectively, and shrouded its provenance in such mystery, that many Romans mistakenly thought that silk was obtained, like cotton, from a tree, or as Roman philosopher Pliny the Elder wrote 'they weave webs like spiders that become a luxurious clothing material for women called silk'.

Perhaps it was in ancient Rome that silk's associations with decadence and excessive luxury began. The emperor Caligula, notorious for his love of luxury and excess, revelled in wearing it. Rich and powerful Roman men aspired to adorn themselves and their wives with silk. This increased demand provoked consternation among the more severe subsequent rulers who considered silk to be decadent and immoral, and vigorous measures were undertaken to restrict its use: men were forbidden to wear it. The Senate, in vain, issued several edicts to try to prohibit the wearing of silk on economic and moral grounds, attempting to characterize it as an excessively frivolous commodity, since this greed for silk had resulted in a huge outflow of gold, threatening the balance of trade. Demand had reached such a pitch that by the end of the third century the finest silk textiles sold for their weight in gold. To counter this demand, silk woven with a warp of an inferior value began to be much more widely worn by both men and women, with pure silk reserved for the upper echelons of society. Silk woven with gold was kept under the control of the imperial family.

The production of raw silk in Europe was first attempted in the sixth century. It is believed that two monks smuggled silkworm eggs in bamboo rods to Byzantium from Central Asia. As in China, silk weaving was restricted by a strict imperial monopoly. The Byzantine church made fabrics for the emperor and was able to develop a large silk industry in the eastern Roman Empire. The legendary magnificence of Byzantine textile techniques was due to the meticulous attention paid to the execution and embellishment, while actual weaving techniques were derived from Egyptian technology.

The cultivation of the white mulberry, the breeding of silkworms and the manufacture of silk textiles had been long confined to Greece, but by the twelfth century this expertise was transported to Sicily, from where it was extended to Southern Europe. In the twelfth century the Normans invaded Byzantium, Corinth and Thebes, centres of silk production, and seized the crops and production infrastructure, as well as deporting all the workers to Palermo, thus prompting the flourishing of the Norman silk industry in Sicily. When Constantinople fell, many skilled silk weavers left for Sicily and Italy and contributed to the development of Italy's increasingly large domestic silk industry.

The sudden boom in the silk industry in the Italian city state of Lucca, beginning in the eleventh and twelfth centuries, was due largely to Sicilian, Jewish and Greek immigration, along with many other immigrants from neighbouring cities of southern Italy.

Venetian merchants traded in silk extensively, and encouraged silk growers to settle in Italy. Italian silk was a significant source of trade by the thirteenth century, with silk produced in **Como** becoming the most valuable in the world. In order to satisfy the demands of the rich and powerful, the cities of Lucca, Genoa, Venice and Florence were soon exporting silk all over Europe. By the late fifteenth century there were over 80 workshops and at least 7,000 craftsmen in Florence alone; its

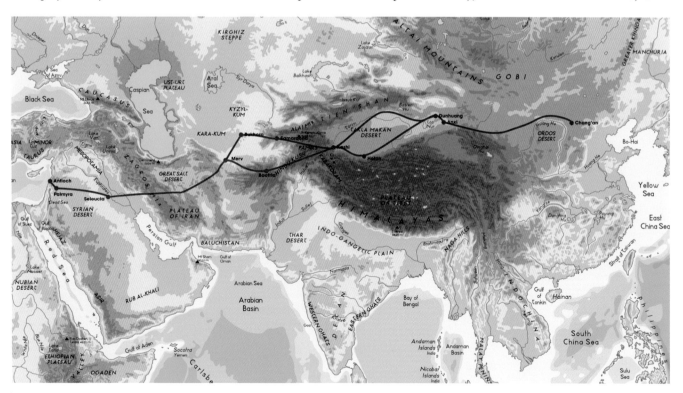

The silk routes, or 'Silk Road' as they are collectively known, are a series of ancient interconnecting trading routes that link China and the West. The map shows the main arterial trading route from East to West, over 4,000 miles long. As well as the luxury of oriental silk, these routes carried other commodities such as tea, spices medicine and were also a conduit for ideas, technical knowledge and cultural exchange, and thus a significant factor in the development of the great civilizations of China, India, Egypt, Persia, Arabia and Rome.

great wealth was built largely on textiles made of wool and silk. Italian silk cloth was very expensive; a result of both the price of the raw material and production costs. Nevertheless, it remained highly prized for its brilliance of colour and elaborate perfection.

Italy's only rival was Spain; however, the expulsion of both the Jews and the Moors in the late 1490s, during the Catholic re-conquest, dealt a blow to the country's silk industry. Some weaving did manage to survive, primarily in Seville, Granada and Valencia, and would be revived again in the 1700s.

In the mid-1400s in France, Louis XI started to develop a national silk industry with the sole objective of reducing France's trade deficit with the Italian city states. In 1535 a royal charter was granted to two merchants to develop a silk industry in **Lyon**. Later a monopoly on silk production was granted exclusively to the city and by the beginning of the sixteenth century Lyon had become the capital of the European silk trade. The oriental style of silk was gradually abandoned for their own Lyonnais textile identity. By the middle of the seventeenth century there were over 14,000 looms in use in Lyon, and the silk industry was so prolific that it fed one-third of the city's population. In the eighteenth and nineteenth centuries Provence experienced a boom in sericulture that would continue until World War I, with much of the silk shipped north to Lyon for production.

In England Henry IV investigated the possibility of developing a domestic silk industry but the lack of expertise did not make it viable. It was not until the 1560s, with the first mass immigration of thousands of French Huguenots fleeing religious persecution, who brought with them their skills in sericulture and weaving, that the silk industry was established. Queen Elizabeth I encouraged them to establish their trades in southwest England. In the north, cities such as Macclesfield saw many high-quality artisan workshops spring up; in London, Spitalfields was the centre of silk expertise. However, the unpredictable British climate prevented England's domestic silk trade from becoming a globally dominant force.

The advent of the Industrial Revolution was marked by a massive boom in the textile industry, and changed much of Europe's silk industry. Remarkable technological innovations galvanized by the cotton industry in England informed the modernization of silk production.

Silk manufacturing benefited from simplification and standardization, as advances followed one another. Bouchon and Falcon invented the punch-card loom in 1775, which was later refined by Jacques de Vaucanson, but ultimately named after Joseph Jacquard, who invented the loom with a string of punch cards that could be processed mechanically in the correct sequence. Skilled workers feared it would rob them of their livelihoods and immediately denounced the jacquard loom, but it swiftly became vital to the industry. By the mid-eighteenth

century the French and English were rivals in design innovation, and, along with the Italians, were producers of the highest quality silks.

In the 1850s the silkworms of Italy and France were virtually wiped out by a ten-year epidemic of the parasitic disease pébrine. Italy was able to rebound from the crisis while France was unable to do so.

Urbanization in the twentieth century prompted many French and Italian agricultural workers to abandon silk growing for more lucrative factory jobs, and raw silk began to be imported from Japan to fill the void. The Asian countries that were once exporters of just the raw material began to develop their own production techniques, enabling them to export higher value finished fabrics and clothing.

Today Italy and France no longer domestically farm silk, however they remain important manufactures of woven and knitted silk fabrics and exceptional clothing. The centres of silk manufacturing remain the regions of Como and Lyon.

This scarlet gown in silk by New York designer Zac Posen features a dramatic rear view inspired by historic corsetry and vintage dresses. The designer uses the geometric lines of layered panels to fuse traditional notions of occasion wear with a contemporary edge.

Japan

Silk cultivation is believed to have spread to Japan around 300 AD. The **yamami silk moth** is thought to be an indigenous species, but exactly when Chinese silk technology reached Japan is unclear.

Japan had become the eastern terminus of the Silk Routes during the early Han period (206 BC–220 AD), and took a step forward in the silk trade at the end of this period by establishing its own sericulture. In the third century, following the Japanese invasion of Korea, important expertise in silk technology was brought back into the country. Succeeding emperors encouraged sericulture, and throughout the following centuries the skills and experience of Korean and Chinese weavers were brought to Japan, ensuring progress in technology. Over time Japan increased the domestic silk rearing it had begun. As a result of this expansion Chinese silk imports became less important, although they still maintained their fine, ultra-luxurious status.

The opening of the Suez Canal in 1869 meant that raw silk imported from Japan became more competitive. In the middle of the nineteenth century **Japonisme** joined **Chinoiserie** and **orientalism** as Western trends, and silk export began in earnest. Attention was turned to the possibilities of expanding silk production for home and exports, and in 1876 Japanese weavers were sent to France to study weaving methods and to copy French **brocades**. The Japanese government invested in the most modern equipment and established a model factory to instruct Japanese weavers in power-driven jacquard looms. Enormous strides in silk production were made throughout the nineteenth century, and this drive towards the modernization of sericulture in Japan rapidly made it the world's foremost silk producer. By the 1880s Japan had supplanted China as the largest supplier of raw silk: for a period until World War II it was the major supplier of raw silk to the West.

After the war Japanese silk production was restored, with vastly improved modernized methods for reeling, inspection and classification of raw silks in place. Japan again became the world's foremost exporter of raw silk – a position it held until the 1970s – and remained the biggest producer of raw silk, until broader industrial expansion led to a decline in sericulture and China made a concerted effort to regain her historic position as the world's biggest raw silk producer and exporter.

Today Japan consumes the greatest amount of silk per person in the world, due in part to its inextricable link with the most important Japanese garment, the **kimono**. Despite the adoption of Western clothing, traditional garments are still culturally important, and synthetic materials have never replaced silk in status. Much of Japan's silk is produced in the narrow width necessary for the uncut loom-width construction of the traditional kimono.

Today a combination of a hand-woven aesthetic fused with modern technology can be found in the innovative textiles produced in Japan. Sophisticated technology employs advances in computerized design and manufacture to reproduce the complex and extraordinary weaves of earlier centuries, as well as to develop new ones.

Extravagant chartreuse silk embroidered dress and coat by John Galliano for Dior from the 2007 'Samourai 1947' collection that celebrated the 60th anniversary of the House of Dior. Galliano paid homage to Christian Dior's revolutionary 'New Look' silhouettes from the iconic 1947 collection, and fused this historical aesthetic with inspirational elements from ancient and modern Japanese culture such as Ikebana floral arrangements, Manga art, Samurai martial arts and the rituals of the Geisha.

The Indian subcontinent

Silk – known as *pattu* or *reshmi* – has a long history in India and is widely produced today. Historically, silk was used by the upper castes, while cotton was traditionally for the poorer castes. Elaborate silk **saris** for Hindus and **lehnga**, **sharara** and **shalwar kameez** for Muslims have a particular significance in celebratory ceremonies such as weddings.

The brocade-weaving centres in India grew in and around the capitals of kingdoms and holy cities in response to the demand for expensive fabrics by the royal families and deities of the temples. The rich merchants of the trading ports further contributed to the development of these fabrics: as well as trading in the finished product, they also advanced money to the weavers to buy the costly raw material. The ancient centres were mainly in Gujarat, Malwa and south India. In the north of the country Delhi, Lahore, Agra, Benares, Mau, Azamgarh and Murshidabad were the main centres for brocade weaving. Ancient traders introduced the complex **jamawar weave** from China, which gained immense popularity among royalty and the aristocracy. Maharajahs and noblemen bought the woven fabric by the yard, wearing it as shawls. Jamawar weaving centres developed in Assam, Gujarat and Malwa.

The region that is now Pakistan has been known for excellent silk weaving since the first millennium. In the Middle Ages the gold and silver silk brocades found eager buyers from Europe, the Middle East and even China.

In 1947 the partition of British India into independent states resulted in mass cross-migration. A large number of Muslim weavers migrated from Delhi and Benares to set up workshops in Lahore, Karachi and Khaiphur, now part of Pakistan. The towns of Orangi and Shershah have emerged as the biggest **khadi hand-loom** markets of Pakistan. The weavers continue to weave brocades in traditional patterns, but have also introduced newer designs deriving inspiration from the old Mughal silks. These weavers mostly fulfil domestic demands using cocoons imported from China and cultivated at Orangi and Shershah.

Islamic teachings forbid Muslim men to wear silk, because it is perceived as feminine and unnecessarily extravagant. The devout were advised 'he who dresses in silks in his lifetime forfeits luxury in the next'. Despite injunctions against silk for men, its popularity for women was retained. A cotton and silk mixture called **mashru** (meaning 'permitted') was developed in this part of the world to allow men access to the luxury of silk. Mashru has silk warps and cotton wefts. The construction is usually of a satin weave, which gives it a smooth silken face and a cotton underside. This satisfies the Muslim edict that silk must not be worn next to the skin.

Today, India and Pakistan produce very competitively priced silk fabrics in traditional and contemporary designs, and are an important source for international designer labels and mass-market high-street retail chains.

A contemporary interpretation of the iconic Indian sari by Anand Kabra. The garment usually relies on complex pleating and draping to achieve an elegant dress made from 6 m of uncut fabric. Here the designer infuses the traditional symbol of Indian femininity with contemporary elements of sheer fabric and a hip belt, and features a triangle bra in place of the usual tailored sari blouse.

Thailand

Silk production in Thailand can be traced back over 3,000 years, to the region of Ban Chiang in the northeast province of Udon Thani. Archaeological discoveries in this area suggest that Thailand's sericulture and weaving history may be as old as that of China.

After the fifteenth century the importance of the Silk Road began to decline as less hazardous sea routes were discovered. This promoted trade between China, Southeast Asia, India and the West. Sea traders reached the Dvaravati Kingdom which controlled the settlements along the Gulf of Siam, and silk was one of the commodities traded.

The Thai silk industry began in the Khorat plateau in the northeast region. Elsewhere, the prevailing Theravada Buddhists' religious belief system forbade the killing of the silkworm inside the cocoon, but the northeast had more relaxed religious views, allowing silk production to flourish. Cultivation is still centred in the Khorat region, and production is mainly in Chiang Mai, the northern capital.

The area known as **Isan** is traditionally famed for its ikat weaves (or mudmee) which use a painstaking **space dyeing** (dyeing sections of continuous yarn in different colours along its length) technique passed down through the generations. Complex weaves and arresting colour combinations typify Thai handloom silks. Elaborate and sophisticated brocades have, over recent centuries, attracted the patronage of the royal families and ensured that the unique variety of local silk weaving techniques has not completely died out.

In the nineteenth century, King Rama V introduced advanced techniques in weaving and created the foundation of the country's expanding silk industry.

In 1901 King Chulalongkorn invited a team of Japanese experts to advise on the modernization of silk production. This marked the beginning of a rapid sericulture development and technological advancement in Thailand. By 1910 more than 35 tons of Thai silk were exported annually. Then in 1948, American entrepreneur Jim Thompson founded the Thai Silk Company, producing distinctive and beautiful hand-woven fabrics that inspired many copies. The artisan appeal of the fabrics was due to their uneven surface, caused by the inconsistencies in the hand-reeled silk from which they were woven. Thompson was a master of public relations, who managed to get his products introduced to fashion luminaries including the influential fashion editor Diana Vreeland, costume designer Irene Sharaff and Parisian designer Pierre Balmain. Custom-made weaves produced for Hollywood epics such as *The King and I* and *Ben-Hur* inspired a craze for his distinctive look in fabrics.

Sustaining growth on a long-term basis, however, proved a problem in the face of cheaper factory-produced fabrics from China and Japan. In 1994 the European Union provided funding for a five-year project to sustain and upgrade sericulture in Thailand. An initiative designed by Prime Minister Thaksin Shinawatra, based upon the Japanese 'one village, one product' model, was launched in 2001. The project has given small villages the opportunity to make a good living keeping traditional Thai arts alive. Queen Sirikit has effectively promoted this initiative and, to this day, silk production in Thailand is still primarily a hand-loom cottage industry, with some larger factories in Bangkok producing cheaper silks.

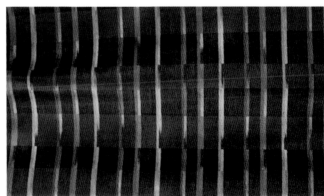

(left) Menswear by Etro from the Spring/Summer 2009 collection. The glowing Asian-inspired saffron tones exemplify the exotic appeal of silk shantung.

(above) This Thai fabric is a typical Jim Thompson design where a traditional fabric has been rescaled and treated with contrasting random raised weft ikat stripes.

The silk market today

By the middle of the 1990s world silk production reached 81,000 tons.

All of the countries with a historical link to the silk trade – China, Japan, India, Thailand, Italy, Spain and France – continue to produce magnificent silks to this day. China, with its recent economic reforms, has once again become the world's largest silk producer, with over 50 per cent of global production. India produces around 15 per cent and Japan a little over 10 per cent.

Other countries producing silk include Bangladesh, Bolivia, Bulgaria, Colombia, Indonesia, Iran, Israel, Kenya, Nepal, Nigeria, Pakistan, Peru, the Philippines, Sri Lanka, Turkey, Uganda, Zambia and Zimbabwe. Brazil, North Korea, Uzbekistan and Vietnam together produce about 4 per cent of the world's raw silk.

The advent of cheaper substitute fibres such as rayon and nylon initially reduced the domination of silk. However, world silk production has more than doubled over the last 30 years, and the total number of people dependent on silk rearing and processing worldwide is rapidly approaching 35 million.

Silk and synthetics

Silk is desirable, but not affordable to all levels of the market. It was therefore inevitable that synthetic copies — artificial or **art silks** – would be developed to satisfy the needs of the less affluent customer.

Nylon was developed in the United States and used as a replacement for Japanese silk during World War II. Its properties and tensile strength when wet were far superior to those of silk and **rayon** – the other major synthetic substitute – making it ideal for military applications, such as parachutes. The use of nylon for stockings revolutionized the hosiery industry. It was not seen as inferior to silk, but rather a modern, more wearable and accessible new product, with its historical connotations of glamour assured by associations with American GIs bearing seductive gifts during World War II.

After World War II, silk, as a commodity, was unable to regain many of the markets lost to the more accessible 'new-age' man-made fibres, which were greeted with great enthusiasm by postwar consumers. The new fibres were not only much cheaper, but far easier to care for. They seemed to represent a future where desirable fashion products were within the grasp of all members of society.

The future for silk

The invention of substitute fibres initially reduced the domination of silk but its status as a premium luxury fibre has endured; despite innovations in man-made fibres it has remained a desirable and luxurious commodity. None of the new fibres has managed to duplicate the breadth of applications that silk can embrace.

Designer Julian McDonald says: 'As far as I'm concerned nothing will ever replace silk. It can look tenderly feminine or high-tech, timeless or cutting edge.'

New York entrepreneurs developed the process of **fibrillation**, or 'sueding' silk in 1982 as a response to the emerging lifestyle trend epitomized by the casual low-key elegance of the 'dress-down Friday' culture. The goal was to achieve a **pre-shrunk**, crease-resistant and machine-washable silk to compete with the easy-care fibres that the consumer was already familiar with.

'The demand for silk garments continues to rise due to growing concern for protecting the environment, particularly among industrial countries which are prohibiting the use of certain dyes and chemicals, and prefer natural to chemical fibres. Thus natural textiles, in particular cotton and silk, are witnessing a new era of global demand.'
Rajatvaty K. Datta and Mahesh Nanavaty, *Global Silk Industry*, Universal Publishers, 2005.

Vintage stockings from the Deutsches Strumpf Museum. Before the advent of nylon, silk was used for stockings. Gifts of nylon stockings helped to endear the American GIs to European women during World War II.

The impact of sand-washed silk

The 1990s witnessed an explosion of sales in **sand-washed silk**, thanks to the consumer's renewed interest in natural fibres. Produced in China, the silk was washed in machines containing sand, pebbles or even tennis balls, resulting in an ultra-soft, peach-skin surface with a familiarly comforting, aged effect. The fabric was perfectly in tune with the dressed-down, luxe sportswear effortlessly interpreted by designers Calvin Klein and Donna Karan.

Shamash and Sons, a New York based converter, and one of the largest importers of silk into the US, launched its own range of washed silks for the 1988 season, using a process developed in Germany. Perfection of the technique for volume (and therefore lower price) was achieved in South Korea. Washed silk products were, at the height of the boom, available at every level of the market, including mail-order and supermarkets. To satisfy the seemingly insatiable demand for sand-washed silk of the late 1980s and early 1990s, the world silk supply doubled to over 1,000,000 tons. Many of these products, promoted as easy-care, proved to be of low quality, pushed onto the market hastily in order to satisfy the demand. The association with low-quality products damaged the noble and precious heritage of silk, and its reputation was in danger of being jeopardized.

The future of worldwide trade in 'the queen of fibres' looks positive. Although silk accounts for less than 10 per cent of the world's fibre market by volume, its importance in monetary value is several times higher, with the US alone importing $2 billion-worth of silk textiles and garments at the end of the twentieth century.

113

(left) Silk stripe top and silk panne velvet pants by Vivienne Westwood from the Spring/Summer 2009 'Do it Yourself' collection.

(above) Sand-washing silk gives the fabric a scuffed and tactile 'peach bloom' surface. The treatment lends this languid full-length crêpe de chine slip dress by Narciso Rodriguez a relaxed elegance.

Silk fibre

Silk fabric has a soft, smooth texture, but depending on the weave can express an almost sculptural structure, a weightless delicacy or a sensuous liquid drape.

Silk is categorized as a **natural protein fibre**, and is naturally produced by the *Bombyx mori* moth **pupa**. Insects that metamorphose primarily secrete silks, but substances categorized by the term silk can also be produced by web spinners, such as spiders. There are over 200 varieties of wild silk moths found in locations all over the world, however most of these produce silk filaments that are generally irregular or flattened in form. Flatter threads tangle more easily and therefore break easily if unwound. It is only the filament of the *Bombyx mori* moth that is capable of producing the much-prized filament, which is smooth, fine and rounder than that of other silk moths.

Properties of silk

Silk is extraordinarily strong in relation to both fibre dimension and the perception of its delicate nature. It is stronger than wool or cotton and weight for weight is actually stronger than steel. It is resistant to mineral acids, but can be dissolved in sulphuric acid. Its high level of absorption lends it superior ability to accept dye. A pure silk textile survives longer than a silk fabric mixed with other fibres.

Silk is a poor conductor of electricity and it is this that makes it comfortable to wear in cool weather. This low conductivity also means it is susceptible to static cling. Its isothermal properties make it feel cool in summer and warm in winter, and its insulative properties have led to fine silk knit undergarments traditionally providing unequalled warmth as skiwear layers. Silk floss or kapok is the lightest and warmest of all quilting materials.

Brilliant fibre

Silk is highly prized for its lustre and shimmering appearance, a result of the fibre's unique triangular, prism-like structure that allows the cloth produced from it to refract incoming light at different angles. When light plays upon a piece of silk fabric the surface appears to glisten, tremble and graduate in colour. For this reason silk can be described as a 'bright fibre', meaning it has a natural lustrous reflectiveness and therefore appears to shimmer. Before the gossamer threads become fabric, complex processing ensures that the brilliance and luminous qualities of the filament are preserved.

Wild silks

A wide variety of wild silks have been known throughout China, India and Europe from the earliest civilizations, however the scale of production has always been smaller than that of cultivated silk. Wild silk cannot be replicated using farmed caterpillars.

Wild silks differ greatly in colour gradation and texture depending on the species, climate and food source, but are generally characterized by an uneven appearance and rough feel, because the single thread that makes up the cocoon has been torn or shredded into shorter lengths by the emerging moth, lending wild silks a characteristic slubby, bark-like effect and dry textured handle. (See also peace silk on page 121.)

(above) Flowing citrus-yellow sheer silk-chiffon kaftan by Etro.

Billowing extreme-proportioned djellaba-style silk chiffon dip-dyed tunic by Antoine Peters.

Raw silk

The term raw silk is often applied erroneously to **silk noil**, or noils, which are the short fibres left over from spinning silk. The fibres are relatively short, weaker and considered far less valuable than spun silk.

A noil is the fibre that remains after the fibres are separated by combing in preparation for spinning. These shorter staple fibres can be used for spinning in the same way as cotton or linen would be spun. Noil fabric is characterized by a dry handle, nubby texture and low sheen. It often has occasional slubs and specks.

Spider silk

Web spinners, such as spiders, produce silks that have been used for medical applications and telescope sights. In the future, genetic modifications may see spider silk being developed as a fibre in its own right.

(left) Hand-spun silk yarn recycled from shredded Nepalese saris. The resulting yarn has an intense colour vibrancy that is informed by the random nature of the raw material. The natural inconsistencies lend it a textured feel, similar to tussah or raw silk. The hand spinning is carried out by women's cooperatives that provide fair wages and generate funds for educational programmes.

(left) Hand-spun silk yarn, also recycled from shredded Nepalese saris, and then over-dyed to a uniform colour.

(above) This elegant raw silk shift dress by A Détacher references the clean silhouettes of the 1960s popularized at the time by such fashion icons as Jackie Kennedy. The textured slubs inherent in the yarn and the pronounced visible weave are desirable characteristic features of raw silk fabric associated with the Indian subcontinent.

Silk production

The best-known of all the natural fibres is produced using the substance secreted by the larvae of the silk moth as a shroud to protect itself while in the cocoon, during the transformation into a pupa and eventually a moth. Several other insects produce silks, but only the silk derived from moth caterpillars has been used extensively for textiles. Silk production today is a combination of both modern technology and ancient techniques first developed and perfected by the Chinese many centuries ago.

Cultivation

Silkworm breeding depends on a highly developed agricultural system capable of sustaining the large-scale cultivation of mulberry trees. One hectare of mulberry trees yields 11 tons of leaves, which will in turn sustain 200 kg of cocoons, which produce 40 kg of raw silk. Specially reared *Bombyx mori* moths are so inbred that they can no longer survive in the wild, and are blind and flightless. They must be raised under careful, temperature-controlled conditions in well-ventilated, closed rooms, because they are unable to live in the open air. The moths lay their eggs on specially treated paper placed on bamboo trays. When the eggs hatch, the caterpillars are fed on the leaves of the white mulberry tree, *Morus alba*.

After about 35 days and four moultings, the silkworms are 10,000 times heavier than when they first hatched, and a little over 7.5 cm in length. The silkworms are removed from the trays and covered with straw, to which they can attach their cocoons. The insect spins a cocoon by secreting a continuous filament of fibroin protein (liquid silk), which protects it while in the cocoon. This liquid silk is coated in **sericin**, a water-soluble protective gum, which is produced in two of the silkworm's glands. Liquid silk is forced through **spinnerets**, openings in the silkworm's head, and as the substance comes into contact with the air it solidifies. Within two or three days the silkworm will have spun approximately 1,600 m of **filament**, and be completely encased in its protective cocoon.

After this entire process the silkworm metamorphoses into a moth. However, in sericulture it is necessary to kill the **chrysalis**, either by steaming, baking in the sun or hot air or by soaking in salt water, before it reaches the moth stage. To obtain the filament, silk cocoons are sorted by fibre size and fibre quality. Defective cocoons are carded and immediately spun, while a certain number of perfect cocoons are set aside for breeding the next generation of silkworms. Approximately 5.5 kg of cocoons will generate 0.5 kg weight of raw silk.

(above) This haunting design from John Galliano for Dior, Autumn 2000, beautifully expresses the crisp sculptural properties of tightly woven silk.

(above) The highly cultivated *Bombyx mori* moth is unique among the moth species in that it produces cocoons that are uniformly pure white in colour and texture. Centuries of in-breeding and controlled cultivation have resulted in colour consistency and a reliably fine filament.

(left) The delicate spectral appearance of the *Bombyx mori* moth highlights its fragility and the expertise required to cultivate it. Centuries of selective breeding have resulted in a creature that is blind, flightless and dependent on a highly regulated environment in order to survive.

(left) The caterpillars of the *Bombyx mori* moth feasting on their diet of white mulberry leaves. Over a month of intensive feeding later, the moths are 10,000 times larger and ready to spin their precious cocoons.

Cooking

The cocoons are first thrown into a cauldron of boiling water, a process called **cooking** or **maceration**, which softens the sericin gum that binds the filaments together. Traditional pan cooking is carried out in open vats, and the cocoons are immersed for several minutes. Cooking is a crucial stage for subsequent reeling; a high proportion of waste can be produced if it is not carried out with sensitivity. Overcooked cocoons increase the number of breaks during reeling, while undercooked cocoons do not unravel easily, thus reducing the efficiency of the reeling process.

The brushing process, by which the reelable end of the filament is located, also produces a considerable amount of filature waste.

Reeling

Reeling, or winding, the cocoons extracts the silk filament, and is a specialist job. Once the reelable ends of the filaments have been secured, known as clearing, the prepared cocoons are transferred to reeling basins and a number of cocoons are unwound simultaneously. Several filaments are grouped together and taken by the **threader**, the machine-feeding device, to the reelers, where they are reeled onto a bobbin to produce one long, smooth thread.

The finest fabrics are woven from threads made by reeling together the filaments from only four cocoons.

Thrown threads

Applying a twist to silk filaments to hold them together is known as **throwing**, and the variety of silk threads throwing produces is extensive.

Leonardo da Vinci (1452–1519) had an avid interest in the mechanics of the silk throwing process, and in 1500 he invented a highly innovative winged, or fly spindle, machine, which performed stretching, twisting and winding operations on three consecutive stretches of thread. With no further major important modifications, his device became the basis for later development of the continuous spinning machine that is still employed in contemporary systems for throwing or silk thread making.

The five general categorizations of **thrown threads** are defined primarily by their intended final use: embroidery; knitting; sewing; wefts; and warps. Within each category a large spectrum of different yarns can be obtained by altering the number of threads, turns and direction of the twist. Common examples include:

Thrown singles: Individual raw silk threads twisted in one direction.

Tram: Weft threads produced by twisting two or more raw silk threads together in only one direction; usually this is a light twist, just sufficient to hold them together.

Organzine: The raw silk is given a preliminary twist in one direction, then two or more of these threads are twisted together in the opposite direction. Generally, **organzine** demands the best quality raw silk and is used for the warp threads, which bear the tension of the loom.

Crêpe: Thrown in a similar way to organzine, but twisted to a much greater degree, resulting in a crinkle effect.

Mommes

Silk is traditionally measured by weight. The **momme** (pronounced mommy) is the unit system used in the silk industry, and quantifies the density of silk as opposed to the thread count, as used for cotton fabrics. It originates from the Japanese cultured pearl industry.

1 momme is equal to approximately 3.6 g of silk fabric per square yard.
A 17-momme fabric would weigh approximately 61.2 g per square yard.

The usual range of momme weight for different weaves of silk are:
Habotai: 5 to 16 mommes.
Chiffon: 6 to 8 mommes.
Crêpe de chine: 12 to 16 mommes.
Gauze: 3 to 5 mommes.
Raw silk: 35 to 40 mommes.
Organza: 4 to 6 mommes.

Isabella Whitworth domestically de-gums silk cocoons in soda and ash solution.

Once the silk yarn has been de-gummed and bleached white, it is wound into skeins and laced up ready for dyeing.

Primary finishing processes

Primary finishing involves several processes that prepare the silk for dyeing. First the silk must be **de-gummed** to remove the sericin, a process that is usually carried out by the dyer and involves boiling the silk in soap, detergent or enzymes. This process has a great effect on the quality of subsequent dyeing. Defects in dyeing can be due to inadequate de-gumming, or fibre damage by overly harsh processing. Bleaching may also be required if a pure white colour is desired.

Fabric weighting

Silk is purchased by weight, and the amount of weight that silk loses in the process of de-gumming (20–25 per cent) is a major consideration. Common practice in the silk industry is that of **weighting** the fabric by loading it with a finishing substance, in order to compensate for the weight lost in the de-gumming process. The loading process increases the volume of the thread and gives the silk a characteristic heavy and supple handle, lending the fabric crispness, lustre and a firm feel. Taffeta is the most common heavily-weighted fabric. Weighting may also lend the cloth better flame-retardant and crease-resistance properties. Weighted silk is generally less compactly woven than unweighted silk, so less silk is used in the manufacture of the cloth.

Weighting is usually done during the dyeing stage. In order to weight a coloured silk, stannic chloride is used, followed by treatment with sodium phosphate. Black silks may be weighted with metallic mordants such as iron salt. Due to the complexity of processes and problems related to chemical pollutants, mineral loading is now almost obsolete. Today weighting is almost exclusively achieved by grafting **acrylic monomers** (usually methacrylic amide) using ammonium persulphate as an initiator.

Weighting can have a remarkably positive effect on the ability of the fibre to take dye, because the types of salts used have been traditionally used as dye mordants. The term **pure dye silk** indicates that weighting was not added at the dyeing stage.

Weaving

Silk weaving follows a similar process to other fibres and yarns.
Warping This prepares the warp by rolling all the warp yarns on to a beam under the same tension, and strictly parallel to each other.
Pirning The weft, or cross-wise yarns are put on to a pirn, which is placed inside the **shuttle** in order to lay the weft yarn between the warp yarns.
Non-stop high-speed weaving has been made possible by the introduction of automatic pirn-changing and shuttleless looms that employ compressed air to shoot the weft yarn between the warp yarns.

Despite technological advances, certain types of silk cannot be made on high-speed machinery, particularly complex novelty fabrics, or those that reproduce the traditional effects that were developed on the original punch-card jacquard looms.

Dyeing

There are two main ways of dyeing silk fabrics. The first method is to dye the yarns before they are woven into fabrics – these are known as yarn-dyed or dyed-woven (eg taffeta, duchesse satin and many pattern-woven fabrics). Multiple colours can be woven together in one cloth. Up until the early nineteenth century, this was the only method of dyeing silk, and today the same basic techniques are used for this process, skeins of raw silk being soaked in tanks full of dyestuff.

The second method is to dye after weaving; fabrics dyed in this way are referred to as piece-dyed fabrics (eg, crêpes, twills, etc). Industrial scale piece-dyeing was introduced in Lyon, France, in the mid-nineteenth century. The fabric is fed into the dye bath through two cylinders, or fixed to a round jig, which is then immersed in the bath. The fabric is then fixed, rinsed and dried.

118

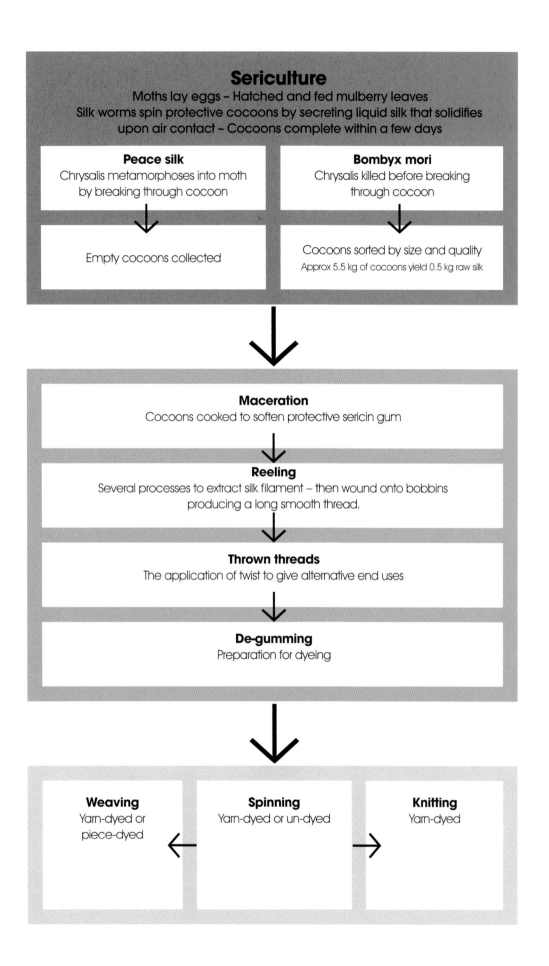

Sericulture

Moths lay eggs – Hatched and fed mulberry leaves
Silk worms spin protective cocoons by secreting liquid silk that solidifies
upon air contact – Cocoons complete within a few days

Peace silk
Chrysalis metamorphoses into moth
by breaking through cocoon

Bombyx mori
Chrysalis killed before breaking
through cocoon

Empty cocoons collected

Cocoons sorted by size and quality
Approx 5.5 kg of cocoons yield 0.5 kg raw silk

Maceration
Cocoons cooked to soften protective sericin gum

Reeling
Several processes to extract silk filament – then wound onto bobbins
producing a long smooth thread.

Thrown threads
The application of twist to give alternative end uses

De-gumming
Preparation for dyeing

Weaving
Yarn-dyed or
piece-dyed

Spinning
Yarn-dyed or un-dyed

Knitting
Yarn-dyed

Additional finishing processes

The purpose of these processes is to restore the fabric's natural brilliance, softness and characteristic handle, counteracting the drying effects of previous treatments.

Calendering: Steel rotary cylinders press the fabric as it passes in between them. By varying the speed of rotation and the heat or pressure, various degrees of glossiness and softness can be achieved.

Tamponing: A very fine, even film of oil is applied to the fabric by machine, to smooth out irregularities and correct any chaffing that has occurred during previous processes.

Breaking: A breaking machine, or breaker, is used to lend a particularly soft handle and brilliance to the surface of the fabric. Two types of machine can be used. The first is known as the 'button', because the fabric is passed rapidly back and forth over small rollers with brass buttons. The alternative machine has slanted knives, and the fabric is similarly passed rapidly back and forth over them.

Steaming: This is applied to pile weaves to encourage them to fluff out and appear more voluminous.

Pressing and lustering: The fabric is passed through heated rollers and then soaked in dilute acid to bring out the lustre. This process removes wrinkles from the finished fabric.

120

(above) Asymmetric hand-painted dress in fluid silk by Antoine Peters.

(above) This close-up of a butterfly's wing illustrates the visual 'morphing' of colour that creates this shimmering array of colours.

The effect is created by light refracting on the structure of the wing. The unique triangular structure of silk fibre responds in a similar way.

Special care

Deterioration of silk is accelerated by exposure to dust and dirt (which will, over time, cut the fibres), and light and grease, so it should always be cleaned and stored in a dark environment. Insects may also attack it, especially if it is left dirty. Silk has a moderate to poor elasticity and can lose up to 20 per cent of its strength when saturated.

Optimum humidity of 50–55 per cent is desirable for silk to retain a supple handle. Dryness makes the fibres brittle, and they break.

Ethical considerations

The process of harvesting silk from a cultivated cocoon kills the larvae, therefore sericulture has been criticized on the grounds that traditional silk production kills silkworms, preventing them from living out their life cycle.

The provenance of silk has not been without controversy to religious practitioners worldwide, dating back many centuries. Chinese Buddhists initially forbade the wearing of cultivated silk because its use violated the prohibition against the taking of life. However, the use of silk in the robes of Chinese and Indian monks is acceptable if the moth has emerged from the cocoon. Similarly, Mahatma **Gandhi**'s criticism of silk production was based on the **ahimsa philosophy** of not hurting any living thing.

In addition to the controversy regarding animal welfare issues, some of the manufacturing procedures, particularly in hand-reeling silk factories, have health and safety implications.

Wild silk and peace silk

Peace silk, also known as vegetarian silk, refers to silk harvested from cocoons from which the silk moths have emerged naturally. Their silk is de-gummed and spun like other fibres. Peace silk moths can be wild, semi-wild or even farmed. The term peace silk is a perfect marketing tool for consumers with ethical concerns who do not want to forego experiencing the beauty of silk.

Thai silk moth

The Thai silk moth is adapted to tropical conditions and is **multivoltine**, producing at least ten batches of eggs per year. The silk is reeled by hand from green cocoons, and traditionally the pupa is not killed prior to reeling. The natural colour spectrum of the silk filament spans a range of shades from light gold to light green. Thai raw silk is characterized by an irregular and bumpy appearance. Although it is soft, it has a relatively coarse texture with knotty threads.

Ahimsa peace silk

Ahimsa peace silk is made from the cocoons of wild and semi-wild silk moths and is promoted in parts of southern India for those who prefer to wear ethical silk. There are several species of silk moth used for ahimsa silk, in addition to the conventional mulberry-feeding silk moth.

Eri silk

The **eri silk moth**, *Philosamia ricini*, is a type of wild moth that feeds on the castor plant. The cocoons are roughly the same size as those of cultivated silk moths, and are characterized by a very light colour, almost as white as the cultivated *Bombyx mori* cocoons. They are gathered from across a large area, then cut to allow the moths to emerge and escape.

The cocoons are made up of several layers of silk. The outer layers are relatively soft and fluffy. The inner layers are glued together like paper. Most cocoons have a hole at one end, where the moth has naturally emerged.

Eri cocoons are raised in a natural situation with minimal interference from man, and are considered to be equivalent to organically grown.

Muga silk

The **muga silk moth**, *Antheraea assamensis*, is a wild and semi-wild species that lives only in a restricted area in Assam, India, and produces a special type of wild silk. The villagers in this forested region gather the cocoons in the wild and then semi-cultivate them from the eggs of the wild moths that emerge.

Tussah silk

Tassah or tassar moths, *Antheraea mylitta* and *Antheraea proylei*, are wild and semi-wild silk moths respectively. Tussah is the most commonly used of all the wild varieties, and lends its name to a particular type of silk.

Grey silk blouse by Danish eco-brand Noir. The fabric used conforms to the stringent 'Oeko–Tex Standard 100' regulation that certifies that the product is free from more than 100 substances known to be detrimental to human health. This initiative reflects the latest in textile chemistry and governmental regulations from around the world. The accreditation does not indicate however that the textiles are necessarily organic.

Silk fabrics

The fabrics listed represent the most popular silks in use and would give any designer or merchandiser an extensive selection for designing a range or building a collection. The list, however is not exhaustive.

The fabrics are all primarily made from silk yarns, though some names are shared with other natural and/or synthetic yarns.

Sumptuous

These dense, three-dimensionally expressive silks feature complex textures.

Brocade An elaborate and richly figured jacquard, often with metallic threads.

Jacquard Refers to both the loom and the resulting patterned fabric.

Damask A reversible self-patterned fabric woven on a jacquard loom. The design is distinguished from the background by contrasting lustre and matt textures.

Velvet A cut warp pile fabric. 100 per cent silk velvet is rare and extremely costly. Silk is usually combined with rayon viscose to achieve a beautiful drape.

Cloqué A woven double cloth where the two sets of warp and weft yarns have a different shrinkage potential that produces a three-dimensional 'blister' effect.

(above) Emerald green jacquard outfit by Markus Lupfer for Armand Basi. The simple silhouette and enlarged proportions of this skirt and top are enhanced by the richly figured raised design of the fabric.

(right) This sumptuous ensemble by Haider Ackermann layers metallics with glowing magenta silk satin in a lurex jacquard brocade coat and waistcoat, worn with violet silk trousers.

(above) The languid drape and lush sheen of viscose silk velvet is apparent in the relaxed glamour of this 'bathrobe' style wrap coat by Kostas Murkudis.

(above) Roksanda Ilincic black satin column evening dress with fluted emerald overskirt that highlights the sumptuous, sculptural properties of the densely woven silk satin duchesse.

Crisply sculptural

Mouldable and architectural, these fabrics are lush or papery to the touch.

Shantung A crisp, slubbed and sheeny silk woven from wild silk originating from the Shantung province of China.

Tussah The name is associated with the wild Antheraea caterpillar that produces a very textured, naturally brown silk.

Dupion A crisp, lustrous silk with a slubby texture that is woven from an irregular silk reeled from the twin filaments of double cocoons.

Taffeta A tightly plain-woven, crisp fabric. Often produced with warp and weft of different colours.

Moiré A structured fabric with a pronounced rib is embossed with rollers in the finishing process, creating a 'watermark' effect.

Satin A weave with the maximum amount of warp showing on the face. The sheen is enhanced by the use of a continuous filament yarn.

Duchesse or Peau de Soie A rich, satiny, medium-weight fabric with fine cross ribs and a moderately stiff drape.

(left) The lush optical qualities of silk moiré are showcased in this late-nineteenth-century corseted evening dress by Mae Primrose, from the Victoria and Albert Museum collection. The distinctive 'watermark' effect that characterizes this fabric is achieved by pressing the ribbed construction of the silk weave with heated rollers. The bow on the bustle of the gown highlights the exceptionally crisp and sculptural quality of the fabric.

(above) A peacock blue and emerald green duchesse silk satin ensemble by Haider Ackermann conveys the incomparable lustre and structural properties of couture-quality silk.

Sheer

Ethereal and whisper-fine or stiff, transparent and gauzy in structure.

Chiffon A very light, diaphanous fabric made with a tightly twisted single yarn in a loose plain weave.

Georgette Made in the same way as chiffon, but with a two- or three-ply yarn.

Tulle A fine, transparent net or mesh construction.

Habotai A smooth and light semi-sheer plain-weave silk with a good drape.

Gauze A thin open-weave fabric with a floppy handle.

Organza An extremely crisp, plain-woven fabric.

Gazar A structured plain-weave, highly twisted double-yarn with a crisp handle and flat, smooth texture.

124

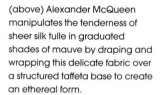

(above) Alexander McQueen manipulates the tenderness of sheer silk tulle in graduated shades of mauve by draping and wrapping this delicate fabric over a structured taffeta base to create an ethereal form.

(left) This lightweight teal silk habotai is an ideal fabric to give sportswear styling a luxe personality, as expressed in this outfit by New York designer Nicholas K. The designer's approach is to blend classic design with a decidedly modern, downtown edge.

(above) French–Chinese designer Yiqing Yin's ethereal sheer Cloud dress, crafted from weightless silk chiffon, references the complex drapery of ancient Greek costume and features skilfully manipulated delicate miniature pleats.

Liquid drape

Sensuous weight and tactile, like a second skin.

Jersey A lightweight knit in silk yarn with a particular drape and handle.

Crêpe A pebbly textured silk woven from high-twist yarns.

Crêpe de chine A lightweight plain-weave crêpe silk made with alternating S- and Z-twist yarns.

Charmeuse A light satin-faced crêpe-backed fabric with a tactile drape.

(above) This ruffled shocking-pink silk dress captures the characteristic liquid drape and fluidity of silk crêpe de chine.

(above) Designer Markus Lupfer glamorizes a super sized T-shirt silhouette by cutting it in a heavyweight silk satin trimmed with a chunky cashmere rib.

(left) Artfully manipulated petrol blue stonewashed silk exploits the structural qualities of the highly twisted double-yarn gazar weave in this couture gown by designer Yiqing Yin. The stonewashed finishing treatment has broken down the crispness of the gazar slightly, and lends the fabric a 'vintage' personality.

Section 2
Plant fibres

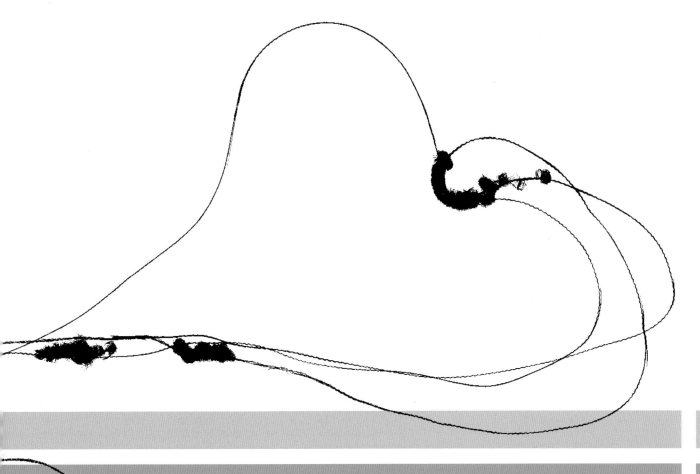

127

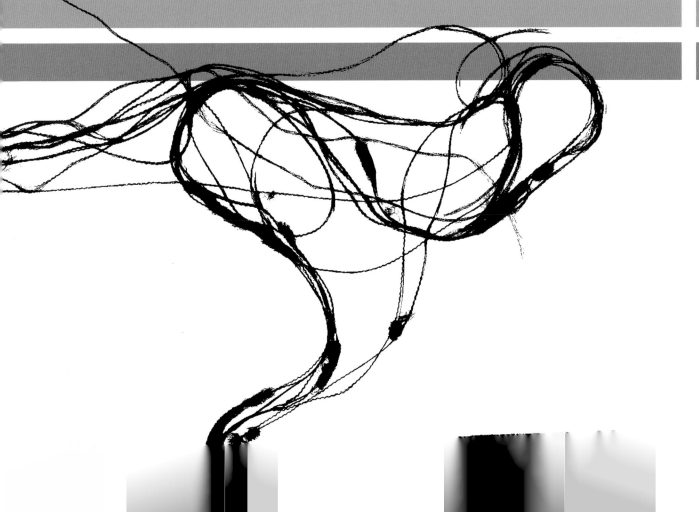

Linen reflects a heritage and aspirational lifestyle that speaks of refinement and quality.

Linen has been highly valued for many centuries for its incomparable handle and unique visual appeal. It embodies a desirable, authentic, low-key luxury that continues to transcend the vagaries of fast fashion.

Linen fibre possesses unique practical properties, which, coupled with a subtle and refined touch, have assured its fashion longevity. It has become synonymous with a classic, relaxed elegance and is the supreme choice for comfort in hot weather. Its cool, absorbent properties are well recognized the world over and are unparalleled by any other natural fibre.

Linen has a very specific tactile appeal; smooth and lustrous to both the eye and hand, the fibre is almost silky in texture, yet embodies a springy freshness. It can also express a robust personality in heavier weaves that may lend it a satisfying drape. Conversely, lighter weights can have an almost featherlight aspect evocative of the draperies of Ancient Egyptian and Greek cultures.

Pure linen will always endure in contemporary fashion. Its natural creasing lends clothing made from it an unmistakable character, while its inherent anti-static properties make it fall away from the body, flutter and undulate in response to movement.

The development of new blends and finishes for linen ensures that this ancient fibre remains relevant to the demands of the modern consumer. Synthetic blends can improve crease recovery, create exciting new textures and offer aspects that appeal to both premium brands and price-competitive markets seeking to experience previously unattainable luxury products.

The history of linen

Linen is the oldest textile in the world, predating cotton and possibly even wool, and is known to have been in use during the Stone Age. Since then its popularity as a clothing textile has risen and fallen with the changing times, but it is thankfully once again being appreciated for all it has to offer the contemporary consumer.

(opposite page) This folded and frayed unbleached linen fabric expresses the natural texture and inherent draping characteristics associated with the finest quality linen.

(above) A collection of contemporary, historically referenced garments, displayed by Masters of Linen to demonstrate linen's quality and authenticity.

Early history

Linen is believed to have first been systematically cultivated in Mesopotamia, in the Middle East region known as the 'cradle of civilization', around 5000 to 6000 BC. The ancient Egyptians and Babylonians cultivated flax, which was then traded with other societies of the region by the Phoenicians. The ancient Egyptians developed a sophisticated linen 'industry'; so valuable was the commodity that it was sometimes used as a form of currency. Linen was seen as a symbol of light and purity, as much as it was a display of wealth for the afterlife. A shroud for an important Pharaoh would often consist of 1,000 m (over half a mile) of fine linen. Some of these shrouds were so finely spun and woven that they still cannot be replicated by modern methods. The linen curtains that shielded the tomb of Tutankhamun were found intact after over 3,000 years, while parts of the shroud of Rameses II were microscopically examined by the British Museum and found to be structurally perfect after almost 3,500 years.

Among the earliest records documenting the manufacturing of linen are the ancient Greek tablets of Pylos. Concurrently, ancient Roman blueprints show that their manufacturing methods closely resembled current manufacturing processes.

Range of uses

Linen is ostensibly a tough fabric. Ancient Greek infantrymen wore protective clothing made of linen, and jackets of padded linen were worn under the chain-mail of medieval knights for additional protection against arrows. Symbolic of purity, Jewish and Christian religious vestments were and are still made from linen.

The structure of woven linen made it a perfect medium for all types of embroidery and drawn thread work. It was also the yarn of choice for fine **needle-** and **bobbin-lace** work. Sixteenth-century **ruffs** were made of heavily starched linen, the best of which was from Flanders (see page 134).

Linen was also used for making paper and bindings for books. The *Liberlinteus of Zagreb* is an intact Etruscan textbook made of linen. It is still today the material of choice for archival quality book-binding, and many artists choose to paint on linen canvas.

130

The meaning of linen

The word linen is derived from the Latin word for the flax plant, *Linum usitatissimum*, which literally translates as 'useful linen', and recognizes the inherent value of this humble plant. Today there are several words in the English language that owe their etymon to the importance of linen. The word 'line' is derived from linen thread, which was used to determine a straight line. Similarly, the word 'lining' developed from the same source, because linen was often used to line woollen and leather clothing. Lingerie, originally a French word, also has its origins in linen, because it was once the fabric of choice for intimate apparel.

(above) A selection of natural linen fabrics in different weights shows its characteristic pronounced weave structure.

Sophistication and practicalities

Throughout Renaissance and Baroque Europe, linen was associated with wealth. In various European courts, periodically, sumptuary laws were passed to curtail the inordinate expenditure on dress, which often referred to the use of linen lace. This was also a useful method of enforcing strict social hierarchy through dress, an early form of dress code.

In the eighteenth and nineteenth centuries the appearance of linen was more restrained, perhaps echoing the new age of enlightenment, but it was still considered an almost obligatory sign of refinement. A gentleman's wardrobe and status was judged by the quantity and quality of his linen. Beau Brummell (1778–1840), the famous Regency dandy and arbiter of taste, had the maxim: 'fine linen and plenty of it, all perfectly starched and freshly laundered'. He considered this to be 'the maximum of luxury in the service of minimal ostentation'. In 1805, at his most fashionable, he ordered 75 yards of fine Irish linen for his shirts and bed sheets, as well as a quantity of Irish linen **damask** for his nightshirts.

In nineteenth-century Europe the status of a gentleman was judged by the quality and quantity of his linens, however flax was also part of the fabric of everyday village life. Prior to the Industrial Revolution and mass urbanization, flax (see 'Linen fibre', page 136) was cultivated, spun and woven by peasant farmers for their own consumption, producing a cloth that was coarser and less refined than the flax that was commercially traded and valued.

(above) This layered chalk white 100 per cent washed linen coat by French designer Marc Le Bihan has a refined historical appeal, reflecting an important part of his approach to design: the appreciation and deconstruction of vintage garments. The designer has a great affinity with fabrics, particularly handmade textiles, having worked as a weaver at the Manufacture des Gobelins in Paris.

(left) Menswear by Rui Leonardes featuring a deconstructed modernized gothic frayed linen ruff.

131

Linen continued to be the fabric of choice until the end of the nineteenth century, used for all intimate apparel, gentlemen's shirts, women's chemises and dresses, as well as for general household textiles. So omnipresent was linen as a household textile that today, in English-speaking countries, the term is generically used to describe bed, bathroom, table and kitchen textiles, even though the majority are now no longer made of linen. Linen cupboards are still in use and retail stores still refer to 'linen' departments.

The last vestige of linen as an essential symbol of a well-dressed gentleman was a neatly folded, well-laundered pocket handkerchief worn in the out-breast top pocket of a suit, a styling detail that was to become a fashion anachronism with the new wave of social changes of the mid-1960s.

The First World War

Until the twentieth century flax cultivation was very much a cottage industry; however, with increased mechanization the demand for factory-scale production became inevitable. Flax was a vital supply during World War I, for both sides. It was used for tents, ropes and canvas for aeroplanes. The scale of production was insufficient to meet the voracious appetite of the war machine, so the supply was supplemented with cotton, which was more readily available due to its faster manufacturing methods. During the interwar years this less expensive, and perhaps more manageable, fabric eventually usurped linen's position as the fabric of choice.

Postwar demands

In the industrialized world, linen, in common with other natural fibres, fell out of fashion after World War II. The new preference was for synthetics, which were more in tune with the contemporary preoccupation for modernity and expectations of an easy-care lifestyle, which better suited women's new role in the workplace. High-maintenance fabrics, together with many other domestic chores, were replaced by anything and everything that could simplify life.

By the 1960s, in Great Britain and North America, linen had developed something of an esoteric status, appealing to only a certain type of consumer. However, in the Mediterranean and South America linen continued to enjoy popularity, because synthetics were not able to offer the same level of coolness and comfort in hot climates.

By the mid-1970s linen as a clothing fabric was at an all-time low, with less than 10 per cent of linen produced being used for fashion textiles. Investment in the industry during the 1980s and into the 1990s resulted in technological developments that eliminated many of the traditional characteristics of linen that were not liked by the average **high-street** retail customer. Mechanical pre-treatments, **enzymes** and ammonia have made linen into a totally modern fabric that can be wrinkle-free, shrink-resistant and sometimes even non-iron.

By the mid-1990s linen's unique appeal was once more appreciated, with around 70 per cent of linen production being again used for fashion fabrics. Today there are special linen and cotton blends being developed for use in denim production, with the aim of improving the feel of this fashion staple in hot and humid climates.

(left) A languid geometric cut cowl-necked linen-and-rayon blend sweater by New York designer Nicholas K exemplifies relaxed urban dressing. Slight slubs and a polished sheen are characteristic of many linen yarns. It is worn with a viscose georgette tunic and cotton poplin trousers.

The development of European linen

The countries that more aptly developed the growing of flax, together with more sophisticated spinning, weaving and manufacturing techniques, are those that today are still recognized as producing the best product. Until the 1950s, Belgium, France, the Netherlands and Ireland were considered the best producers and manufacturers of linen. Italy, alongside other Mediterranean countries, was valued for producing good, handmade linen products.

Irish linen

It is believed that the Phoenicians first traded Egyptian linen fabric and flax seeds with Ireland long before the advent of Christianity, although evidence of an organized industry was not apparent until the twelfth century. Fifteenth-century English travellers remarked on how 'the wild Irish wore chemises of 30 to 40 **ells** of linen, dyed with saffron'.

Huguenots

In 1685 Louis XIV revoked the Edict of Nantes resulting in religious persecution against the Protestant Huguenots. The majority of Huguenots lived in northeast France and Flanders and were predominantly skilled silk and linen weavers. Many of the silk weavers fled to London, settled and set up their looms in Spitalfields. By contrast, the linen weavers migrated to Ulster (Northern Ireland). The British government knew that their skills in weaving fine linen would benefit the existing industry, so encouraged the Huguenots to the province with privileges and financial incentives. Louis Crommelin (1652–1727) was invited by the government of King William (of Orange) to join fellow Huguenots and further develop the industry. He introduced new industry methods, such as mass bleaching, and developed the commercial export trade. His lasting legacy was the foundation of today's modern linen industry.

Linen has been so fundamental to the region that it was often described as the 'fabric of Ireland'.

The classic pea coat is reinterpreted here in a textured Irish linen with deconstructed multi-fabric decoration by John Rocha.

(left) Fluid Irish linen jacquard dress with swerving seams by John Rocha expresses the natural ease and relaxed wearability of this luxury fabric.

Irish Linen Guild logo, an assurance of quality. Yarn or fabric must be either spun or woven in Ireland to carry the logo of authenticity.

Linen industry

In 1711 the Board of Trustees of the Linen Manufacturers of Ireland, also referred to as the **Linen Board**, was established. This, together with the introduction of tariff protection, further encouraged the development of the industry. By the mid-eighteenth century around 500 Huguenot families had the controlling influence in the Irish linen trade, by now firmly established in the northern provinces between the rivers Bann and Lagan, collectively known as the 'linen homelands'. Flax needs well-prepared ground and was therefore usually planted after a potato crop. This rotation of crops saved the region from the potato blight and famine that adversely affected the rest of Ireland.

The region further profited from the American Civil War, because the resulting shortage of cotton increased the demand and price of linen. At its height almost two-thirds of the linen produced was destined for export, of which nearly 90 per cent was to England. By this point Belfast was known as **Linenopolis**.

The Industrial Revolution came late to Ireland. Labour was cheaper here than in mainland England, so the linen industry developed more slowly than that of cotton, giving cotton the competitive edge. However, when the Revolution did reach Linenopolis, the province's engineering developed quickly around the requirements of its most important industry.

Up to and including World War I, Ulster was the largest linen producer in the world, and strategically very important to the war effort. By the early 1920s almost every town or village had a mill or factory, and 70,000 people, which represented about 40 per cent of the workforce of Northern Ireland, were directly involved in the linen industry. Today there are only about ten significant companies, and fewer than 4,000 people directly employed in producing linen. Very little flax is now grown in Ireland; the majority is imported from Eastern Europe. The expertise that was once the backbone of the linen industry is now the driving force behind design and technology in spinning, dyeing and weaving.

Luxury linen

Irish linen is a valuable and desirable commodity and if spun or woven in Ireland can carry the Irish Linen Guild's logo of authenticity. This assures it is a luxurious product worthy of global recognition.

In the mid-1990s the **Living Linen Project** was set up to record first-hand information about the linen industry in the twentieth century, since it is considered integral to the country's cultural identity.

(Notes from a lecture by Mr Daniel McCrea to students of the Irish Linen Guild, 1971)

Flemish (Flanders) linen

Historically Flanders is the geographic region that now overlaps parts of northeast France, Belgium and the adjoining Netherlands. Today Flanders designates the Flemish community of these regions. The cities of Ghent and Bruges in Belgium and Lille in France were all once part of Flanders.

The climate and geography of the region make it ideal for the cultivation of flax, which was originally an ancillary crop grown to be woven during the long winter months, while the farmers waited for the next crop-growing cycle to begin.

During the fourteenth and fifteenth centuries – the golden age of Flemish fabrics – the linen trade flourished. Linen fabric and yarn for lace was especially valued, bringing prosperity to the region, which became one of the most urbanized parts of Europe. Tielt in West Flanders was the centre of the linen industry. Around the 1790s nearly 20 per cent of households were involved in linen production, a figure that grew to over 70 per cent by the 1840s.

Flax was cultivated in the region around Ypres using seeds from both Holland and Riga, which produced better crops.

Spain and its South American colonies formed the primary export market, however trade barriers were later imposed that dramatically affected the industry – as did the mechanization of cotton production – which fell into decline.

Today, through design, technology and the merging of several companies, Belgian linen is once again a desirable commodity and a competitive product equalling that of Irish linen.

Guaranteed traceability

Club Masters of Linen is a collective mark registered by the European Confederation of Linen and Hemp (CELC, Confédération Européenne du Lin et du Chanvre). The mark guarantees 100 per cent European traceability to each stage of processing flax into linen fabric. Spinners and weavers must follow a stringent set of rules to be able to use the mark of authentication.

The seal of excellence is available for three categories of fabric:
- Pure linen
- Linen union (cotton warp and linen weft)
- Linen-rich fibre (51 per cent linen; 49 per cent other fibres)

Italian linen

While not important in the cultivation of flax, Italy is very important within the linen industry as a whole. It is singularly the largest converter of flax fibre into yarn and fabric for both the export and domestic markets. Although linen represents approximately 5 per cent of Italy's textile production, it is an important percentage because it represents high value, export-led merchandise.

As with other Mediterranean countries, Italy has a long heritage in working fine linen for both clothing and household textiles. These were once cottage industries, where designs and techniques were passed down from mother to daughter. Today, Italy's preoccupation with design-led technology has resulted in the development of sophisticated machinery that can produce competitively priced fine linen products. Although much of the lace work, embroidery and pulled thread work is now machine made, the results continue to echo the handcrafted linen work of previous generations.

Linen market

Approximately 70 per cent of linen is used for the clothing industry, while approximately 30 per cent is used for household textiles.

The principal countries that process flax into high-quality yarn and fabric are Italy, France, Belgium, Northern Ireland, Germany and Japan. Eastern Europe and the Baltic countries are now important producers of flax, as is China. However, the most desirable linen, whether yarn, fabric or manufactured goods, still remains in the domain of Belgium, France, Ireland and Italy. The European Community's agricultural policies department sets European flax prices, which are prevented from falling below a certain level.

The major consumers of linen clothing and household textiles are the United States, Italy, Germany, Japan, France and Great Britain. Italy is the single largest consumer of flax. The country produces yarn and woven fabrics and has one of the most sophisticated linen knitting industries producing fully-fashioned knitwear.

Languid milk-white double-breasted summer suits, cut to optimize the draping qualities of the luxurious silk-and-linen mix designed by Italian brand Corneliani.

CELC (Confédération Européenne du Lin et du Chanvre) is a non-profit-making trade organization for linen (flax) and hemp in Europe. Masters of Linen, based in Paris, is a subsidiary of CELC, providing information and promoting European quality linen.

Linen fibre

Grades of flax differ, with flax cultivated in Western Europe usually of a better quality.

Linen is the yarn and fabric made from the fibres of the stem of the flax plant, the only cellulosic plant indigenous to Western Europe. Flax, also referred to as linseed, is a commercial field crop plant grown for its fibres, which are used to manufacture cloth, rope or paper. Flax grows in many parts of the world but prefers temperate maritime climates and good soil to flourish well.

Flax stems vary from 60 to 120 cm in height, and the individual **bast** fibres are held together in 'bundles' by **pectin**. It takes about 100 days for planted flax seed to grow to maturity and be ready for harvesting. The plant has small, five-petal flowers that are either blue or white and that blossom for only one day: the plants with blue flowers tend to yield better crops. The fruit capsules contain the seeds, which are converted to linseed oil.

Properties of linen

Flax fibres are the strongest of all the vegetable fibres, two to three times stronger than cotton. They vary in length from approximately 20 to 130 cm, with a micron count (diameter) of 12 to 16. The cross section of the fibre is made up of irregular polygon shapes, which give it a coarse and crisp appearance.

Natural flax colours range from shades of ivory, tan and grey. White or pure white is only achieved through various bleaching processes.

After the impurities have been removed the fibre becomes hygroscopic, absorbing up to 20 per cent of its weight in moisture or perspiration, which it quickly releases into the atmosphere, making it dry to the touch. The fibre does not lock in or trap air or have any insulative properties, allowing the linen wearer to feel cool. It is thermo-regulating, encouraging the body to acclimatize in hot environments. For this reason it is believed that in hot climates linen bed sheets give you a far more restful sleep than cotton sheets. Flax is also believed to have therapeutic properties that promote sleep.

The slight stiffness of the fabric stops linen from clinging to the body, instead it tends to billow away, thus drying more quickly and eliminating perspiration. Linen can be blended with more insulative fibres, such as cashmere or wool, to become trans-seasonal.

Linen has a longer staple relative to cotton, is **lint**-free and does not **pill**. It is resistant to stains, which can be washed out at lower temperatures than cotton due to the smoother surface of the fibre. Although good-quality linen carries a premium price tag, products made from this precious fibre are regarded as investments because they can endure regular use by many generations. Durable and practical, the more often it is worn and laundered, the softer, smoother and more beautiful it becomes. The surface of linen fabric responds well to steaming and pressing, acquiring an almost polished finish. It is believed to be unharmed by germs and resists humidity.

Linen does not have any natural give or stretch, but is resistant to damage from abrasion, however it can 'break' if constantly folded in the same place.

The natural absorption properties within linen mean that it is able to absorb a good depth of colour in the dyeing process, and remains colourfast for a long period.

The slubs along the length of the yarn are sometimes considered a characteristic of linen, but are technically a defect that denotes a lesser quality of fabric.

136

Flax flowers are either blue or white and bloom for one day; plants with blue flowers tend to yield better crops.

Ecological considerations

Linen is a more expensive fibre than cotton, with much more of a niche market, making it an ideal vehicle for organic cultivation and ecological production methods.

Flax is or can be an ecologically pertinent and sustainable crop. It grows best when crops are rotated annually, a sound method of crop production that does not strip the soil of all its nutrients. Flax is environmentally friendly, requiring little irrigation and energy to process, and is fully biodegradable. With crop rotation it is not necessary to use chemical fertilizers and pesticides, and even when these are used flax requires only one-fifth of the pesticides and artificial fertilizers required for commercially grown cotton. Additionally, linen is up to 12 times stronger than the equivalent cotton product, which dramatically increases its life span, which means it does not need to be replaced so often.

Linen absorbs dye well, especially natural dyes, and does not require chemical treatments. It can be sun bleached to avoid the use of artificial agents.

A paper bag neckline 'Galaxy' dress by Icona Vera in coral-pink linen showcases the crisp weave structure, desirable natural irregularities and natural sheen of the fibre.

Linen production

The fundamental principles of producing linen yarn from the flax plant have changed little since early Roman times. However, modern technology has revolutionized the efficiency and flexibility of the yarn, and the speed at which it can now be produced.

Flax processing is labour-intensive, requiring skilled workers; however several by-products are also produced – including linseed oil for linoleum, soap, fuel and cattle feed – meaning there is minimum wastage.

Today's technology

Until recently linen production was in the domain of specialist manufacturers, however today's advanced technology has allowed it to be more widely produced. Technologic advances have also improved the quality of the crops at both the growing and finishing stages, so fungal attacks are now averted in the field. The shuttleless loom means that smaller weaving sheds can be used, while mechanical pre-treatments have made linen into a modern fabric that maintains its age-old advantages. Enzymes smooth out the fibres making them softer and ideally suited for knitting single jersey fabric with less propensity to shrinkage. The use of liquid ammonia makes linen into a wrinkle-free and non-iron fabric, while pre-washing stops it shrinking.

Cultivation

Flax is one of the few crops still produced in Europe. Russia, alongside other countries of the Federation, is currently turning much of its land over to flax production. The majority of the production is **tow**, the lower-grade shorter fibres. France sows about 60 per cent less but produces a much greater quantity of **long-line fibres**. Flax production in Northern France, Belgium and the Netherlands is relatively small by global production standards but it is considered to be by far the best quality. Of the three countries France is the largest producer.

Canada and China are two of the principal flax producing countries, between them producing just over 50 per cent of total global production. India and the United States are also important producers. In Africa both Egypt and Ethiopia produce flax while in Eastern Europe, Russia, the Ukraine, Belarus and the Baltic countries of Latvia and Lithuania are expanding their flax production.

138

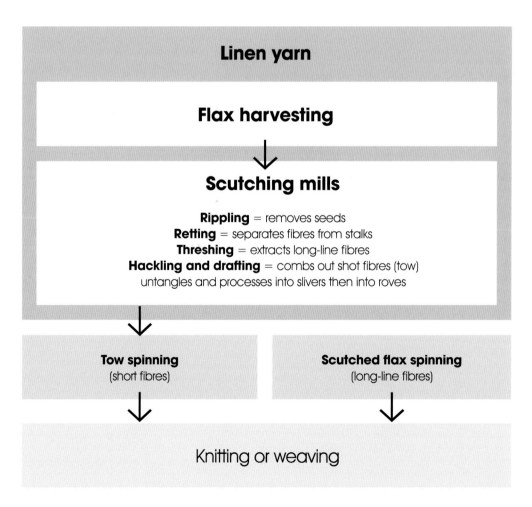

Harvesting

The quality of the final linen yarn and fabric is dependent on flax's growing conditions and harvesting methods. Flax needs well-prepared ground and is sensitive to weeds. It is a renewable resource needing little fertilization in the form of chemicals or pesticides, and is harvestable after a single growing season.

The shoots are ready for harvesting approximately 100 days after planting. This is about four weeks after the plant has flowered and two weeks after the seed capsules have formed. The shoots are 80–120 cm (31–47 in.) long and start to yellow at the base. If they are allowed to go brown the fibre will be degraded.

Harvesting can be mechanized using combines, or it can be carried out manually which maximizes the fibre length and thus the quality of the eventual yarn.

Mechanized harvesting involves cutting the plant and raking it into windrows. When sufficiently dry, a combine harvests the seeds.

Hand harvesting involves pulling the complete plant with root from the ground – this gives the longest and most desirable fibres, since the fibres go all the way to the root. The second-best option is cutting the plant stalks very close to ground level.

Scutching

This process extracts and cleans the fibres contained within the stalks, with the objective of producing long-line fibres. The entire process involves up to ten successive operations that fall into two principal categories. The first is separating the different elements that make up the plant to enable the extraction of the fibres, and the second is the cleaning processes that eliminate all the other materials. **Scutching** mills represent an important part of the manufacturing process. The short tow fibres are used for coarser fabrics and household textiles, while the long-line fibres are used for fine clothing and bed linen.

Rippling

Rippling as part of the scutching process is the removal of the seeds, which is done by metal-toothed comb machine. The process also aligns all the stalks parallel to each other for easier separation. The seeds are then kept for the next season's sowing. After rippling, the flax is passed through a further series of speeding toothed rollers that reduces the thickness. The next process, referred to as breaking, crushes the woody fibres into small particles known as shive.

139

Cottonizing

Traditional cotton machinery is sometimes used to process linen fibres in a similar way to cotton, an alternative and faster production process that requires less equipment. However, the fibres tend to lose their linen characteristics.

Long fibres (linen flax) processed through a turbine after scutching.

Retting

Retting is a process used for all bast vegetable fibres, to separate the fibre from the stalk. This can be achieved through the use of chemicals, although these are harmful to both the fibres and the environment. Alternatively, and ecologically more prudent, the stalks can be immersed in warm water tanks. Through sufficient soaking and the introduction of enzymes, bacteria will form and decompose the pectin that binds the fibres together.

Historically, the stalks were left in the fields in the autumn where nature would naturally decompose the binding agent. This process was known as 'wind retting'. In some areas the stalks were left to soak in shallow river areas, however this may contaminate the water.

The flax is then collected and pressed into large bales and stored until it is time to extract the fibres.

Threshing

The process consists of beating or threshing the material in turbines, which extract the long flax fibres from the epidermis, shive and short fibres known as tow. The resulting long fibres of scutched flax are also referred to as long-line flax; this is then hand-sorted and classified according to colour and cleanliness.

Hackling and drafting

Hackling combs out the short broken fibres or tows as well as untangling the bundles, rollers then process and divide the bundles to form continuous **slivers** which are further processed by means of doubling and drafting; this evens out the weight and produces **roves** which are ready for the final spinning process.

(above) Sliver of flax obtained during drafting and preparation, after combing and before spinning.

(above right) Weaving linen yarn.

(right) Flax stems, linen fibres and finished woven fabric.

Spinning

There are two methods of spinning flax. One involves spinning the long fibres and is known as scutched-flax spinning. The other is tow spinning and is used for the shorter fibres or tows. Spinning is the final process that turns the roves into yarn. Both the long fibres and the tow can be spun using wet, dry or semi-wet techniques. Wet spinning long-line fibres will achieve a very fine-quality yarn used for fine clothing and the best bed linen. Dry spinning will result in a coarser, less regular yarn with some naps, and is mainly used in household textiles. A final process eliminates defects and impurities and then joins the yarn by a means of knotting and splicing.

Finished linen fabric can range from rough and stiff to fine and smooth.

(above) An exquisite Grès gown inspired by the Parisian couturier Madame Grès. Designer Yiqing Yin has deftly created sculptural organic forms that snake effortlessly around the body, constructed from finely pleated linen and mounted on an almost invisible Sophie Hallette 'illusion' tulle.

Units of measurement

Using a **yarn count** is a way of grading linen according to the fineness of the fibre.

In the United States linen yarn is measured in **LEA**. The finer the yarn the higher the LEA number.

**1 LEA = 1 x 300 yards (yarn) to the pound weight,
40 LEA = 40 x 300 yards to the pound weight
(i.e.12,000 yards)**

In Europe the metric system is used, represented by the letters **Nm**, indicating the number of 1,000-metre lengths per kilogram.

In China the English **cotton-count** system is used, indicating the number of 840-yard lengths or hanks per pound weight.

Cotton

Cotton is the most egalitarian and practical of all natural fibres.

The democratic appeal of cotton allows it the scope to be relevant to myriad marketing possibilities, from the most value-driven price categories through to cutting-edge designer fashion. It may be woven or knitted, superfine and as gossamer light as voile, lending it a luxurious personality. Conversely, its perennial appeal can be expressed by hardwearing canvas-type weaves or drill constructions, which provide the ultimate democratic classic fashion fabric: denim.

Cotton possesses the qualities of comfort and natural absorbency, and can embody, depending on processing, either cool or warm aspects that make it truly trans-seasonal. The raw fibre in its natural state is visually evocative of its potential usefulness to man, the small cloud-like formations of the cotton **bolls** suggestive of a comforting end product.

The history of cotton

Cotton cultivation is said to have started almost simultaneously in India and South America. The Harappans, living along the banks of the Indus river valley (now Pakistan), first produced cotton fabric 6,000 years ago, and exported it to Mesopotamia (now Iraq) during the third millennium BC, from where it was introduced to the Egyptians of the Nile valley. Dating back over 7,000 years, fragments of fabric found in Mexican caves prove that cotton was also indigenous to early South and Central American people. It was important to the Moche and Nazca cultures of pre-Spanish Peru, who grew it upriver then made it into nets that they traded with the fishing villages along the coast.

The usefulness of cotton spread, and in late medieval Europe it was acknowledged as an important fibre. It was initially used in its relatively raw state as wadding for padded protection, before being developed as a yarn.

(opposite page) Cotton is the most commonly used natural fibre. The production and export of cotton extends to more than 100 countries, with an estimated 350 million people involved in its production, farming, transportation and manufacturing.

(above) Freshly picked raw cotton.

(right) Organic jeans by Dutch brand Kuyichi. Cotton denim is the ultimate democratic fashion fabric, eternally desirable to all consumers.

The Spanish conquistadors in Mexico noted the wearing of clothes made from cotton by the indigenous peoples of the region. By the 1500s cotton was well known around the globe, and by the close of the sixteenth century it was being fully cultivated throughout the warmer regions of Asia and the Americas.

It is an ironic tragedy that India's once important cotton-processing industry was actively sabotaged during the period of British Raj and colonial rule in the eighteenth and nineteenth centuries. The British East India Company had a policy of de-industrialization in order to force the closure of cotton processing and manufacturing workshops throughout India. This was purposefully done to ensure that the Indian markets supplied only the less valuable raw material and in turn were then obliged to buy more expensive manufactured textiles from Britain.

(above) Cotton weaving on a traditional hand loom. Cotton was actively farmed and used for clothing by the indigenous peoples of South and Central America long before the arrival of the Spanish conquistadors in the early sixteenth century.

Tree wool

Greek historian Herodotus (c. 484–425 BC), observing Indian cotton, wrote: 'there are trees which grow wild there, the fruit of which is a wool exceeding in beauty and goodness that of sheep'. These early poetic observations endured, as cotton was popularly believed to be some form of 'tree wool'. This concept continues today: in the Germanic languages the word for cotton, Baumwolle, literally translates as 'tree wool'.

Industry

The Industrial Revolution boosted cotton manufacturing and made textile production Britain's leading export. New machines were invented, such as the roller spinning machine and the flyer-bobbin system that were used to draw cotton to a more even thickness. The **spinning Jenny** was invented in 1764, followed by the **spinning frame** in 1769. Both machines enabled the spinning of multiple yarns at one time, and revolutionized the Lancashire cotton industry. In North America, Eli Whitney (1765–1825) was credited with the invention of the **cotton gin** (1794), which was fundamental to the mass production of cotton fibre. Small gins were hand powered, while larger ones were powered by horse or water. The cotton gin facilitated much larger-scale harvesting and only required an unskilled labour force, which in the southern United States consisted of slaves. The gin is credited for vastly increasing the financial assets of the economy of the United States. An Indian machine called a **charkha** or churka predated the American cotton gin but was unsuitable for shorter-staple cotton.

English weavers were now able to produce cotton yarn and fabric to higher and more consistent standards, at faster speeds with increased productivity. A contemporary slogan of the time read, 'Britain's bread hangs by Lancashire threads'. Manchester's wealth was founded and further prospered on the manufacture and export of cotton; as the undisputed capital of the global cotton trade it acquired the nickname of **cottonopolis**.

(above) John Smedley Mill in Matlock, Derbyshire. While the area was important for knitting cotton hosiery it was Manchester (Lancashire) that enjoyed the sobriquet of 'cottonopolis' as the undisputed capital of the nineteenth-century global cotton trade.

American cotton

Improved technology and the increased control of world markets allowed British traders to develop a commercial chain where raw cotton fibres were purchased cheaply from colonial plantations, then processed in the Lancashire mills and re-exported on British ships to captive colonial markets in West Africa, India and China via Shanghai and Hong Kong, all at a considerable profit. Such vast quantities of raw cotton fibre were required that by the 1840s India, the then principal supplier, was no longer able to meet the insatiable appetite of the Lancashire mills. Shipping low-cost bulky raw cotton was both expensive and time-consuming, so British merchants turned to the emerging cotton plantations of the southern states of America. The advantage of American cotton was threefold: the two varieties of domesticated Native American species produced a longer-staple fibre of superior quality; the cotton production was far less expensive because it was picked and grown by a slave labour force; and finally, it incurred a shorter shipping time, because the sea route did not entail the lengthy and arduous Cape of Good Hope. By the mid-nineteenth century the commodity known as 'King Cotton' had become the backbone of the Confederate States of America.

Egyptian cotton

When the southern US ports were blockaded by the northern Union during the American Civil War (1861–1865), Britain and France, the main buyers of Confederate cotton, had to find an alternative source. They found it in Egypt but at the end of the Civil War they turned their allegiances back to the cheaper American cotton. Through the British, the Egyptians made heavy economic investments in their cotton industry, and the sudden departure of their two primary buyers sent their economy into spiralling deficit and eventual bankruptcy. To protect its investment, Britain seized control of the government and later made Egypt a British protectorate. Cotton remained an important commodity and was one of the reasons Britain held on to Egypt, until it seized full independence in 1956.

Indian cotton

In 1869 the Suez Canal opened to shipping, connecting the Red Sea to the Mediterranean and halving the journey time from India to Britain. This renewed an interest in Indian cotton, and cultivation in turn increased. However, the British government imposed heavy tariffs to discourage the production of cotton yarn or fabric in favour of the less valuable raw fibre.

Mahatma Gandhi (Mohandas Karamchand Gandhi 1869–1948) was the political and spiritual leader of India during its struggle for independence from colonial rule. He pioneered non-violent resistance by means of mass civil disobedience, non-cooperation and the boycotting of British goods, especially fabrics. He symbolically wore a cotton **dhoti** and shawl, woven with yarn he hand spun on a charkha. He recommended that all Indians spend time each day spinning khadi (homespun and woven cloth) in support of the independence movement. The charkha is fundamental to India's cultural heritage and is symbolic of its long struggle for independence – its symbol was incorporated into the Indian flag, which should, in principal, be made of cotton khadi.

Mahatma Ghandi wearing a dhoti and spinning khadi cloth on a charkha. The term khadi can be applied to any fibre that is hand-spun and hand-woven.

American cotton after the Civil War

The emancipation of slaves at the end of the American Civil War did not diminish the importance of southern cotton as a key crop. Black farmers continued to work on the white-owned plantations in return for a share of the profits, known as **sharecropping**. Vast labour forces were required for cotton picking, which was all done by hand. In the 1920s some basic machinery was introduced, however it was not until the 1950s that mechanisms reached any level of sophistication as to not damage the fibre (see page 148).

The United States is still a major exporter of cotton, the majority of which is of the long-staple variety.

The 1950s and early 1960s in North America, and to a lesser extent in Northern Europe, were periods enamoured with synthetic materials, which were seen as desirable, sophisticated and worldly. Cotton production plateaued sharply, and by the mid-1960s the American cotton producers had initiated a self-help programme to research and promote the use of cotton, a proactive policy intended to counteract the rapid decline in cotton consumption. In 1966 The Cotton Research and Promotion Act was passed, aimed at combatting the rise in popularity of synthetic fabrics and re-establishing the market for cotton. Concurrently, the socio-political undercurrent of the time, in the guise of the flower-power movement, helped create a 'new' interest in natural produce, from which cotton benefited substantially, reborn as a seminal fabric.

Modern material

Today, technology works harmoniously with cotton's natural characteristics, giving us a product that surpasses expectations. Oiling and waxing were early 'low-tech' applications to weatherproof cotton, and today, **bonding**, lamination and chemical treatments can turn a basic fabric into a performance fabric.

Summer or winter, cotton is now a fashion perennial at all levels of the market, from designer to high street. Its pan-global appeal has seen its demand increase at an average of about 2 per cent per year over the last 50 years, and by approximately 4 per cent over the last decade. Cotton is the best-selling fibre in the United States, and one of the best worldwide.

Cotton market

The production and export of cotton extends to more than 100 countries; it is believed to employ an estimated 350 million people in its production, farming, transportation and manufacturing.

The largest producer and consumer of raw cotton is China. It consumes around 40 per cent of the world's raw cotton output, for both domestic consumption and export of its manufactured goods. Although the largest producer, China has to supplement its domestic production with additional imported raw material, in order to feed the insatiable appetite of its garment manufacturing industry and the demand for Chinese-made clothing. India, Pakistan and Turkey also supplement their domestic raw cotton production with imported raw material to, similarly, fulfil their export production orders.

The southern United States, known as the **cotton belt**, is the second largest producer of raw cotton. California has the largest global yield per acre, while Texas leads in production. After China and the US, other primary global cotton producers are India, Pakistan, southern Brazil, Burkina, Uzbekistan, Australia, Greece and Syria.

Israel and the USA are the two highest-cost cotton producers in the world. Australia, China, Brazil and Pakistan are among the world's lowest-cost cotton producers.

One-third of all global raw cotton production is traded internationally, the majority of which will go to countries that do not have domestic crop production to supply their spinning, knitting and weaving industries. These manufacturing hubs include: Bangladesh, Indonesia, Thailand, Taiwan and Russia.

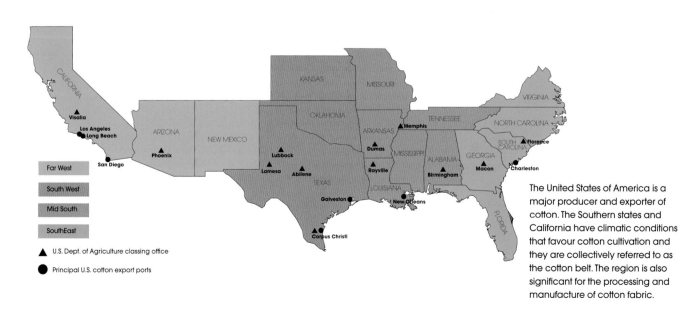

Far West

South West

Mid South

SouthEast

▲ U.S. Dept. of Agriculture classing office

● Principal U.S. cotton export ports

The United States of America is a major producer and exporter of cotton. The Southern states and California have climatic conditions that favour cotton cultivation and they are collectively referred to as the cotton belt. The region is also significant for the processing and manufacture of cotton fabric.

146

Cotton fibre

Cotton is the most commonly used natural fibre.

Cotton is a soft fibre that grows around the seeds of the cotton plant, which is grown between latitudes 45 degrees north and 35 degrees south. In tropical climates cotton is a perennial crop.

The cotton plant is a small shrub with greyish green tri-lobed leaves. The flower is cup-shaped with creamy white to yellow petals that have purplish to red spots near the base. The cotton fibres are the white hairs that cover the seeds in the 'fruit' capsules (the bolls).

As a native of tropical and subtropical regions, the cotton plant produces flowers and 'fruit' throughout the year. It takes approximately two months after the seeds have been planted for the flower buds to appear, which then blossom after a further three weeks. These last about three days before they start to fall, leaving the remaining pods or 'cotton bolls'.

Cotton's aesthetics vary depending on the applied treatments and the grade of the fibre. A typical untreated cotton fabric has a matt lustre, soft drape and a smooth touch, making the fabric comfortable to wear. Cotton garments have a good level of moisture absorption and can typically be machine washed and dried. Dyed cotton retains its colour longer if washed in warm or cool water.

Cotton is susceptible to acids such as lemon juice and should be rinsed quickly. Sunlight causes oxidization, turning it yellow. If the fabric has not been pre-treated with shrink resistant finish then it is liable to shrink.

Cotton plant

There are 43 species of cotton plant, including four primary domesticated species.

Although cotton is native to many regions, the vast majority of the cotton grown today is from one of two principal varieties of the American species *Gossypium hirsutum* and *Gossypium barbadense.*

Cultivation

Cotton cultivation requires long, frost-free periods, plenty of sunshine and a moderate rainfall. The soil needs to be fairly heavy and does not require high levels of nutrients. These conditions tend to be best met within the seasonally dry tropics and subtropics, in both the southern and northern hemispheres. However, today cotton is also cultivated in areas with far less rainfall, the water being obtained by means of irrigation.

Production of the crop starts soon after the autumn harvesting of the previous season's crop. Planting time in the northern hemisphere varies from the beginning of February to the beginning of June.

147

Once in full bloom, the flowers (left) last approximately three days before dropping, leaving the remaining pods, or cotton bolls (right). The white hairs that cover the seeds are the cotton fibre.

The four principal cotton varieties

Gossypium hirsutum
Maya civilization, Central America

Gossypium barbadensa
Inca civilization, South America

Gossypium herbaceum
Harappan civilization, South Asia

Gossypium arboreum
Egyptian civilization, North Africa
Indo Pakistan subcontinent

Processing cotton
From raw material to finished yarn and fabric

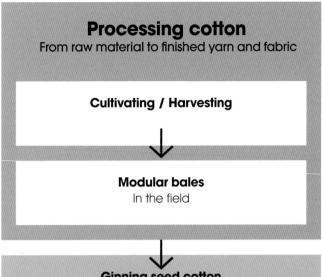

Cultivating / Harvesting

↓

Modular bales
In the field

↓

Ginning seed cotton
Fibres separated from seed pods,
linters and unwanted matter
Usable cotton = about 35% of pre-ginned weight

Cleaned cotton referred to as
lint cotton

Fibre Classification for pricing purposes

↓

Spinning mills
Further cleaning processes to form batts.
Carding to produce slivers then combined to equalize
thicker and thinner parts to consistent size.
Rovings then spun into yarn

Optional combing processes

↓

Fabric mills
(Weaving / Knitting)

Cotton production

The production of cotton is generally efficient, with less than 10 per cent of the picked weight lost in the subsequent processes of converting the raw cotton bolls (seed cases) into pure fibre.

Harvesting

One hundred million rural households around the world are involved in cotton production, the majority of which happens within the developing world where cotton continues to be picked by hand. In Europe, Australia and the United States, on the other hand, it is mechanically harvested by one of two types of harvesting machine, depending on the cotton variety grown. A **cotton picker** removes the cotton from the boll without damaging the plant, while a **cotton stripper** machine strips the entire boll from the plant. Strippers are used in climatic regions that are too windy to grow the 'picker' varieties of cotton.

In some cases a chemical defoliant is first used to remove the leaves; alternatively natural defoliation would occur after a temperature freeze.

After harvesting the land is tilled. The conventional method is to cut down the reaming stalks and turn the soil ready for the next round of seed planting. The alternative method, known as the 'conservation method', leaves the stalks and the plant residue standing on the surface of the soil, and the new seeds are planted through the 'litter' that remains.

After harvesting a machine known as a **module builder** compresses the cotton into large modular blocks that are covered and temporarily stored in the fields. These are collected by specially designed trucks and transported to the **gin**.

Ginning

Ginning is the generic term used for the complete process of turning the cotton bolls into fibre, and the building in which these processes occur is referred to as the gin. The name was originally used as an abbreviation of the word 'engine', and is now part of cotton vocabulary. At this stage, and until the ginning process has been completed, the cotton is referred to as **seed cotton**.

Once the cotton blocks have been delivered to the gin they are broken apart and fed into the ginning machine, which efficiently separates the cotton fibres from the seedpods, removing leaves, burs, dirt, stems and the fuzzy down known as **linters**. Usable cotton fibres will make up about 35 per cent of the pre-ginned cotton weight. The balance of the pre-ginned weight is made up from 55 per cent removed seeds and 10 per cent waste. The seeds are refined and made into cottonseed oil for human consumption. The linters are used in the manufacture of paper, as well as within the plastics industry.

The ginning machine also cleans the cotton, which is now referred to as lint instead of seed cotton.

Classification

The next stage is the classification of the cotton for the purpose of pricing. The lint is formed into bales from which samples are taken to establish fibre quality. Staple length, colour, cleanliness and **micronaire** are the four principal aspects by which the ginned cotton is judged. Micronaire represents fibre fineness and maturity, which is influenced by the climate during the growing period. A poor micronaire count affects the processing and therefore the value of the cotton. After pricing the bales are sold to cotton merchants who in turn sell them on to textile mills or spinners.

Processing and spinning

Once processed to remove traces of wax, protein and seeds, cotton fibre consists of nearly pure **cellulose**, which is a **natural polymer**. The arrangement of the cellulose is such that it gives cotton fibres a high degree of strength, absorbency and durability. Each fibre is made up of between 20 to 30 layers of cellulose coiled in a neat series of natural springs. The fibres of the open boll dry into flat, twisted, ribbon-like shapes that become kinked and interlock together. It is this interlocked form that is ideal for spinning into fine yarn.

Spinning is a generic term for all the processes the fibres will pass through to become yarn, ready for eventual weaving or knitting.

Once at the spinning mill, which may also be referred to as the 'spinners', the bales are opened and further cleaned to remove any residue vegetable matter and short lint. A machine called a **picker** beats, loosens and mixes the fibres, which are then passed through toothed rollers of varying sizes to remove the residue vegetable matter. The fibres finally come off the machine in batts, large bundles of multiple strands of fibres, which are then ready to be carded. The short lint is sold on for other processes and end uses.

The **carding machine** lines up the fibres evenly to make them easier to spin. This is done by passing the batts through different-sized rollers that produce what is termed slivers (pronounced sly-vers), or untwisted ropes of fibres. Several slivers are then combined to equalize the thicker and thinner parts of the slivers, thus making a more consistent size. These are now too thick, so are separated into **rovings**, long, narrow bundles of fibre with twist to hold them together.

In addition to carding, fibres can also go through an optional combing process to make them smoother (see page 13). Finally, the rovings are spun into yarns.

149

(opposite page) Mechanized cotton harvesting in the United States.

(above) Seed cotton ready for the ginning process.

Naturally pigmented Peruvian Pakucho™ cotton from Ecoyarns.

Luxury cotton

Luxury cotton is defined as cotton with characteristics far superior to those of the standard varieties and finishes.

A longer-staple fibre tends to be more desirable, because it can withstand additional combing processes that in turn will make it smoother and finer to the touch. Long-staple cotton may be obtained from many different countries or regions.

Egyptian, **Sea Island** and **Pima** are all names that denote a traditionally luxurious and fine-quality product. The pedigree of their heritage assures the consumer that the product they are buying has an added value. They also provide a USP (unique selling point) for brands targeting a more discerning customer.

Egyptian cotton

Egyptian cotton is used for clothing and household linens alike; however, it is possibly for bed and bath linen that the name most evokes a product of luxury and quality. The term is applied to all cotton grown in Egypt; however, less than half of Egyptian cotton has the desirable extra-long staple length.

Ironically, the cotton species that best produces this extra-long staple is an indigenous American plant, *Gossypium barbadense*. The French and English introduced Native American cotton into Egypt at the time of the American Civil War, when the northern Union ships were blockading southern ports to stop the export of Confederate cotton. Egyptian cotton became a realistic alternative, with the advantage of shorter shipping times to that of cotton from India. Today the term Egyptian cotton is also applied to another indigenous American species, *Gossypium hirsutum*.

In summary, the term 'Egyptian cotton' can be applied to either of the two long-staple varieties. Most importantly the term Egyptian used as a prefix implies luxury and refinement and is considered the ultimate in cotton.

Grey cotton jersey-dress featuring undulating three-dimensional 'landscaping' detailing by Ria Thomas. The easy and comfortable drape expresses one of cotton's many versatile characteristics.

Sea Island cotton

The term 'Sea Island' is applied only to extra-long-staple cotton. However, unlike Egyptian cotton, it is not applied to the *Gossypium hirsutum* species but only to *Gossypium barbadense,* also known as Pima and **Creole** cotton. This species grows as a smaller bush requiring full sun and high humidity and rainfall; it is also sensitive to frost. The plant has a natural anti-fungal property that contains the chemical gossypol, making it naturally insect-repellent and therefore an ideal candidate for organic cotton. The cotton fibres are particularly long and silky.

The species is now cultivated widely across many countries, although its pedigree can be traced back originally to pre-Spanish conquest Peru, then subsequently to the West Indies. Barbados was the first British colony to export cotton and is possibly the original source of the name.

Whereas Egyptian cotton conjures up the idea of luxurious woven fabric, Sea Island cotton applies to luxurious fine-gauge knitwear.

Luxury cotton types

Egyptian cotton

Gossypium hirsutum
and
Gossypium barbadense

Two long-staple cotton varieties grown in Egypt

Sea Island cotton

Gossypium barbadense

A long-staple cotton that is widely grown in several geographic regions. (Caribbean origins)

Pima cotton

Gossypium barbadense

A long-staple cotton grown by Pima Indians in southwest United States

Pima cotton

Pima cotton is silky smooth and is the popular name for *Gossypium barbadense,* which is the same species marketed under the Sea Island prefix, and also one of the two species of the extra-long-staple Egyptian cotton. The progenitors of American Pima cotton were indigenous Egyptian plants interbred with earlier South American varieties that became known as Yuma cotton in the early 1900s and then finally named after the Pima Indians that helped to first grow it. In the United States Pima cotton is grown in the southwestern states of Texas, New Mexico, Arizona and parts of southern California where the climate is dry and hot. Many plantations are run or owned by Native American Pima Indians. Supima® (superior Pima) cotton is a registered trademark of the Supima Association of America and is exclusively 100 per cent American-grown Pima cotton. It is often considered better than Egyptian cotton because it has a guaranteed staple length of more than 3.5 cm. Only a very small percentage of the world's cotton is Supima. The Calvin Klein brand is an active exponent of Pima cotton for its products.

Pima cotton is also grown in Peru, together with a similar variety called **Tangüis cotton**. Both are grown organically. Some species of Tangüis cotton are naturally pigmented and can create natural mélange effects when mixed with white.

Today thousands of Indian peasant farmers are benefitting from the revival of native organic cotton.

Mercerized cotton

Mercerized cotton is not a type or variety of cotton but a treatment applied to the cotton to give it a more lustrous and smoother appearance. Named after John Mercer, who invented the technique in the mid-nineteenth century, it was not popularized until the 1890s, when the processing technique was improved.

Mercerizing can be applied either to the yarn or to the fabric, or for ultimate luxury it may be applied to both, when it is then referred to as double mercerized.

Mercerizing is a series of processes that exposes the yarn or fabric to caustic soda while under tension. The caustic soda 'burns' off superfluous surface fibres or lint to create a 'rounder', smoother yarn, resulting in a lustrous effect achieved by light reflection on the improved yarn. Long-staple cotton is an ideal candidate for mercerization. The end product results in a finer fabric that is also cooler and more comfortable to wear, sometimes with an almost silk-like appearance.

(left) This gown by Rhode Island School of Design graduate Abbey Glass was inspired by the desert colours of Idaho. It expresses the luxurious aspect of Supima cotton, a brand that designates an elite variety of American cotton prized for its lustre and strength. The gown was created for the annual Supima Design Competition, created to showcase emerging talent.

(above) A crisp ensemble by Haider Ackermann emphasizes the luxury aspects of cotton in this structured organdie jacket, paired with a silk jumpsuit.

Cotton lisle

Cotton lisle is similar to mercerized cotton in that all the lint and threads are burnt off to give a smoother touch. It is used for expensive cotton underwear and socks.

Filo di Scozia

Filo di Scozia® is a registered trademark that represents the highest grade of cotton fabric or yarn. It is two-ply, combed, long-staple, double-mercerized cotton. It has the unique characteristics of brilliance, softness and a silky touch and, above all, the ability to maintain these characteristics over time. Filo Di Scozia® is used for the very best cotton knitwear and hosiery.

Cotton cupro

Cupro is made from pure organic cellulose fibres reborn from the discarded linters that are a by-product of processing cotton. The fuzzy down, when processed, is perfectly round in cross section with a naturally silky smooth finish, and possesses many of the attributes of cotton, such as moisture management.

The history of cupro

Cupro fibre was first developed and produced in Germany in the late 1890s and was first used for filaments of 'copper silk' for light bulbs. By the early 1900s manufacturer J.P. Bemberg had converted production to the more lucrative product of artificial silk for the clothing and textile industries. Bemberg Seide (silk) was finer than the finest silk and stronger than viscose silk; it was used for clothing, internal padding, linings and stockings, as advertised by Marlene Dietrich (see viscose rayon, page 217).

The manufacturing process was taken to Japan, where by the early 1930s cupro was being manufactured by the Asahi Kasei. The company is today one of few producing cupro fibres, trademarked as Bemberg™.

Cupro fibre properties

Cupro makes a perfect lightweight lining; it is far cooler to wear than both silk and man-made linings, provides the gentleness of a natural fibre with the functionality of a man-made, and is also biodegradable.

Bemberg produces excellent cupro linings, which are favoured by many of the prestige Italian tailoring houses.

Cupro production

Linters are ultra-fine silk-like fibres that remain stuck to the seeds of the cotton plant after it has been ginned. The cellulose that constitutes the cotton linters is dissolved in an ammoniac copper oxide solution and processed with caustic soda before being passed through a spinneret. The regenerated solution is hardened, the copper and ammonia are removed and the caustic soda neutralized. Cupro is usually manufactured as fine filament yarns, and is both hypoallergenic and anti-static. The name cupro is derived from the **cuprammonium** process used to make the fibres.

Ecological sustainability

Cupro makes use of a by-product from harvested cotton, recycling what would otherwise be waste material, from a renewable raw material. However, the chemicals used in processing can cause concern.

Ecological and ethical considerations

The increasing demand for cotton at competitive prices has resulted in what may be considered mass-exploitation of poor cotton farmers and the land upon which cotton is cultivated. However, there are alternatives that allow the consumer to choose a product from an ethically and environmentally sound source.

Approximately 30 per cent of the cotton harvested and knitted for T-shirt production is shipped to a second country for manufacturing, impacting on cotton's carbon footprint.

Some cotton cultivation is known to make use of a variety of pesticides and insecticides. These are especially prevalent in the developing world and some sources attribute deaths within the cotton industry to their use. Cotton Incorporated is a company with offices worldwide that offers extensive information regarding all aspects of cotton, from farming and 'green issues' to design and manufacturing. It also has an extensive list of fabric resources.

The American and Australian cotton industries have invested in **biotechnology** to try to combat the excessive use of insecticides associated with standard commercial cotton production. However, this has resulted in much of the cotton grown today being **GM cotton**.

There are two types of GM, or transgenic, cotton in use. Bollgard® is obtained from a naturally occurring soil bacterium, *Bacillus thuringiensis*, referred to as **Bt cotton**. This naturally occurring soil organism is used as a spray, which reduces the use of insecticides by up to 85 per cent compared to conventionally grown cotton. It gives the plant an in-built tolerance to its main pest, the *Heliothis* caterpillar, and in North America the boll weevil. The alternative product is **Roundup Ready®**, which is obtained from the soil bacterium *Agrobacterium tumefaciens*. This herbicide-tolerant cotton reduces the amount of soil cultivation and herbicides needed to control weeds. It also promotes healthier soil through less disruption and a reduction in herbicide residues.

Organic cotton

GM cotton shares with **organic cotton** the same issue of chemical usage in the growing cycle, however the similarities stop there as organic cotton has a completely different ethos.

Slowly but steadily there are now a growing number of farmers moving towards a more organic, ecologically sound and socially sustainable method of production. Organic agricultural methods rely upon crop rotation and the use of natural enemies, such as ladybirds, to suppress harmful insects, rather than the use of agrochemicals, artificial fertilizers and other toxic-persistent chemicals. Organic cotton does not use genetically modified organisms but seeks to build a biologically diverse agricultural system, replenishing and maintaining the soil's fertility.

Organic cotton is far more expensive to produce; however it does not pollute and there is no over-production. Unfortunately, currently it only represents a small percentage of global cotton production.

Organic cotton is grown in around 20 countries, with Turkey the primary producer. The United States, India, Peru, Uganda, Egypt, Senegal, Tanzania, China and Israel also produce organic cotton.

(opposite page) Relaxed men's suit and tunic by Kostas Murkudis in a silk and cupro mix.

(right) G-Star RAW blends its own post-consumer reclaimed denim with organic cotton to give a unique character to this ubiquitous fabric. The use of recycled cotton generates savings on raw materials, water, chemicals and energy, and provides the previously owned products with a second life.
© G-Star RAW C.V.

Water consumption to produce 1 tonne of fibre

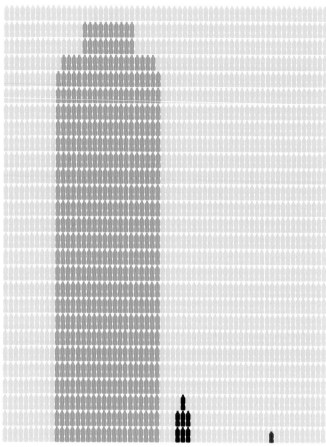

1 bottle = 50 litres
cotton = 25,000 litres
viscose = 350 litres
polyester = 7 litres

Swedish high-street brand H&M is the largest user of organic cotton in the world, and has pledged to use only cotton from sustainable sources for all production by 2020. This crinkled, raw-edged organic cotton ruffled dress from the 'Conscious' collection was part of a range designed to highlight and promote sustainability in the fashion industry.

Water

Cotton is a thirsty crop, a fact that is fast presenting problems to countries whose economic growth overly relies upon the cotton industry but whose geographical position suffers from water shortages. Uzbekistan and Kazakhstan, both once part of the former Soviet Union, have in parts been turned into a desert through the excessive cultivation of cotton, which in turn has also led to the shrinking of the Aral Sea.

Developments are now being made in the cultivation of new plant varieties that include drought-resistant, flame-resistant and wrinkle-free genetically modified cotton.

154

Naturally coloured cotton

Peruvian Pima and Tangüis cotton is naturally coloured and grown organically.

Five millennia before the advent of European settlers, Native American peoples of the Peruvian coastal valleys cultivated **naturally coloured cotton**, the principal colours being (then as now) cream, beige, brown, chocolate and mauve. Many varieties and landraces of New World cotton plants were identified and named in the following two centuries, describing the wide range of both fibre lengths and natural pigmentation.

Europe's Industrial Revolution saw an explosion in commercial cotton manufacturing, where the contemporary concern was with printing and dyeing, processes for which white cotton was preferred. Furthermore, the shorter fibres of the coloured plant species were more difficult to spin commercially. This lack of financial incentive meant naturally coloured cotton remained commercially dormant until the early 1980s.

Algodón pais, as the traditional farmers call the naturally coloured cotton plants, continues to be farmed for domestic use, artisan textile crafts, traditional medicinal cures and religious rituals. In traditional communities infants wear pads of naturally coloured brown cotton, as it is believed to protect their fragile skulls. It has recently been discovered that cotton seeds contain modest amounts of natural antibiotic substances.

155

(above) Children's knitwear by Stella James. The range of cotton colours featured in this outfit is naturally occurring. Naturally coloured cotton offers an extra benefit in that it has inherent flame-retardant properties.

(left) A naturally coloured Peruvian cotton boll, showing the pod and seeds, which contain small amounts of natural antibiotic substances. Naturally coloured cotton requires little maintenance or water following sowing; it is far more resistant to insects and diseases than conventional cotton and needs no fertilizers or pesticides.

Naturally coloured cotton requires minimal maintenance after sowing: compared to other varieties, it is far more resistant to insects and diseases, does not require fertilizers and pesticides, needs far less water during its growing cycle and so can grow successfully in desert soils. Brown cotton does not require chemical treatment because it has natural fire-retardant properties and is ideal for children's clothing.

In Peru, Peru Naturtex Partners offers local farmers a lucrative cash crop – organic **Fairtrade**-certified Pakucho, naturally pigmented cotton – as an alternative to growing coca, the natural ingredient of synthesized cocaine. The company is the first in Latin America to develop naturally coloured organically grown cotton on an industrial scale.

In the US, Fox Fibre produces naturally coloured cotton in a range of colours that include browns, greens and rusts. Most of the cotton is organically grown and has been engineered to have a longer fibre that can be commercially spun. It is grown in Texas, New Mexico and Arizona.

(Source: James M. Vreeland Jr., www.perunaturtex.com)

Naturally coloured cotton rovings.

(opposite page) Relaxed jumpsuit in naturally coloured lightweight crinkled cotton by New York brand A Détacher.

Ecological and ethical considerations

Fairly traded cotton

Cotton is one of a number of cash crops. A cash crop, in agricultural terms, is grown for money as opposed to domestic subsistence. In the United States cotton is the leading cash crop and is the number one **added value crop** – a crop grown under a written contract with the intent of receiving a premium because of its special attributes. Cotton is a very important global commodity; however many farmers in the developing world are paid very little for their produce. They find it difficult to compete with the developed countries, especially when government subsidies artificially depress the global price of cotton; it is estimated that the price would be at least 15 per cent higher if the market was not manipulated. In 2004 West African cotton farmers were paid approximately 30 per cent of the true market price for their cotton. By contrast, US producers (who currently receive subsidies equal to their total crop value) were paid 70 per cent above the market price. In 2003/4 60 per cent of US cotton was dumped on the global market, this figure rising to 76 per cent in 2003/4.

Fairtrade cotton is defined as cotton which has met the international Fairtrade standard for production of seed cotton (harvested with seed and fibre attached) and is therefore eligible to carry the FAIRTRADE mark. It is an independent product certification label that means the farmers receive a fair and stable market price, as well as benefiting from longer term and more direct trading relationships. Cotton farmers are at the bottom of the supply chain and therefore susceptible to price exploitation within the trading system. The Fairtrade certification helps to redress the situation by basing the Fairtrade price on the actual cost of sustainable production. If the market price is higher than the minimum price then the market price applies.

Fairtrade food products were first launched internationally in 1994. Cotton carrying the certified FAIRTRADE mark was launched in the United Kingdom in November 2005 and cotton farming groups currently selling into the UK market include India, Mali, Egypt, Cameroon, Burkina Faso and Senegal. There are plans to extend certification to include Peru and East Africa.

53 per cent of global cotton is government subsidized. Unsubsidized countries find it difficult to trade at a fair price.

Tackling subsidies

In 2002 Brazil was the first country to make a formal complaint to the United States under the world trade disputes process of the World Trade Organization (WTO) regarding the issue of government subsidies and their ethical implications. Australia acted as a third party mediator. The resulting recommendation was to withdraw export credit guarantees and payments to domestic users and exporters, and to remove the adverse effects of mandatory price subsidies. Although little has been done to redress the situation it has led to a fair trade in cotton clothing. Fairly traded footwear was added to the rapidly growing market for organic clothing.

An outfit made from ethically traded organic cotton designed by Elsien Gringhuis, a graduate of the ArtEZ Institute of the Arts in Arnhem. The designer's approach is characterized by a reductive aesthetic. Her clothes represent a minimalistic simplicity underpinned by a complex and innovative construction, using Zero Waste pattern-cutting techniques to realize her sustainable principles.

Ethical trading

Fairtrade clothing is not to be confused with ethical trading. Ethical trading or sourcing is a business model that aims to ensure that acceptable minimum labour standards are met in the **supply chain** for the whole company and their range of products.

Fairtrade

There is now an international Fairtrade fortnight in the UK, and schools are encouraged to join the Fairtrade schools scheme.

For a cotton product to be eligible to carry the FAIRTRADE mark, the cotton must be sourced wholly from a certified Fairtrade source, while a blended product (cotton plus other fibre) must be at least 50 per cent Fairtrade certified cotton.

Fairtrade certified cotton farmers receive a stable and fair price for their cotton and better access to the cotton market.

Fairtrade standards encourage a greater respect for the environment.

Fairtrade encourages closer links between shoppers and producers.

White organic cotton jacket by Danish brand Noir. The brand was founded upon ethical and ecological principles by Peter Ingwersen in connection with textile company Illuminati II, which was created 'to prove that organic and ethical fabrics can be used in luxurious and sexy designs'.

159

The Australian cotton industry is a leader in sustainable production, and growers do not receive any government subsidies. As a body it self-funds environmental audits.

Organic Fairtrade cotton

Clothing made with Fairtrade cotton is not to be confused with ethically traded clothing, as they are quite different things. Fairtrade specifically aims to improve the position of marginalized producers in the developing world by empowering them to invest in sustainable development projects that have a wider community benefit.

Not all Fairtrade certified cotton is organic. At present only about 20 per cent of the Fairtrade cotton producers are farming organically, although those that are not organic producers must implement a system of integrated crop management to establish a balance between environmental protection and business results. Organic fertilizers and biological disease control methods are used to replace industrialized methods of farming. The Fairtrade standards prohibit the use of genetically modified seeds as well as encouraging appropriate water management. (Source ICAC 2004)

Peru Naturtex is the first company of its kind in the Americas to deal in organic cotton on a Fairtrade basis.

160

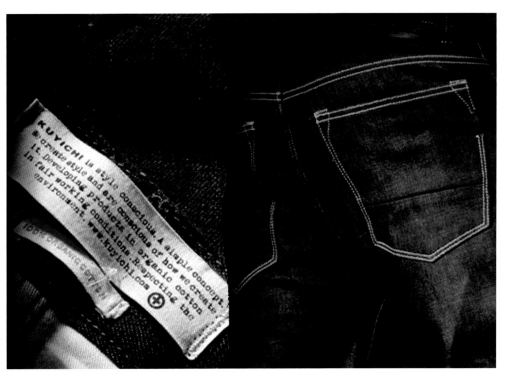

(left) Organic jeans by Dutch design brand Kuyichi. Cotton denim is the ultimate democratic fashion fabric, eternally desirable to all consumers.

(below) Hand-printed cotton boots by Como No. The products are handmade in Argentina from transitional cotton, which will be fully certified as organic in 2009. This transitional cotton comes from small producers from northern Argentina. All processes, from the growing of the cotton to the finished product, are manufactured under Fairtrade. The exclusive prints are eco-friendly and heavy-metal free.

Layered jeans dress from the 'Persona' project designed by Jeffrey Wang of BLANQ. The main purpose of the project was to showcase the reuse of denim. This piece was constructed using only safety pins; the 'raw' personality of the jeans was retained and treated as sculpture.

Ecological and ethical considerations

Cotton fabrics

The fabrics listed represent the most popular cottons in use and would give a designer or merchandiser an extensive selection for a collection. It is not, however, exhaustive.

The fabrics are primarily made from cotton yarns, though some names are shared with other natural and synthetic yarns.

Furry

These cotton fabrics have three-dimensional, tactile, rough textures.

Chenille French for 'caterpillar', which it closely resembles, this fabric has a fur-like texture.

Corduroy Cut-pile fabric, usually cotton. The original French name, corde du roi meant 'cloth of kings'. Corduroy is described by the size of its wales (ribs).

Flannelette A soft-brushed surface on a basic cloth.

Moleskin Medium-weight firm fabric with a fine-brushed nap to one side.

Towelling Woven fabric with uncut loops to one or both sides. Knitted towelling is usually referred to as terry towelling.

Velvet Straight or diagonally woven fabric with a cut pile. The choice of yarn to make velvet will greatly influence its visual appearance, more so than with many other fabrics.

Velveteen A lighter and often finer version of velvet.

Velour May be woven or knitted fabric with a close-cropped velvet effect.

Textured

Raised surface effects.

Aertex A cellular fabric constructed with tiny 'air holes' for warmth.

Bedford cord A flattened warp ribbed effect without the usual raised surface of a classic corduroy.

Cloqué A double-cloth weave where different shrinking factors achieve a figured or blistered effect. Also known as 'blister fabric'.

Crêpon The yarn has been heat crêped before weaving, creating an uneven crêpe effect.

Crinkle All-over heat-pleated or crinkled fabric.

Seersucker Yarns with differential shrinkages are woven then washed to create a crinkle effect. May be plain, check or stripe.

Piqué or piquette Has a bird's-eye raised effect. May be woven or knitted.

(right) This 100 per cent cotton washed denim (Italian) with darker blue weft and whitish warp has been washed with chemicals to achieve a smooth finish. The different shades were achieved by twice hand over-dyeing the original denim, achieving three shades of the same colour. The long shirt worn underneath is made of a 100 per cent worsted wool (Italian), usually used for men's suits with a shiny finishing.

(left) This oversized coat, designed by London College of Fashion graduate Mary Binding, was made from a loosely woven, lemon-and-cream cotton–viscose tweed. The fabric, which has a pronounced weave, was made by British mill Linton Tweeds.

Sheer

These are more fragile fabrics.

Batiste Very finely woven and almost sheer.

Gauze A very light, straight weave that is semi-translucent.

Muslin Very lightweight, plain-weave fabric that is almost transparent.

Voile Fine, sheer and semi-transparent plain weave using tightly twisted yarns.

(above) Crisp cotton poplin shirt and skirt by Kris Van Assche.

(above) Inspired by Elizabethan costume, designer Nabil El Nayal has cut this voluminous 'six-sleeve' dress from 16 metres (52 ft) of cotton shirting.

(left) Menswear by Kris Van Assche. This outfit exploits the crisp and airy qualities of pure white cotton and lends them a fresh, contemporary edge.

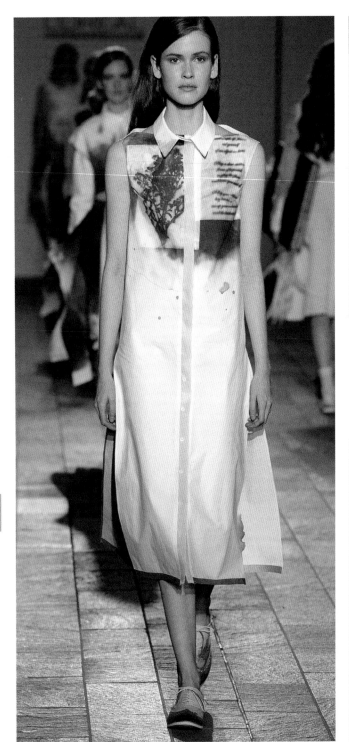

Smooth

These fabrics have a polished effect.

Chintz A Hindi word for printed cloth with a **glazed** surface, originating in India in the seventeenth century and made popular during the Raj. Now generically used to imply flower-printed fabric.

Ciré French in origin. A high-gloss look is achieved by impregnating the fabric with wax and heating and pressing it.

Lawn Very fine, lightweight plain-weave fabric with a crisp finish originating in Laon, France.

Sateen Satin-weave fabric with a polished sheen to the face side.

(above) A poetic, elongated white cotton open-shouldered shirt-dress, featuring a faded-effect blue cyanotype print and weighted hem, by Japanese designer Nayuko Yamamoto.

(right) Knitted head-wrap created by London College of Fashion graduate Rebecca Thorpe using mercerized and single-ply fine cottons, elastomeric yarns, silk and viscose. The use of LYRCA® and folding techniques allowed the flat knitted fabric to become distorted and asymmetric, creating a dramatic three-dimensional effect. The graduated colour was created entirely with yarn changes.

Functional

These fabrics are grouped by weave and construction rather than weight. For example, twills, drills and denims come in many different weights and finishes, ranging from pristine to aged and from smooth to **brushed**.

Chambray Light- to medium-weight plain weave using alternate **indigo** and white yarns.

Denim Usually a twill weave using both white and indigo dyed yarns.

Drill Heavier-weight twill weaves with a workwear feel.

Gabardine Diagonal weave with clearly defined diagonal rib effect to surface.

Gingham Lightweight plain weave with yarn-dyed stripes or checks of an even size.

Madras Originally a vegetable-dyed hand-woven fabric from Madras, India. Today it is suggestive of any bold check or stripe.

Poplin A strong plain-weave fabric with a very light cross-rib effect. The fabric was originally made for the pope and referred to as 'Papalino'.

Twill Diagonal weave.

Authentic

Utility cottons.

Calico Generic name for lighter-weight plain-weave, coarse-yarn fabric, often used for making a toile.

Canvas Generic name for plain-weave coarse fabric, often un-dyed, in many different weights.

Cheesecloth Thin, loosely woven, plain-weave Indian cloth originally used in the food trade but made into an iconic 1960s hippy fabric.

Duck Plain weave with a canvas-like feel.

Hopsack Straight-weave construction using roughish yarns, often with a slub.

Repp Has a pronounced weft rib effect.

Ticking A heavy diagonal-weave fabric striped with a coloured yarn.

Toile Generic name for a straight-weave fabric, as well as implying a prototype/sample made in a workroom.

(above) The functional styling of this cotton twill jacket by designer Walter Van Beirendonck references authentic World War II flight jackets, and has been garment dyed in colours specially selected by the designer.

(above) Youthful tunic dress in different shades of cotton chambray by New York brand A Détacher. The casual denim-like appearance of chambray is created using a white yarn in the weft and an indigo yarn in the warp of the weave.

Alternative plant fibres

There are many plant alternatives that can readily produce fibres. Some have a pedigree as long and eventful as that of cotton, while others are relatively new and are being developed as sustainable alternatives that focus on ethical sourcing and ecological issues.

The variety of sustainable plants now being grown commercially is encouraging to both the designer and the consumer.

Some have long been part of Asian cultural identity, but it is only with modern technology that they can be produced in a commercially viable manner. Other plant species needed modern processing techniques to render them of a suitable quality as fibres for contemporary fashion purposes. This section considers alternative bast fibres, leaf fibres and the stem fibre bamboo.

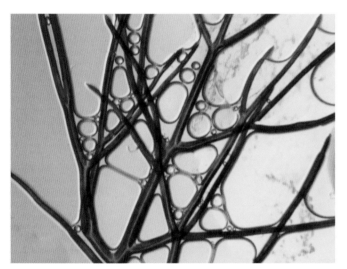

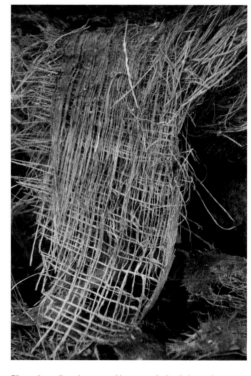

Fibres from the stems and leaves of plants have been in use for thousands of years as textiles. Some are processed direct from the stem of the plant, including linen, hemp and even nettle. Other sources of cellulose, such as wood or algae, are converted into fibres using processes similar to those used to make viscose.

Alternative plant fibres

Bast fibres

A bast fibre, also described as a soft fibre, is obtained from the **phloem** or inner skin of a plant. The fibre needs to be separated from the xylem or woody core and sometimes also from the epidermis, the outermost layer of cells carrying nutrients to the leaves. Bast fibres tend to have good tensile strength.

Jute

Jute, or **hessian** as the fabric is better known, is one of the cheapest natural fibres to produce and is the second most important vegetable fibre after cotton in terms of usage, global consumption, production and availability.

Jute is native to the monsoon regions of the world, growing during the monsoon season. The most important region for jute has always been Bengal in the Ganges delta, where it was an integral part of the local culture.

The history of jute

During British rule of India in the nineteenth and early twentieth centuries jute was shipped to Dundee in Scotland to be processed and woven, and was an important part of their economy until the 1970s, when it was usurped by synthetics. In Bangladesh it was once referred to as the 'golden fibre', because it represented the largest foreign currency into the country. Demand dropped and local farmers burnt their crops rather than sell at unsustainable prices; however, recently there has been an increase in demand and prices have risen steadily. Bangladesh and West Bengal, in India, are still the principal producers of jute, while China and Thailand also have a strong jute production.

Today jute is an important component in the automotive industry because it is high in both **tensile** and **ductile strength**: its strength and lightness of weight make vehicles more fuel-efficient and thus a better ecological proposition. The fibre is also used for paper, film, **composite materials** and **geo textiles** in environmental engineering.

In North America it is referred to as **burlap**.

Jute fibre

Jute is a long, soft, shiny vegetable fibre that is coarse and strong. Jute fibres are composed of mainly cellulose but also **lignin**, a wood fibre. It could therefore be described as a fibre that is part textile and part wood.

The plant is of the *Corchorus* genus and is native to tropical and subtropical regions. The two varieties are white,

or Indian, jute (*Corchorus capsularis*), and tossa jute (*Corchorus olitorius*), an Afro-Arabic jute. Tossa jute is also now grown in India. Tossa jute is softer and silkier than white jute; the more lustrous the fibre the higher the quality of the product.

Jute fibres have a high tensile strength and blend well with other natural and synthetic fibres. When dyed they retain colour well, being both colour and light **fast**. Jute is anti-static, has low thermal conduction and a high level of UV protection. It is mostly used in the furnishing textile industries; however, due to its many advantageous properties, it is also now being developed for high-performance technical textiles.

Jute production

The fibre is produced from the outer skin or stem of the plant. The first process is retting, which involves immersion in running water. Stripping follows, usually done by women and children, and involves removing the non-fibrous matter to reach the fibres on the stem.

Ecological sustainability

Jute has very strong environmental credentials, because it does not require excessive watering, fertilizers or pesticides. It is a fast-growing plant with a good yield ratio of fibre to weight and acreage. It can be recycled several times within its life cycle and also has important biodegradable properties.

Tussah silk shoe with hemp rope ties by Indian designer Rohit Khosla. The shoe shape reflects a French rococo influence reinterpreted in hand-loom, raw and humble materials. The natural colours and texture of the hemp and raw silk complement each other.

168

Ramie

Ramie is a very old fibre crop used for textiles and believed to date back over 7,000 years. In Ancient Egypt mummies were sometimes wrapped in inner layers of linen with outer layers of ramie, while in China the fibre was mainly used for farm workers' clothing. In English-speaking countries it is pronounced either as RAY-mee or rah-mee.

China is the largest ramie producer, and it is also produced in Taiwan, the Philippines, Indonesia, Thailand, South Korea and India. In the western hemisphere, Brazil is the only important producer, the majority produced for domestic consumption with little being traded internationally. The principal consumers of the fibre are Japan, France, Germany and the United Kingdom. Ramie is also an important woven and knitted fabric for the North American market, where it is seen as a cheap 'linen-look' alternative.

Ramie fibre

Ramie is a strong fibre with a tensile strength between three and five times tougher than cotton and at least twice that of linen (flax), although it is brittle and will break if consistently folded in the same place. It holds its shape well but does tend to wrinkle easily, and is often **blended** with cotton and wool.

Fabric woven from ramie has a thick and thin horizontal appearance, giving it many of the visual characteristics of linen, and has often been used as a linen alternative because it costs far less to produce.

Ramie production

Ramie (*Boehmeria nivea*) is a flowering plant of the **nettle** family, native to Eastern Asia. It flourishes best in warm, humid temperatures, but is also able to withstand droughts. The two types of ramie are **China grass**, also known as true ramie or **white ramie**, and **green ramie**, believed to have originated in Malaysia. The fibres are produced from the bark or stalks of the plant, which are harvested on average two to three times each year, although under some growing conditions may be harvested up to six times in a year.

The plant is harvested soon after flowering, when it will produce the maximum amount of fibre. It is either cut just above the root, or bent at ground level where it can be stripped while still in the field, a process called **de-cortication** that removes the hard outer bark. Further scraping reveals the fibrous parts while also removing some of the gums and pectin. The third stage involves washing, drying and de-gumming, ready to extract the fibre for spinning. The de-gumming process requires chemical processing, which will eventually reduce the original dry weight by about 25 per cent. Ramie is a very absorbent fibre that also dries quickly, making spinning and weaving difficult due to the brittle characteristics of the fibre; good utilization depends on improved processing techniques.

Ecological sustainability

Ramie is a sustainable plant that has a long fibre-producing lifespan of up to 20 years and can be harvested up to six times a year.

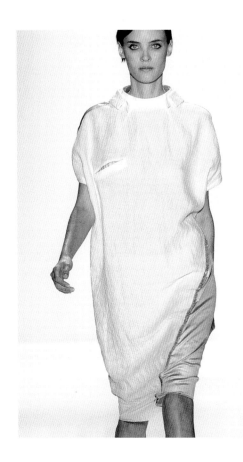

(left) Designer Son Jung Wan creates collections with an easy contemporary elegance, exemplified by this tailored collar dress that features the linen-like appeal of ramie at the front of the dress and tactile washed silk at the back.

(above) A structured outfit made by Finnish designer Saara Lepokorpi, who focuses on sustainability. The 'floating' effect of the jute-fibre yarns is created with an open warp technique.

Hemp

Hemp is the generic name for the entire *Cannabis* family of plants. There are several cultivated varieties and subspecies, as well as wild and feral cannabis. *Cannabis sativa* L. subsp. *sativa*, commonly known as **industrial hemp**, is the variety grown for fibre and other non-drug related purposes. Conversely, *Cannabis sativa* L. subsp. *indica* is the variety grown for both recreational and medical drug use. By contrast to its 'industrial' relative, this variety has poor fibre qualities. The principal difference between the two varieties is the level of THC (tetrahydrocannabinol) that each secretes.

The production of hemp in Western countries is growing steadily to meet the growing eco-demands of contemporary society. In Canada the export of hemp seeds increased by over 300 per cent during 2007–2009.

The history of hemp

China has the oldest tradition for hemp cultivation, where it was used for rope, clothing, shoes and early forms of paper. Hemp remains have been found in ancient Chinese pottery dating back 10,000 years. In Japan many traditional kimonos were decorated with images of hemp because it was considered a beautiful plant. In medieval Europe hemp was first cultivated on a small-scale domestic basis, and most communities would have had access to a hemp field for domestic cloth and rope production: hemp was easier to produce than flax for linen. In Germany and Italy, hemp was also used for culinary purposes, in soups and as fillings in pies. Under the reign of Elizabeth I of England (1558–1603) all landowners were obliged to grow hemp for sails and rope for naval use. Commercial hemp production in Europe vastly expanded in the eighteenth century with colonial and naval expansion, and it was popularly said that the British Empire was built on hemp. It was an essential element of shipbuilding, being used for sails, ropes and oakum (tarred fibre preparation used to pack joints of timber ships). During the Napoleonic Wars many military uniforms were made of hemp, favoured for its strength and low cost. Hemp was considered a commercially viable plant because it produced a high volume of fibre to the ratio of land used for its cultivation.

The term 'money for old rope' was coined after old hemp rope was recycled to make early bank notes.

In North America, hemp was primarily grown in Kentucky and the Midwest. The American Declaration of Independence was drafted on hemp paper, and Betty Ross made the first American flag from hemp canvas. America's first president, George Washington, was a hemp farmer and recommended 'that it be planted everywhere'. The early republic became an important Western producer, inventing and developing machinery to better produce the fibre and its importance in nineteenth-century America was second only to King Cotton.

In the nineteenth century 80 per cent of the world's fabric was made from hemp.

The advent of steam-driven iron ships using steel cables rendered hemp almost redundant for naval purposes. In addition, the development of synthetic fibres in the twentieth century further reduced its reign. **DuPont** and William Randolph Hearst, industrialists who had financial interests in the petrochemical and timber industries respectively, were major adversaries of hemp cultivation, viewing it as a financial threat and lobbying the government until The Marijuana Tax Act was passed in

Black eco hemp shift dress by designer Elsien Gringhuis. The stark, reductive styling challenges the reputation of hemp as an unsophisticated artisanal material. The contrasting fabric is a viscose polyamide mix.

1937, which caused prices to plummet. The fibre fell out of service, in part due to the paranoia linked with its association with marijuana and illicit drug use, although the fibre-producing species and drug-producing species are quite different.

The Japanese invasion of much of the South Pacific during World War II meant that **Manila hemp**, or **abacá**, which the US navy used for ropes and canvas for uniforms, was unobtainable, and American domestic hemp was once again essential. Advertising propaganda of the time read 'Hemp for victory'.

Hemp's importance is now back in ascendance because it is seen as a viable and sustainable alternative crop for mass-cultivation for a variety of uses, including textiles.

Hemp fibre

Industrial hemp is an efficient crop that has multiple uses. The most valuable part of the plant is its fibres for production for the fabric industry, and it is also extensively used for biodegradable plastics and biofuels. It contributes to the construction and automotive industries as well as the health-food and cosmetics industries. It is second only to soy in its nutritional value, is highly digestible and an effective unsaturated oil. Hemp has good thermal values and resists decay and infestation.

Colours range from creamy white, shades of brown and grey as well as green and black. The fibres are strong and durable, resist mould, have good absorbency and offer protection against ultraviolet light.

Hemp production

Years of selective breeding have produced many different-looking varieties of hemp plant. Since the 1930s the focus has been on the production of strains that offer poor sources of drug material. The plants are long and slender with fibres that are between 1 and 5 m (3–16 ft) long running the full length of the plant. If the plant is harvested before it flowers it will produce finer fibres and be less effective as a potential drug source, although the THC is already much lower in industrial hemp. Male and female plants need to be planted together because it is the female plants that produce seeds for the next crop. Good seeds are integral to successful hemp production.

In some parts of the world hemp is still harvested by hand, otherwise the greater majority is now machine harvested. It is cut 2–3 cm (about 1 inch) above ground level and left to dry. Traditional methods of separating the fibres included dew and water retting. One involved floating the bundles of harvested hemp in water, while the other made use of natural ground dew and bacterial action. Modern retting involves mechanical thermo-pulping. Hemp can also be **cottonized** by a process similar to that used for flax.

Hemp is not easy to spin but does make for a very good blend when used together with cotton in a 50:50 ratio.

Hemp can be made into fabrics as diverse as the finest lace through to heavyweight industrial canvas.

The contemporary styling of this wedding dress by Nepalese designer Sanyukta Shrestha belies its fabrication from hemp, which is usually associated with casual wear. The London College of Fashion graduate combines a sustainable approach with hand-crafted luxury. Most of the natural fibres used in her bridal collections are hand-spun and woven by village women in Nepal. She adheres to ecological and social sustainability guidelines, with fabrics sourced from ethical and fairtrade-certified manufacturers.

171

Hemp market

Hemp is cultivated all over the world, although in the United States it is still illegal to grow hemp; however some states have granted licences for industrial hemp. Canada, the United Kingdom and Germany lifted the ban in the 1990s but within the European Union and Canada a licence has to be issued for its cultivation, described as 'industrial hemp for non-drug purposes'. Japan, under American influence, restricted the growth of hemp in 1948 and is one of the few Eastern countries to have prohibited its cultivation.

Up until the mid-1980s the old Soviet Union was the largest hemp producer, much of it being cultivated in Ukraine and the parts of Russia close to Poland. The world's premier institute for the development of hemp is still situated in Ukraine, where it develops new varieties with improved fibre content, increased yield and low THC.

Other important producers of hemp include China, North Korea, Romania and Hungary.

India produces a variety of hemp known as **Sunn** or **Bombay hemp**.

Ecological sustainability

Hemp is ecologically and sustainably important, and is often referred to as the world's most useful plant. It is non-toxic in use, renewable and non-polluting during its life cycle. It needs few if any pesticides, crops grow quickly, and around 100 days after harvesting the soil is left in better condition as it has been replenished with nutrients and nitrogen. In addition hemp controls topsoil erosion and produces a great amount of oxygen.

The seeds and stalks, as well as the general fermentation of the plant, produce an oil that may be used as biodiesel: as a low-energy fuel it is better than other similar crops. It can also be used for biodegradable plastics.

Hemp paper is eco-friendly because it does not require the bleaching processes of wood pulp. About 1 acre of hemp will produce the same paper quantity as around 4 acres of trees.

Kenaf

Kenaf is a species of hibiscus with visual similarities to jute. The word kenaf has Persian etymology, however in different parts of the world it is known by several other names, including **bimli, ambary, ambari hemp, deccan hemp** and **bimlipatum jute**.

Kenaf has a long history of cultivation in parts of Africa, India and Thailand. Today the major producers are China and India. The traditional uses for kenaf have been rope, twine and coarse cloth, as well as fuel and nutrition. It is an ideal candidate for sustainable ecological cultivation because it requires the minimum use of pesticides and fertilizers. The emerging uses for it today span engineering applications, insulation paper and clothing-grade cloth, as well as providing vegetable oil from the seeds. The fibres are naturally white and do not need to undergo any bleaching processes for either paper or cloth uses.

Kenaf is not produced in vast quantities and may not become commercially viable without financial investment and enthusiasm.

Nettle

Fabric made from nettle dates back at least 2,000 years, but lost its popularity with the growth of the commercial cotton industry. During World War I it was used to make German military uniforms after blockades made cotton unobtainable.

The common stinging nettle has potential for fibre crop production; it is far stronger than cotton and finer than other bast fibres. It is an ecologically sustainable plant requiring far less water and no chemical pesticides or fertilization. It also sustains many varieties of invertebrate species.

Investigations into nettle as an alternative eco-fibre are currently limited to a specialist clothing market. Fabrics are perceived as being of good quality because of their long staple lengths, sometimes matching that of Egyptian cotton. Nettle yarns and fabrics can be mercerized; the fibre is also naturally biodegradable.

(right) These jeans by G-Star RAW are made from a fabric that combines new developments in nettle plant fibre with organic cotton to create a unique and more sustainable denim with a reduced environmental footprint. Nettle plants can flourish on land unsuitable for food production and require much less water and chemical intervention than conventional cotton.
© G-Star RAW C.V.

(far right) Nettle yarn from Habu Textiles.

Banana

Bananas and plantains grow in the hot climate of tropical regions, where the two names are used synonymously. They are a significant food crop harvested every six to nine months.

During harvesting the stems are cut down to allow for new growth; these are often discarded but can be used to produce alternative sustainable fibres.

The fibre is strong and versatile with an appearance that can resemble bamboo and linen or, depending on processing method, silk. The plant has a long history of high-quality textiles in several Asian countries, especially Japan and Nepal. Banana fibre has been harvested in Japan for centuries, where it is called *bashofu*.

Banana fibre

Banana is a bast fibre (known as lignocelluloses) obtained from the pseudo-stem of herbaceous plants of the genus **Musa**. Fibres differ depending on which part of the stem they have been taken from: outer layers are tougher and may be used as a jute substitute (the extreme outer layers may even be too tough); the inner layers can be very fine. Fibres expand when wet, allowing moisture and perspiration to be absorbed and dry quickly. Banana fibre dyes well and fabrics can easily be printed. Blends are sometimes made with cotton or viscose.

Banana fibre production

The two traditional methods of producing fibres in Japan and Nepal differ.

Japan
The Japanese method uses younger stems that provide finer fibres. The stems are boiled in an alkali solution (saltwater), and then washed. The fibre is then pared away from the outer skin; soft fibres are destined for use as wefts, harder fibres for the warps. After selection the fibres are joined and spun to make a continuous thread, and then dyed. The finished woven fabric goes through several more washing, drying and setting processes before being stretched, straightened and pressed.

Nepal
The Nepalese method generally involves mechanical crushing of the stems of the banana plant and produces fibres that are often referred to as 'banana silk'; with its crisp texture it closely resembles local silks.

Commercial production
Contemporary large-scale fibre production tends to use one of two alternative methods, either enzyme retting or chemical processing. Enzyme retting allows for a natural breaking down of the fibres from the shaft. While a lengthy process, it does not impact on the environment. The faster commercial chemical processing method may cause pollution. About 37 kg of banana stem yields 1 kg of good-quality fibre.

173

(right) These banana-fibre 'tops' are skeins ready for spinning. The inner fibres of the banana plant are soft and smooth and often referred to as 'banana silk'.

Bamboo

In China, bamboo is often referred to as the plant of a thousand uses.

Bamboo is a stem fibre, a perennial evergreen of the grass family. It is of great cultural significance in many East Asian countries, where it has been used for thousands of years as a building material, for ornamental garden design and also as a source of nutrition. Today, through technology and a will to find sustainable organic products to meet the demands of the textile industry, it has been developed as a fibre by Beijing University.

Bamboo fibre has several unusual characteristics that help to reduce greenhouse-gas emissions and to re-enrich land that may have been drained of its nutrients through non-sustainable methods of cultivation. The yield per hectare of bamboo is greater than that of most tree plantations – because the plants can grow close together – and exceeds the yield for cotton on the same size of plantation.

Moso bamboo is China's most important bamboo crop, for which the Hebei Jigao Chemical Fibre Company has the patent for a key processing method. Moso is the Chinese word for the giant bamboo *Phyllostachys pubescens*. Crops can be grown without chemical intervention, and fibres, yarns and fabrics are sold under the trade name of Shanghai Tenbro®, the majority of which is exported.

Bamboo fibre

Bamboo fibre is strong and durable with good stability and tensile strength.

At microscopic level bamboo has a round cross section, making it smooth to wear next to the skin. In the United States its softness has earned it the description of 'cashmere from plants'. The surface of the cross section is covered with micro-gaps and micro-holes. The microstructure allows fast absorption and evaporation, and bamboo fabric beats cotton's absorbency rate more than threefold. It will wick away and evaporate perspiration instantly, keeping the wearer drier and cooler. It is also believed that the fibre will keep the wearer one or two degrees cooler in a summer climate than other natural fibres, which is perhaps why it is marketed in some Asian countries as 'air-conditioning' dress.

Bamboo kun is a natural substance within bamboo that protects the plant from pests and pathogens (biological agents causing disease in the host plant), and it is this substance that prevents bacteria from surviving in bamboo fabric that has not been chemically processed.

Bamboo also has anti-static characteristics that make it sit well next to the skin and not cling. These qualities are used to promote bamboo as an ideal fabric for active sportswear clothing, especially for sports that generate a high degree of perspiration. It is for these reasons that it is described as the perfect eco-performance fabric.

Bamboo fibres naturally block out over 90 per cent of both UVA and UVB rays. Bamboo textiles are soft and have a natural sheen.

Bamboo production

Bamboo is one of the world's most prolific and fastest-growing plants; it can reach maturity in about four years, compared to the typical 20 to 70 years of many commercial tree species. There are around 90 genera and 1,000 species of bamboo spread across extensive native habitat, ranging from the high altitudes of Asia down to the north of Australia, and west to India and parts of Africa and the Americas. Bamboo for commercial use is plantation-grown and not harvested from tropical forests. The variety grown for conversion into textile fibre is **moso bamboo** or *Phyllostachys*, which was and still is used in construction and food industries.

Bamboo fibres are stem fibres, so, unlike bast fibres, the entire stem or culm is used. The stems can be either naturally converted into fibre or chemically processed into bamboo viscose.

Bamboo's 'green' credentials are widely recognized, but the conditions under which it is grown and harvested vary widely. In addition, the major processes for converting bamboo into yarn employ the use of toxic chemicals, leading to concern about the sustainability of the finished fabrics.

Processing bamboo fibre

There are two ways of processing bamboo into fibre, producing different end products of varying quality, with divergent environmental and marketing implications.

One resulting fabric is referred to as **viscose** or **rayon bamboo**. The United States uses the term rayon while in Europe the term viscose is applied (see page 217). The alternative production process results in a fabric often marketed as bamboo linen, implying that the fibres have been mechanically processed without the use of chemicals.

The majority of bamboo is, however, produced using the viscose method, by which cellulose is processed from the pulp of the cane. The United States has strict regulations regarding the transparent labelling of bamboo fibre. The FTC (Federal Trade Commission) requires that yarns produced via this route must be referred to as **bamboo rayon** or rayon bamboo. Only yarn that has been mechanically processed directly from the plant may be called bamboo without the application of the designation 'rayon'.

The 'Bamboo Collection' range of T-shirts by Wear Chemistry is made from a tactile blend of 70 per cent bamboo and 30 per cent organic cotton jersey. The range is sustainably focused, and its garments have been independently tested, meeting the requirements of the Oeko-Tex® Standard 100, which is a guarantee of the safety of textiles and dyestuffs to human health and to the environment. The collection is also ethically manufactured. The concept stand was designed for Clothes Show Live in consultation with Catherine Carpenter of Folk of London.

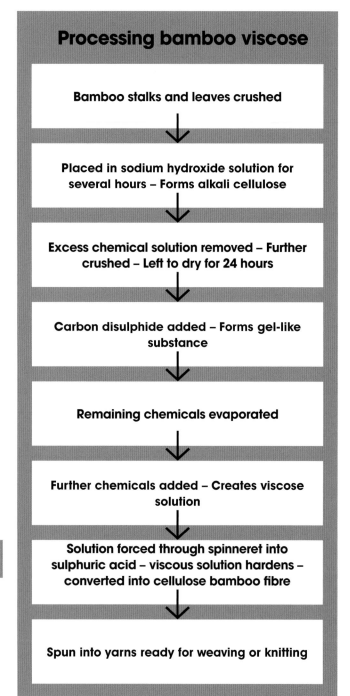

Processing bamboo viscose

Bamboo stalks and leaves crushed

↓

Placed in sodium hydroxide solution for several hours – Forms alkali cellulose

↓

Excess chemical solution removed – Further crushed – Left to dry for 24 hours

↓

Carbon disulphide added – Forms gel-like substance

↓

Remaining chemicals evaporated

↓

Further chemicals added – Creates viscose solution

↓

Solution forced through spinneret into sulphuric acid – viscous solution hardens – converted into cellulose bamboo fibre

↓

Spun into yarns ready for weaving or knitting

Bamboo viscose

Bamboo viscose (or rayon in the United States) is produced in a similar way to other wood pulp celluloses, with the use of chemicals. Some companies use **closed-loop-processing** methods to capture and reprocess the solvents used, but unfortunately this method tends to remove the antibacterial properties and ultraviolet (UV) protection present in the original plant.

Bamboo linen

The term 'bamboo linen' is used for what is also referred to as 'mechanically processed bamboo'. The leaves and soft fibrous inner parts of the stalks are extracted by means of high-pressure steam and mechanical crushing; natural enzyme retting and washing are used to decompose the bamboo to enable the extraction of the fibre.

Litrax, a Swiss company, has pioneered 100 per cent eco-friendly processing of bio-bamboo fibre yarn and textiles. Its Litrax-1® natural bamboo is enzymatically extracted. It is classified as a bast fibre and credited with a high level of softness. Depending on the final product requirement, Litrax recommends blending Litrax-1® natural bamboo with merino wool, Supima® or Egyptian cotton, silk or with Lenzing TENCEL® or lyocell fibre.

Processed bamboo fibre, referred to as tops, ready for the final spinning process. The fibre's natural smooth sheen is evident in the image and will remain apparent in the finished fabric. Bamboo wicks away and evaporates moisture efficiently, keeping the wearer drier and cooler in hot, humid climates.

Lyocell bamboo fibre

Shanghai Tenbro® is a lyocell bamboo. Lyocell is a processing technique that implies that the cellulose has been obtained by an organic solvent process and is free of chemicals (see page 220). The product targets the United States market where misleading labelling is closely monitored.

Ecological sustainability

Bamboo is a naturally grown and sustainable resource that does not require pesticides or chemicals, partly because of the anti-microbial and anti-fungal bamboo kun (also spelled kuhn). Bamboo biodegrades naturally through exposure to soil and sun. It is a naturally regenerative tropical grass with an extensive root system that self-replenishes, and some species can grow as much as 140 cm (55 in) a day. It also has the ability to improve and replenish soil in degraded or eroded areas, as well as generating more oxygen than the same acreage of trees. Bamboo offers a far greater rate of conversion of greenhouse gas to oxygen than any other plant, as well as regenerating itself almost immediately after each harvesting. The more bamboo that is planted the greater the photosynthesis, resulting in a reduction of greenhouse gases. Garments made from bamboo are completely biodegradable at the end of their life cycle.

A structured jacket silhouette made from bamboo-fibre fabric teamed with organic cotton jersey Zouave pants by Ada Zanditon.

Leaf fibres

Leaf fibres can be produced from the strands of fibre that run through the leaf and hold it in place, and are classified as 'hard' fibres, as opposed to bast or 'soft' fibres. The classification is fluid, because some may actually be softer than bast fibres.

Fibres such as raffia and **piña** may never make commercial sense on a global scale, however they do represent interesting alternatives as well as, in the case of piña, being inherently linked to cultural identity.

Abacá

Abacá, also spelt abaká and pronounced ah buh KAH, is the plant from which Manila hemp, also known as **daveo** and **cebu hemp**, is produced. The fibre has been produced in the Philippines since the 1800s; however commercial plantations were started by Britain and the Netherlands in the early 1920s in Borneo and Sumatra. It is also cultivated in Central America, where it has been sponsored by the United States Department of Agriculture.

It is not commercially used as a clothing fibre but there are developments underway hoping to unearth its viability as a sustainable alternative.

Abacá production
The abacá leaves form a sheath that grows from the trunk of the plant. The fibres range in length from 1.5 to 3.5 m and are extracted from the sheaths in a three-stage process. The first, **tuxing**, is the separation of the outer and inner sheaths of the leaves, followed by stripping the fibres then sun drying. Once the fibres have been separated they are sold as Manila hemp, named after the country's capital.

Piña

Piña is obtained from the leaves of the pineapple plant. Although native to several parts of the world, it is in the Philippines that it is used as a fibre for clothing purposes. Strands are hand scraped from the leaves of the plant then hand knotted, one by one, to form a continuous filament. The fibre is soft and lightweight, easy to care for and has a good translucent lustre. It is usually white or ivory in colour.

The filaments are traditionally woven on a hand loom into **piña cloth** and made into the **barong Tagalog**, an embroidered shirt worn for formal occasions and wedding ceremonies by Filipino men, and sometimes women.

Raffia

Raffia palms (*Raphia*) are native to the tropical regions of Africa, Madagascar and Central and South America. The fibres are long and thin and absorb dye well. Raffia is used for shoe, hat and bag production, as well as for decorative textiles.

(above) Abacá fibre is produced from the sheath-like leaves that grow from the trunk of the abacá plant (*Musa textilis*, a species of banana).

(right) This crisp one-shouldered raffia-fibre dress by Joaquín Trías expresses a sophistication not usually associated with the artisanal roots of this palm fibre. The natural springy quality of the raffia weave allows the designer to create an almost 'moulded' form.

(right) A bias-cut raw-edge-finished raffia tweed dress with open-shouldered cable-knit sleeves designed by Son Jung Wan. The velvet flower appliqué ornamentation forms a yoke, and a band of velvet trim snakes around the hip, forming a diagonal line of contrasting texture.

(below) This whimsical sculptured cape by Rachel Caulfield is formed from a cane basket weave. The aesthetic for the collection of which this piece forms a part was influenced by Scandinavia, furniture design and also an interest in combining different elements: the wearable and unwearable, natural and artificial, to produce challenging clothing concepts.

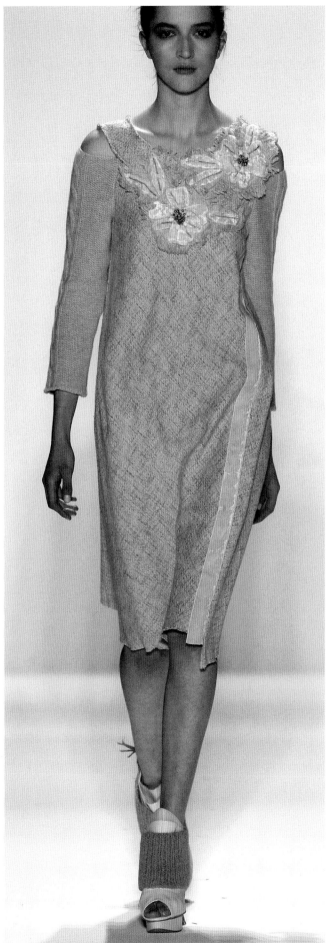

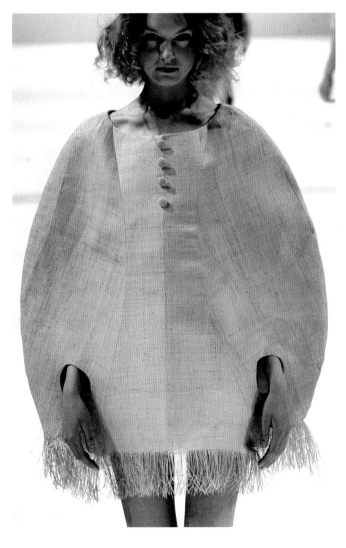

179

Section 3
Man-made
fibres

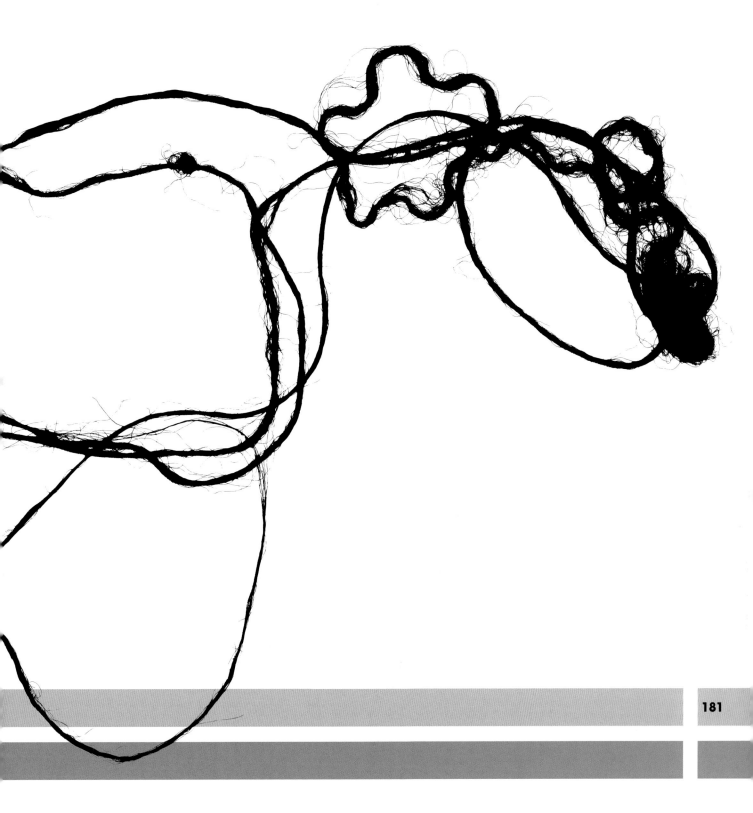

181

Man-made fibres can be formed to render the exact properties and functions required for their end use.

Natural fibres, in contrast, generally maintain the characteristics of their original source, sharing the coding of its DNA even after undergoing modern processing techniques. Man-made fibres may also be blended with natural fibres to give the finished fabric the benefits of both the characteristics of nature and the application of science.

Global Market

Early 1990s

50%

2010s

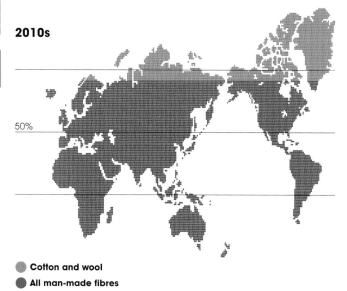

50%

● Cotton and wool
● All man-made fibres

Global market

Man-made fibres and fabrics represent a significant force within global production, and their production continues to increase each year. By the early 1990s the two principal natural fibres – wool (animal) and cotton (plant) – represented just over half of global production, and man-made fibres just under half. In 20 years the balance has switched, with man-made fibres now representing nearly 70 per cent of all global fibre production.

China is the principal producer of man-made fibres, with Europe, collectively, being the second largest producer. Other key countries include India, Japan, South Korea, Pakistan, Taiwan, Brazil, the United States and the Commonwealth of Independent States (CIS, comprising countries that were once part of the Soviet Union).

Sustainability

It is wrong to assume that man-made fibres are not eco-friendly; the next generation of man-made fibres could be a way towards completely sustainable production. Many new raw materials come from renewable or recycled resources; are light and durable; use clean energy sources; and require little land usage or water consumption in their production, furthermore representing a low carbon footprint.

Categorizing man-made fibres

To help clarify the ambiguities and complexities of the different types of man-made fibre this book groups man-made fibres into two principal chapters: synthetic and artificial. The chapter on synthetics covers fibres made from chemicals and derived from such fossil fuels as oil and coal (excluding metallic yarns). The artificial fibres chapter is subdivided into plant cellulose and bio-engineered fibres. Plant cellulose fibres are regenerated from such natural sources as wood; the term artificial implies that they cannot be converted into fibre without chemical intervention.

The section on bio-engineered fibres describes a new generation of fibres that bridge the gap between fibre and polymer science and may use proteins, sugars or starches as their starting point.

This table shows the dramatic growth in production of man-made fibres over a 20-year period. In the early 1990s, man-made fibres represented under half of all fibre production, but by the 2010s they comprised nearly three quarters of all fibre production.

182

Man-made fibres

Synthetic
Chemical compounds from fossil fuels

↓

Polyester

Polyamide – Nylon

Aramids
(aromatic polyamides)

Acrylic and Modacrylic

Olefin
(polyethylene and polypropylene)

Elastane and Synthetic rubber
(polyurethane)

Artificial
Regenerated from natural sources

↓

Cellulose
Naturally occurring polymers

↓

Acetate – triacetate

Viscose rayon

Lyocell
TENCEL® – Modal® – Seacell®

Biopolymer fibres
Bio-engineered proteins

↓

Corn fibre

Soya fibre

Milk fibre

Castor oil fibre

Mined
↓
Metallic

T-shirt label by Wear Chemistry. Consumers are becoming increasingly aware of raw materials and their effect on health and our environment. The garments in the Wear Chemistry range have been independently tested, meeting the requirements of the Oeko-Tex® Standard 100, which is a guarantee of the safety of textiles and dyestuffs to human health and to the environment.

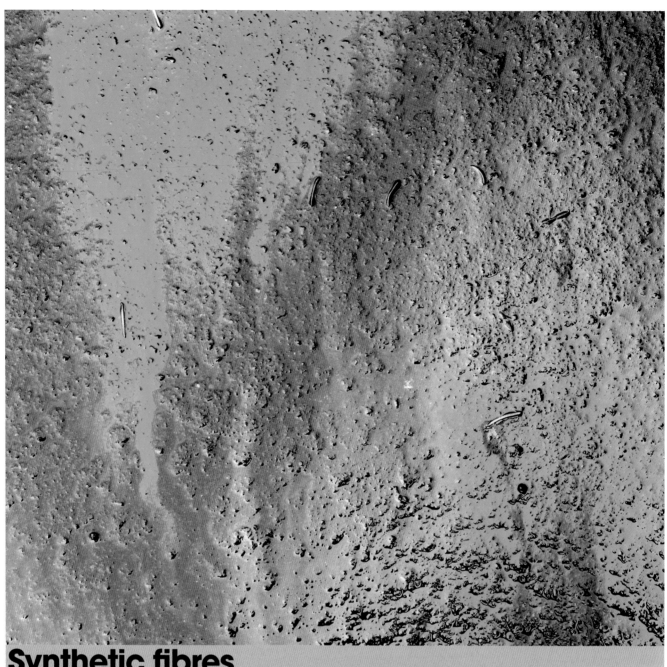

Synthetic fibres

'Synthetic' describes the outcome of combining separate elements, either material or abstract, into a complex whole; synthesizing is the process.

Unfortunately, today the term 'synthetic' is used rather liberally and often with negative connotations. In relation to fibres and fabrics, 'synthetic' applies to the synthesis that artificially creates a new compound, either single or multiple, through the chemical reaction of two or more elements.

Synthetic fibres are a group of man-made fibres, where synthesis has been chemically carried out. Synthetic fibres are composed of chains of small unit **hydrocarbons** synthesized (joined together) as **polymers,** and are sourced mainly from petroleum that has been processed from crude oil.

The contemporary meaning of synthesis, in the context of a chemically developed substance, is generally attributed to the German chemist **Adolph Wilhelm Hermann Kolbe** (1818–1884). Kolbe developed the idea that organic compounds could be derived from inorganic sources. His theory of the existence of secondary and tertiary alcohols was successfully confirmed by the later synthesis of these substances.

The history of synthetic fabrics

Synthetic fibres and fabrics trace their origin to the early development of cellulose acetate in the 1860s and to the artificial silk developed at the end of the nineteenth century. Artificial or 'art' silk was initially referred to as viscose, but by the mid-1920s it had become known as rayon. However, these are artificial fibres – they are not synthetics; the first commercial truly synthetic fibre was nylon, which, rather like its earlier artificial cousins, was developed as a cheap and plentiful alternative to silk.

The United States, Great Britain and Germany were at the forefront of experimental research into synthetics.

Germany
In Germany, Professor Dr Hermann Staudinger's work during the 1920s on the atomic structure of wool was pioneering. This was followed in the 1930s by the discovery at I.G.-Farben, a chemical company, of a method to spin a substance made from coal tar, believed to be the first fully synthetic staple fibre. Trademarked as PeCe, the polyvinyl chloride fibre's low melting point made it unsuitable for textile production. **Perlon** (nylon) stockings were first made in 1942, but were not sold commercially.

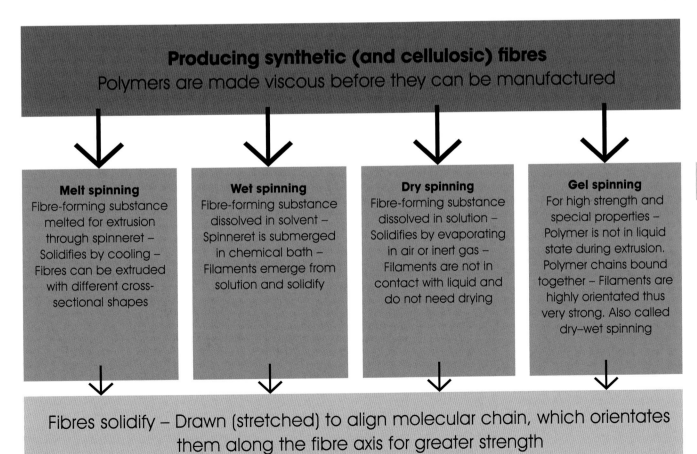

Producing synthetic (and cellulosic) fibres
Polymers are made viscous before they can be manufactured

Melt spinning
Fibre-forming substance melted for extrusion through spinneret – Solidifies by cooling – Fibres can be extruded with different cross-sectional shapes

Wet spinning
Fibre-forming substance dissolved in solvent – Spinneret is submerged in chemical bath – Filaments emerge from solution and solidify

Dry spinning
Fibre-forming substance dissolved in solution – Solidifies by evaporating in air or inert gas – Filaments are not in contact with liquid and do not need drying

Gel spinning
For high strength and special properties – Polymer is not in liquid state during extrusion. Polymer chains bound together – Filaments are highly orientated thus very strong. Also called dry–wet spinning

Fibres solidify – Drawn (stretched) to align molecular chain, which orientates them along the fibre axis for greater strength

United States of America

Nylon was first produced by Wallace Carothers in the 1930s at the DuPont research facilities in Delaware. Piloted as a substitute for silk for stockings, the fabric made its debut in the United States just prior to that country's entry into World War II.

Market dominance

Synthetic fibres represent over half of all the textile fibres in current global production. The four fibres that dominate the synthetic fibre market are nylon, polyester, acrylic and polyolefin. Together they are believed to represent around 90 per cent of the total volume of global synthetic fibre production; polyester alone is estimated to represent around two thirds of this figure.

Polymers and polymerization

The chemicals used to make synthetic fibres are derived from oil, coal and natural gas, all of which are fossil fuels. They are artificially produced from synthesized polymers, many of which are not biodegradable.

Polymers are formed by the polymerization of monomers. (Monomers are large molecules of repeating structural units, bonded to each other with **covalent bonds**.) Through a synthesis process these molecules are combined into longer polymer chains. Polymers have a high molecular weight and consist of thousands of atoms.

A mix of different chemical compounds is used to produce a range of synthetic fibres, all of which generally share similar properties, such as low moisture absorbency, resistance to insects and fungi and, for the most part, heat sensitivity.

186

(above) Man-made fibres are made from polymers that first need to be melted, dissolved or chemically treated to produce a pourable viscous liquid before being processed into filaments and fibres.

(right) Beakers containing Trevira PES fibres and the chips that are the feedstock for polyester production. Photo: Trevira GmbH.

(previous page) This image of oil on water shows the raw material of most synthetic fibres: petroleum, which is processed from crude oil.

Production methods

Man-made fibres generally begin life as pellets, flakes or chips, which need to be made into a **viscous** liquid before processing. Depending on the type of polymer this can be achieved by one of several methods: principally melting, dissolving in a solvent or chemically treating the polymer to form a soluble derivative. Once fluid, the syrup-like substance is processed by extrusion, which means forcing the viscous liquid through a **spinneret** to form a continuous semi-solid polymer filament. (The spinneret, possibly named after a spider or silkworm's silk-spinning organ, is a device rather like a showerhead with many small holes through which the viscous liquid is forced or **extruded**.) The emerging semi-formed polymer solidifies as it extrudes, in a process called **spinning** (not to be confused with the age-old term *spinning* as used to describe the twisting of fibres together to form yarns).

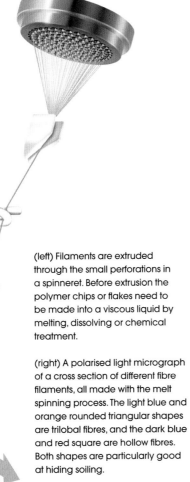

(left) Filaments are extruded through the small perforations in a spinneret. Before extrusion the polymer chips or flakes need to be made into a viscous liquid by melting, dissolving or chemical treatment.

(right) A polarised light micrograph of a cross section of different fibre filaments, all made with the melt spinning process. The light blue and orange rounded triangular shapes are trilobal fibres, and the dark blue and red square are hollow fibres. Both shapes are particularly good at hiding soiling.

Spinning

There are four principal methods of spinning (in this context). Melt spinning is the most common. As the name implies, the substance is melted for extrusion through the spinneret, solidifying as it cools. This method allows for different cross-sectional shapes – for example, round or octagonal – each of which will give different characteristics to the fibre and resulting fabric. Wet spinning is used when the substance has been dissolved in a solvent; in these cases the spinneret is submerged in a chemical bath and fibres solidify as they emerge and make contact with air. In dry spinning, solidification is achieved by evaporating the solvent in air or **inert gas** – as the filaments do not come into contact with a liquid, they do not need to be dried. For high-strength fibres the gel spinning method is used. The liquid crystals are aligned along the fibre axis during extrusion, producing filaments of high tensile strength. Gel spinning is sometimes called dry–wet spinning, as the filaments pass through both air and a liquid bath.

Yarn

After extrusion, while or after the fibres are solidifying, the filaments are drawn (stretched), which aligns the molecular chains orientating them along the fibre axis, making them considerably stronger. Groups of filaments are joined together to form fibre bundles, which then become the filament yarn.

Fibre properties

Most synthetic fibres are round in cross section, but they can also be oval, star-shaped, trilobal or hollow. Trilobal cross sections have optically reflective properties, while hollow fibres help to trap air for added warmth and lightness. Synthetic textile fibres are often crimped to provide more bulk. Fibre surfaces can manufactured to be dull or bright; dull surfaces reflect more light than bright ones, which tend to transmit light and render the fibre more transparent.

Ecological sustainability

Non-cellulosic synthetic fibres are not biodegradable, but that is only one part of the eco-sustainability debate. Synthetics ease the strain on agricultural land usage: virtually no land is required to produce synthetic fibres, whereas by contrast a similar volume of wool fibre requires between 60 and 70 hectares of grazing land for the sheep, land that arguably could be used for food production.

While it is a major concern that petroleum, from which most synthetic fibres are produced, is not a limitless resource, the reality is that less than 1 per cent of petroleum is used for the global production of all man-made synthetic fibres. Polyester, the predominant synthetic fibre, requires only a few cubic tonnes of water for its production; in excess of 20,000 cubic tonnes is required to produce the same amount of cotton.

Polyester

Polyester is the most widely used man-made synthetic material, either as a single fibre or as a blend with natural or other fibres.

Fashion has had a love–hate relationship with polyester, from the peak of its popularity during the 1950s through its lowest point at the end of the 1980s to a rebirth (or rebranding) today. Polyester has always been perceived as the ultimate low-maintenance and, to some extent, low-cost fabric, and it has become a ubiquitous material.

The early love affair with polyester was rooted in the English-speaking world – its credentials were perfectly in tune with the attitudes of the postwar boom years, the appetite for mass consumerism and the desire for modernity.

It could be said that polyester freed the 1950s housewife from the drudgery of ironing; its easy care could even be credited with engaging men with the taboo of domestic chores.

Mainland Europe and South America were, perhaps, more sceptical of polyester's merits, as social emancipation was generally less evident and natural fibres prevailed.

From fashion and social class perspectives, polyester was the victim of an image problem. It was seen by many as synonymous with cheap fashion and questionable taste; it was the fabric by which the social classes were separated. Recent innovative developments in fibre and fabric and its use by creative designers have raised polyester's profile. Today it is judged without prejudice on its own merits, especially where and when 'intelligent' or performance fabrics are in demand: polyester is the world's major man-made fibre.

Trademarked fabrics made from polyester include Terylene/Dacron®, Ultrasuede/Alcantara®, Nanofront®, Sorona® and S.Café®. Polyester is also used to make micro- and nanofibres.

188

(above) An ice-blue tulle creation by designer Walter Van Beirendonck from the 'Cloud' collection. The garment was constructed from multiple layers of hand-cut flowers in polyester tulle, stitched onto a structure similar to a historic crinoline, a technique inspired by the construction of couture dresses.

(right) Yellow up-cycled bag by Bag To Life, made from recycled aeroplane life vests. The coated polyester material is very strong and water-resistant. The mouthpiece becomes a pencil holder inside the bag, and seat belts are used as straps.

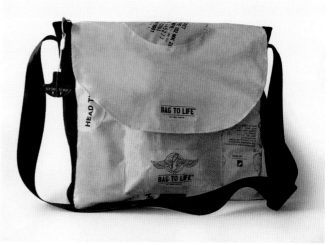

The history of polyester

The polymer that became polyester was discovered and patented in 1941 by the British chemists John Rex Whinfield and James Tennant Dickson. Both worked at the research laboratories of the Calico Printers' Association in Manchester (Great Britain), better known today as Tootal Ltd. In 1946 and under the trademark name of **Terylene**, the polymer was sold to ICI (Imperial Chemical Industries – defunct in 2008).

Research into the fibre can also be traced to Wallace Carothers (at DuPont) during the late 1920s, although DuPont's research focused on nylon, as it was believed to be a more promising fibre. DuPont did, however, purchase the US rights several years later, and after further work started production in the early 1950s using the trade name of DACRON®; mass production was in full swing by the middle of the decade.

Because of its low cost and multiple applications, polyester has been the most commonly used man-made fibre since the early 1970s. In spun form its use ranges from clothing to automotive tyres, and in its non-woven format it is used as a filling for soft furniture.

Polyester properties

The noun polyester is comprised of two parts, poly, meaning many, and **ester**, a basic chemical compound derived from oil, and denotes a group of polymers made from this base. It is most commonly used to refer to the synthetic polymer poly ethylene terephthalate, which for academic clarity is referred to as poly (ethylene terephthalate), the principal ingredient of which is ethylene, a petroleum-derived polymer.

Over 50 per cent of polyester produced is destined for fibre production.

Bottle and packaging materials represent a further large percentage of production of poly ethylene terephthalate, and are referred to by the acronym PET.

Wool and cotton blends
In the early years of manufacture, polyester was seen as an alternative to both cotton and wool, as the fibre could be made to mimic many of the visual characteristics of both. Polyester for tailoring and shirts was then, and is still, popular for inexpensive corporate wear. Once the novelty value had passed, it was difficult for polyester to be seen as a serious long-term competitor to either of these two natural fibres, as it shared somewhat fewer of their tactile properties. However, as a blend with either wool or cotton, polyester does give exceptional added benefits; the best blends for tailoring use a smaller percentage of polyester, allowing the natural fibre greater prominence while the synthetic contributes strength, stability and serviceability to the garment.

Sportswear
For sportswear and performance clothing, polyester is an ultra-efficient fabric; there is almost no limit to what technology can build in to the fibre. Polyester fibres are strong and do not absorb moisture, making them perfect for the application of chemical treatments and finishes, such as waterproofing and fire-retardant finishes. The fibre has low absorbency, making it resistant to staining; fabrics can be pre-shrunk and will not stretch out of shape.

Future fabrics
Textile researchers in the United States are currently developing a form of polyester as a 'super fibre' to rival Kevlar® in strength, to produce bulletproof vests.

Red bouclé sleeveless jacket designed by Romanian London College of Fashion graduate Dinu Bodiciu. The extraordinary moulded shape is realized in a wool-and-silk-mix bouclé strengthened with the inclusion of elastane and polyester. The design expresses a protective and powerful silhouette.

189

Processing polyester filament yarns

↓

Polymerization
Dimethyl terephthalate and ethylene glycol with a catalyst are heated to high temperature – Resulting chemical, a monomer alcohol, is added to terephthalic acid and heated to higher temperature – Resulting clear molten polyester is extruded through slot to form long strands

↓

Drying
Strands are cooled – Cut into tiny chips – Dried to prevent irregularities

↓

Melt spinning
Polymer chips are melted to syrupy liquid – Forced through tiny holes of spinneret – Emerging fibres are united to form single strand – Yarn diameter determined by number of holes in spinneret – More chemicals may be added for additional finishes (NNO3-retardant, anti-static or other)

↓

Drawing
Once extruded from spinneret, it is pliable and stretched to five times its original length – This aligns molecules for stability – As fibres dry and solidify they strengthen – Diameter and length dependent on end purpose of yarn

↓

Winding
After drawing, yarn is wound onto large bobbins or flat-wound onto packages ready for knitting or weaving into fabric

190

Polyester production

Polyester is manufactured in several ways: commonly as **filament** yarns (individual fibre strands of continuous length) or **staple fibres** (filaments that are cut to short predetermined lengths) that are easier for blending with natural fibres. Staple fibres are processed like filaments, but a spinneret with more numerous holes is used during the melt spinning process.

The emerging fibre-forming substance extruded from the spinneret is first cooled and then drawn on heated rollers to three or four times its original length. It is then compressed, forcing the fibres to fold and crimp, and reheated to set the crimp. **Tow** is filament that has been loosely drawn together and is used for staples that are cut into different lengths for blending. When blending with cotton, polyester is cut into 3.2 to 3.8 cm lengths (1.25 to 1.5 in); when blending with rayon the lengths are 5 cm (2 in). Alternatively, polyester can be manufactured as fibrefill, often referred to as wadding, which is a voluminous mass used as padding in quilts and for cold-weather clothing.

Elegant, relaxed styling by Italian brand Corneliani. The single-breasted jacket is made from a tactile synthetic microsuede, and features a zipped removable inner chest piece of self fabric, worn with soft trousers made from bouclé cotton jersey and a mélange wool turtleneck.

Microfibre and nanofibre

The original and most common **microfibre** is made from polyester, although other man-made fibres and blends are also used. The term microfibre refers to synthetic fibres that measure less than one denier or one Decitex per filament. (*Textile Terms and Definitions,* 11th edition, published The Textile Institute.) Denier and Decitex are units of linear mass density used to describe the diameter or fineness of fibre. Microfibres are finer than any natural fibre and many times finer than human hair; even invisible to the naked eye. Yarns can be knitted or woven into any fabric construction. Microfibres produce durable, soft fabrics with good absorption and wicking characteristics; they wash well and dry quickly, making them popular for sports and athletic clothing.

Ultrasuede®/Alcantara®

Research into ultra-fine fibres began in the late 1950s, but the early results lacked the consistency required for commercial production. The first successful ultra-microfibre was invented in 1970 by Drs Miyoshi Okamoto and Toyohiko Hikota at Toray Industries Japan. Ultrasuede® is a registered trademark of Toray (America), which markets the product in the Americas. In Europe the trademark name is Alcantara® and it is produced by the Italian company of the same name, which is co-owned by Toray Industries.

Nanofront®

Recent nanotechnology has allowed Japanese chemical company Teijin to pioneer research into and development of the first nano-fibre, produced commercially since 2008, which is 7,500 times thinner than a human hair. Nanofront® is used in sportswear, particularly anti-slip footwear that benefits from its frictional properties.

(above) Navy blue functional jacket made from Teijin's Blue Eco recycled fabric and designed by Henri Lloyd, with high-performance styling features: waterproof zips, reflective detailing and drawcord security.

(right) 'Green we go', a conversation piece by Myka Baum. While the scourge of environmentalists, the much-maligned plastic bottle can today be recycled into fleece fabric.

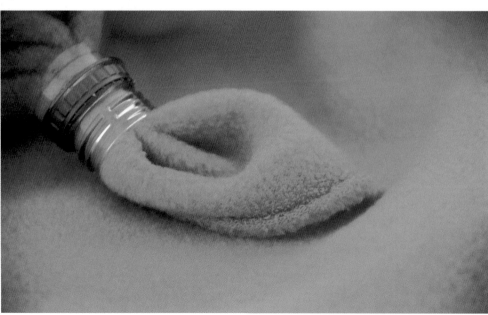

Ecological sustainability

The source of fibres is only one part of environmental concern. It can take 700 years before plastic bottles in landfill start to decompose. While polyester does not biodegrade, it can at least be recycled almost to its virgin state.

Recycled polyester production has the potential to keep billions of plastic (PET) bottles from landfill by using post-consumer plastic instead of virgin materials for fibre and clothing production.

US manufacturer Foss uses seventeen PET bottles to produce sufficient fibre for one sweatshirt made from its Eco-fi fibre (1 lb of fibre is produced from ten bottles). In 2010 Issey Miyake collaborated with Teijin on a collection using their recyled polyester. The large Japanese chemical company has developed specialized equipment to revert used polyester back to its original source material of dimethyl terephthalate, removing all impurities, such as colour dyes. These impurities had until recently been the obstacle to producing longer and softer fibre threads (and a more luxurious feel) than those of conventional recycled polyester, seen frequently in outdoor sportswear; without them, the material can also be used repeatedly. Miyake is quoted as saying that he 'felt that it could be used for something more' if the impurities in recycled polyester could be removed. (From an article by Michiyo Nakamoto, *Financial Times*, 8/12/2010.) Patagonia and Henri Lloyd are two out of more than a hundred companies that collect their products from customers and pay Teijin to recycle them.

The Euro 2012 football strips (kit) designed by Nike for France, Croatia, Holland, Poland and Portugal were said to be the most environmentally sustainable to date, made almost entirely from discarded plastic bottles with the inclusion of a small percentage of organic cotton. Nike said that using discarded plastic saves a third of the energy it would take to produce the same product from virgin polyester.

Triexta

Triexta is a generic designation assigned to a sub-group of polyester fibres that include naturally occurring polymers in their make-up. The chemical name for the polyester in use is **polytrimethylene terephthalate** (PTT); the organic compound component is propanediol (PDO).

PTT was first patented in the early 1940s and used to make carpet fibres, being commercially unsuitable for clothing. DuPont has researched and further developed the fibre, resulting in the marketing of its **Sorona®** branded product.

The fibre can be used for knitted or woven fabrics, and is ideal for sportswear as it is exceptionally durable, stain-resistant and softer and smoother than traditional polyester. For performance clothing it offers exceptional recovery from stretch deformation, said to be at least twice that of traditional polyester or nylon. Izod, Timberland and Calvin Klein have all used Sorona® in their collections.

The fibres are in part made from ingredients from renewable sources; production is also more energy efficient as fibre extrusion is carried out at a lower temperature than that of traditional polyester extrusion, resulting in fewer greenhouse-gas emissions.

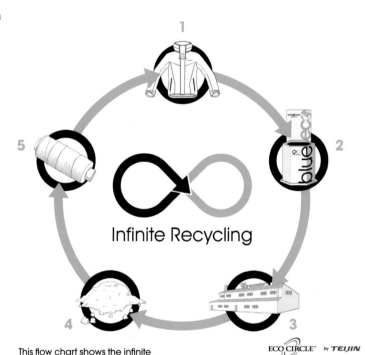

This flow chart shows the infinite recycling loop of Teijin corporation's innovation Eco Circle®, and its Blue Eco fabrics. Recycling post-consumer polyester products results in significant reductions in CO_2 emissions and energy consumption compared to creating polyester from raw material.

S.Café®

The S.Café® yarn is a high-performance polyester that comprises 3 per cent post-consumer waste coffee. Waste grounds are converted into nanoparticles, which are embedded in the core of the yarn; as little as half a cup of waste coffee will produce the fibre equivalent of one T-shirt. Processing removes all odour, and by-products can be used to manufacture soap. The properties within roasted coffee are naturally deodorizing, absorb perspiration and offer protection against UV rays. S.Café® ICE-CAFÉ is a sister yarn with additional cooling properties that dissipate body heat. Both yarns can be knitted or woven; they are ideal for sportswear fabrics and have been used by Nike, Patagonia, The North Face and Puma.

The product meets bluesign® standards for environmentally responsible textiles and is produced by Singtex® of Taiwan.

Post-consumer coffee grounds are the raw material for a new fibre development, in which ground coffee waste is converted into nanoparticles, which are embedded into yarn. Innovative Taiwanese company Singtex® has created a recycled polyester using the coffee nanoparticles, branded S.Café®.

193

Polyamide (nylon)

Polyamide (nylon) was the first commercially successful synthetic polymer.

Nylon is a generic term for a family of synthetic polymers called linear polyamides. TACTEL® fibre and CORDURA® fabric are just two of the trademarked products made from nylon; GORE-TEX® and ripstop frequently use nylon in their production processes.

Nylon fibre was so synonymous with stockings and so fundamental to postwar fashion that the term 'nylons' became the term by which all stockings were known.

The invention of nylon is attributed to Wallace Carothers, working at DuPont. The fibre in its yarn and fabric form was intended as a replacement for silk. It made its debut in the United States in 1935; however, it did not go into general production until 1940 – and no consumer item ever before had caused such nationwide excitement. After eighteen months of making stockings, the United States entered World War II and all nylon production was diverted to the war effort, primarily for parachutes. This created a black market for nylons (stockings).

Although the United States is credited with the invention of nylon, fibres made from polyamide were also being developed in Germany during the same period.

The US development, which was eventually called nylon, was 'polyamide 6,6', while the German development, containing only six carbon atoms, was referred to as 'polyamide 6' and was eventually manufactured under the trade name of **Perlon**.

The first German test stockings were produced a few months after Perlon's invention in 1938. The fibre was also used as reinforcement for German military socks; that apart, it was decreed a military material and kept a secret. Postwar, manufacturers of nylon (in the United States) and Perlon (in Germany) reverted to stocking production. Demand outstripped supply, riots were commonplace when shops had an intake of stock, and it took more than a year for production to catch up with global demand.

194

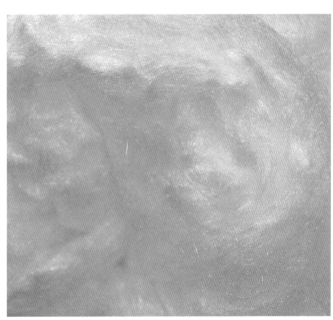

(above) Rainbow-coloured trilobal nylon 'tops' fibres featuring the intense colours and reflective shine typically associated with synthetic fibres.

(right) Trilobal nylon fibres from The Handweavers Studio and Gallery. Trilobal refers to the rounded triangular profile of the fibre.

Polyamide properties

For academic and scientific purposes it is referred to either as polyamide 6,6 or as polyamide 6 – the numeric expression denoting the number of carbon atoms in each monomer unit, the base materials of which are coal and petroleum. Both fibres are formed from polyamide polymers of repeating units, which are held together by amide bonds.

Polyamide fibres are light and fine but also very durable and resistant to abrasion. They are lustrous with a high elasticity, easy to wash and especially quick-drying, and have good shape retention – all qualities that have made nylon (for stockings) far more desirable than its predecessor, silk. In its woven guise the main use for polyamide nylon is in performance outerwear and technical fabrics.

GORE-TEX®

GORE-TEX® is a breathable waterproof laminate patented by Bob Gore in the United States in 1980. It is based on **fluoropolymer** products and thermo-mechanically expanded polytetrafluoroethylene (PTFE), which is a fluorine fibre and the chemical constituent of Teflon®. The 'Gore' membrane is laminated onto any one of a number of high-performance fabrics, frequently nylon, which are then sealed with a solution that renders the membrane both waterproof and breathable. GORE-TEX® fabrics protect against the wind and can be extremely light in weight.

The expanded PTFE component of the GORE-TEX® membrane contains millions of microscopic pores, each one smaller than a drop of water, thereby creating a barrier to the liquid, but bigger than a molecule of moisture vapour, allowing the gas to escape.

Garments manufactured using GORE-TEX® (including boots and gloves) must have taped seams to prevent water ingress through the sewing-machine needle holes. The tape is glued or heat-sealed and placed over all the internal **seam turnings**.

A sister product called WINDSTOPPER® employs similar technology in that it is breathable and windproof; however, it is not fully waterproof.

The patent has since expired and there are now several other products available with similar characteristics that use the same technology.

TACTEL®

TACTEL® is a registered trademark for nylon 6,6 fibres produced by INVISTA. The name is derived from the Latin *tactum*, to touch, which also gives us tactile. The versatile TACTEL® fibre combines the durability of nylon with the added bonus of incredible softness. The fibre was introduced in the early 1980s by DuPont. It is produced today by INVISTA, a privately owned company that was formed from the DuPont Textiles and Interiors division, and which is now one of the largest integrated fibres, resins and intermediaries companies in the world. TACTEL® fibre has proven to be a popular alternative to cotton within the women's lingerie market because of its noticeable softness, breathability and easy-care appeal. It is regularly used in seamless garments. It is a high-performance synthetic, dries fast (typically much faster than cotton) and resists creases and wrinkles.

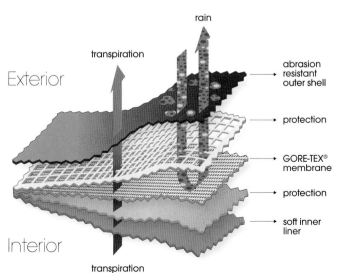

(left) Cross-section diagram of the layers of fabric required to achieve optimum performance in a range of temperatures and weather conditions. The GORE-TEX® membrane prevents moisture from penetrating the inner layers, while allowing the wearer's skin to breathe.

(above) Two high-durability woven fabrics. The green one has been finished with a heavy-duty water-repellent coating. The blue one has been treated with a finish that offers slight moisture proofing. This additional functionality is provided purely by the coating on the fabric and is not a function of the weave, yarn or fibre used in the manufacture of this particular fabric.

CORDURA® fabric

CORDURA® fabrics are durable woven or knitted fabrics with an exceptional strength-to-weight ratio. Constructed from high-tenacity nylon fibre, weight for weight the fabrics are said to offer best-in-class tear and abrasion resistance. Introduced by DuPont in the late 1960s as a development of more robust nylon, the fabric trademark is now owned by INVISTA.

CORDURA® fabric was first used in military applications where durability and performance were an advantage. In the 1970s brands such as Eastpak started to use the fabric for backpacks and luggage. By the late 1980s lighter weight fabrics had been introduced for clothing; these now classic fabrics are widely used today as reinforcement panels in workwear, skiwear and motorcycle clothing by labels including Dickies, Jansport and Dainese, where maximum abrasion resistance is required.

Today there are many different CORDURA® fabrics, available in a wide variety of weights, blends, constructions and finishes including laminates, double weaves, two- and four-way stretch knitted and woven fabrics. CORDURA® Denim and CORDURA® NYCO fabric ranges are based on blends of cotton and INVISTA nylon, which offer the added comfort advantages of cotton; CORDURA® Naturalle™ fabrics have the appearance of cotton; CORDURA® Lite fabrics are often pack cloths, ripstops and dobby weaves. All can be coated, uncoated or laminated depending on end use requirements, which include fashion, outdoor clothing, workwear and military uniforms.

Nylon ripstop

Ripstop is a term given to any type of lightweight woven fabric (including silk, cotton, polyester or polypropylene) that has a visible, slightly raised-rib crosscheck surface – a thicker thread in a diamond pattern. While any fibre can be used to weave ripstop, nylon is the key yarn used in its production. The interlocking nylon thread pattern, woven through the lighter material at regular intervals, stops any tear from spreading. Ripstop fabrics with Nomex® fibres, a kind of aramid fibre, are used by firefighters; with a camouflage print it has military applications; and it is also used in everyday clothing with or without functional requirements.

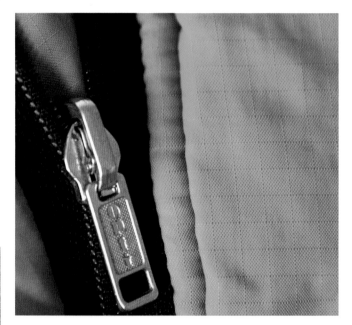

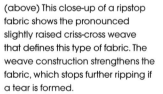
(above) This close-up of a ripstop fabric shows the pronounced slightly raised criss-cross weave that defines this type of fabric. The weave construction strengthens the fabric, which stops further ripping if a tear is formed.

(above) Microscopic cross section of woven CORDURA® fabric, showing the structure and density of the filament bundles. Constructed using high tenacity fibre technology, weight for weight, CORDURA® fabrics are exceptionally durable. © INVISTA. CORDURA is a trademark of INVISTA for durable fabrics.

(right) CORDURA® fabrics come in many different constructions and textures. They provide durable tear and abrasion-resistance performance for a variety of end uses including apparel, luggage and footwear.

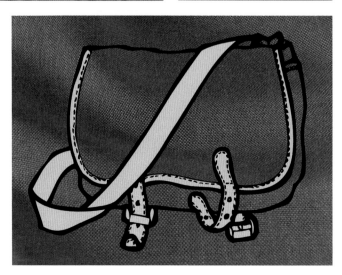

Polyamide production

There are two distinct methods to produce nylon fibre.

Nylon 6,6

The first employs molecules with an acid group on each end (adipic, or hexanedioic, acid); these react in water with molecules containing amine groups (hexamethylenediamine), also on each end. The resulting fibre is named nylon 6,6 on the basis of the number of carbon atoms (a total of 12) separating the two acid and the diamine groups. The compounds form a salt, known as nylon salt, which is then dried and heated to eliminate the water, forming the polymer.

Nylon 6

The second method employs a compound containing an amine at one end and an acid at the other (caprolactam). This is polymerized through heating, during which it breaks down to form a chain of repeating units. The resulting polymer fibre (polycaprolactam) is referred to as nylon 6, also based on the number of carbon atoms processed.

Polymer to yarn

The primary material is chemically processed into granulate (tiny grains), which are then dissolved into a liquid and heated to produce a molten syrup-like mass. The molten polymer is then pumped through holes in a spinneret at a very high temperature to form the filaments, which are then cooled to solidify.

The process, the type of spinneret and the choice of additives to the mass determine the end product; in both cases the polyamide will be melt spun and drawn after cooling. Fibre strands are finally stretched to four or five times their original length, forcing the molecules to align, thus making the fibres stronger and rendering some elasticity. Filament yarns are then oiled and wound onto bobbins.

Ecological sustainability

Nylon is a petrochemical synthetic that does not biodegrade. It also creates greenhouse gas (nitrous oxide) in its production. However, with the notable exception of stockings, fabrics and apparel created from nylon are frequently durable and reusable. Some nylon polymers, such as TACTEL®, can be recycled to create household plastics.

Aramid fibres (aromatic polyamides)

Aramid fibres are man-made high-performance fibres that are exceptionally strong, have excellent resistance to heat and do not combust under normal levels of oxygen.

The term aramid is a portmanteau of the words aromatic and polyamide. As fabrics, aramids are used in the protective and performance clothing industries. Concerns have been raised that some aramid fibres are said to exhibit similar characteristics to asbestos, but the fibre is still in demand.

The most common commercial aramids are poly (paraphenylene terephthalamide), traded as Kevlar®; and poly (m-phenylene isophthalamide), known as Nomex®.

The history of aromatic polyamides

Aromatic polyamides were developed in a corporate science laboratory and first applied commercially in the early 1960s. By the end of the decade, DuPont had developed a meta-aramid fibre, which it marketed under the trade name of Nomex®. Further experimentation resulted in the discovery of a para-aramid fibre. The first was poly (parabenzamide) (PpBA), sold as 'Fiber B'. This was soon superseded by poly (paraphenylene terephthalamide) (PpTA), discovered at DuPont by Stephanie Kwolek and marketed from the early 1970s as Kevlar®.

Other manufacturers are now producing competitors to both Kevlar® and Nomex®. Notably, the Dutch chemical company Akzo developed Twaron®, a para-aramid fibre derived from polyphenylenediamine (PPD), which is now produced by industrial giant Teijin of Japan along with meta-aramid fibres Technora® and Teijinconex®.

Properties of aramid fibres

An aramid fibre is an aromatic polyamide of which there are two principal types: meta-aramid and para-aramid. Fibres are formed from a long chain of synthetic polyamides that are related to polyamide nylon (PA), although with a differing main chain structure composed of molecules that are characterized by relatively ridged polymer chains. The molecules are linked by strong hydrogen bonds that efficiently transfer mechanical stress.

Meta-aramid fibres have exceptional thermal and fire-resistant properties: they do not ignite, melt, deform or degrade and are resistant to chemicals as well as offering protection against radiation. In addition to this, they have relatively soft handle and can be processed as ordinary fibres.

Para-aramid fibres share many of these characteristics, adding exceptional strength-to-weight ratio. The key structural feature of Kevlar® is a **benzene ring**; the symmetry of the molecules forms a strong chain structure.

Nomex® and Kevlar®

Nomex® is a **meta-aramid** polymer fibre while Kevlar® is a **para-aramid** polymer fibre. The two brands dominate the market for aromatic polyamides. They share a similar basic chemical structure, both are manufactured by DuPont and both are produced in either fibre or sheet form.

In its fibre form, Nomex® is used to make fire-protective material used for clothing for racing drivers, firefighting crews and military personnel. Nomex® is manufactured in the United States and Spain, and has the most visible market exposure of the meta-aramids.

Kevlar® is an extremely strong para-aramid polymer fibre; on a weight-for-weight basis it is said to be five times stronger than steel.

Kevlar® is a cut-resistant fibre used for industrial and protective clothing such as bulletproof vests and components in motorcycle protective clothing, including gloves and protectors for the elbow, knee and spine. It is much lighter in weight and thinner than the traditional materials it replaces, and therefore more comfortable to wear. **Kevlar®** has arguably cornered the market in para-aramid fibres; it is manufactured in the United States, Northern Ireland and Japan, and has entered popular consciousness in the form of Batman's bodysuit.

Aramid fibre production

Aramids are generally prepared by the reaction between an amine group and a carboxylic acid group to dissolve the aromatic polymer. Kevlar® is made from the reaction of para-phenylenediamine (PPD) and molten terephthaloyl chloride (TPC), which is wet spun in sulphuric acid. Nomex® is created by the reaction of m-phenylenediamine (MPD) and isophthaloyl chloride (IPC). Technora® is created by condensation polymerization of two diamines, PPD and diaminodiphenyl ether (ODA), with TPC.

In the spinning solution, the stiff molecules become liquid and the polymer molecules align. The solution is wet spun, producing the filament yarn, which is forced through a spinneret. The remaining solvent is evaporated. After extrusion the liquid filaments pass through an air gap and enter a coagulation water bath. Additional processes include washing, neutralizing and drying before winding onto bobbins (see page 185).

These high-performance ergonomic leather motorcycling gloves by OSX London incorporate the extremely protective properties of Kevlar® at the knuckles to prevent injury in the event of impact.

Acrylic fibres

The boom years for acrylic fabrics were the 1950s. As with polyester and nylon, acrylic was synonymous with postwar modernity, of which the North American market was the most advanced.

The 1950s consumer wanted not only labour-saving machines, but also easy-care clothing – and acrylic was one of the materials that fitted the bill.

With its high **loft** and generally warm wool-like touch, acrylic was used widely as a wool substitute, especially for knitwear and across almost all market levels. By the late 1960s, however, consumer taste had evolved and acrylic was a victim of the changing times: it was now perceived as a cheap substitute with a tendency to pill (bobble). Today an array of exciting novelty yarns is available that makes acrylic a 'must' blend with wool and other natural fibres. As a pure fibre, acrylic has greatly advanced the popularity of sportswear clothing for daily use in the guise of fleece tops and training and jogging clothing.

During acrylic's 1950s heyday, popular US brands included Orlon®, Acrilan® and Creslan®; in Europe there was Dralon® and Courtelle™. The current market is dominated by LEACRIL®.

The history of acrylic fibre

Acrylic and methacrylic acids were first synthesized in the mid-nineteenth century, but the potential of the materials derived from these compounds became apparent only at the turn of the twentieth century with a publication on polymers of acrylic esters by German chemist **Otto Röhm**. Throughout the 1930s research developments ran in parallel in Germany and the United States; acrylic paints and clear resins including Perspex and Plexiglas were produced. DuPont scientists were working on improvements to rayon fibre when, in the early 1940s, they discovered a means of spinning acrylic polymer through a solution. They called the substance 'Fiber A'. Shortly afterwards DuPont began limited production.

Commercial production
Early difficulties in development of the material, in spinning and dyeing, delayed commercial production in both the United States and Germany until the early 1950s, when it went into full flow. DuPont marketed Orlon®; Acrilan® (polypropenonitrile) was made by Monsanto, and Creslan® (also known as Fiber X-54, or Exlan, a copolymer of acrylonitrile with acrylamide) by American Cyanamid. In Great Britain, Courtaulds produced Courtelle™; while in Germany Dralon GmbH manufactured its eponymous Dralon®, still in production today.

Future fabrics
Because of economic factors, production of acrylic fibres today is centred in the Far East, Turkey, India, Mexico and South America, although a number of European manufacturers continue to produce; production in the United States has ended. The largest producer of acrylic yarn is the Spanish–Italian company Montefibre SpA, first formed in 1957 and now producing acrylic fibres under the trade name of LEACRIL® in both Spain and Italy and with a joint-venture company in China.

199

want easy care? You want casuals made with
ACRILAN
So smart, they'll go from cram session to cake session. So carefree... they'll never show the strain. Wrinkles? Droop? Bagginess? Forget 'em. From now on you're living easy... fresh, unwrinkled, pleated and pretty... with Acrilan acrylic fiber. Casuals styled by *Bill Atkinson* for **glen of michigan**

This US advertisement from the mid-1950s, intended to appeal to collegiate youth and the newly defined teenage market, showcases carefree, casual styling. It emphasizes the use of the new man-made fibre, extolling the virtues of the wrinkle-free, easy-care Acrilan® in these separates by Glen of Michigan.

Acrylic properties

Acrylic (PAN) can be defined as fibres that are composed of linear macromolecules with 85 per cent or more (by mass) acrylonitrile repeating units in the chain. Acrylonitrile, an oil-based chemical obtained by reacting propylene with ammonia and oxygen in the presence of a catalyst, is polymerized to form polyacrylonitrile, a synthetic resin, which is then used to make acrylic fibres.

Additional chemicals are used to improve the fibres' ability to absorb dye. Acrylic benefits from a good level of heat- and shape-retention (it is crease-resistant) and has a low level of water absorption. It is a resilient, durable and low-maintenance fibre with the added benefit of quickly wicking moisture to the surface where it evaporates and dries.

The majority of acrylic fibre production is destined for the garment industry; a lesser percentage is for furnishing fabrics and a further small amount has an industrial end use. It is a common substitute for wool.

Modacrylic

Modacrylic (MAC) fibres are a modified form of acrylic, which have less than 85 per cent and more than 35 per cent (mass) acrylonitrile repeating units in the chain and are formed from a combination of coal, air, water and oil. Modacrylic is used for flame-retardant garments, children's wear and baby wear, and in soft toys; also fake fur and wigs. It is primarily a German development, first introduced in the early 1940s and produced on a large scale from 1954 by Bayer AG, a German chemical and pharmaceutical company. It was also produced in the United States during a similar period, in the forms of Eastman Kodak Company's Verel (acrylonitrile and vinylidene chloride), Dynel (acrylonitrile and polyvinyl chloride) and Monsanto's SEF. Because of their low moisture content, fibres can build up static charges, but modacrylic fabrics are resistant to moths, mildew and creasing during wear.

A beaded polyester organza dress by designer and Central Saint Martins graduate Maia Bergman. The granular texture of the acrylic beads appears to 'grow' over the base fabric in clustered and spaced formations resembling pixellated organic forms. The strength of the polyester fibre and structure of the organza support the weight of the beading.

Acrylic production

Propylene reacts with ammonia and oxygen to produce acrylonitrile. Acrylonitrile is then polymerized to produce polyacrylonitrile (PAN) polymer, from which fibres can be produced by either wet or dry spinning methods (see page 185).

In wet spinning the fibres are formed by forcing the polymer (fibre-forming substance) through a multi-hole spinneret, while submerged in a chemical solution; filaments solidify as they emerge. In dry spinning, the polymer is forced through the spinneret into a hot-air chamber where the fibres solidify through evaporation. Additional processes include washing, stretching, drying and fixing. After an additional finishing process, fibres are steamed and crimped and are finally ready as filament tow. An additional cutting process is required if filament tow is to be turned into staple fibres.

Acrylic can be produced in a range of deniers.

Ecological sustainability

Acrylamide is recognized as a probable carcinogen, although investigations into whether wearing it causes cancer have been inconclusive because of its prevalence in the environment – in many processed foods it forms naturally (during baking and roasting, for example). In the 1950s and 1960s it was identified as a potential source of occupational neurotoxicity for manufacturers who might inhale fumes.

Using non-renewable petrochemicals, acrylic production is also energy-intensive and the fibres do not degrade. Researchers at The Hong Kong Polytechnic University in China, assessing the environmental impact and ecological sustainability of ten types of textile, concluded in a report published report in 2011 that acrylic was the worst offender. Production techniques can be improved – 1 tonne of Dralon uses only 5 m³ of water, significantly less than for natural fibres (Dralon company) – but it is clear that acrylic is not the most sustainable choice.

Olefin fibres – polyolefin or polyalkene

Polyolefin fabric is extremely lightweight, having the lowest specific gravity of all fibres.

Olefin (polyolefin) fibres are manufactured from polyethylene and polypropylene, the most common manufactured plastics in the world today. Polyolefin has great bulk and cover while having low specific gravity – which means warmth without the weight. (Sara J. Kadolph, *Textile*, Prentice Hall.) Fabrics made from olefin fibres are used in sports and active wear, thermal underwear and socks, and as insulative linings for outerwear. Fabrics are also used for home furnishing, automotive interiors and for industrial and geo-textiles.

Olefin fibre brands include Tyvek® and Thinsulate™.

The history of polyolefin fibres

The Italian chemist Giulio Natta is credited with successfully formulating olefins for textile application. The catalysts he developed with German Karl Ziegler enabled precise and low-cost polymer manufacture, further developing the uses of polyethylene, which had been in production since the 1930s. The two men were awarded the Nobel Prize for Chemistry for their work. Commercial production of olefin fibres was in progress by the end of the 1950s in both the United States and Italy.

Commercial production
Today numerous manufacturers produce olefin fibres, of which the two best known are made by DuPont and 3M. DuPont produces a fibre called Tyvek®, a high-density polyethylene fibre finer than human hair.

The discovery of Tyvek® was accidental – a researcher at DuPont's experimental laboratories noticed a polyethylene fluff coming out of a pipe.

The material that caught Jim White's attention was developed and investigated, and flash spun polyethylene went into production in the late 1960s.

A decade later, 3M began commercial production of its well-known brand Thinsulate™, a thermal insulating material.

Olefin fibre properties

Olefin fibre is a synthetic fibre made from either **polypropylene** or **polyethylene** polymers. Olefins are also known as alkenes. Polyethylene is generally used for ropes and utility fabrics while polypropylene is used for clothing (especially protective clothing), furnishing fabrics and industrial products. Today fibres are often blended with cotton.

The fibre-forming substance is a simple structure of long-chain carbon atoms; polyethylene polymer is composed of at least 85 per cent by weight of ethylene, propylene or other olefin units and is created when ethylene and propylene gases are polymerized. The fibres are very strong and resistant to abrasion as well as being stain, sunlight, fire and chemical resistant. Olefin is flammable and thus requires spot cleaning at low temperatures.

Olefin fibres have a lower melting point than nylon or polyester, hence fabrics can be thermally bonded – which is one reason the fibre has been used in developments in competitive swimwear, as the process eliminates the need for sewing, reducing drag and making the fabric more aerodynamic.

Other factors include low moisture absorbency; also, olefin has the lowest specific gravity of all fibres and is therefore able to float.

Tyvek®

Tyvek® is a polyethylene non-woven fabric, made of randomly distributed fibres heat-bonded together, that provides a protective membrane and resembles waxy paper. It has a wide range of industrial applications, including construction and packaging; as a garment fabric, Tyvek® is used in protective apparel (limited-use bodysuits). A lightweight, comfortable microfibre that resists oil and water, it provides an effective barrier for workers dealing with such hazardous materials as asbestos, carbon fibres or paint. Tyvek® is very difficult to tear but can be cut.

Thinsulate™

The word 'thinsulate' is a portmanteau of the words thin and insulate. The fabric is made from a range of polymers, mostly polyethylene terephthalate and polypropylene. It was launched onto the skiwear market in the 1970s, following development over the previous decade. The fibres are said to be thinner than polyester fibres. As with most insulative materials, the gaps between fibres trap air and help to reduce heat flow while allowing moisture to wick away. The manufacturers say that it provides insulation twice as effective as duck down, is less water-absorbent and more resistant to crushing. The product is used by such brands as Tommy Hilfiger, The North Face and Woolrich as well as both the US and Canadian ski teams.

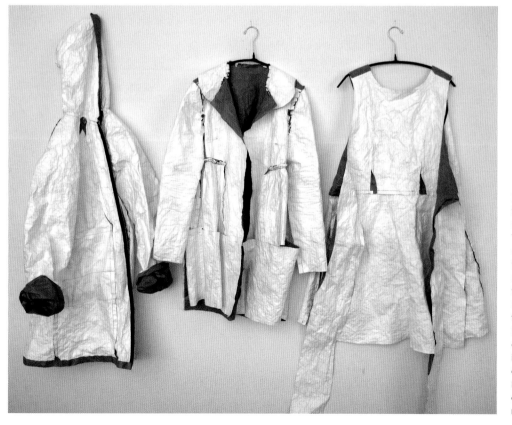

Monochrome garments from the 'Post-industrial Folk Wear' collection by New York brand Mau. This collection of practical and adaptable street wear is made from the ubiquitous packaging material Tyvek®. The material is a featherweight high-performance non-woven material, usually used for protective suits in industry. Tyvek® looks and feels deceptively fragile and perishable, like paper, but is in fact waterproof, oil-resistant and extremely difficult to tear. It is produced in the US, and is composed of 25 per cent recycled material.

Olefin fibre production

Fibres are produced in a similar way to polyester and nylon: they are formed by polymerization of propylene and ethylene gases in the presence of a catalyst. Karl Ziegler initially used a mixture of titanium tetrachloride and an alkyl derivative of aluminium; the Ziegler-Natta catalyst group also includes halides of chromium, vanadium and zirconium with the alkyl aluminium compounds.

Because of its higher melting point, polypropylene (rather than polyethylene) is preferred for textile applications. Different fibre characteristics can be created by additives and processing conditions. The polymer can then be wet or dry melt spun through a spinneret, into water for wet spinning, or air-cooled for dry spinning. Polyethylene yarn resists dye once it has gone through the manufacturing process; colour is added to the melt at extrusion, thus rendering the finished fibres, yarn and fabric colourfast. Fibres are stretched to five or six times their original spun length. Olefin can be produced as filament, staple and tow fibres.

Ecological sustainability

Olefin fibres are inexpensive to produce and said to be relatively environmentally friendly owing to the few by-products of the manufacturing process (particularly during dyeing); they are also easily recycled. Tyvek® ProtectiveWear by DuPont is an olefin material that is already 25 per cent recycled.

The quirky, up-cycled 'Launderette' collection by Central Saint Martins graduate Hayley Grundmann uses strips of laundry bags knitted using an e-wrapping technique, in which strands are looped around selected hooks on a domestic knitting machine. Other recycled materials were woven around a box loom, making the resulting fabric seamless. The designer used all man-made or up-cycled fibres, apart from silk organza.

Polyurethane (elastomers)

Elastane is the generic term used to describe a yarn or fabric with exceptional elasticity. In North America the generic name **spandex**, an anagram of the word expands, is in common usage. Elastomeric yarns were first developed as a replacement for latex rubber elastic as used in corsetry and underwear; ultimately they are far more durable than the non-synthetic (organic) competitor they were introduced to replace.

In popular culture elastane has been the fabric of choice for decades of comic-strip superheroes, heroines and arch-villains.

Superheroes and athletes

From superhero- to fetish-wear, the smooth, body-contoured clothing that can be achieved only with elastomeric yarns has gained the material a cult status and following. In the process a genre of fetish and semi-bondage **zentai** clothing (full-body covering) has been fostered.

From a more practical perspective, elastane has been a major driving force in the development of sportswear performance clothing and ultimately has revolutionized the way we all wear clothing today. A small amount of elastane added to a fabric enables the garment to return to its original shape after any amount of stretching. During the 1980s leggings and bodywarmers became ubiquitous; body-con fashion owes its genesis to the development of stretch fabrics, showcased by designers including Azzedine Alaïa.

LYCRA® is arguably the best known of all global elastane yarns, so much so that the term 'Lycra' has been appropriated for all stretch fabrics regardless of brand.

(above) Skin-tight zentai bodysuits (worn here under coats) employ the stretch and recovery of elastomeric yarns, which have revolutionized our expectations of comfort and the way we wear clothing. The second-skin fit made possible by elastic yarns has entered our contemporary fashion vocabulary in a wide range of products.

(right) Microscopic image showing the structure of a unique fabric designed and developed by PUMA for use in football uniforms. The fine loose fibres are coated microfibres that channel away moisture. The strong loops featured in the knit construction are from an elasticated material that allows performance-enhancing stretch and recovery.

204

The history of elastane fibre

Otto Bayer discovered and patented the chemistry of polyurethane in Germany in the 1930s, inventing the basic diisocyanate polyaddition process. But it is William Hanford and Donald Holmes at DuPont who are credited with inventing the modern process to develop multi-purpose polyurethane, in the early 1940s, and their process that forms the basis for the elastomeric fibres created later in the 1950s by American chemist Joseph Shivers. The fibre was first envisaged as a more reliable and readily obtainable replacement for latex rubber elastic as used in the corsetry and underwear industries, and was known as 'Fiber K'. DuPont marketed its revolutionary new yarn from 1962 under the trade name of LYCRA®, which today is produced by INVISTA. Other elastane brands include Creora® from Hyosung Korea, ESPA® from Toyobo and Linel® from Fillattice.

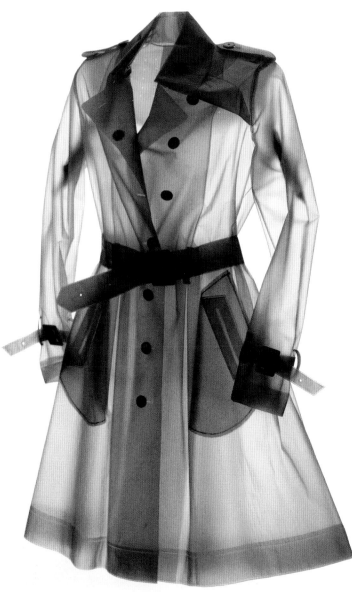

Elastane fibre properties

Elastane yarns and fabrics stretch under tension to at least three times (even as much as seven times) their relaxed measurement, and can revert to their original measurements once the tension has been removed.

Elastane does not stretch a fabric; the stretch is in the fabric construction – the elastane provides the recovery.

Elastane is not a fabric in itself; elastane yarns must be used in conjunction with other yarns, natural or man-made, to form a fabric with elastomeric qualities. The traditional use of elastane is in the production of knitted fabrics, as the construction of interlinking loops that forms a knitted fabric already has an element of built-in stretch and is therefore a perfect vehicle for a stretch yarn. Woven fabrics, by contrast, have more stability and therefore were not ideal early candidates. However, with today's technology elastane yarns are also used for woven fabrics. These are referred to as either weft- or warp-stretch fabrics depending where exactly the elastane yarn has been used, and are likely to be marketed as '**comfort stretch**' fabrics, implying a limited stretch ability more suited to leisurewear than to sportswear; woven fabrics with both weft and warp stretch are also available.

Muscle performance factor

In addition to the freedom of movement made possible by stretch fabrics, elastomeric yarns also enhance muscle recovery while reducing muscle fatigue in active sports. Sportswear fabrics are for the most part of a knitted construction. Knitted fabrics generally have the greatest stretch (yarn elongation) across their width; while the stretch in the length of the fabric is limited, a high elastane content increases the power of the fabric or its **elastic modulus**. The fabric stretches and contracts in tandem with the body's muscle movement, which helps to reduce muscle fatigue through garment support. As it decreases muscle strain it enhances performance.

205

(left) The classic trench coat is revisited by Terra New York and constructed from a sheer polyurethane membrane. The properties of polyurethane allow the seams to be welded, with no stitch perforations to allow water in, resulting in a completely waterproof garment. Perforated ventilation systems at key points under the storm flaps allow breathability.

Elastane fibre

Elastane fibres are elastic or rubber-like fibres that are used in a variety of garments to improve fit and function. Elastane is differentiated from other fibres by its high stretch and recovery. Elastane fibres are composed of long polymer chains that are networked together. In the unstretched or relaxed state, these long polymer chains are randomly coiled. As the fibre is stretched the coils straighten out, allowing the fibre to elongate without breaking. When the force stretching the fibre is removed, the polymer chains quickly return to the normal coiled state and the fibre returns to essentially its original length. To be called an elastane, a fibre must be composed of at least 85 per cent (by weight) segmented polyurethane and when stretched to three times its original length and released, it recovers rapidly and substantially to its initial length.

Elasticated yarn may be constructed with an elastane fibre core and a covering fibre. This can provide bulk, improve abrasion resistance, and provide a final fabric with the appearance and feel of the covering fibre, but with a level of elasticity that will not be achievable with the covering fibre alone. Elastane fibre can also be incorporated directly into a fabric structure composed predominantly of another fibre type. In this case the elastane fibre will be hidden within the fabric structure, while providing the desired fit and comfort.

LYCRA®

Today there are many different variants of LYCRA® elastane fibre, each designed to excel in a specific end-use, from Xtra Life LYCRA® fibre, which is said to have up to a tenfold greater resistance to chlorine compared to ordinary elastane yarns, to Easy Set LYCRA® fibre, which is especially suited for use with heat sensitive fibres. Proprietary, brand-specific process distinguish LYCRA® elastane and its competitor brands from generic elastane fibres.

The LZR Racer®

The LZR Racer® swimsuit (made from elastane-nylon and polyurethane) was developed as a collaboration between Speedo®, the Australian Institute of Sport, NASA's low-speed wind tunnel testing facilities and ANSYS' fluid-flow analysis software system. Comme des Garçons worked on the design of the swimwear, which was tested by Olympic athletes. The FASTSKIN® material is designed to mimic sharkskin. The suit allows better oxygen flow to the muscles; its compression panels hold the body in a hydrodynamic position; it repels water and increases muscular flexibility. The seams of the suit are ultrasonically welded and the material quick-drying (eliminating drag); the suit is also chlorine-resistant.

The success of the LZR Racer® in improving competitive swimming times (up to 5 per cent) at international level caused a re-evaluation of apparel rules by FINA, swimming's governing body worldwide.

(left) High-stretch elasticated bandage-like strips made from rayon, nylon and elastane form the iconic signature aesthetic of French designer Hervé Léger. The designer employs the tension of the strongly elasticated bands to wrap the strips around the form, then stitches them together, sculpting and constricting the body to create an almost corseted effect.

(above) This structured swimsuit by London College of Fashion graduate Diana Auria Harris is made from recycled LZR Racer® suits. Following a review of apparel rules by FINA, swimming's governing body, Speedo® held a competition among several colleges to encourage the creative up-cycling of the suits. Inspired by corsetry, Harris's version has inflatable plunge cups.

Polyurethane (elastane) production

The elastane polymer is typically formed in a two-step reaction process. In the first step, a macroglycol and a diisocyanate monomer are mixed, creating a pre-polymer. This pre-polymer is diluted with a solvent and further reacted with a diamine or diamines mixture to form a polymer solution. This solution of polymer and solvent may also contain various additives to improve the performance of the elastane for specific applications. The final elastane thread is most commonly produced from this solution in a process called dry-spinning. In the dry-spinning process, the polymer solution is delivered into a dry-spinning cell where the solvent is evaporated and recovered for re-use. Lastly, the fibres may be treated with a finishing agent to improve the downstream textile processing.

(above) High-performance running gear designed by Sweaty Betty. The fabric is a high-stretch polyamide/elastane fabric, developed specifically for the demands of sportswear. It has thermo-regulating capabilities, and is sweat-wicking and quick-drying.

Polyurethane (elastane) production

Macroglycol and diisocyanate monomer mixed – Prepolymer created

↓

Prepolymer further reacted with diamine – Diluted with solvent – Spinning solution created

↓

Pumped into fibre-producing cell – Forced through spinneret

↓

Fibre is coalesced by removal of solvent – Solvent is evaporated and recovered for re-use

↓

Fibres produced – sticky texture enables strands to adhere

↓

Fibres treated with finishing agent for better textile manufacturing – Spooled and shipped

Synthetic rubber

The two principal synthetic rubbers used in the fashion industry are **neoprene** and Ariaprene™. Neoprene is commonly associated with wetsuits but today has applications in many areas of fashion.

Ariaprene™ is the biodegradable alternative to neoprene – it is solvent- and toxic-free and also available in a wide selection of lightweight rubber fabrics.

Louis Vuitton, Chanel, Michael Kors, Balenciaga, Lanvin and Vera Wang have all used a synthetic rubber in their collections.

The history of synthetic rubber

Experimentation with synthetic rubber was in progress in Germany and Russia at the turn of the twentieth century, but it was the increase in price of natural latex rubber that concentrated research to find a synthetic, inexpensive replacement, leading to the development of neoprene by DuPont. The invention was based on the research work at Notre Dame University of **Julius Nieuwland**, from whom DuPont purchased the rights to the patent. Arnold Collins, a chemist in Wallace Carothers' unit, first produced neoprene while investigating by-products of divinylacetylene. The name of neoprene was adopted in the late 1930s; it is a generic not a trade name, as it is sold as a raw material for compounding rather than as a final product. Following an intensive marketing campaign, neoprene was in great demand by the end of the same decade.

Future fabrics
Today's eco-friendly, non-toxic alternative is Ariaprene™, developed at the turn of this century, which has been designed for reuse several times within closed-loop recycling processes, after which it will safely decompose.

208

(above) Synthetic rubber materials were originally created for industrial applications. They were never intended for mass-produced consumer products, and as such are not made to be recycled or to break down in landfill. By contrast, Ariaprene™ was specifically designed to be reused many times. The manufacturing scraps can be recycled back to the next-generation product or to create something entirely new. Once the waste reaches maximum processing, it will safely decompose in landfill, taking two to five years to degrade completely.

(above) Esoteric 'Wrapping shoe' by Japanese designer Takuya Takizawa. The construction features a sole and upper formed from spirals of spaghetti-like latex cord wrapped and woven around a neoprene inner sock.

(left) This spongy-textured Ariaprene™ material provides breathable cushioning against impact, making it particularly suitable for sports footwear.

Synthetic rubber properties

Synthetic rubber is an artificial elastomer (see page 204) and is made by the polymerization of a variety of petroleum-based monomers. In active sportswear synthetic rubber is often used as a component to act as a shock absorber, while in leisure sportswear it has often been bonded to knitted fabrics, such as jersey and velour. Laminating synthetic rubber to lightweight unstable fabrics adds stability and strength, and therefore allows more and alternative applications including outerwear styles that would not have been possible with the base fabric. Synthetic rubber and fabric-laminated synthetic rubber may be sewn, glued or heat-taped together depending on the end requirement of the product. It does not degrade in sunshine and resists damage from flexing and twisting; it is used as an insulation material for aquatic sports (wetsuits for diving and waders for fishing).

Synthetic rubber production

Neoprene (polychloroprene, chloroprene rubber, CR) is produced from the polymerization of chloroprene (obtained from the chlorination of butadiene), using potassium persulfate as a reactor. The presence of chlorine lends the fibre resistance to heat, flame, abrasion and oil. The production processes for making neoprene can provoke allergic reactions, as they include chemical solvents and heavy metals. Ariaprene™ is hypoallergenic, odour-free and solvent-free.

Ecological sustainability

Traditional synthetic rubbers were designed not to degrade; while this has advantages during use, discarded material is destined for landfill. Extensive research into production processes that avoid solvents and metals now means recyclable, biodegradable alternatives are available.

(right) The light, sculptural qualities of neoprene are apparent in the undulating peplum of this red tailored suit by Lanvin. The nature of the material allows the designer to create forms that stand proud of the body, without the need for extra stiffening.

(below) The compact and smooth qualities of the Ariaprene™ used for this eco-sports shoe showcase the sleek futuristic aesthetic made possible by moulding technology.

(above) Futuristic white two-piece by designer Eileen Pang. The super-light spongy and sculptural qualities of neoprene, a honeycomb-structured airtex and LYCRA® are exploited to create an outfit that embodies a modern, functional glamour.

Metallic yarns

Although not a synthetic substance, metals are discussed in this chapter because, just as oil needed for synthetic fibre production is extracted from the ground, metals are also mined.

Today, aluminium or 'aluminized' yarns have generally replaced gold and silver, the metallic filaments being coated with transparent films to minimize tarnishing.

The most common fabrics in use today that utilize metallic threads are **lamé** and **brocade**.

The history of metallic fibres

The ancient world
Fabrics with golden threads have been produced for millennia. There are biblical, Ancient Greek and Roman references to these precious fabrics; mythological accounts of the Golden Fleece may have implied fabrics woven through with gold.

The ancient Greek city of Byzantium (today Istanbul) was a centre of production for these exotic fabrics, as were neighbouring areas of the Muslim world. Metallic fabrics made their way into Europe by way of trade with the Italian city-states of Genoa, Venice and Lucca, which in turn became the centres of medieval European weaving for 'cloth of gold' and greatly contributed to the Italian Renaissance. Yarns were produced using very thin gold or silver strips, which were spirally wrapped or spun around a core yarn of silk, linen or wool.

Samite
The most luxurious of all the cloths of gold was **samite**, a heavy silk fabric interwoven with gold and silver threads. It was so important to the economy of the Venetian Republic that the silk-weaving guilds distinguished samite weavers from all other silk weavers.

Samite was the fabric of kings, high-ranking nobility and the clergy; its high status included it among the luxuries forbidden to the urban middle classes under various sumptuary laws of the Middle Ages and Renaissance Europe.

Samite has also been discovered along the Silk Road and is especially associated with **Sassanid Persia**, the last pre-Islamic Persian Empire.

Zari
Cloth of gold should not be confused with gold embroidery-work. **Zari** (**Jari** or **Zardozi**) is gold and silver embroidery threadwork or supplementary weft-threads, which has its origins in Mogul India and Persia and is still in use today in India, Pakistan and parts of Iran. Threads of gold and silver were also used in weaving and supplementary threadwork in China and numerous other regions of South-east Asia, Sumatra and the Malaysian peninsula. The Dobeckmun Company (USA) is credited with the first production of modern metallic fibre, shortly after the end of World War II.

The thread of the story is LUREX

Lurex...black as shining jet, woven in silk by Rémond-Holland ...in a gown designed by Jean Dessès for Nanty Frocks. At Gunther Jaeckel, New York; Neiman-Marcus, Dallas. Lurex, non-tarnishing metallic yarn, made only by The Dobeckmun Company, Cleveland 1, Ohio...New York; 250 West 57 Street.

This advertisement from the 1950s brings the non-tarnishing metallic LUREX™ yarn to the forefront of the visual composition, marketing it as an elegant luxury fibre blended with silk. The manufacturers of both the yarn and the fabric are credited along with the Parisian designer, Jean Dessès.

Metallic fibre properties

Metallic fibres are composed of metal, plastic-coated metal, metal-coated plastic, or a core completely covered by metal. Yarns produced from **ductile** metals, such as gold, silver, **Nitinol** or copper, are thinly drawn, whereas brittle metals, such as nickel or aluminium, are **extruded** during a melt spinning process; alternatively, yarns can be bonded to a core yarn. Garments with metallic fibres should be dry-cleaned; the fibres are also at risk of melting if ironed at high temperatures.

LUREX™

LUREX™ is a British company known for its metallic and metallized yarns, which it has produced for more than fifty years. Its range includes yarns that when dyed have sparkle or iridescent effects. It also produces laminates that absorb light and then shine in the dark.

The company also produces retro-reflective yarns and yarns that have colour-change effects under ultraviolet (UV) lighting. Alternative producers of metallic yarns include Metlon in the United States and Samlung, a Hong Kong Chinese company that markets Suncoco metallic yarns.

Production of metallic fibres

There are several different ways to manufacture metallic yarns.

Lamination

The most popular production method is by lamination. This method seals a coloured aluminium film around a core fibre of acetate, nylon or polyester. The rolls of resulting fibre are first slit into narrower rolls and then **gang-slit** across their full width into micro-widths to form yarn, which is then wound onto spools ready for shipment to textile mills. Yarns may also be produced by vacuum-coating a synthetic film with metallic particles. Both processes minimize tarnishing from salts, chlorinated water or climatic conditions. Metallic yarns may also be made by twisting a strip of metal around a core natural, man-made or blended yarn to produce novelty-effect yarns.

Metallizing

An alternative manufacturing process is called metallizing. This process involves heating the metal until it vapourizes and then adding it to the polyester film. Although a less popular method, it produces a thinner, more flexible fibre, which is both more durable and more comfortable.

Finally, metal fibre may also be thinly drawn (shaved) from large-diameter gold, silver, Nitinol, stainless steel or nickel to form wire-wool bundles.

A striking bronze corset by Dutch designer Iris van Herpen is composed of intricate geometric layers of metallic-coated material. Van Herpen shows her couture collections in Paris and has pioneered innovative moulded garments created by a type of three-dimensional printing technology that allows the construction of slices of material from a polymer cured by laser technology.

Artificial fibres

The term 'artificial' is used to discuss man-made fibres that have their genesis in nature but require either chemical or bio-chemical intervention to be converted into fibre.

The first part of this chapter considers fabrics produced from plant **cellulose**, processed by either organic or non-organic means, while the latter part looks at fabrics that bridge the gap between fibre science and polymer science and may be broadly described as bio-engineered.

Cellulose

Fibres can be made from the naturally occurring polymer cellulose, which is present in all plants. Cellulose forms the basic structure of plant cell walls, making up a third of all plant matter: it is the most common organic compound on Earth.

Cellulose fibres can be either natural or regenerated and for technical accuracy are referred to as **cellulose I and II** respectively. Natural cellulose fibres look like the plant from which they have been manufactured, having undergone minimal processing (for example, cotton or linen). The second group of fibres and fabrics can be designated as either artificial or cellulosic, with equal effectiveness.

Wood and, to a lesser extent, cotton **linters** are the principal source of artificial cellulose fibres; the term 'artificial' implies that they cannot be converted into fibre without some form of chemical intervention.

(above) Trees are the principal source of cellulose for viscose production. These wood chips provide the feedstock for the chemical processing, which converts them into a viscous liquid ready for extrusion.

(right) The fine, silky shorter fibres that surround the seed of the cotton plant are known as cotton linters. They remain stuck to the seed after the cotton bolls have undergone the ginning process. As the staple length of the linter is typically less than 3 mm, making it difficult to spin, linters are used to make the artificial fibre cupro, as well as in the manufacture of paper.

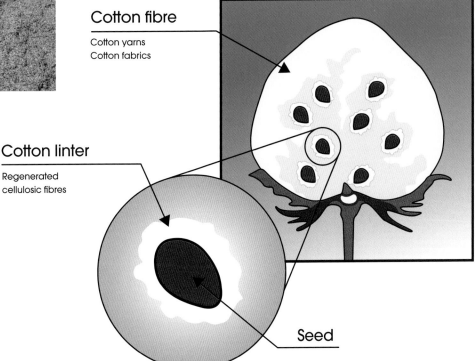

Cotton fibre

Cotton yarns
Cotton fabrics

Cotton linter

Regenerated
cellulosic fibres

Seed

213

The history of artificial cellulose fibre

Early experiments

The term 'cellulose' has been used since the late 1830s, when the French chemist **Anselme Payen** discovered the substance, having isolated it from plant matter and determined its chemical formula. Hermann Staudinger established in the 1920s that cellulose is a **linear polymer**, a polysaccharide.

The development of cellulose acetate during the 1860s was the earliest of the investigations into cellulose's practical application, although the first spun acetate yarn did not appear until the 1920s. It was 'artificial silk', also known as viscose or rayon, that was the first artificial fibre and had several incarnations from the end of the nineteenth century.

The development of artificial fibres could accurately be described as both a social commentary on the fickleness of fashion and the genesis of the mass fashion we all enjoy today.

Without these early experiments to find inexpensive alternatives to natural fibres, there might not have been the impetus or imperative to experiment further and develop the technically more sophisticated synthetic fabrics of the second half of the twentieth century.

New generation plant cellulose fibres

Early man-made fibres, termed artificial, focused on using regenerated plant (wood) cellulose. By the middle of the twentieth century the focus of attention, for man-made fibres, had turned to oil and the resulting synthetic fibres (polyester, polyamide nylon, aramids, acrylics, polyolefins, elastanes and synthetic rubbers). Today the tide is turning; current concerns regarding our dependency on oil and the increasing shortage of arable land has instigated developments that embrace a new breed of 'clean' man-made (artificial) fibres, which are made into technically sophisticated fabrics, often for a premium high-profile market sector. These new cellulose fabrics are no longer seen as substitutes for natural fabrics, but as desirable in their own right.

Ecological sustainability

In contrast to previous production, the new generation of cellulose artificial fibres is made from sustainable wood sources, usually grown in forests or on marginal land. There is no need for synthetic fertilizers or pesticides; irrigation is reliant purely on rainfall. The yield of cellulose from beech and eucalyptus is efficient; new processing methods have resulted in sustainable production methods with reduced carbon footprint and limited pollution – all of which help to protect the environmental.

Acetate and triacetate

Acetate is produced from wood pulp or **cotton linters**. It is a low-cost fibre that can be smooth and soft, with good draping qualities. It is favoured as a substitute for silk in such fabrics as satins, brocades and taffetas, and can be blended with cotton and silk. The noun acetate is made up of the stem 'acet', meaning acetic acid or vinegar, and the suffix '-ate'.

Cellulose acetate was developed as early as the mid-nineteenth century; the first yarns at the beginning of the twentieth.

Acetate and triacetate are separate chemical compounds. Acetate fibre is a modified (secondary) acetate; triacetate is a primary acetate, without a cellulose hydroxyl group and with a higher ratio of acetate to cellulose fibres.

Acetate fibres have been sold as Setilithe®, Plastiloid® and Bioceat® (Mazzucchelli); triacetate as Tricel™/Arnel® (Celanese Corporation).

214

This coloured scanning electron micrograph (SEM) shows the fibres of a sweat-absorbent fabric magnified 1000 times. The man-made fibres are covered with different coatings on the outside and inside. These prevent the cloth from becoming wet during wear, by absorbing the moisture and then wicking it away from the body.

The history of acetate fibre

Acetate was first introduced in the early years of the twentieth century, although initial developments date back to several sources in the 1860s.

In the Lombardy region of northern Italy, Santino Mazzucchelli and his son began experimenting on cellulose nitrate sheets with the intention of producing hair accessories for the fashion industry. Mazzucchelli 1849 SpA is today the largest producer of celluloid acetate and cellulose nitrate sheets worldwide; the company is most famous for eyewear frames and costume jewellery.

First commercial production

Swiss brothers **Camille and Henri Dreyfus** fully exploited the commercial production of acetate. Their first applications, in the 1910s, were cellulose diacetate as a non-flammable lacquer (called 'dope'), which they sold to the fledgling aviation industry; and plastic film, which they sold to the motion picture (celluloid) industries. By World War I they had opened chemical manufacturing plants in both the United States and Great Britain.

By the mid-1920s the two corporations had acquired elements of the name by which the international company is known today: the **Celanese Corporation.** The British factory produced the first commercial cellulose acetate yarn in the early 1920s, with the American company following later the same decade.

Although the acetate yarn was aimed at the stockings business, its greatest success in the early years was in the production of moiré fabric, as the thermoplastic quality of the fabric made watermark designs permanent.

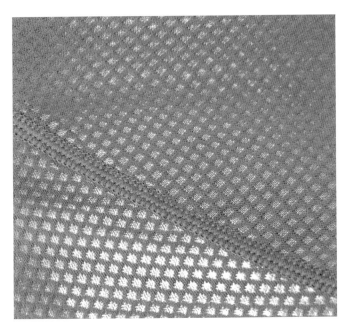

(left) Recent technologies in synthetic sports textiles have seen multiple properties embodied in a single fabric. High performance and constant innovation are demanded by the major sports brands, which work directly with mills to develop fabrics that will provide them with a competitive edge.

(above) A striking large-scale moiré effect resembling geological rock formations on a structured gown, shown in Moscow by Russian designer Valentin Yudashkin.

Demand for acetate fabrics, which could take permanent pleating, also increased during the 1920s following the vogue for pleated styles popularized by Chanel. DuPont began production of acetate fibres at the end of the 1920s.

Triacetate was developed in the 1950s and produced by Courtaulds and British Celanese as Tricel™ (Arnel® in the United States).

Mass appeal
Acetate was initially blended with both silk and cotton, bringing affordable fabrics to a wide audience, part of the democratization of fashion. Today, acetate is blended with many different fibres, both natural and man-made, to give a strong wrinkle-free fabric that dries easily and drapes well.

Acetate and triacetate properties

Acetate and triacetate fibres have a similar appearance, since both are comprised of cellulose acetate, albeit with differing ratios of acetate to cellulose. Triacetate is sometimes described as a primary acetate and acetate as a secondary acetate. The cellulose in triacetate is almost entirely acetylated and the fibre shows greater heat resistance. In nature, acetate is a common building block for **biosynthesis**.

Acetate and triacetate fabrics both have good draping characteristics; acetate has a softer touch than triacetate. Both have relatively poor abrasion resistance but show excellent resistance to **pilling**. The two fibres have similar strength when dry, but when wet, triacetate is stronger, with a higher melting point and better resistance to sunlight. Both fabrics dry quickly, have poor thermal retention but are hypoallergenic. Acetate wicks moisture and is therefore favoured as a lining, as it allows perspiration to dissipate quickly.

Acetate cannot be dyed with the traditional dyes used for cellulose fibres, and is therefore generally dyed using **disperse dyes** that give a high degree of lustre to the fabrics.

The main end uses for acetate filament yarns are as linings and other similar lightweight fabrics. Acetate is often used as an inexpensive silk-like replacement; there is little demand for acetate staple fibres.

Acetate and triacetate fibre production

Cellulose acetate is produced from wood pulp or **cotton linters**. Wood pulp is swollen and degenerated using **acetic acid** and then converted into purified cellulose acetate using a related chemical compound called acetic anhydride. If the process is allowed to complete, the result is triacetate; if it is partially hydrolized (treated with water) it becomes secondary cellulose acetate (cellulose diacetate).

The pure cellulose, in the form of resin flakes, is dissolved in **acetone** producing a viscous resin, which after filtering is ready for extrusion through spinnerets. As the acetate filaments emerge, the acetone solvent is evaporated in warm air; filaments are then stretched and wound onto cones or bobbins.

Both acetate and triacetate fibres are sometimes finished with surface saponification (application of sodium hydroxide), which removes the acetyl groups from the surface and leaves the fibres with a cellulose coating that is less likely to pick up electrostatic charge.

Environmental sustainability

Both acetate and triacetate are made from a renewable resource that can be composted or incinerated at the end of the garment's life cycle.

216

Viscose rayon

The invention of viscose rayon, the very first man-made fibre, is a testament to the desirability of the fibre that it sought to copy: silk.

The high price of silk has historically confined it to niche markets, or for special occasion use. Low-cost 'art silk' enabled a more democratic experience of the silky **drape** and glamour of its natural counterpart throughout the first half of the twentieth century, and is arguably the most popular cellulose fabric to date.

In continental Europe it is known as viscose, in Great Britain it may be referred to as viscose or viscose rayon, and in the United States the preferred popular term is rayon. The designation 'rayon' was once applied to all cellulose fibres including acetate; however, in the early 1950s it was redefined and now it refers only to fibres made from regenerated cellulose that are produced by the viscose process, which excludes acetate.

The history of viscose rayon

Early experiments
There is a long list of names associated with the invention of viscose fibre, as it appeared in various guises before emerging in its current form. **Georges Audemars**, a Swiss chemist, is credited with inventing the first artificial silk in the 1850s. His technique (dipping a needle into a pulp and rubber mix) was too slow and crude for commercial use, but it was the genesis of something revolutionary.

French aristocrat and industrial chemist Hilaire Bernigaud, comte de Chardonnet, took up the gauntlet, creating fibres from a nitrocellulose solution extruded through spinnerets and hardened in air jets. By the mid 1880s he had patented a cellulose-based artificial silk that he named **Chardonnet silk**. While a beautiful fabric, it was very flammable and had to be removed from the market.

Cuprammonium rayon
Around the same time as Chardonnet submitted his patent, another Frenchman, Louis-Henri Despeissis, patented the process to produce fibres from dissolving cellulose in a solution of copper salts and ammonia. His work was based on discoveries by Eduard Schweizer in the 1850s. Cuprammonium rayon went into production in the early years of the twentieth century, as Bemberg silk.

217

One-shouldered violet viscose crêpe de chine knotted dress by New York brand A Détacher exploits the supple drape and silk-like characteristics of rayon viscose to create a sophisticated and sensuous form.

Modern commercial viscose rayon

In the 1890s a group of British inventors (Charles Cross, Edward Bevan and Clayton Beadle) patented a commercially viable method of producing artificial silk.

Manufacture began in England at silk firm Courtaulds around the turn of the twentieth century.

Large-scale commercial production was launched in the United States in the 1910s. There, the fabric was first referred to as artificial silk, followed by the unpopular name of glos; but by the mid-1920s the term rayon had been officially adopted. In French rayon means ray or beam of light, which is an evocative description of the fabric's visual appearance. By contrast, the European designation, viscose, is more pragmatic, being descriptive of the processing method used to produce the fibre: production of a highly viscous solution.

Mid-century developments

During the 1940s the physical properties of rayon were changed to produce **high-tenacity rayon (HTR)**, which is extremely strong and used for industrial purposes. Further developments in the 1950s resulted in the production of **high-wet-modulus rayon (HWM)**, which has greater strength when wet, allowing it to be machine-washed.

Viscose rayon properties

Viscose rayon is a man-made artificial fibre also described as a semi-synthetic; it is produced from regenerated cellulose usually obtained from wood but, depending on processing technique, also from cotton linters (short fibres). It shares some properties with its base organic materials.

Viscose is absorbent and has a soft and smooth touch, but lacks insulative properties. In both yarn and fabric form, it dyes well, resulting in rich, bright colours that are perfect alternatives to silk and linings, especially for tailoring and outerwear. Rayon fibres are naturally bright, but can be given a matte finish with the addition of a delustring agent during dyeing. Traditional viscose rayon is not especially durable, losing up to half its strength when wet, and therefore it is best dry-cleaned; it has very low elastic recovery. Fabrics are distinguished by their lengthwise (warp) lines, referred to as **striations**.

Production of viscose rayon

The traditional method of production uses cellulose from both wood and **lignin**, while newer methods need lignin-free cellulose as a starting point.

Chemistry

Processed cellulose (ground from wood pulp) is dissolved in sodium hydroxide (caustic soda). Excess liquid is removed by passing it through rollers. The resulting pulp is shredded, creating a crumbly substance called white crumb, which is then exposed to oxygen, then reacted with carbon disulphide – a process known as **xanthation**. The result of this process is yellow crumb (cellulose xanthate). Caustic soda is again used to dissolve the substance, which in turn produces a viscous yellow solution: viscose (sodium cellulose xanthate).

Post-formation

After ripening, viscose is filtered to remove any undissolved particles, and air bubbles are removed. The viscose solution is finally extruded through a spinneret into sulphuric acid to form rayon filaments, which are drawn to straighten the fibres and then washed to remove chemical residues. If staple fibres are required, the filaments are cut to determined lengths.

Production of cuprammonium rayon

Production of cuprammonium rayon shares certain similarities with viscose, however the cellulose is mixed with copper and ammonia for processing. If cotton linters are used, it is referred to as cupro and has the greatest similarity to silk (see page 152).

Ecological sustainability

Viscose rayon production and use is in decline, in part because of environmental concerns. Production processes release carbon disulphide into the atmosphere and salt into water supplies. Cuprammonium rayon is even less environmentally friendly and is no longer produced in the United States. Korean researchers claim that rayon decays more easily than cotton; Korea and India are both important producers of rayon fabric. Rayon production has been linked to the destruction of rainforests, although production is possible from sustainable plantations. Attention is turning to a new generation of renewable and eco-friendly alternatives, such as lyocell (see page 220).

Striking red suit made from a coated cotton and rayon pile fabric by Romanian designer Dinu Bodiciu, from his 2011 London College of Fashion graduate show.

Viscose rayon

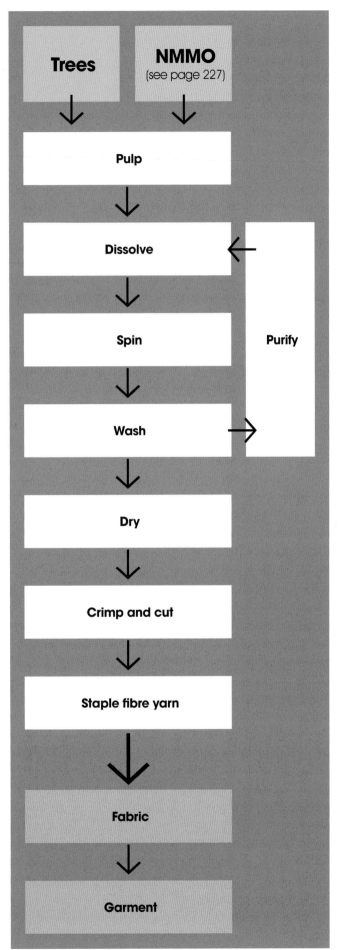

Lyocell

Lyocell is a cellulose fibre made from wood pulp.

In broad terms, lyocell can be described as a new generation viscose rayon.

In the United States the fibre has been given its own (rayon) sub-category, defined as 'cellulose fabric obtained by an organic solvent spinning process' *(U.S. Federal Trade Commission).* 'Solvent' here implies the agent into which the fibre-forming substance is dissolved as part of the spinning process (see polymers and polymerization, page 186).

    The process by which the fibre is produced is said to be eco-friendly; the raw materials used are from sustainable sources. The finished fabric has an advantage over traditional rayon in that it is less prone to shrink and is far stronger.

The history of lyocell fibres

TENCEL®, Modal® and Seacell® yarns and fabrics are all produced under the lyocell umbrella process by the Austrian company Lenzing AG. Each fabric has its own characteristics, but for the most part lyocell fibres share the same eco credentials and sustainable manufacturing processes.

In the early 1940s British chemists were among the first to experiment with processing seaweed into fibre. Today, Lenzing produces Seacell® fibres and yarns that have been developed by the German company smartfiber AG (Smartcel™ fibres).

Modal® was first produced commercially by Lenzing during the 1960s and is considered a second-generation HWM rayon. Initial production methods used harsh chemicals, but gradual improvements by the manufacturer in recovering recyclables during the production process and alternative methods of bleaching have improved its sustainability credentials.

TENCEL® was developed by British firm Courtaulds during the 1980s. Chemists found a method of dissolving cellulose directly, in a non-toxic and recyclable solvent, as an alternative to the harsh chemicals used to produce viscose rayon. Lenzig purchased the TENCEL® division from Courtaulds and launched the fibre during the early 1990s.

(left) Supple TENCEL® chambray tunic dress by G-Star RAW. © G-Star RAW C.V.

(above) Eucalyptus trees grow rapidly and thrive on poor-quality land, needing no irrigation or pesticide control. The wood from these trees is the raw material feedstock for the production of TENCEL®, which uses FSC (Forest Stewardship Council) certified trees.

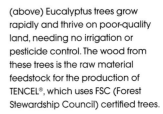

221

Properties of lyocell fibres

The fabrics have a highly crystalline structure continuously dispersed along the fibre axis. This gives good tensile strength, that can match that of polyester while sharing cotton-like qualities; it has good volume and a soft touch. Long filament fibres are used to manufacture silk-like yarns, and so the finished fabrics have a good lustre and drape well. Untreated, the fabric is prone to pilling and has a natural reluctance to absorb dye.

TENCEL®

Lyocell is better known by the brand name TENCEL®. The fibre is made from eucalyptus, an evergreen plant that grows to a height of up to 40 metres (131 feet). Eucalyptus grows quickly and does not require artificial irrigation, use of pesticides or gene manipulation. It is cost-effective, providing a good yield ratio of cellulose per acre of land; the trees grown for TENCEL® production are from sustainably managed plantations.

Fabric processing is closed-loop but does require a substantial amount of energy. Eucalyptus trees are shipped from South Africa to Europe, which has carbon footprint implications. The processes used to dye or texture lyocell sometimes include toxic chemicals, although this is dependent on the **converter**.

Applications

There are several versions of the fibre, one of which features **chitosan**, which is derived from the **chitin** found in crab shells (treated with alkali sodium hydroxide). Chitin is the second most abundant natural polymer and, if of medical grade, has no allergenic potential. In fabrics such as Lenzing TENCEL® C, chitosan is marketed as providing a cell-regenerating effect, creating what the company calls 'pure cosmetics from textiles'. The fibre is well-suited for lingerie and bedlinen as it inhibits bacterial growth and is anti-inflammatory.

TENCEL® is also used within the automotive sector, in carpets, seat covers and as a fibrous powder to reinforce injection-moulded components. It is also available as a 50–50 blend with either standard or organic cotton.

(left) Abundant supplies of post-consumer waste from crab, lobster and prawn shells are the unlikely raw material for new soft and drapeable fabrics. The chitin that makes up the shells is compatible with cellulose, with which it is combined in a closed-loop process similar to making viscose.

(above) 'Origami' skirt and top by Céline Faizant in 55 per cent TENCEL® and 45 per cent hemp. The transparent fabric of the 'Ori' shirt is 100 per cent organic cotton.

(above) The top of this outfit by Ada Zanditon is organic cotton, while the trousers are made from crustacean fibre. This new development is a mix of TENCEL® and processed waste from the food industry, which when combined produce a strong and durable jersey that has natural antibacterial, hypoallergenic and anti-static properties. These properties are inherent in the crustacean fibre, and are usually applied as a finishing treatment to other fabrics. Mario Boselli produces this naturally dyed and woven fabric in Italy. It is also completely biodegradable.

223

Lenzing Modal®

Modal® is processed from beech trees, which are thought to be unbeatable when it comes to improving soil quality. Beech is extremely resistant to pests and environmental damage. Lenzing's Austrian beech groves are sustainable and need no artificial irrigation; the wood is not transported over long distances. Processing is said to be carbon neutral, and any chemical used is recovered and recycled; bleaching today is done through oxygen technology. The fabric is biodegradable. Their inherent softness means that Modal® fabrics retain their touch after repeated washes. Particularly well suited for blending with cotton (as both have similar properties), Modal® is seen in lingerie, sleepwear and socks.

Applications

There are several varieties of the fibre, including Lenzing Modal® LOFT, which has great loft (fibre thickness) and is ideal for towels. ProModal® is a combination of Modal® and TENCEL®, offering both softness and performance.

Spun-dyed Modal® is dyed during processing, the pigment (colour) being embedded directly into the fibre matrix. This eliminates the need for the yarns or fabrics to be dyed later by a 'third party' converter, saving water and energy and reducing the possibility of harsh chemicals being used.

(above) Outfit by Ada Zanditon. This extreme silhouette employs the tactile drape of this finely gathered TENCEL® jersey by Lenzing to form a 'skin' over the underlying boned structure of the outfit.

Seacell®

Seacell® is made from seaweed and cellulose fibre, using a type of lyocell process. The cellulose-based fibre acts as the carrier ('functioning substrate') for active ingredient seaweed's health-promoting properties. The porous structure of seaweed fibres allows an active exchange between body and garment; in short, the fabric absorbs what the body expels, while the skin absorbs the beneficial vitamins and mineral-rich elements of the seaweed (approximately 5 per cent of fabric composition, locked permanently into the fibre and still in evidence after numerous washings). The seaweed used is the North Atlantic brown seaweed *Ascophyllum nodosum*, also known as Norwegian kelp and knotted wrack.

Applications

Fabrics are soft and smooth and breathe, offering the most benefit when worn next to the body: Seacell® fabrics are ideal for intimate apparel and bedding.

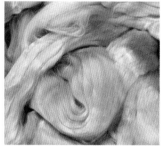

(above) Brown kelp is an abundant and renewable source of alginate, a natural biopolymer and polysaccharide, which forms the raw material for recent alternative fibre development Seacell®. It is biodegradable and nutrient-rich and is also said to possess inherent antibacterial properties.

(above) Skeins of silky Seacell® fibre 'tops' ready for spinning.

(right) Ensemble by German designer Christine Zillich for The Seaweed Fashion Project's 'Flow' collection, inspired by the movement and colours of the ocean. The top and skirt are made from Seacell® single jersey, and both printing and fabric are GOTS (Global Organic Textile Standard) certified. The knit cardigan is a Seacell®-and-cotton-blend single jersey.

225

'"It is a question of discipline" the little prince said to me later on. "When you've finished your own toilet in the morning, then it is time to attend to the toilet of your planet, just so, with the greatest care."' Antoine de Saint Exupéry, *Le Petit Prince*. Lingerie made from discarded pine branches by French brand g=9.8.

The raw material for the production of TENCEL® is wood harvested from rapidly renewable FSC certified eucalyptus trees, which are chipped and then pulped and broken down with solvents, which are then recovered for reuse in a closed-loop process. The fibres are extruded and then spun. The final image shows the finished fabric, a soft chambray with a light sheen and good drape.

226

Lyocell processing

Eucalyptus trees

Pulped wood TENCEL® sheets

Balls of TENCEL® fibres

Dyed TENCEL® fibres

Carded and spun fibres

Finished woven fabric

Production of lyocell fibres

Small chips around 25 by 25 millimetres (1 square inch) are cut from hardwood logs. These are chemically dissolved to remove the lignin and to soften sufficiently for mechanical milling. A wet papery pulp is produced, which can then be bleached if required, dried as sheets and rolled onto spools.

The rolls of dried pulp are broken up and dissolved in an organic compound, N-methylmorpholine-N-oxide (NMMO) at high temperature and pressure, producing the filtered cellulose solution. The solution is pumped through spinnerets into an organic compound bath of diluted amine oxide to set the strands, which are at this stage referred to as dope. The fibres are washed and dried (remaining water residue is evaporated). The strands are often finished with lubricants such as silicone or soap as appropriate to the end use. The tow (bundle) is crimped to compress the fibre for added texture and bulk, and finally the fibres are mechanically carded, cut and baled for shipment to fabric mills.

Lyocell can be spun with cotton or wool.

Ecological sustainability

Lyocell is generally regarded as an eco-friendly fabric: it derives from renewable sources and is manufactured in a closed-loop system that recycles almost all the chemicals used. The raw material utilizes less land and water than is needed for comparable materials; when disposed of appropriately, it is fully biodegradable. There is, however, a debate over the amount of energy used in heating, milling and drying, and over the fact that some solvents may have a petrochemical origin. The fibre's natural reluctance to absorb dye and its tendency to **fibrillate** (pill) when wet have also been debated, as both are sometimes remedied by using harsh chemicals; this, of course, is dependent on the manufacturer of the end fabric.

Biopolymer fibres

Biotechnology could be defined as making use of organisms and their components to create industrial products and processes. The European Federation of Biotechnology has defined it as 'integrated use of biochemistry, microbiology and chemical engineering in order to achieve the technological application of the capacities of microbes and cultured tissue cells'.

Research in the textile sector has centred on several issues, which include improving and expanding plant varieties used for fibre production and their specific properties; replacing harsh energy-inefficient chemicals with natural enzymes; and friendlier processing treatments for finishing fabrics as well as better effluent management.

Adoption of biotechnology can cut processing costs and helps towards a cleaner environment. New applications will one day form the basis of new commercial intelligent fabrics – for example, fabrics that literally eat odours by using genetically engineered bacteria, and self-cleaning fabrics that repel dirt.

Azlon is a group of man-made fibres made from regenerated naturally occurring proteins, such as those found in corn, soya and milk.

227

Corn fibre

Plentiful supplies of corn (also known as maize) grown in the heartlands of the United States are now a source of commercially viable man-made fibres obtained from 100 per cent annually renewable resources.

PLA (polylactic acid) fibre can be derived from any naturally derived sugars. It is mostly produced from corn but can also come from beets.

Cargill–Dow-branded PLA resin NatureWorks® is sold as Ingeo™ fibre. Originally an American development, Ingeo™ is now a joint venture with a Japanese company. Other fibres, yarns and fabrics produced from or containing corn sucrose include Biophyl™ from Advansa (Germany), Lactron® and Ecodear® from Kanebo and Toray respectively (Japan), and Sorona® from DuPont.

The history of corn fibre

Corn fibres were first developed during the 1940s at the USDA Northern Regional Research Laboratory. Corn proteins were dissolved in alkali, extruded through spinnerets and cured with formaldehyde. Production was discontinued in the 1950s owing to the popularity of high-performance synthetic fibres.

The possibility of producing fibre from corn was revisited in the 1990s by Dow Chemical Company and agricultural commodities company Cargill. This second generation of corn fibre is processed from sugars and carbon in corn to create the polymer (poly)lactic acid. The new fibre designation PLA was assigned in 2002 by the Federal Trade Commission, which ruled that while technically a type of polyester (created from repeating units linked by esters), the fibre exhibits significant differences from the generally understood existing definition.

Corn fibre properties

The fibre is high in strength and stability, has low flammability, is more resistant to ultraviolet (UV) light and is more hydrophilic (attracting water) than common synthetics. Once blended with cotton or wool, it forms a fabric that is light and wicks moisture away from the skin. Corn fibre is spun into yarn for woven or knitted textiles. Diesel is one of several fashion companies using Ingeo™ yarns.

Maize, or corn, is a naturally renewable raw material that grows plentifully in the United States. The natural sugars stored in the corn provide the polylactic acid for a range of recent branded bio-synthetic fibre developments.

Corn fibre production

By means of photosynthesis, the starch naturally stored in corn is broken down and converted into dextrose sugar. The carbon and other elements of these natural sugars are used to make a **biopolymer** by means of fermentation and separation to produce the lactic acid. The water is then removed and the resulting PLA resin is extruded into high-performance fibre. Fabrics have a fluid drape and soft touch with excellent stretch and recovery. They are ideal for casual- and workwear because they are low-maintenance and easy to care for.

Ecological sustainability

Producing fibre from corn is a low-cost process involving little fossil fuel; it is not derived from petrochemicals; and it uses abundantly available raw material. A lower level of energy is required than in the manufacture of other artificial fibres, producing significantly fewer greenhouse gas emissions. Additional energy reductions are achieved during dyeing and finishing fabrics through lower temperatures and shorter processing times. Garments made from corn fibre, once discarded, can be returned to the earth, degrading into natural compost with the passage of time. However, there is concern that an increasing amount of the corn cultivated in the United States is genetically modified.

(left) Processed cellulose fibres, known as 'tops', ready for the spinning stage.

(above) Scandinavian designer Maxjenny exploits the light, drapeable qualities of Ingeo™ fabric in this large-scale-print dress. The designer's approach to pattern cutting is inspired by a Zero Waste philosophy, intended to reduce the use of seams, and the collection reflects a strong environmental commitment through design innovation, wearability and function.

Soya fibre

It is believed that soy (or soya) was first harvested in China more than 5,000 years ago.

The soya bean was widely grown throughout Asia and remains a major crop in China, Japan and Korea, where it is a common food source; cultivation has spread worldwide since the nineteenth century. It was introduced into the United States almost by accident in the early 1800s when Yankee clippers, trading with China, often used soya beans as inexpensive ballast. Today the United States is the largest producer of soya beans. Branded soya fibres include SOYSILK®.

The history of soya fibre

Soya fibre was first pioneered by Henry Ford in the mid-1930s and referred to as soy wool. Chemists Robert Boyer and Frank Calvert were employed by the automobile manufacturer to produce an artificial silk, which resulted in the fibre known as Azlon. As with most early bioengineered fibres, its popularity was overtaken during the 1950s by synthetics. Modern methods of production, using soya bean proteins and polyvinyl alcohol, were developed at the turn of the twenty-first century by Guanqi Li at the Huakang R&D Centre in China. Today garments made of soya fibre tend to be targeted at a mid-market consumer, however as demand increases it should become inexpensive to produce.

Soya beans are an abundant and renewable source of the protein biopolymers that are synthesized to produce recent developments in fully biodegradable fibres.

Processed cellulose fibre.

Soya fibre.

Processed soya fibre, referred to as 'tops', ready for the spinning stage.

Soya fibre properties

Soya is a renewable botanic **protein fibre** consisting of 16 amino acids that are considered beneficial when worn next to the skin. Clothing made of soya is moisture absorbing, and the structure allows good ventilation. The fabric drapes well and is often considered to be as smooth as cashmere, while its lustre can resemble that of silk. Fibres can hold dye and repel ultraviolet (UV) better than cotton or silk. It is also believed to synthesize the qualities of natural fibres with the physical properties of synthetics.

Soya fibre production

Soya bean protein fibre is an advanced textile fibre produced by bioengineering technology from soybean 'cake'; the protein is distilled from the cake and refined. Through various processes, and by the use of auxiliary agents and biological enzymes, the structure of the protein changes into a confected substance that can then be extruded into fibre by means of a wet spinning process. Finally the fibre is stabilized and cut into short staples.

Environmental sustainability

Soya fibre is often marketed as the green fibre of the twenty-first century that is completely biodegradable. The manufacturing process does not pollute, because the auxiliary agents used in producing the fibre are non-poisonous. The residue that remains after the protein has been extracted may be used as animal feed. However, in many countries soy production is non-organic and genetically modified. This means that crops may be treated with chemicals to enhance production and deter weeds, and this is believed to affect the welfare of neighbouring livestock.

Soya fabric is softer and more durable than cotton, but is quicker drying. It has similar thermal qualities to wool and its touch is often likened to that of silk or cashmere. Its inherent absorbency and breathability make it the ideal fabric for this retro-inspired jersey underwear range by Soyshorts™.

Milk fibre (casein)

Milk proteins have been extracted since Ancient Egyptian times. Casein paint, similar to tempera, was used extensively until the advent of acrylic in the 1960s.

Research into milk fibre production dates back to the 1930s in both Italy and the United States, and resulted in fibre production later in the decade.

Lanatil was the first Italian fibre patented, followed by the American brand Aralac. During the 1940s milk fibre was used as a wool substitute, but it fell victim to the rise of the low-price synthetics marketed during the 1950s. Early milk fibre suffered from weaknesses when introduced to water; the introduction of acrylic and blends has produced stronger contemporary fibres. Japanese company Toyobo produced Chinon® from 30 per cent casein and 70 per cent acrylonitrile in the 1960s.

Branded milk fibre yarns include Milkofil®, made from organic milk; Milkotton, a cotton and milk protein fibre; Milkwood (Lenpur®), a milk and wood cellulose; and QMilch®, produced from waste milk, which is an exceptionally smooth fibre more akin to silk than to wool.

Milk fibre properties

Milk protein fabrics have certain wool-like characteristics, and so the preferred fibres for blending are wool and cashmere. Fabrics breathe, capture and dissipate moisture, supposedly, as efficiently as wool.

Milk fibre production

The main component of milk fibre is casein, a type of protein found mainly in cow's milk; it is most often combined with acrylonitrile, the chemical compound used to make acrylic.

The casein (or protein) is first dissolved in water and alkali. The fibre-forming substance is extruded through a spinneret; the resulting viscous solution is then immersed in an acid bath to neutralize the alkali, and additional solutions are used to treat the fibre. Finally, the fibre is stretched to align the molecules for added strength. The process is similar to those for producing other viscose fibres.

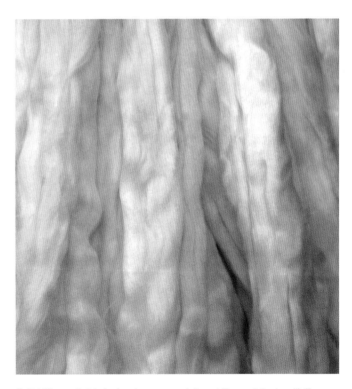

(left) Milk unsuitable for food production provides the raw material for recent milk fibre developments. The casein is extracted from the milk and processed to form a regenerated protein fibre.

(above) The proteins in milk fibre have characteristics similar to those of animal hair fibres, and fabrics made from it behave much like wool. The fibres are fluffy and springy and work well in blends with wool, cashmere and Lenpur™.

232

Castor oil fibre

The castor oil plant, *Ricinus communis*, is a non-GM crop that grows in semi-arid regions and needs minimal irrigation. Oil is extracted from the castor bean (seed for the sake of botanic accuracy), which contains a toxic but naturally occurring protein called ricin. Once the toxins have been neutralized by heating, the viscous substance is processed in much the same way as other man-made fibres. The resultant fibre is marketed as a non-fossil fuel alternative to polyester, with which it shares many characteristics. Greenfil®, produced by Sofila and Arkema, is a high-performance **bacteriostatic** fibre with good thermo-regulating properties ideal for knitted fabric applications, especially for sportswear. It has dimensional stability and is abrasion resistant.

(above) The castor bean plant is a non-food crop source of biopolymers (part biomass, part conventional polyester) produced through 'hybrid' engineering. Greenfil® castor-oil-based yarn is five to ten times more durable than conventional nylon, making it ideal for technical clothing.

(above) This elegant milk fibre gown by Nepalese London College of Fashion graduate Sanyukta Shrestha references vintage lingerie and exploits the delicate draping characteristics of this fabric, which also has inherent antibacterial and humectant qualities.

(right) Shoe mould and three-dimensional sketch of a biodegradable polymer shoe designed by 01M. An injection technique allows varied thicknesses for the shoe body, heel and sole, enabling a skintight fit and a higher level of comfort. The inspiration for the shoe comes from Amazon tribespeople, who painted their soles with natural latex from the Hevea rubber tree (*H. brasiliensis*), protecting their feet during the rainy season.

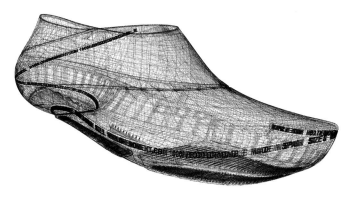

Useful
information

235

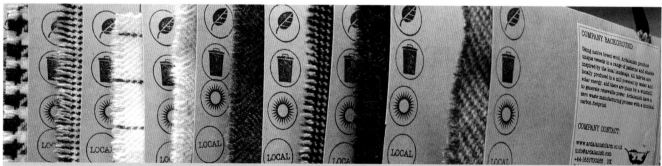

Fabric and the fashion industry

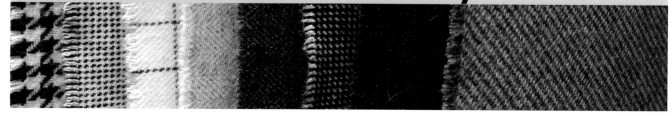

Working with fabrics

The selection of fabric is fundamental to the creative and commercial viability of a collection and should realistically precede any design development work. Fabric is the medium that expresses two of the essential ingredients of fashion design – colour and tactile appeal. Both are key considerations at the conceptual stage of designing and planning a collection.

A mood board is usually compiled at this stage to consolidate a variety of inspirational sources, and to communicate a concept or theme; it helps to focus direction and to make objective and strategic design decisions. This is especially important when working as part of a team.

Sourcing fabrics

Trade fairs

These are shows or fairs where international fabric mills come together to showcase all their new fabric designs and developments for the forthcoming season. Generally designers and buyers will request samples, which are then forwarded for sampling, prior to ordering bulk fabric for production.

Mills

Fabric is woven or knitted in a textile mill. Mills often tend to specialize in specific types of fabric, or are known for their expertise with certain processes. Popular fabrics and colours are usually held in stock, while others are made to order and will need to meet production minimums. These vary depending on fibre type, fabric construction and finish. For example, screen-printed silk from a mill in Como, Italy, may only require a 50m (164-ft) minimum while a yarn-dyed cotton from a mill in China may require a 1,000m (3,280-ft) minimum.

Agents

An **agent** is a 'middle' person or company that represents the interests of a fabric mill or mills. Agencies enable mills to show their fabric collections to designers and buyers internationally.

The fabrics are shown on **header cards** which consist of a large swatch of fabric used as a feeler for touch and drape, a range of colour options and all the information regarding construction and composition. Agents do not carry stock but help organize the ordering and delivery of sample lengths and eventual production.

Importers and stock houses

These are fabric wholesale companies that buy fabrics from domestic and foreign mills in large quantities and then sell the fabric on, usually without any minimum requirements.

Converters

Converters buy large volumes of greige piece goods (unfinished fabrics) directly from the mills, then dye, print and finish the fabric into smaller quantities, according to market trends. They work closely with designers and manufacturers to allow a quick response to trends in colour and print, without the commitment required from large fabric minimums.

Jobbers

Jobbers specialize in buying stock fabrics from mills or garment manufacturers that are in excess of their requirements. They sell these fabrics at competitive prices; it is unlikely that, once sold, the fabric can be repeated.

Internet

The Internet offers a quick way to source fabrics on both a domestic and a global scale. It is particularly useful if fabrics are needed midway through a season with no trade fairs available. The disadvantage is that you are not able to feel the quality of the fabrics, or to compare suppliers, qualities and prices at a single venue. This method of sourcing is best suited to a designer or brand that knows exactly what fabric is required, rather than a designer looking for inspiration.

The Première Vision fabric trade show (top) takes place in Paris. A bi-annual exhibition of textiles from mills all over the world, in addition to showcasing fabrics it also provides fashion industry players with a 'first view' of future trends in colour and texture. The Future Fabrics Expo (middle and bottom), presented by the Sustainable Angle, is a smaller, specialized textile fair that promotes the sustainability credentials of fabrics.

Sourcing considerations

Fabric type

Sourcing fabrics requires an informed sensitivity to the different personalities that fabrics possess, coupled with an instinctive creative approach. Consideration of the suitability of different fibre types for specific products underpins effective sourcing.

To work with the inherent nature and properties of the fabric, manipulate a large piece of cloth and drape it; observe how it relates to the body and consider how it feels next to the skin. It may be stiff, structured and hold pleats crisply, or it may be dense, fluffy and sculptural, or conversely have a tactile and supple drape that clings to the body. The structure and tightness of the weave is important as it will affect the handle and drape, the way the fabric behaves and its potential durability.

Purpose and market

Another important aspect is the suitability of the chosen fabric for its intended purpose. The lifestyle of the **target consumer** needs to be taken into consideration to identify how the products will be used, laundered and the expected level of wear and tear. Fabrics from reputable mills are usually pre-tested for an identified range of uses. Alternatively fabrics can be sent for independent testing to specialist laboratories. This is especially useful for high-performance clothing.

Useful fabric sampling vocabulary

Colour-ways alternative fabric colour options.

Drape the way the fabric hangs and moves.

Dye lot minimum meterage required to dye to a specific colour.

Handle/Touch describes the characteristics of a fabric eg soft, firm etc.

Lead times the length of time it takes to receive the fabric (usually applies to bulk fabric).

Minimums minimum meterage required to place an order to produce a fabric.

Print runs minimum meterage required to print a design or colour.

Sample colour for sampling purposes; not all colour options may be available, sample colour implies the available colour.

Sample lengths small meterage required to make a prototype sample.

Swatches small fabric pieces used in pre-selecting a fabric range.

It is also important that the selected fabrics reflect the brand image and the target consumer's perception of the brand. Certain consumers respond to specific types of fabrics positively. For example, natural fibres may give added value, or high-tech performance fibres may provide a unique selling point for certain categories of products.

Sustainable considerations

The geographic origin of the fibre and processing of the fabric may also be relevant considerations. The carbon footprint and ethical and fair-trade issues regarding manufacture may make certain choices inappropriate. How a fabric needs to be looked after throughout its life cycle and, ultimately, how it will be disposed of are growing concerns that are impacting on all levels of the market. Awareness of these issues is on the rise, as shown by the recent founding of the Sustainable Apparel Coalition, which includes over 80 powerful global brands (including Marks & Spencer, Nike, PUMA, Gap, H&M and Burberry) representing more than a third of the world's apparel production, as well as government, educational and non-profit organizations.

Cost, sizing and fabric direction

Pricing awareness is vital in today's competitive market, and the price per metre or yard needs to consider the width of the fabric in the costing.

The standard widths for different fabric types have until recently been 36, 45 or 60 in wide (90, 112 and 150 cm), with some specialist fabrics as narrow as 18 in or as wide as 150 in (45 or 375 cm). Today most fabrics are made to a standard 60 in (150 cm) wide, which is a more cost-effective width for a **lay planning** (economical arrangement of garment pattern pieces onto the fabric) and also best suited for general factory production.

Further cost considerations when selecting fabrics include **one-** and **two-way** directional fabrics and fabric matching.

A one-directional fabric implies that the design (printed or woven) needs to be cut in a single direction. Alternatively, a one-directional fabric may imply that it has a pile or raised surface and that the fabric must be cut with all garment pattern pieces following the same direction. One-directional fabrics are less cost effective than two-way fabrics. Fabric matching further increases fabric usage or costing.

Testing

Fabrics from reputable mills will have been pre-tested with all the relevant information available for the buyer, designer or merchandiser. Alternatively fabrics may be sent for testing to independent laboratories, which is particularly useful for performance clothing.

Standards

Transparent information and the assurance of recognized certifications can be useful in evaluating the environmental and social impact of fashion products. The 12 principles outlined in the Green Chemistry section (page 244) take into consideration the impact of material production at a chemical level, and the most widely recognized sustainable certifications, which assure various aspects of more responsible production, are compiled in the certifications chart (overleaf). Some of the certifications are consumer-facing (such as the FAIRTRADE mark), and are used almost as a 'brand' in their own right, as a mark of integrity and added value. Others, such as the Better Cotton Initiative, actively unite those involved in fibre production into a global community. Some of these standards are owned by umbrella organizations that strive to inspire the acceleration of sustainable practices throughout the textile value chain; for example, Textile Exchange (formerly Organic Exchange), owners of the Organic Exchange and the Global Recycling Standard, focuses on minimizing the harmful impact of the global textile industry, and maximizing its positive effects.

Buyers sourcing denim at The Future Fabrics Expo in London. The header cards at the top of the fabric hangers provide detailed information about the fabric, such as fibre content, weave, weight and fabric width, as well as certifications and information about the sustainability credentials of the fibre and its processing.

Fibre designation codes

Animal

SE Silk
WG Vicuña
WO Wool
WV Virgin fleece wool
WP Alpaca wool
WL Llama wool
WS Cashmere
WM Mohair wool
WA Angora wool
WK Camel hair
YK Yak hair

Plant

AB Abacá
BF Bamboo fibre
CO Cotton
CU/CUP Cupro
HA Hemp
JU Jute
LI Flax/Linen
RA Ramie

Man-made

AC/CA Acetate
AR Aramid
CLY Lyocell
CMD/MO Modal
CR Neoprene
CTA/CA Triacetate
EL/EA Elastane/Elastomer/Rubber
LY Lycra
MAC/MA Modacrylic
ME Metallic/Lurex
MTF Metal
NY Nylon
PAN/PC Acrylic
PA Polyamide (Nylon)
PES/PL Polyester
PE Polyethylene (olefin fibres)
PET Polyethylene terephthalate
PLA Polylactide
    (usually corn fibres)

PP Polypropylene (olefin fibres)
PR Protein
PTT Polytrimethylene terephthalate
PU Polyurethane
PUR Polyurea
SPF Soya protein fibres
VI/CV Viscose

Other

AF Other fibres
TR Unspecified

Certifications

Standard	Covers	Products
BCI Better Cotton Initiative	Social, economic and environmental aspects of cotton production.	The Better Cotton Initiative (BCI) brings together producers, ginners, mills, traders, manufacturers, retailers, brands and civil society organizations in a unique global community committed to developing Better Cotton as a sustainable mainstream commodity.
bluesign®	Water effluent, air emissions, energy consumption, worker safety, consumer safety, RSL/chemical residues, responsible use of resources.	The bluesign® system uses 'Input Stream Management' process to assess textile products, from fibres and yarns to fabrics and final products; components for textile products, chemicals and dyestuffs, and textile processing techniques.
cradletocradle®	Water effluent, air emissions, energy consumption, worker safety, consumer safety, social criteria, RSL/chemical residues, responsible water use.	Materials, sub-assemblies and finished products.
FAIRTRADE® Certified Cotton	Worker safety, social criteria, environmental impact.	Certifies producer organizations and traders, helping them to capitalize on market opportunities.
GLOBAL ORGANIC TEXTILE STANDARD · GOTS ·	Organic, GM, water effluent, worker safety, consumer safety, social criteria, RSL/chemical residues.	GOTS includes but is not limited to fibres, yarns, textiles and garments.\n\nFrom 2014 post-consumer recycled polyester will be allowed.
Global Recycle Standard	Water effluent, energy consumption, worker safety, consumer safety, social criteria, responsible water use.	GRS covers products containing pre- and/or post-consumer recycled raw materials.
I.W.T.O.	IWTO offers standards and test methods for the measurement of wool fibre, yarn and fabric properties.\n\nSince 2012, IWTO collates various Life Cycle Analysis data and information from across the wool industry to provide a better-informed assessment of the environmental attributes of wool fibre.	Full Test methods provide the objective, technical and scientific measurements required for issuing IWTO test certificates.\n\nAs regards wool's environmental credentials, wool's LCAs now look at all areas of the industry on a cradle-to-cradle basis.
MADE-BY	Organic, worker safety, social criteria.	Made-By applies to environmental and working conditions throughout the entire supply chain of products, covering affiliated fashion brands.

240

Stages include	Requirements
BCI focuses on cotton production at farm level. BCI principles outline that Better Cotton is grown by farmers who: 1. Minimize the harmful impact of crop protection practices 2. Use water efficiently and care for the availability of water 3. Care for the health of the soil 4. Conserve natural habitats 5. Care for and preserve the quality of the fibre 6. Promote decent work.	Growing Better Cotton means initially meeting a set of minimum requirements including pesticide use, water conservation, habitat protection, fibre quality and decent work principles. Once the minimum criteria are met, farmers need to show continuous improvement to remain qualified. www.bettercotton.org
Primarily rates • resource productivity • consumer safety • air emissions • water emissions • occupational health and safety throughout the textile supply chain, focusing on testing initial raw materials.	The bluesign® system indicates improvement of all environmental, health and safety aspects throughout the textile supply chain, assessing components based on their toxicological and ecological properties and risks. 'Intelligent' chemistry is acceptable for best product functionality, quality or design. These must be managed using Best Available Technology (BAT). www.bluesign.com
A multi-attribute standard covering five categories. C2C certifies products made with materials that are safe for humans and the environment, designed for reutilization (e.g. recycling or composting), and manufactured using renewable energy, water stewardship and social fairness. Materials are designed for reuse in biological or technological cycles.	Basic, bronze, silver, gold or platinum product rating to reflect continuous improvement. Products must be optimized over time to reach higher levels of certification and become ideal C2C products. All materials in a finished product and their chemical ingredients must be identified, then scored on their impact on human and environmental health, and cyclability. Materials are scored on their ability to be reused in biological or technological cycles. The product manufacturing process is evaluated for renewable energy use, water stewardship and social fairness. www.c2ccertified.org
Fairtrade standards for producers ensure the farmers receive a fair and stable price and the Fairtrade Premium, which they choose how to invest in their businesses and communities.	Farmer organizations as well as Fairtrade licensees (businesses selling finished products) are inspected regularly and are required to report on sales. www.fairtrade.org.uk
GOTS-licensed farms and fibres are certified to internationally recognized organic standards by an accredited certification body. GOTS covers the entire processing chain, including manufacturing, dyeing, weaving, knitting, CMT, finishing, packaging, labelling, distribution and wholesale.	Products must meet all the standards throughout the entire supply chain to be certified to GOTS. Companies trading in GOTS certified products must be certified and inspected by an accredited certification body. www.global-standard.org Soil Association Certification is one body which can certify to GOTS. If a textile company is certified to GOTS by Soil Association Certification, they can use the trusted Soil Association symbol on their approved products, as well as the GOTS symbol. www.soilassociation.org
Tracks and documents the purchase, handling and use of pre- and/or post-consumer recycled raw materials. Environmental processing impact and social criteria are also assessed. Pre-industrial waste is now not included.	GRS-labelled products must contain a minimum of 5 per cent pre- and/or post-consumer recycled raw materials. Labels state: 'Made with recycled [raw material] – x% pre-consumer and x% post-consumer.' www.textileexchange.org/content/standards
Standards and test methods cover all stages of the wool supply chain, from greasy wool to scoured wool, carded wool, sliver, top, yarn and fabric. IWTO collates and analyses LCA data from various stages of the supply chain including co-products within the sheep production system, water footprints, product wear life, recycling and carbon cycles.	IWTO test certificates can be obtained from IWTO licensing labs. All standards and specifications can be found in the IWTO Red and White Book. The report on wool's LCAs can be downloaded from the IWTO website. www.iwto.org
Environmental impact of raw materials, social conditions in factories, product distribution.	Each partner brand has a scorecard published online and in Made-By's annual report. Supply bases are thoroughly analysed to custom develop targets with brands, culminating in an action plan to improve the supply chain through training and workshops. www.made-by.org

241

Certifications

Standard	Covers	Products
CONFIDENCE IN TEXTILES — Tested for harmful substances according to Oeko-Tex® Standard 100 — 00000000 Institute	Consumer safety, RSL/chemical residues.	Textile raw materials, intermediate products and end products at all stages of production, including textile accessories, dyes and textile auxiliaries.
CONFIDENCE IN TEXTILES — Eco-friendly factory according to Oeko-Tex® Standard 1000 — 00000000 Institute	Water effluent, air emissions, energy consumption, worker safety, consumer safety, social criteria, RSL/chemical residues, responsible water use.	Tests, audits and certifies environmentally friendly production sites throughout the textile processing chain including spinners, weavers and knitters, yarn dyers and textile finishers, and garment manufacturers.
CONFIDENCE IN TEXTILES 100 plus — Tested for harmful substances according to Oeko-Tex® Standard 100 + Oeko-Tex® Standard 1000	Water effluent, air emissions, energy consumption, worker safety, consumer safety, social criteria, RSL/chemical residues, responsible water use.	Predominantly yarn producers and fabric producers.
ORGANIC 100 Content standard	Organic raw materials, genetic modification.	The Organic Content Standard (OCS) covers the use of certified organically grown materials in any product. The 100 logo may be used for products with at least 95 per cent organically grown material, as long as the remaining percentage is not the same type of material.
ORGANIC BLENDED Content standard	Organic raw materials, genetic modification.	The Organic Content Standard (OCS) covers the use of certified organically grown materials in any product. The Blended logo may be used for products containing at least 5 per cent organically grown material. The remaining percentage may be the same variety of material.
CERTIFIED TO OE 100 STANDARD	Organic cotton, genetic modification. (Formerly called Organic Exchange)	OE 100 covers the use of 95–100 per cent certified organically grown cotton fibre in yarns, fabrics and finished goods.
CERTIFIED TO OE BLENDED STANDARD	Organic cotton, genetic modification.	OE Blended covers the use of 5–95 per cent certified organically grown cotton fibre in blended yarns, fabrics and finished goods for suppliers starting to introduce organic cotton.
SOIL ASSOCIATION ORGANIC	Organic, genetic modification, worker safety, consumer safety, social criteria, RSL/chemical residues.	Soil Association certification is awarded to producers, processors and suppliers according to GOTS standards.

Stages include	Requirements
Every stage of production of raw materials, intermediate products and end products is measured against required criteria, which must be met without exception.	Products are allocated to one of four product classes based on how intensively they will come into contact with the skin. Testing parameters include banning lawfully prohibited, regulated and harmful substances, and ensuring colourfastness and a skin-friendly pH-value to safeguard consumer health. www.oeko-tex.com
Textile processing elements audited include: • no use of environmentally damaging auxiliaries and dyes • waste water and exhaust air treatment • optimization of energy consumption • avoidance of noise and dust pollution • introduction of environmental management system • quality management system.	Evidence must be provided that at least 30 per cent of total production is already certified under Oeko-Tex® Standard 100, and manufacturing processes must in general meet stipulated criteria for environmental friendliness. Social criteria stipulated in Oeko-Tex® Standard 1000 must be fulfilled. www.oeko-tex.com
Every production and processing stage at all sites is assessed. Certification can be for any stage up to and including garment manufacture.	All production sites involved in the production chain for an Oeko-Tex® 100 plus garment must fulfil the requirements of Oeko-Tex® Standard 100 and Oeko-Tex® Standard 1000. www.oeko-tex.com
Tracks and documents the purchase, handling and use of certified organically grown material in any product, but does not cover production processes.	Products meeting the OCS and containing 95–100 per cent organically grown material should be labelled as: 'contains organically grown [raw material]' or 'contains 100% organically grown [raw material]' as long as the product does not also contain conventional ingredients of the same raw material. www.textileexchange.org/content/standards
Tracks and documents the purchase, handling and use of certified organically grown material in any product, but does not cover production processes.	Products meeting the OCS and containing 5–95 per cent organically grown material should be labelled as: 'contains X% organically grown [raw material]' www.textileexchange.org/content/standards
Tracks and documents the purchase, handling and use of 95–100 per cent certified organic cotton fibre in yarns, fabrics and finished goods, but does not cover production processes.	Must use at least 95 per cent certified organic cotton fibre, exclusive of thread and non-textile trims or accessories. Can label goods 'Contains organically grown cotton' if they are 95 per cent or more cotton, and the remaining material is not cotton. www.textileexchange.org/content/standards
Tracks and documents the purchase, handling and use of certified organically farmed cotton fibre in blended yarns, fabrics and finished goods, but does not cover production processes.	Certified goods must contain a minimum of 5 per cent organic or organic in conversion cotton. Labels state: 'Contains x% organically grown cotton.' www.textileexchange.org/content/standards
Harvesting of raw materials, production, processing, manufacturing, packaging, labelling, exportation, importation and distribution of all natural products including fibres, yarns, textiles and garments.	Certified goods must meet the requirements outlined by the GOTS standard. They can then be labelled with the Soil Association Organic symbol, which is the most widely recognized organic symbol in the UK.

Green chemistry

There are 12 principles that explain what **green chemistry** should mean in practice, as set out by Paul Anastas and John Warner. They help to define the true ecological, ethical and sustainable credentials of a raw material or product. These should be considered seriously by anybody looking to source or work with green fabrics for ethical reasons rather than pure marketing potential.

Prevention Preventing waste is better than treating or cleaning it after it is formed. This is self-explanatory. Currently there is a whole industry built on cleaning waste. It is very expensive to treat waste and contain it. The waste has to be monitored even after it has been contained.

Atom economy When creating materials it is important to maximize the incorporation of all the materials used into the final product. In other words, waste as little material as possible. For example, if the process has 50 per cent atom economy, then half of the materials that are used turn out to be waste. Only half of the materials actually end up as product.

Less hazardous synthesis Processes should be designed to use and generate substances that have little to no toxicity. Plan the process of creating the materials to use substances that are not toxic and to produce substances that are not toxic. This is often easier said than done!

Designing safer chemicals Chemical products should be designed to function well while reducing toxicity. Reducing toxicity of the products reduces hazards to people and to the environment.

Safer solvents Whenever possible, avoid the use of additional substances such as solvents and separating agents. When these substances are needed, they should be non-toxic.

Energy efficiency Energy efficiency should be considered when designing and producing a product. The energy requirements should be minimized since they impact the environment and raise cost. When possible, processes should be conducted at room temperature and pressure.

Use renewable resources When possible the feedstock (or material used to make the product) should come from renewable resources. For example, there is research being done to make chemicals out of products such as corn instead of coal or oil. Also, when choosing a feedstock look at waste from other reactions being made in the lab.

Reduce derivatives Derivatives are chemicals that are used to cause a temporary effect in the process. This could be a chemical that protects a certain part of the substance that is later removed, or it could be a chemical that causes a temporary change in a property so that a reaction can take place. Using derivatives should be avoided when possible. They do not end up in the final product and only increase waste.

Catalysis Use selective catalytic reagents over stoichiometric reagents. A catalyst helps a reaction occur with less energy, and also speeds the reaction.

Consider the end Design for the proper disposal of the item. The product that is made should break down into non-toxic substances after it has been used. This way the product will not remain and build up in the environment.

Use real-time pollution prevention Methods need to be further developed to allow real-time monitoring of chemical processes. This includes monitoring while the process is happening, detection and control of the formation of hazardous substances and monitoring after the substance has been disposed.

Accident prevention The substance and the form of the substance (liquid, gas, etc.) should be carefully chosen to minimize accidents during the chemical process. Accidents include fire, explosion and accidental release.

Source: *Green Chemistry: Theory and Practice*, Paul T. Anastas and John D. Warner, Oxford University Press, 2000

Biodegradable

'Degradable' and 'biodegradable' have different implications

- **Biodegradable implies that materials degrade in a given length of time. The time frame depends on the product and the right biodegradable conditions.**

- **Biodegradable materials in landfill sites degrade very slowly as they are deprived of oxygen, light and moisture and create methane gas in the process.**

- **Degradable implies that materials will eventually decompose with no clear time frame set.**

244

Seasonal Cyclical Industry Process

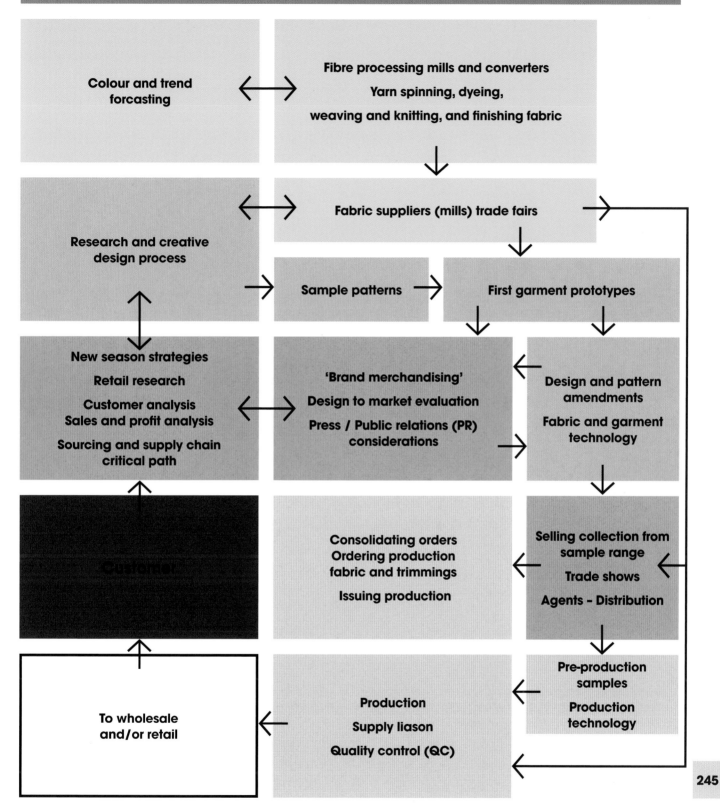

Colour and trend forcasting ⟷ **Fibre processing mills and converters / Yarn spinning, dyeing, weaving and knitting, and finishing fabric**

Research and creative design process ⟷ **Fabric suppliers (mills) trade fairs**

Sample patterns → **First garment prototypes**

New season strategies / Retail research / Customer analysis / Sales and profit analysis / Sourcing and supply chain critical path ⟷ **'Brand merchandising' / Design to market evaluation / Press / Public relations (PR) considerations** → **Design and pattern amendments / Fabric and garment technology**

Customer

Consolidating orders / Ordering production fabric and trimmings / Issuing production ← **Selling collection from sample range / Trade shows / Agents – Distribution**

To wholesale and/or retail ← **Production / Supply liason / Quality control (QC)** ← **Pre-production samples / Production technology**

245

Manufacture and processing

The structure of the fabric industry has changed considerably in the last 30 years, although many of the disciplines within it have remained the same.

Design

In a competitive, consumer-savvy market good design is instrumental to a company's success. Today's designer needs a wide skill and knowledge base, from marketing knowledge to manufacturing skills. Design schools produce multi-talented graduates that are ripe for French, Italian and American design companies.

Design product management

This is a wide area, which has gone through radical changes and expansion in recent years. There is now a need for more graduates within merchandising, buying and product development departments, dealing with anything from sourcing to branding; range-building and line-planning to product distribution.

Liaising with **offshore** manufacturers creates problems with communication even if the accepted *lingua franca* is English. At retail, information technology has made information instant: once it took a few weeks to know a bestseller, now it's possible by return.

Pattern cutting

Pattern cutting for higher-end products and **tailoring** is still usually carried out domestically. However, for the greater majority of clothing the patterns are cut in the country of manufacture, the advantages being cost and proximity to the factory.

Garment technology

Technologists were historically linked to the factory, where they could be hands-on with issues as they arose. Today they deal with problems long distance, requiring greater accuracy of information and better communication.

Sample making

Similarly to pattern cutting, where samples are made is dependent on the product level; an expensive dress manufacturer may have domestic sampling whereas a multiple brand will sample at its offshore factory. The advantage is twofold, cost and production manufacturing techniques. A factory will always produce a tailoring sample, irrespective of level.

Manufacturing

Today offshore manufacturing is not only the domain of inexpensive volume brands, but also many high-profile labels take advantage of the cheaper labour costs the developing world has to offer. The choice is between **manufacturing hub** and the quality level of the factory. Better brands will be more selective with their trimmings and may well have these transported from other global sources. For example, today around 60 per cent of men's tailoring is made from fabric sourced in a different country from where the production is based. Thirty per cent of T-shirt cotton is grown and knitted into fabric, then shipped to be manufactured in another country or even continent. While this travel increases a company's carbon footprint and questions its ethics, the lure of a better **margin** does nothing to dampen its resolve.

Quality control

Once this was only a component discipline of the manufacturing process, today, with the explosion in offshore manufacturing, it has become all-important. **QC** is now as much a part of buying or product development as it is a manufacturing component.

Fabric suppliers

The majority of Far East manufacturing takes advantage of its domestic fabric production, especially with cotton piece goods. Therefore, fabric sourcing would be part of the same exercise as sourcing the manufacturing production.

Sales

Once the collection is ready or launched, it is the task of the sales department to generate sales. Depending on the size of the company this could be handled in-house or by an agent/representative. Sales to foreign countries can be via a fashion trade fair or given over to an agency or **distributor** in the respective country that has a better understanding of national characteristics and requirements that may be an issue.

Trade fairs

Yarn trade fairs

The purpose of a yarn trade fair is to showcase a new season's yarn and colour direction.

Expofil Paris, France. Yarns, textile fibres and fashion services.

Indigo Paris, France. Prints. Same time as Premier Vision.

Intercot Changing venue. Global approaches to organic yarns and textiles.

Pitti Imagine Filati Florence, Italy. Yarns and fibres.

Peru Moda Lima, Peru. Luxury yarns such as vicuña and alpaca.

Printsource New York, USA. Tri-annual international print design and finishing.

Yarn Expo Beijing, China. Centralized for the whole of China.

Fabric trade fairs

These showcase all new fabrics and colour directions for the next season. Trend directions tend to be six months ahead of the wholesale fashion trade fairs, although many companies also show stock or short lead-time fabrics.

Fabric trade fairs are now global. Fairs of varying sizes can be found in any country that has a textile and/or garment industry. In some cases these fabric fairs are combined with parallel fairs promoting industry and commerce.

Internationally acclaimed fairs can be found in all the fashion capitals of the world. The most important, from a fashion perspective, remain the traditional fairs of France, Italy, Germany, Japan and the United States.

Première Vision Paris, France. Very important bi-annual fair with forecasting, accessories and print halls. Also Moscow, Tokyo, Shanghai and New York.

Denim By Premier Vision Paris, France. Smaller shows concentrating on denim and related materials.

Fabric at Magic New York, USA. Fabrics, trimmings and colour trends.

Idea Como Milan, Italy. The very best fabrics, predominance of silks.

Interstoff Frankfurt, Germany. Bi-annual fair showing international fabrics.

Interstoff Asia and Interstoff Russia Derivatives of the original, exhibiting in Hong Kong and Moscow.

Intertextile Beijing, Shenzhent and Shangai, China. Part of the Interstoff organization for the Chinese markets.

Japantex Tokyo, Japan. International fabrics.

Modatisimo Porto, Portugal. National and international fabrics.

Moda in Tessuto e Accesori Milan, Italy. Bi-annual, fabrics and accessories.

Prato Expo Florence, Italy. Important fair due to the sheer number of new ideas showcased

Texworld India and Texworld USA Part of the Interstoff organization exhibiting in Bombay and New York.

Texbridge/Turkish Fashion Fabrics: Bi-annual shows held in London, Milan and New York.

Resources/Glossary

Useful organizations and publications

The following organizations, services and publications can provide useful information regarding a variety of different aspects of the fibres and fabrics discussed in this book, from the raw material to the finished product.

Fabric and colour publications

There are many textile and colour journals published worldwide. Some are factual while others are creative and inspirational, and of great use when starting a design collection.

Eco Textile News, UK, 6 issues.
Journal Du Textile, France, 42 issues.
Mood Textiles, Italy, 4 issues.
Noa Colour, Japan, 2 issues.
Provider (View On Colour), The Netherlands, 4 issues.
Selvedge, UK, 6 issues.
The Society of Dyers and Colourists, UK, 10 issues.
T Design Living Textile Tendence, Italy, 4 issues.
Texitura, Spain, 2 issues.
Textil Wirtschaft, Germany, 52 issues.
Textile Asia, Hong Kong, 12 issues.
Textile Forum, international, 4 issues.
Textile History, UK, 2 issues.
Textile Horizons, UK, 6 issues.
Textile Month, UK, 6 issues.
Textile Outlook International, UK, 6 issues.
Textile Report, France, 4 issues.
Textile Research Journal, US, 12 issues.
Textile View, The Netherlands, 4 issues.
Textiles Eastern Europe, UK, 1 issue.
Textiles, UK, 4 issues.
View Point, The Netherlands, 2 issues.

Wool

Australian Wool Innovation Ltd:
www.wool.com.au; and
Australian Wool Services:
www.wool.com
Both are part of the Australian Woolmark Company, which is considered to be the world's leading wool fibre textile authority, with more than 60 years of experience.

British Wool Marketing Board:
www.britishwool.org.uk
Central marketing system for UK fleece wool.

International Wool Textile Organization:
www.iwto.org
Representing the world's wool textile trade and industry, including spinners, weavers and garment manufacturers.

Merino Advanced Performance Programme MAPP:
www.mapp.co.nz
Performance-based fabric developments incorporating New Zealand merino wool.

Merino New Zealand:
www.nzmerino.co.nz
Represents the merino producers of New Zealand, promotes the merino characteristics of brightness/whiteness, strength, extra staple length and thus advanced manufacturing efficiency, and is associated with the highest quality manufacturers.

Uruguay: Wool Secretariat/Secretariado Uruguayo De La Lana (SUL):
www.wool.com.uy
Works to promote and develop all aspects of Uruguayan wool in a similar way to the larger Australian Woolmark Company.

Wool is Best: www.woolisbest.com
A factual guide to the Australian wool industry.

The Woolmark Company:
www.wool.com.au
The aim of the company and organization is to improve the profitability of wool growers by building and sustaining demand. It also aims to increase productivity through research, development and marketing. It has offices in approximately 20 countries and representation in 60. It also has design and development centres in Biella, Italy, and Ichinomiya, Japan. It also encourages industry partner projects. Central to the company is the Woolmark, which is an international trademark that promises high-quality performance and fibre content. It also confirms that the products on which it is displayed are of pure new wool.

Wools of New Zealand:
www.fernmark.com
Works to promote and develop all aspects of New Zealand wool. It originally promoted interior textiles, and since 1996 includes apparel textiles.

Zque™ Fibre: www.zque.co.nz
Ethically sourced New Zealand merino wool with an accreditation programme that ensures environmental, social and economic sustainability as well as animal welfare, with traceability back to the source.

Luxury animal fibres

Australian Alpaca Association:
www.alpaca.asn.au
Comprehensive information on the Australian alpaca industry.

Australian Cashmere Breed and Fleece Standard:
www.acga.org.au
Information on the Australian breed evolved from the bush goat.

British Alpaca Society:
www.bas-uk.com
Comprehensive information on the British alpaca industry.

Canadian Llama and Alpaca Registry:
www.claacanada.com
Comprehensive information on the Canadian llama and alpaca industry.

Cape Mohair Wool:
www.cmw.co.za
A group of South African mohair textile production companies.

Cashmere and Camel Hair Manufacturers Institute:
www.cashmere.org
US-based international institute for research into and promotion of camel hair and cashmere.

Coloured Angora Goat Breeders Association:
www.cagba.org
Promotes the development and marketing of coloured angora goats and fibre.

Import and Export of Vicuña (US Wildlife Services): www.fws.gov
Information on legalities in and restrictions on the trade in vicuña fibre.

International Alpaca Association (Peru):
www.aia.org.pe
Peruvian-based association with extensive information on all South American camelids and their hybrids.

Pygora Breeders Association:
www.pygoragoats.org
US-based association dedicated to the 'advancement' and well-being of pygoras.

Roseland Llamas:
www.llamas.co.uk
Informative site regarding llama attributes.

Yampa Valley Yaks:
www.yampayaks.com
Colorado-based site dealing with yaks.

Silk
Peace Silk suppliers:
www.ahimsapeacesilk.com
Suppliers of peace silk.

Silk Association of Nepal:
www.nepalsilk.org
European Union-funded trade organization for silk producers and exporters.

Silk Mark Organization of India (SMOI):
www.silkmarkindia.com
Silk quality mark organization sponsored by the Textiles Ministry.

Linen
CELC: Confédération Européenne du Lin et du Chanvre (Linen and Hemp):
www.belgianlinen.com
A non-profit-making trade organization for linen in Western Europe. Affiliated countries are Austria, Belgium, France, Germany, Italy, Holland, Switzerland and the UK.

The Irish Linen Centre and Lisburn Museum:
www.lisburncity.gov.uk
Information and artefacts relating to the Irish linen industry. Lisburn, Northern Ireland.

The Irish Linen Guild:
www.irishlinen.co.uk
Founded in 1928, promotes and monitors quality Irish linen. Gives a seal of quality to fabrics or yarns that are made and finished in Ireland.

249

The Linen Dream Lab: Showcasing textile innovations, trend publications, yarn and fabric sourcing – sponsored by CELC 15, rue du Louvre, Paris, France 75001 and Via Orti 2, 20122 Milano, Italy.

Maison du Lin: www.lin.asso.fr
Organization promoting French linen.

Masters of Linen:
www.mastersoflinen.com
Paris-based subsidiary of CELC. Provides information on and promotes European linen.

Saneco: www.saneco.com
Statistics and information on the flax industry.

Cotton

Cotton Australia:
www.cottonaustralia.com.au
Organization servicing Australian cotton growers, dealing with environmentally conducive and sustainable production issues.

Cotton Foundation:
www.cotton.org
US cotton export and research foundation.

Cotton Incorporated:
www.cotton.inc
A company with offices worldwide that offers extensive information on all aspects of cotton from farming and green issues to design and manufacturing. It also offers extensive fabric resources.

International Cotton Advisory Committee:
www.icac.org
Association of governments of cotton producing and consuming countries.

International Cotton Association:
www.ica-ltd.org
International trade association and arbitral body.

National Cotton Council News and Current Events:
www.cotton.org/news
Global news and information site.

Plains Cotton Cooperative Association:
www.pcca.com
Largest producers and suppliers of Texan-style cotton.

The Seam: www.theseam.com
Online trading and interactive marketplace for cotton agriculture.

Spinning the Web:
www.spinningtheweb.org.uk
Comprehensive information on the history of the cotton industry.

United States Cotton Board:
www.cottonboard.org
Information for producers, buyers and importers.

100 Per Cent American Supima cotton:
www.supimacotton.org
Information on American Pima cotton.

Naturally coloured cotton producers

Peru Naturtex Partners:
www.perunaturtex.com
Organic production with sustainable processing for textile products. The site has good information on the origins of cotton, organic and naturally coloured cotton. It also has several links to fashion companies using organic cotton.

Facts and figures on the cotton trade
www.cottonorg/econ/cropintfo/cropdata/rankings.cfm
www.pbs.org/now/shows/310/cotton-trade.html

Sustainability; ethical and fair-trade issues

Ecological, Fairtrade and organic organizations

ASTM International
www.astm.org/Standard/interests/textile-standards.html
Textile standards organization.

BCI (Better Cotton Initiative):
www.bettercotton.org
Since 2005 the BCI has worked across the supply chain and aims to improve the economic, environmental and social sustainability of cotton cultivation worldwide. The first Better Cotton products became available in 2011.

The Centre for Sustainable Fashion:
www.sustainable-fashion.com
London College of Fashion's sustainable research, education and business consultancy centre.

C.L.A.S.S. (Creative Lifestyle and Sustainable Strategies):
www.c.l.a.s.s.org
An international organization with its own dedicated materials library. C.L.A.S.S. works to promote eco-textiles, materials and services.

The Clean Clothes Campaign:
www.cleanclothes.org
Aims to improve working conditions and to empower workers of the global clothing industry.

A Deeper Luxury:
www.wwf.org.uk/deeperluxury
A report on the findings of WWF-UK's analysis of the environmental and social performance of the luxury goods sector.

DEFRA (Department for Environment, Food and Rural Affairs):
www.gov.uk/defra
DEFRA invests in supporting farming, protecting biodiversity and encouraging sustainable food production. It launched the Sustainable Clothing Action Plan in 2009 with 300 stakeholders. The UK Sustainable Clothing action plan can be seen here:
http://www.gov.uk/government/publications/sustainable-clothing-action-plan.

Environmental Justice Foundation:
www.ejfoundation.org
Information on empowering those affected by environmental abuse.

Ethical Fashion Forum:
www.ethicalfashionforum.com
Network of designers, businesses and organizations focusing on environmental and social sustainability in the fashion industry.

Ethical Trading Initiative:
www.ethicaltrade.org
Information on the promotion of ethical trade.

The Fairtrade Foundation:
www.fairtrade.org.uk;
www.fairtrade.net
Registered charity that licenses the FAIRTRADE mark to products that meet internationally recognized ethical standards.

Fair Wear Foundation:
www.fairwear.org
International verification initiative dedicated to enhancing workers' lives all over the world.

Fibre 2 Fashion:
www.fibre2fashion.com
A US organization covering sustainable issues through the entire value chain from fibre to fashion products.

FTC (Federal Trade Commission):
http://ftc.gov
US consumer protection agency.

Helen Storey Foundation:
www.helenstoreyfoundation.org
A London-based, project-funded, not-for-profit arts organization. It aims to inspire new ways of thinking across art, science, design and technology, incorporating ethical and sustainable thinking.

International Fairtrade:
www.ifat.org
Information on members practising fair trade in business.

Labour Behind the Label:
www.labourbehindthelabel.org
Resources and information on clothing labels.

No Sweat: www.nosweat.org.uk
Information on the global campaign against sweatshops and child labour.

OCIA (Organic Crop Improvement Association): www.ocia.org
Organic certifications.

Organic Trade Association:
www.ota.com
Organization listing members using organic cotton.

Pesticide Action Network UK:
www.pan-uk.org
Working to eliminate pesticides and to promote fair trade and organic alternatives. Website has many related links.

Positive Luxury:
www.positiveluxury.org
An organization offering the first consumer guide to positive living. It licenses and awards the 'blue butterfly', a global interactive trust mark, providing information about recommended brands' social and environmental status at the point of sale and on its website.

Rite Group: www.ritegroup.org.uk
Founded by UK retailer Marks & Spencer, University of Leeds and *Ecotextile News*, it provides advice and information to drive forward sustainable and ethical production of textiles and fashion products.

SCP (Sustainable Cotton Project):
www.sustainablecotton.org
Founded in 1996, the SCP encourages information-sharing among farmers, about biological farming techniques, and educates manufacturers and the consumer about the importance of supporting local industry in order to develop a Cleaner Cotton™ industry.

The Sustainable Angle:
www.thesustainableangle.org
A not-for-profit organization dedicated to education and the promotion of sustainability in the fashion industry. The Sustainable Angle presents exhibitions, manages an extensive fabric library and liaises with the fashion industry on responsible sourcing strategies.

Sustainable Apparel Coalition:
www.apparelcoalition.org
An international trade federation founded in 2011 that aims to reduce the environmental and social impact of the fashion industry.

Sustainable Cotton Initiative:
www.wwfpak.org
The initiative focuses on some of the most important, and poorest, cotton-producing areas (e.g. Australia, Pakistan, India and Central Asia). The Sustainable Cotton Initiative is aimed at reducing water use for the irrigation of cotton, while safeguarding the livelihood of the local farmers. As such, the project will contribute to the biological, economic and social sustainability of these focal regions.

Textile Environmental Design (TED):
www.tedresearch.net
Chelsea College of Art and Design's collaborative projects looking at creating textiles with a reduced impact on the environment.

Textile Exchange:
www.textileexchange.org
A charitable organization committed to expanding organic agriculture, with a specific focus on organically grown fibres, such as cotton.

Vote Hemp: www.votehemp.com
US advocacy group which holds comprehensive information on all aspects of hemp, from legislative and sustainable issues to production and retail information.

World Fair Trade Organization:
www.wfto.com
Global authority on fair trade.

Recycling organizations

Cardato: www.cardato.it
Italian organization for recycled and regenerated CO_2-neutral wool fabrics produced in the Prato region of Italy.

Eco Circle: www.ecocircle.jp/en/
Polyester fibre producer Teijin has developed an innovative eco-recycling system, Eco Circle, to reuse post-consumer garments to make new fibres.

Ragtex, Textile Recycling Association:
www.textile-recycling.org.uk
The Recylatax Bonded scheme helps local authorities, charities and other organizations set up recycling services for reuse of clothing and shoes.

TRA (Textile Recycling Association):
www.textile-recycling.org.uk
The association has members internationally, and facilitates the work of second-hand shoe and clothing collectors, graders and reprocessors.

TRAID: www.traid.org.uk
Charity recycling organization.

Waste Online:
www.wasteonline.org.uk
An overview of recycling with facts, figures and details of what happens to the clothes we recycle. Run by Waste Watch.

Man-made fibres

AFMA (American Fiber Manufacturers Association):
http://fibersource.com/afma/afma.htm

BISFA (Bureau International pour la Standardisation des Fibres Artificielles):
www.bisfa.org
International association of man-made fibre producers.

CIRFS (Comité International de la Rayonne et des Fibres Synthétiques): www.cirfs.org
European Man-made Fibres Association

Further reading and exhibitions

The Book of Silk, Phillippa Scott (Thames & Hudson, 1993)

Chinese Silk: A Cultural History, Shelagh Vainker (The British Museum Press, 2004)

Colour, Edith Anderson Feisner (Laurence King, 2006)

Colour, Helen Varley, ed. (Marshall Editions, 1998)

Colour: A Workshop for Artists and Designers, David Hornung (Laurence King, 2005)

The Colour Eye, Robert Cumming and Tom Porter (BBC Books, 1990)

Cradle to Cradle: Remaking the Way We Make Things, William McDonough and Michael Braungart (Vintage, 2009)

Cotton, Beverly Lemire (Berg, 2011)

Cotton: The Biography of a Revolutionary Fibre, Stephen Yafa (Penguin, 2006)

The Chemistry of Textile Fibres, R.H. Wardman and R.R. Mather (RSC Publishing, 2010)

Eco Chic: The Fashion Paradox, Sandy Black (Black Dog, 2008)

An Economic History of the Silk Industry, Giovanni Federico (Cambridge University Press, 1997)

Fair Trade, A. Nicholls and C. Opal (Sage Publications, 2005)

Fashion and Sustainability: Design for Change, Kate Fletcher and Lynda Grose (Laurence King, 2012)

Fashion and Textiles, Colin Gale and Jasbir Kaur (Berg, 2004)

Fashion Zeitgeist, Barbara Vinken (Berg, 2005)

Fashioning the Future, Suzanne Lees (Thames & Hudson, 2005)

Global Silk Industry: A Complete Source Book, R. Datta and M. Nanavaty (Universal Publishers, 2005)

Green Chemistry: Theory and Practice, Paul T. Anastas and John D. Warner (Oxford University Press, 2000)

The Green Imperative, Papanek, Victor (Thames & Hudson, 1995)

Green Is the New Black, Tamsin Blanchard (Hodder & Stoughton, 2007)

Hemp for Victory: History and Qualities of the World's Most Useful Plant, Kenyon Gibson (Whitaker Publishing, 2006)

An Insider's Guide to Cotton and Sustainability, Simon Ferrigno (MCL Global, 2012)

Mantero 100 anni di storia e di seta, Guido Vergani (Fos Editoria e Communicazione, 2002)

Seven Deadly Colours, Andrew Parker (Free Press, 2005)

Silk, Jaques Anquetil (Flammarion, 1995)

Silk, Mary Schoeser (Yale University Press, 2007)

Small Is Beautiful: Economics as if People Mattered, E.F. Schumacher (Vintage, 1973)

Sustainable Fashion and Textiles, Kate Fletcher (Earthscan Publications, 2008)

Techno Textiles 2, Sarah E. Braddock Clarke and Marie O'Mahony (Thames & Hudson, 2005)

The Sustainable Fashion Handbook, Sandy Black (Thames & Hudson, 2012)

251

Glossary

A

Abacá: The leaves of the abacá plant (*Musa textilis*) which produce **Manila hemp** fibres.

Acetate: An **artificial fibre** derived from **cellulose**.

Acetic acid: A colourless liquid, classified as a weak acid, used to process **acetate**.

Acetone: Colourless, flammable organic compound. A common building block in organic chemistry, acetone is used to dissolve **cellulose** resin in order to process **acetate** fibres.

Acrylic: The generic name for a **synthetic polymer** fibre.

Acrylic monomers: Methacrylic amide is commonly used as part of the **weighting** process of silk production, and facilitates the absorption of dye.

Added value crop: A crop grown under a written contract with the intent of receiving a premium because of its particular attributes.

Additive colour: The process of mixing coloured light, as in theatrical or retail applications.

After-image: The reaction seen on a blank surface when the viewer's brain supplies the opposite colour after staring at a particular **hue** for a few seconds.

Agent: A representative showcasing and selling a brand or company's products either domestically or abroad.

Ahimsa peace silk: Made from the cocoons of several species of wild and semi-wild **silk moths** and promoted in parts of southern India as ethical silk.

Ahimsa philosophy: A rule of conduct not to harm any living thing. Ahimsa is a Sanskrit term meaning non-violence, and the philosophy – part of the 3,000-year-old Indian Jain philosophy, and important to Buddhism and Hinduism – supports the philosophy of karmic consequence.

Alpaca: *Vicugna pacos*, a domesticated species of the *Camelidae* family. It is the principal South American fibre-producing animal.

Alpaca fleece: The term for marketing fibre from huacaya alpacas (see also **alpaca suri**).

Alpaca suri: The term for marketing fibre from suri alpacas (see also **alpaca fleece**).

Ambari hemp: See Kenaf.

Ambary: See Kenaf.

Ammonia: A colourless gas compound used as a building block to process **acrylic**.

Analogous hues: Colours that are adjacent to each other on the **colour wheel**.

Angora: A specific breed of goats, rabbits and cats that share a similar type of hair fibre. The name is derived from the city of Angora (Ankara) in Turkey. The fibre of the angora goat is called **mohair**.

Appliqué: Decorative technique using pieces of fabric or other materials stitched or embroidered onto a base cloth to create designs.

Aramid fibre: A man-made, high-performance fibre. The word 'aramid' is a portmanteau of **aromatic polyamide**.

Aran: A style of Gaelic fishermen's knitwear originating from the Aran Islands off the west coast of Ireland. Typically features raised **cable**-stitch patterns and uses **Aran wool**.

Aran wool: Undyed wool that still contains its natural lanolin.

Argyle (also Argyll): A Scottish knitwear pattern made up of diamond blocks of colour.

Aromatic polyamide: A synthetic **polymer** related to **nylon**, capable of being spun into **aramid fibres**.

Artificial fibres: Made from **cellulose** and not to be confused with **synthetic** fibres, which are man-made.

Art silk: A textile term originally coined to describe artificial silk. See also **Rayon**.

Audemars, Georges: Swiss chemist who, in 1855, was awarded the first patent for artificial silk.

Australian cashmere goat: A hybrid, and a different breed from the 'standard' **Himalayan mountain goats**, that produces **cashmere**.

Azo or azoic dye: Petroleum-based dye typically used on **cellulose** fibres.

B

Bacteriostatic: Inhibits growth or multiplication of bacteria

Bactrian: *Camelus bactrianus*, a species of camel from which camel-hair fibre is produced.

Bamboo kun: Natural **cellulose** contained within bamboo, which is used in fibre processing. It also protects the plant from pests and biological pathogens, which can create disease in the host plant.

Bamboo linen: Mechanically-processed bamboo fibre, made without chemical intervention.

Bamboo rayon: Term used in the United States for bamboo fibre produced by the **viscose** method, with chemical intervention.

Bamboo viscose: Term used in Europe for bamboo fibre produced by the viscose method, with chemical intervention.

Barong Tagalog: A traditional embroidered shirt from the Philippines, made from **piña cloth** and worn for formal occasions and ceremonies.

Bast fibres: These are obtained from the **phloem** or inner skin of a plant, and are separated from the xylem or woody core.

Bat: A flat, orderly mass of fibres formed by machine **carding**.

Batik: Wax is applied to fabric prior to **dyeing** to produce a pattern that resists the dyeing process.

Batt: A large bundle of multiple strands of fibres partway through the **spinning process**, also known as a **web**.

Benzene ring: A six-carbon-atom closed ring, with a single hydrogen atom attached to each to carbon atom.

Bergello: A form of **canvas-work** embroidery.

Bias: Fabric cut at 45 degrees to **warp** and **weft**. This cut exploits the natural stretch of the fabric so that it **drapes** well over the curves of the body.

Biella: An important textile-producing town – primarily woollens – near Milan, Italy.

Bimli: See Kenaf.

Bimlipatum jute: See Kenaf.

Biodegradable: The process by which organic substances are broken down by **enzymes** produced by living organisms.

Biopolymers: Naturally occurring polymers produced by living organisms such as starch and sugar.

Biosynthesis: The formation of complex molecules within the cells of living organisms.

Biotechnology: The term used for any technology that uses biological systems, living organisms and derivatives to make, modify or process products for specialist use.

Bleeding: A loss or transfer of colour in printed fabric.

Blend: A yarn mixed from two or more different fibres.

Block printing: Wooden blocks carved with a design in relief are used as a means of transferring **dye** onto fabric. Originated in China.

Blowing: A treatment that uses steam to remove creases from fabric.

Blue collar: Manual work.

Bobbin lace: A textile made by braiding and twisting threads, wound on bobbins and held in place by pins on a pillow.

Boll: The 'fruit' capsule of the cotton plant, containing the seeds covered in white hairs – the cotton fibres.

Bollgard®: A registered trademark for a quality of **GM cotton**.

Bolt: A complete piece of fabric folded over a card. Cotton is rolled, so a bolt will usually be woollen/worsted fabric.

Bombay hemp: See Sunn.

Bombyx mandarina moore: Believed to be the wild ancestor of the cultivated *Bombyx mori*.

Bombyx mori: The cultivated silk moth, which feeds on the leaves of the mulberry tree. It is both blind and flightless.

Bonding: Attaching two or more layers of fabric together, often by an adhesive heat treatment.

Botany wool: Merino wool originating from Botany Bay, where the first merino sheep in Australia landed .

Bouclé: Yarn or fabric with a curled, looped surface.

Breaking: (1) The process of adding a soft *handle* and brilliance to the surface of silk fabric. (2) One of several processes in flax production, which converts the raw material into linen yarn.

Brightening agent: Increases whiteness or brightness of fabric.

British Colour Group (BCG): British colour consultancy.

Broadcloth: A term for fabric over 150 cm wide, cotton or woollen.

Brocade: Rich fabric with woven raised pattern.

Brushed: Fabric with a brushed, raised surface.

Brushing: Process that removes loose fibres and can raise the surface of the fabric for warmth.

Bt cotton: Naturally occurring soil bacterium *Bacillus thuringiensis*.

Burlap: American-English term for jute or hessian.

C

Cable knitting: Knitted three-dimensional twisting effects that mimic ropes.

Calendering: The process of adding sheen to fabric using heated steel rotary cylinders.

Canvas work: Form of embroidery that completely covers the under-fabric.

Carding: Process of brushing raw or washed fibres to ensure that they are thinned out and evenly distributed to facilitate spinning. Carding can also be used to create mixes of different fibres or of different colours.

Carding machine: A device featuring a series of rollers that straighten and align fibres into an orderly mass. See also Carding.

Cash crop: Crops grown for money as opposed to domestic subsistence.

Cashgora: A blend between cashmere and mohair, one of three types of fibre produced by nigora goats.

Cashmere: The fine, downy undercoat produced primarily, but not exclusively, from the Himalayan mountain goat (*Capra hircus laniger*), popularly known as the cashmere goat for its fine, downy undercoat.

Ccara: One of two 'light wool' types of llama. See also Curaca.

Cebu hemp: See Manila hemp.

Celanese Corporation: The producer of the first commercial acetate yarn, originally called American Cellulose & Chemical Manufacturing Company; today a global chemical company.

Cellulose: This organic compound is the primary structure to all green plants, forming the primary cell wall and also part of the secondary wall.

Cellulose fibres: Natural and man-made fibres regenerated from plants, such as viscose and modal.

Cellulose I and II: The correct designation for natural and regenerated cellulose.

Chacu: An inca ritual involving the communal rounding up of vicuña, once every three to four years, for shearing and releasing back into the wild. This practice continues today as part of the Peruvian government's vicuña conservation policy.

Changeant: Different colours in the warp and weft threads produce a fabric that appears to change colour depending on the angle it is viewed at. Also referred to as two-tone or shot fabric.

Chardonnet silk: An early cellulose-based artificial silk, which was highly flammable.

Charkha (or churka): An Indian precursor to the cotton gin, used for long-staple cotton but not adequate for short-staple varieties.

Chenille: Yarn or fabric with a furry, velvety 'caterpillar' appearance.

Chemical finishes: Treatments applied to fabric to give a specialist finish.

Chrome dye: Type of dye typically used on wool.

China grass: One of two types of ramie, a bast vegetable fibre of the nettle family, also known as white ramie.

Chinoiserie: Eighteenth- and nineteenth-century trend influenced by orientalism.

Chintz: A finishing process on cotton fabric that produces a glazed surface.

Chitin: A natural polymer that can be found in crab shells, among other places.

Chitosan: A fibre substance produced from chitin.

Chroma: The saturation or brightness of a colour. The term also defines the purity and strength of a colour.

Chromatic: Having a hue.

Chromatics: The science of colour. Chromatics considers the human perception of colour, colour theory, and the eyes' and brain's perception of colour.

Chrysalis: Pupa case, the third of four life stages (embryo/larva/pupa/imago) of the silk moth.

Circular knitting: Knitted on a circular machine resulting in tubular fabric.

Clip: A generic term applied when clipping or shearing a herd of angora goats. Also refers to the amount of wool cut from a flock of sheep at one shearing.

Closed-loop processing: In textiles, usually refers to methods of capturing and reprocessing the solvents used in the manufacturing of man-made fibres.

CMYK system: The four-colour screen system used to reproduce colour photographs: cyan, magenta, yellow, black.

Cocoon: Pupa casing made by the silk-moth larvae.

Color Association of the United States (CAUS): Colour standards and forecasting organization, established in 1915. Its current title dates to 1955.

Colourant: Dye or pigment colouring substance.

Coloured angoras: Hybrid angora goats.

Colour fade: Loss of colour due to light, washing or other agencies.

Colourfast: Fabrics dyed in colours that resist fading.

Colour harmony: Colour relationships in proportion to each other.

Colour Marketing Group (CMG): A colour forecasting service.

Colour migration: Colour moves from one part of the fabric to another.

Colour value: See Value (colour).

Colour-way: One of several alternative colour combinations.

Colour wheels: The colour spectrum organized into wheels to help rationalize and predict colour interactions.

Combing: Process of making fibres smooth prior to spinning.

Comfort stretch: Implies approximately a 2 or 3 per cent stretch in a fabric, provided by the knit or weave structure, or by the inclusion of an elastane yarn.

Commision Internationale de L'Eclairage (CIE): Founded in 1931 following the exploration of the need for a standardization of colour.

Como: Italian city and region famous for manufacturing silk, and still the centre of the Italian silk industry.

Complementary hues: Opposite colours on a colour wheel.

Composite materials: Engineered materials made from two or more constituent materials with significantly different physical or chemical properties, that remain separate and distinct on a macroscopic level within the finished structure.

Concession (retail): A dedicated retail space within a large department store that is rented or allocated to a specific brand. This gives the brand a retail presence it may not normally be able to obtain.

Condensers: Machines that separate the web or batt into predetermined weight strands as part of the spinning process.

Contrast: The visual difference between colours. For example black and white are high-contrast colours.

Converter: A company that buys greige fabric then dyes, prints or finishes it.

Cooking: A term in silk processing that refers to the cocoons being immersed in boiling water to soften the sericin, also referred to as maceration.

Cotton belt: Term used to describe the cotton-growing regions of the US.

Cotton count: Numerical expression for size of yarn, denoting a certain length of yarn for a fixed weight, in this case the number of 840-yard lengths or hanks per pound weight.

Cotton gin: An abbreviation of cotton engine, this machine separates the cotton fibres from the seedpods. The American inventor Eli Whitney (1765–1825) is credited with inventing the modern gin in 1792, patented in 1794.

Cottonizing: Method of processing linen or hemp fibres using cotton processing machinery.

Cottonopolis: A term used to describe Manchester, England, as the most important city for cotton manufacturing in the world in the nineteenth century.

Cotton picker: A machine used to remove the cotton from the boll without damaging the plant.

Cotton stripper: A machine that strips the entire boll from the cotton plant.

Counted-thread embroidery: The warp and weft threads of the base fabric are counted and bear a relation to how the surface is embroidered.

Course: In knitting, the row of loops that runs across the width of the fabric, equivalent to the weft in a woven fabric.

Covalent bond: A chemical bond characterized by the sharing of pairs of electrons between atoms forming a **polymer**.

Crease-resistant: Fabric that has been treated to improve its recovery.

Creole cotton: *Gossypium barbadense*, a luxurious long-**staple** cotton.

Crêpe: Yarn or fabric with a high **twist** that has a granular texture.

Crewel-work: A form of freehand embroidery.

Crimp: A natural or artificial wave to the fibre or yarn.

Crocheting: Decorative technique that creates fabric by using a hooked needle to pull loops of yarn through other loops.

Crocking: A rubbing test for **colourfast**ness.

Cross-dyeing: The dyeing of a component in a mixture of fibres where at least one is coloured separately to produce a mélange effect.

Cross stitch: Style of **counted-thread** embroidery.

Cuprammonium: A compound composed of copper sulphate and ammonia used to produce cellulose fibres such as **cupro**.

Cupro: A fibre derived from the discarded **linters** that are a by-product of processing cotton, frequently used for linings.

Curaca: One of two 'light wool' types of llama. See also **Ccaca**.

Cured: In the printing process, a term for a colour that has been fixed.

Cut-and-sewn knitwear: Knitted garments made by stitching together pre-knitted fabric, in much the same way as woven garments are made.

D

Damask: Figured fabric, with the **figure** (design) of a contrasting weave. Usually constructed with **satin-weave** warps and wefts in sateen weave. Named after Damascus in modern-day Syria.

Daveo: See **Manila hemp**.

Deccan hemp: See **Kenaf**.

De-cortication: The removal of the hard outer bark from plants such as **ramie**.

De-gumming: The removal of **sericin** as part of silk production. In the production of **ramie** it is the process of extracting the fibres prior to **spinning**.

De-hairing: The removal of coarse outer **guard hairs** from the soft under-down of animal fibres in preparation for **spinning**.

Denier: A unit of measurement used to measure the linear mass density of fibres. Several **filaments** together are referred to as 'total denier'. The system is used in Britain and the US for hosiery.

Denim: A cotton **twill-weave** fabric where the **wefts** pass under two or more **warps** producing a diagonal rib effect. The fabric was originally called serge de Nîmes from the French town where it was made.

Design repeat: A complete unit of a textile design, which may be repeated in one of several ways.

Devoré: A partially sheer fabric containing two or more fibre types. One of the fibres is 'eaten' away to produce a pattern by screen printing with an acid that 'burns out' or 'devours' the natural fibre to reveal the sheer **synthetic** base filaments.

Dhoti: Traditional unstitched cloth garment worn wrapped around the lower body. Considered authentic formal attire for men in the Indian subcontinent.

Direct printing: Commonly used industrial printing method. **Dyes**, thickeners and mordants are printed directly onto the fabric.

Discharge printing: Colour is chemically removed from parts of the fabric to reveal the base colour. Alternatively, adding an additional colour that is unaffected by the discharging agent.

Disperse dyes: Mainly used for polyester, disperse dyes contain particles that scatter on the fibre to produce the colour.

Distributor: A person or organization involved in making a product or service available for use by a consumer or other retailer.

Double-cloth weaving: **Weaving** technique that creates a fabric with two **face** or right sides and no wrong or reverse side.

Double face: Any fabric that has two **face** sides and no reverse side.

Double jersey: All needle rib-knitted fabric where both the **face** and reverse side are the same. See also **Jersey**.

Drape: The behaviour of the fabric, how it handles, falls and hangs.

Drawing and finisher drawing: Two processes that further improve the evenness and regularity of yarn, prior to final **spinning**. Each technique gives a uniquely different character, in both appearance and feel, to the fabric and end product.

Dreyfus, Camille and Henri: Swiss industrialists; early producers of **cellulose acetate** yarn.

Dromedary: *Camelus dromedarius*, the single-humped Arabian camel, not used in the production of camel-hair fibre. See also **Bactrian**.

Dry prints: Pigment-printed fabric with colours that have been heat-set.

Ductile: Easily moulded or shaped.

Ductile strength: The mechanical property describing how much deformation a material can sustain before fracturing.

DuPont: American chemical company founded in 1802. In the twentieth century it led the **polymer** revolution by developing successful materials such neoprene, **nylon**, **Lycra** and Teflon.

Dye: **Pigment** dissolved in a fluid for **dyeing**.

Dyeing: The process of transferring **colourant** to fibres, **yarns**, fabrics or ready-made garments.

Dye lot: A batch of **yarn** that has been **dyed** together in the same vat.

E

Egyptian cotton: *Gossypium hirsutum* and *Gossypium barbadense*. All cotton grown in Egypt is called Egyptian cotton, however it is these two cotton species, with an extra-long **staple**, that produce the luxury fabric synonymous with the name.

Elastane: The generic term for stretchy fabrics and yarns.

Elastic modulus (modulus of elasticity): The mathematical description of a substance's tendency to be deformed elastically (non-permanently) when a force is applied.

Elastomer: A rubbery material composed of **polymers**, capable of recovering its original shape after being stretched.

Ells: English measuring system from the Tudor period, whereby 30–40 ells was equal to 35–50 yards (32–46m).

Embossing: A relief pattern is embossed onto the fabric, usually by a heated press.

Embroidery: Handicraft surface decoration. Designs are stitched onto fabrics using threads and yarns. Beads, sequins and other applied decorative **trimmings** can be embroidered onto the fabric.

Ends: **Warp** threads.

Enzymes: Proteins that catalyse/accelerate chemical reactions.

Eri silk: A type of **wild silk** gleaned from the eri silk moth.

Eri silk moth: *Philosamia ricini*, a type of wild **silk moth** found only in India, it feeds on the castor plant and producing silk yarn from its **cocoon** is considered to be ethical and equivalent to organic rearing.

Ester: Any of a class of organic compounds that react with water to produce alcohols and organic or inorganic acids.

Extrusion (extruded): Forcing a **viscous** liquid through a device to form filament fibres.

F

Fabric dyeing: **Dyeing** process that occurs after **weaving** the fabric. Also known as piece dyeing.

Face: The correct side of the fabric.

Fair Isle: A traditional, complex hand-**knitting** technique featuring horizontal patterns using five to seven different colours, and originating in Fair Isle, north of Scotland.

Fairtrade: An independent labelling scheme, initiated in the Netherlands for food production, it has now been extended to textiles; particularly cotton. The label assures the consumer that the product has met the international Fairtrade standard for production and is eligible to carry the FAIRTRADE mark, which guarantees that the farmer has been paid a premium above the market value of their commodity.

Fashioned: In knitting, increasing or decreasing stitches forms the garment shape.

Fast (colour and light): Does not lose colour with exposure to light or after washing.

Felt: A non-woven fabric made by matting and condensing fibres together.

Felted: A matted appearance.

Felting: Process of making **felt**.

Fibre: A long, thin, flexible structure. Plant and animal fibres are spun to create yarn.

Fibrillation: A natural defect to which silk is prone, and which occurs if the outermost layer is roughened up off the filaments by harsh washing or abrasion. The resulting fibrils reflect light, giving a 'peach bloom' effect. This effect is also purposely reproduced over the whole surface of the fabric by 'scuffing' with an enzyme treatment or mechanical abrasion. The result is a desirable, tactile, 'sueded' or 'sand-washed' silk.

Fibrils: Nanometre fibres.

Figure/figured: A motif or raised part of the design that contrasts with the ground fabric.

Filament: A single, continuous strand of fibre. Any man-made yarn of one or more strands running the entire length of the yarn.

Fire-retardant: Able to delay or prevent combustion.

Fixing: Method of making a dye colourfast on a fabric by use of a mordant.

Flax: *Linum usitatissimum*, an annual herb of the Linaceae family used to make linen.

Float: A portion of yarn that extends under or over adjacent warps or wefts. The term is also used in knitting when the yarn 'floats' across several stitches.

Fluoropolymer: An organic polymer with large, multiple-unit molecules that consist of a chain of carbon atoms to which fluorine atoms are appended.

FTC (Federal Trade Commission): The US regulatory body for consumer protection, which monitors accurate labelling in that country.

Fulling: A finishing process that compresses fabric by means of heat, steam and pressure.

Fully fashioned: A term applied to knitwear when each piece is knitted to the exact shape required by increasing and decreasing stitches.

G

Gandhi, Mohandas Karamchand: (1869–1948) A major political and spiritual leader of India and its independence movement, commonly known as Mahatma (Great Soul). He exhorted Indians, both rich and poor, to spin khadi (homemade cloth) in support of the independence movement, which resulted in a boycott of British textiles.

Gang-slit: One of several slitting processes in the production of metallic yarn, producing micro-width yarns.

Garment dyeing: Dyeing ready-made garments.

Gauge: Describes the fineness or chunkiness of a knitted garment achieved by needle size and spacing.

Geo textiles: Permeable fabrics that, when used in association with soil, have the ability to separate, filter, reinforce, protect or drain; usually made from polypropylene or polyester.

Gin: The building where cotton is processed. See also Cotton gin.

Ginning: Generically implies the complete process of preparing cotton.

Glazed: Smooth, glossy surface on fabric.

GM cotton: Genetically modified or transgenic cotton.

Grease-wool: The term used to describe wool before it has been cleaned and scoured, also known as wool-in-the-grease.

Green chemistry: Twelve principles that aim to help define the true ecological, ethical and sustainable credentials of a raw material or product.

Green ramie: One of two types of ramie, a bast vegetable fibre of the nettle family.

Greige: Fabric in its raw state, before it has been bleached, dyed or finished.

Ground colour: Usually a print term indicating the background or main colour of the fabric.

Guanaco: *Lama guanicoe*, a member of the South American *Camelidae* family.

Guard hairs: Coarser outer hairs that protect the finer under-hairs or down on many animals.

H

Hackling: Process by which the short, broken linen fibres, or tows, are combed out, leaving only the desirable long fibres, ready for spinning.

Hair sheep: A type of sheep that does not produce wool.

Halo effect: The effect created by the fine downy surface of angora yarn that, in pale colours, appears slightly luminous in the light.

Handle: The touch or feeling of the fabric.

Hank: Unsupported coil of yarn. The ends are tied together to maintain the shape. Also called a skein.

Hank dyed: Dyed as yarn.

Header cards: Also known as a fabric 'hanger', the header card is a large fabric swatch, or 'feeler', used for displaying and demonstrating the quality of a fabric. Information regarding fibre types, yarn count, width, weight and finish appear on the card that supports the swatch.

Hemp: The generic name for the entire *Cannabis* family of plants.

Henduan: A breed of yak from the alpine regions of Tibet, producing the best fibre yield. See also Jiulong.

Hessian: See Jute.

High street: A generic marketing and retail term implying competitive mass-market fashion.

High-tenacity rayon (HTR): An extremely strong rayon developed in the 1940s for industrial purposes.

High-wet-modulus rayon (HWM): A strong rayon that retains its strength when wet, developed in the 1950s.

Himalayan mountain goat: *Capra hircus laniger*, popularly known as the cashmere goat.

Hollow fibre: A tube-like man-made fibre that provides good insulation.

Homespun: Cloth woven on a small domestic scale. The term can also suggest a desirable rustic craft appearance that implies a handmade authenticity.

Horsehair: Originally tail and mane hair, now a generic term for canvas interlining generally used in tailoring.

Huacaya: Pronounced wua'ki'ya, one of two types of alpaca, producing a dense, soft, sheep-like fibre with a uniform crimp. See also Suri.

Huarizo: An alpaca-llama cross breed.

Hue: Colour. Pure hue has no other colour mixed in with it.

Hydrocarbon: Any chemical compound that consists of only hydrogen and carbon.

I

Icelandic wool (sheep): Wool from the fleece of Icelandic sheep, which is double layered, made up of fine cashmere-like inner fibres and coarser, medium outer fibres.

Ikat: A weaving technique where the wefts and/or warps are dyed different colours at predetermined intervals. The designs produced when using this technique appear to have a blurred effect.

Indigo: A naturally derived plant dye still in popular use for denim products to provide the distinctive shade of blue that fades desirably.

Industrial hemp: The term given to the variety of hemp (*Cannabis sativa* L. subsp. *sativa*) grown for fibre and other non-narcotic purposes.

Inert gas: A gas that does not chemically react under a set of given conditions.

Ingeo™: A high-performance trademarked biopolymer fibre made from corn.

Inkjet printing: Droplets of ink are transferred or propelled onto almost any medium. Common means of printing on home computer printers.

Inlaid yarn: Yarn that is held in place by the loops of the knitting rather than being knitted in.

Intarsia: A knitted fabric with several solid colours in one row of knitting. The pattern is formed by stopping one colour and twisting in a new colour over the needles each time there is a colour change.

Interlining: A firmer fabric that is applied to parts of the outer fabric of a garment to give a stronger handle or firmer shape, usually on collars and cuffs and chest panels in tailoring.

International Colour Authority (ICA): Colour prediction organization.

Isan: Northeastern area of Thailand where ikat weaving is traditionally a speciality.

Itten wheel: Colour wheel devised by Johannes Itten (1888–1967) to document a logical format for working with colour.

J

Jacquard: A type of weaving or knitting process and a type of fabric. In woven fabric the process allows for an unlimited variety of designs, in knitwear it implies that every colour of yarn used is knitted into the back of the fabric when not in use on the face side.

255

Jacquard loom: Developed by French inventor Joseph Jacquard (1752–1834), the loom features a string of punch cards that can be processed mechanically in the correct sequence.

Jamewar weave: An intricate Kashmir weaving technique producing expensive shawl fabrics worn, originally, by nobles.

Japonisme: Eighteenth- and nineteenth-century trend influenced by orientalism.

Jersey: Generically used to describe many types of knitted fabric. Single jersey is plain knit on one side and purl on the reverse and is used for tops. Double jersey is plain on both sides and can be double in weight. It does not unravel when cut so is fine for cutting and sewing more complicated styles.

Jerseywear: Generic term for various garments, such as T-shirts and polo shirts, that are cut and made from fabric that has been previously knitted.

Jiulong: A breed of yak from the plateau regions of Tibet, producing the best fibre. See also Henduan.

Johnstons of Elgin: The oldest cashmere mill still in operation, located in Elgin, Scotland.

JIT (just-in-time): A production strategy aimed at reducing stock by manufacturing only when necessary.

Jute: A coarse, strong, bast vegetable fibre.

K

Kapok: Vegetable seed fibre from the kapok tree.

Karakul: Also known as Persian lamb, this sheep has a tight glossy curl, often in black or grey.

Kasuri: Japanese type of ikat weave.

Kemps: Short, thick, coarse, stiff, hollow fibres on coarser wools, such as those of angora goats, usually unaffected by dye.

Kenaf: A species of hibiscus with visual similarities to jute.

Keratin: Animal protein found in wool, hair, nails, feathers and horn.

Khadi: Indian hand-spun, hand-woven cloth made from cotton, silk or wool, traditionally spun on a domestic spinning wheel called a charkha.

Khadi hand-loom: Indian hand-spun, hand-woven cloth of either cotton, silk or wool.

Kimono: Traditional Japanese costume made from silk.

King Cotton: A term used to describe the financial importance of cotton production to the US economy in the nineteenth century.

Knitting: Method of constructing fabric from yarn by a series of interlinked loops. Refers to hand and machine techniques.

Kolbe, Adolph Wilhelm Hermann (1818–1884): German chemist credited with the understanding of synthesis in the context of a chemically developed substance.

L

Lab dips: Small pieces of yarn windings or fabric swatches sample dyed for approval prior to larger dye lots and bulk production dyeing.

Lace: Fabric or trim made up of intertwined or embroidered threads.

Lamé: Fabric woven with metal laminate, often gold in colour.

Lamination (1): Part of a manufacturing process to produce metallic yarn; the process seals a metal layer between two layers of a selected fibre.

Lamination fabrics (2): Bonding or sealing two or more fabrics together.

Lanolin: Produced from wool grease. Medical-grade lanolin is hypoallergenic and bacteriostatic.

Lanuda: One of two 'heavy wool' types of llama. See also tapada.

Lay planning: The placement of garment pattern pieces onto the laid fabric in the most economical format prior to cutting. In mass production, this process is usually executed by computer.

LEA: A US measuring system for grading the fineness of linen – 1 LEA = 1 x 300 yards (yarn) to the pound weight.

Lead time: The amount of time it takes to manufacture fabric and or garments and the delivery transport time.

Lehnga: Long skirt and top traditionally worn by Muslim women in India and Pakistan.

Light wheel: Based on the additive colour system, this wheel shows information concerning light rays and transparent colour. Used for lighting and as the basis for video and computer graphics.

Lignin: A chemical compound commonly derived from wood and an integral part of the cell walls of plants.

Linear polymer: A polymer in which the molecules form long chains without branches or cross-linking; all fibre-forming polymers are linear in structure.

Linen Board: Established in 1711, The Board of Trustees of the Linen Manufacturers of Ireland was set up to develop the Irish linen industry.

Linenopolis: A term used to describe Belfast in the nineteenth century.

Linen union: Fabric with a linen weft and a cotton warp.

Lint: Cleaned cotton. Also describes a fuzzy surface. Linen is lint-free.

Linters: Fuzzy down removed from cotton as part of the ginning process.

Living Linen Project: Records first-hand information about the linen industry in Northern Ireland in the twentieth century.

Llama fibre (or llama wool): Referred to as fibre because, technically, llama hair is not wool due to its particular structure.

Lofty (or loft): Descriptive of the appearance of woollen fibre or fabric, meaning voluminous, supple, soft and springy.

Long-line fibres: One of two categories of flax fibre, the short fibres are called tow fibres.

Loop-back fabric: Type of pile-woven fabric, with the loops left intact, such as towelling.

Luminosity: Refers to colour value. The lighter a colour the greater is the reflection of light back to the eye, lighter colours are therefore more luminous than darker colours.

LUREX™: The brand name of a type of metallic yarn, usually a synthetic fibre, with a vaporized layer of aluminium. The term may also refer to fabric that contains metallic yarn.

LYCRA®: A trade name for an elastane fabric made by DuPont and now produced by INVISTA.

Lyon: French city and region famous for manufacturing silk, and still the centre of the French silk industry.

M

Maceration: See Cooking.

Machine embroidery: Automated embroidery.

Macramé: Fabric created by the interlinking of knots.

Manila hemp: Also known as daveo and cebu hemp and produced from the leaves of the abacá plant.

Manufacturing hub: Describes an important centre of manufacturing, and is often used in reference to the developing world.

Margin: A gross margin implies the difference between buying and selling a product before overheads have been deducted. Net margin is the profit after overheads have been deducted.

Marl yarns: Two different-coloured yarns twisted together.

Mashru: Meaning 'permitted', a fabric development using silk warps and cotton wefts, which allowed Muslim men to wear silk.

Mauvine: First synthetic dye, discovered in 1856 by William Perkins.

Medulated fibres: Intermediate fibres on an angora goat, less coarse than the kemp fibres but coarser than the true mohair fibres.

Mélange: A mix of colours worked together in yarn or fabric form.

Mercerized cotton: See Mercerizing.

Mercerizing: A caustic soda solution is applied to cotton yarn and/or fabric to give it a more lustrous and smoother appearance. Named after John Mercer who invented the technique in the mid-nineteenth century.

Merino: A distinctive breed of sheep originating in Spain but now the source of the bulk of Australian wool production. A luxury wool.

Meta-aramid: One of two aromatic polyamide fibres (the other is para-aramid), primarily used for fire-protective clothing.

Metallic yarns: Yarns containing metal threads or metallic elements.

Microfibre: Fine man-made fibre or filament that is under 1 denier. Ten kilometres should weigh less than one gram.

Micronaire: A system for assessing cotton fibre fineness and maturity. A poor count affects the value of the cotton.

Microns: Unit of measurement, one micron is one-millionth of a metre.

Mill: The place where yarn and fabric are manufactured.

Milled: Fabric that has been treated to age or soften its appearance, or to blend colours together.

Milling: A treatment that ages and softens the appearance of fabric by blending the colours, obscuring the weave and making the fabric more compact.

Modal: Generic name for regenerated natural polymer cellulose fibre.

Module builder: Machine that compresses cotton into large modular blocks.

Mohair: The fleece of the **angora** goat and fabric produced from it.

Moiré fabric: Fabric with a watery, wavy or rippled appearance. Usually silk or rayon.

Molecule: The smallest identifiable unit into which a material can be divided and still retain the composition and chemical properties of that material. A molecule must contain two or more atoms held together by a chemical bond.

Momme/s: System of weight measurement for silk, quantifying the density of silk as opposed to the thread count.

Monochromatic: Of one **hue** or colour. One hue harmony combines colours derived from a single hue, graduated shades of the same base colour.

Monomer: A molecule that can bind chemically to other molecules to form a **polymer**. The word comes from the Greek 'mono' for one and 'meros' for part.

Mordant: Chemical compound used as a **dye** fixative.

Mordant printing: A design pattern is printed using a **mordant** that resists colour when **dyed**, thus forming the pattern.

Moso bamboo: *Phyllostachys*, the species of bamboo cultivated for textile production.

Muga silk: A variety of **wild silk** gleaned from the **muga silk moth**.

Muga silk moth: *Antheraea assamensis*, a wild and semi-wild species of **silk moth** living in a restricted area in Assam, India.

Mulberry silkworm: See Silkworm.

Multivoltine: Term applied to **silk moths** that produce at least ten batches of eggs per year.

Munsell wheel: A **partitive colour** system based on five **primary hues** and **after-image** perceptions that are derived from hues we see in nature.

Muted colour: A subdued version of a **hue**.

N

Napa (or nappa): Sheep leather.

Narrow fabric: Fabric less than 45 cm (18 in.) wide (UK) or 30 cm (12 in.) wide (Europe/USA).

Naturally coloured cotton: Cotton that is naturally plant pigmented. Peruvian **Pima** and Tangüis cottons are naturally coloured.

Natural polymer: See Polymer.

Natural protein fibre: See Protein fibre.

Natural resin: A **viscous** liquid substance, formed by hydrocarbon-based plant secretions, that hardens over time. Resins are usually transparent or translucent, and they are typically soluble but not in water.

Needle lace: Handmade **lace** using a needle where all the stitch work is based on **buttonhole** or **blanket** stitch.

Needlepoint: A form of **canvas-work embroidery**.

Neoprene: A synthetic rubber.

Neps: Entangled fibres or knots.

Nettle: A **bast** fibre.

New Zealand cotton: Fibre from the **bast** of the New Zealand ribbon tree. It has a strong fibre that resembles **flax**.

New Zealand flax: *Phormium tenax*, or *harakeke* in Maori, native of New Zealand and not related to linen **flax**, *Linum usitatissimum*.

Nieuwland, Julius (1878–1936): Belgian-born American chemist whose research led to the invention of **neoprene**.

Nigora: A cross between an **angora** goat and **cashmere**-producing Nigerian dwarf goat. The fibre it produces is known as **cashgora**.

Nitinol: A nickel–titanium alloy distinguished by its shape memory: if deformed while below a particular temperature, an object made of Nitinol will return to its original shape when heated.

Nm: Metric measuring system used for linen/**flax** – the number of 1,000-metre lengths per kilogram.

Noils: Short fibres left over from **combing** wool or **spinning** silk. These fibres are weaker than normal fibres and considered inferior.

Nylon: The first **synthetic** fibre from the **DuPont** chemical company, used as a replacement for silk for stockings during the Second World War. It is also a generic term for synthetic **polymers** also known as polyamides.

O

Off-grain: The garment pattern pieces are not correctly placed on the straight **grain** of the fabric (unless **bias** cut).

Offshore: A term used to describe manufacturing in a foreign country; it usually implies production in the developing world.

Oiled wool: Undyed, unscoured wool containing natural **lanolin**.

Oiling (cloth): Water-repelling treatment applied to fabric.

Olefin fibre: A man-made fibre known for strength and resistance to staining, mildew, abrasion and sunlight.

One-way fabric: Implies the fabric has a single direction and that all the pattern pieces must be cut in the same direction to avoid noticeable **shading**.

Organic cotton: Cotton grown without pesticides from plants that are not genetically modified.

Organzine: Twisted threads used as **warps** in silk **weaving**.

Orientalism: A generic term applied to trends and fashions inspired by oriental art and culture.

Oshima: A Japanese type of **ikat** weave.

Over-dye: To apply the same or different **dye** colour as a second process over the initial dyeing. Can be used to produce a deeper intensity of colour, to correct or darken an unwanted colour instead of **stripping**, or be applied over an existing printed fabric.

Over-print: An additional design or motif printed over an existing all-over print.

P

Paco vicuña: A vicuña–alpaca cross breed.

Pantone Professional System: An international colour matching and referencing system.

Para-aramid: One of two aromatic polyamide fibres (the other is **meta-aramid**). Weight-for-weight, para-aramid fibres are stronger than steel.

Partitive colour: The process of placing colours next to each other in order to produce different reactions.

Pashmina: A Kashmiri word for shawls made of **cashmere**. The term is derived from the Persian word *pasham*, meaning 'goat wool'.

Pattern cutting: The art or science of interpreting a drawing or design into a two-dimensional pattern, which when translated into fabric and sewn together becomes a three-dimensional representation of the original design drawing.

Payen, Anselme (1795–1878): French chemist who discovered **cellulose** in the 1830s.

Peace silk: Refers to silk that has been produced without harming the moth that has produced the silk **cocoon**. The moth is allowed to emerge naturally, before the cocoons are harvested. Also known as vegetarian silk.

Pectin: Light substance derived from the cell walls of plants (the non-woody parts). Pectin helps to bind cells together.

Percale: Denotes a close weave, high thread count, irrespective of yarn type.

Perlon: Trade name for a German polyamide developed as a competitor to the American **nylon** in the build-up to World War II. Because Perlon's monomer unit has six carbon atoms, Perlon is also referred to as nylon 6, as opposed to nylon 6,6 for the original version.

Peruvian alpaca: Alpaca marketed with its own distinctive branding.

Petit point: A form of **canvas-work embroidery**.

Phloem: Living plant tissue that carries nutrients. See also **Bast fibres**.

Photosynthesis: The process by which green plants use carbon dioxide, water and sunlight to produce sugars.

Picker: A machine that beats, loosens and mixes cotton fibres.

Picks: **Weft** threads.

Piece: A complete or full length of fabric, which may be in the form of a **bolt** or a **roll**.

Piece dyeing: See Fabric dyeing.

Pigment: Insoluble colour.

Pigment print: Printed with **pigment** and binder rather than **dyes**.

Pigment wheel: A 12-step **colour wheel** for working with **subtractive colour**, showing how colours react when used in combinations to create the other **hues**.

Pile fabric: Generic term for a raised surface fabric, such as velvet or corduroy.

Pile weaving: **Weaving** technique that uses rods to make loops on the surface of the resulting fabric. The loops can be cut to create **pile fabric**, or left intact to create **loop-back fabric**.

Pill or pilling: Entangled fibres after washing or wearing form little balls known as pills.

Pima cotton: Indigenous American long-**staple** cotton (*Gossypium barbadense*) named after North American Pima Indians.

257

Glossary

Piña: Fibres obtained from the leaves of the pineapple plant.

Piña cloth: Fabric woven from **piña** fibres.

Plain knit: The **face** side of basic **jersey**, the reverse side is known as **purl**.

Plain weave: A basic weave construction of **warps** and **wefts** criss-crossing each other at right angles.

Ply: Two or more single yarns twisted together.

Polyamide: Any **synthetic polymer** that consists of amides (nitrogen-containing compounds) joined by peptide bonds (chemical bonds between groups of amino acids, which are the primary linkage of all protein structures).

Polymer: A substance composed of molecules with a large molecular mass linked by repeated structural units or monomers. It can be naturally occurring or have a **synthetic** substance. DNA and plastics are well-known examples.

Polyester: Generic name for **synthetic polymers**.

Polyethylene: One of two polymers used to make olefin fibres, polyethylene is the most common plastic and is usually used to make ropes and utility fabrics.

Poly(ethylene terephthalate): Synthetic polymer used to make **polyester** and PET (the stiff, transparent plastic usually used for containers).

Polymerization: Any chemical process in which **monomers** are fused to create longer **polymer** chains.

Polypropylene: One of two polymers used to make olefin fibres, polypropylene is often used to make clothing and furnishing fabrics.

Polyurethane: A polymer used to make **elastane** as well as many types of flexible and rigid foam.

Prato: An important centre for the Italian wool industry, near Florence in Italy.

Premier Vision: A bi-annual fabric **trade fair** in Paris, France, and also at other international venues.

Pre-shrunk: Fabric that has been shrunk at the **weaving mill** and should not shrink further.

Primary colours: Red, yellow and blue, the three colours that cannot be made from other colours.

Primary triad: The three **primary colours**.

Print run: In textile printing, a term that usually refers to the amount of fabric to be printed but may also refer to the time frame.

Process wheel: A 12-step process for the three basic primaries that when mixed result in purer **hues**.

Production run: The total number of garments of a style that is manufactured at one time. The number of pieces given as an order to a factory.

Protein fibre: Animal hair/wool or silk.

Pupa: An insect between the usually passive stage of larva and adulthood.

Pure dye silk: Indicates that **weighting** was not added to silk at the **dyeing** stage.

Pure new wool: See Virgin wool.

Purl knit: The reverse side of basic **jersey**, the face side is known as **plain**.

Pygora: A cross between an **angora** goat and a **cashmere**-producing pygmy goat.

Q

QC: Quality control of fabric and clothing manufacturing.

Qiviut (or qivent): The under-wool of a musk ox, *Ovibos moschatus*, whose habitat is the Arctic regions of Canada, Alaska and Greenland.

Quilting: A method of stitching a layer of fabric to a layer of insulative **wadding**, commonly in diamond patterns, but often with decorative stitch patterns. This produces a light and warm material, often used for linings.

R

Raffia palms: Used to make raffia fabric.

Raker: A component design line in an **Argyle** design.

Rambouillet or French merino: A cross between a Spanish **merino** and an English long-wool sheep, originally bred at Rambouillet, near Paris, France.

Ramie: (*Boehmeria nivea*) a **bast** vegetable fibre of the nettle family. See also **China grass** and **Green ramie**.

Raw silk: The short fibres left over from **spinning** silk.

Rayon: A manufactured, regenerated **cellulose fibre**. The name was first used in the US in 1924, in Europe it was referred to as **viscose** or **art silk**, because it was an inexpensive alternative to real silk.

Rayon bamboo: See Bamboo rayon.

Reactive dyes: **Dyes** used primarily on **cellulose** and **protein fibres**.

Reeling: Process of extracting the silk **filament** from the silkworm's **cocoon**.

Repeat: One complete unit of a design, either printed or woven.

Resist dyeing: Generic term for the different methods of patterning fabric by preventing **dye** reaching certain parts of it.

Resin: See Natural resin and Synthetic resin.

Retting: Process used on all **bast** vegetable fibres to separate the fibre from the plant's stalk.

Reversible: Fabric that can be used either side up, or a style of garment that can be turned inside out.

Ribs: Usually on the waist and cuffs of a sweater for better elasticity and closer fit. May also be used as an all-over knit effect.

Rippling: A process in the production of **flax** fibres for making linen, entailing the removal of the seeds by a mechanical process.

Röhm, Otto (1876–1939): German scientist whose doctorial publication on the **polymers** of acrylic **esters** spurred understanding of the practical potential of **acrylics**.

Rolag: A loose roll of fibres produced by **carding**.

Roller printing: Commercial printing using engraved rollers to transfer colour and design onto fabric.

Roundup Ready®: A registered trademark for a quality of **GM cotton**.

Roves: Continuous lengths of fibre ready for **spinning**.

Roving: A long narrow bundle of fibres with a slight twist to hold it together.

Ruff: Item of clothing worn around the neck, usually of linen. Prominent in Europe from the mid-sixteenth to mid-seventeenth centuries.

Run (print): A complete, continuous length of printed fabric.

S

Samite: A heavy silk fabric woven with gold and silver threads, worn by individuals of high status, that originated in early Byzantium and has also been found in medieval Italy and along the Silk Road in Persia.

Sand-washed silk: Silk fabric washed with sand or other abrasive materials to 'scuff' the surface and produce a tactile, suede-like **handle** and peach-bloom appearance.

Sari: Traditional Indian women's costume.

Sassanid Persia: The last pre-Islamic Persian Empire, which lasted from the third century CE to the seventh century CE.

Sateen: Satin-weave fabric with a polished sheen to the **face** side.

Sateen weave: A weave construction with the maximum amount of **wefts** on the face of the fabric, achieving a soft touch and a smooth finish.

Satin weave: A weave construction with the maximum amount of **warps** on the face of the fabric, achieving a flat, smooth and lustrous finish. Satin weave is not to be confused with satin, which, while of a satin weave construction, refers to the fabric itself.

Saturation: The purity or intensity of a specific colour.

SCOTDIC (Standard Color of Textile Dictionnaire Internationale de la Couleur): A worldwide colour codification system for fabric. The system is applicable to **polyester**, cotton and wool. The coding defines **hues**, **value** and **chroma** for thousands of colours. Head office in Kyoto, Japan.

Scouring: Removal of natural fats, oils and dirt from a yarn, giving fullness to the fibre and bulking up the fabric.

Scutchers: See Scutching.

Scutching: Process of separating fibrous stalks from the woody stems of **bast fibres** using metal rollers.

Sea Island cotton: *Gossypium barbadense*, a luxurious long-**staple** cotton.

Seam turnings: Seams, once sewn together and turned inwards to face the inside of the garment.

Secondary colours: The colours that result from mixing two **primary colours**. The secondary colours are green, orange and violet.

Secondary triad: The three **secondary colours**.

Seed cotton: Pre-cleaned cotton. i.e. before the harvested cotton has gone through the **ginning** process.

Selvedge: The firm side edges of the fabric running parallel to the **warp**.

Sericin: A water-soluble protective gum produced from the glands of the **silkworm**.

Sericulture: The process of breeding and cultivating **silk moths**.

Shalwar kameez: Traditional dress worn, principally, by Muslim women in Bangladesh, Sri Lanka, Pakistan and Afghanistan. *Shalwars* are loose pyjama-like trousers; a *kameez* is a long shirt or tunic.

Sharara: Traditional Muslim women's garment popularized in India since the time of the Mughal invasion.

Sharecropping: In agriculture, a landowner gives a share of the profits to a tenant who works the land. In particular applied to black farmers (ex-slaves) in the US working on white-owned cotton plantations after the American Civil War.

Shatoosh: A shawl made from the down of the chiru or Tibetan antelope, *Pantholopas hodgsonii*.

Shearing: The process of removing the fleece of a sheep or other fibre-producing animal in one piece.

Shetland sheep: Of Scandinavian origin, with a fleece featuring distinctive fine fibres.

Shoddy: Recycled or re-manufactured wool made by tearing apart existing wool fabric and re-spinning it.

Shot: Fabric that appears to change colour when viewed from different directions.

Shous: Woody stems prior to their separation from the fibrous part of the stalk in processing bast fibres.

Shuttle: A weaving tool designed to store and pass weft yarns back and forth through the shed (space between two warps) in order to weave in the wefts.

Silk moth: The cultivated silk moth, *Bombyx mori*, feeds on the leaves of the mulberry tree and is blind and flightless. Silk is harvested from the cocoon of the caterpillar.

Silk noil: See Raw silk.

Silk Road: Ancient trade routes connecting China with Asia Minor and the Mediterranean.

Silk-screen printing: Technique using a screen and ink to print a design, by hand or mechanized. Synthetics are now used for the screens.

Silkworm: The larva or caterpillar of *Bombyx mori*, the cultivated silk moth that feeds exclusively on mulberry leaves.

Single coat: Implies there are no guard hairs in the coat of the animal.

Single jersey: Plain knit on the face side and purl on the reverse. See also Jersey.

Skein: Coiled yarn with tied ends to keep the shape.

Skirted: Angora fibres when clean, with all stains removed.

Slivers: (Pronounced sly-vers) untwisted ropes of fibres.

Smocking: Decorative stitch-work or embroidery technique used to gather and hold fabric together. See also Hank.

Space dyeing: Dyeing technique. Colours are applied at random or regular intervals along the yarn, creating a random multicolour effect when woven or knitted.

Spandex: Generic term for stretch fabrics and yarns, used in North America.

Spinneret (1): Openings in the silkworm's head that secrete the protective sericin gum.

Spinneret (2): Multi-holed device used to extrude viscous polymer filament fibres.

Spinning (1): The singular specific process of applying twist to yarn.

Spinning (2): Manufacturing process used in producing polymer filament fibres, in which they are extruded through a spinneret.

Spinning frame: An eighteenth-century invention often credited to Richard Arkwright (1733–1792), however others developed the invention while under his employment. It was later developed into the water frame (patented 1769) increasing textile production and producing stronger threads than the earlier spinning Jenny.

Spinning Jenny: A multiple yarn-spinning machine invented by James Hargreaves (1720–1778) in Lancashire, England, in 1764 (patented 1770). It enabled the spinning of eight and later up to 80 yarns simultaneously. Considered a factor in starting the British Industrial Revolution. It was named after his daughter.

Spinning process: A generic term for several separate processes, including carding, combing, drawing and spinning.

Spiralling: Knitted fabric distortion.

Staple: Quantifies textile fibre characteristics of length, quality and grade.

Staple fibre: Fibre of finite length.

Stitches: Individual linked loops that form the fabric.

Stock houses: Wholesale companies that hold stock fabrics from a variety of sources, with the advantage of dealing in smaller quantities than placing an order directly with a mill.

Striation: One of a number of parallel grooves or ridges.

Strike-off: Preliminary small-print sample for approval of colour and print.

Stripping: Removal of unwanted colour from printed fabric.

Subtractive colour: A method of creating colours based on pigments or dyes from natural or chemical sources. The colours mix by absorbing some wavelengths of light and reflecting others.

Sunn: A variety of hemp produced in India and also known as Bombay hemp.

Super 100's: An international system that identifies a range of fine worsted fabrics from Super 100's through to Super 210's, the higher the figure the finer the yarn. Ideal for good tailoring.

Supply chain: All the separate disciplines, services and people involved in processing a product from concept to retail.

Suri: Pronounced soo'ree, one of two types of alpaca. They have silky, pencil-fine, mop-like locks. See also Huacaya.

Synthetics: Man-made fibres derived from petrochemicals (which may be produced in staple or filament yarns). Not to be confused with artificial fibres (part natural and part synthetic), which are chemically treated cellulose derivatives.

Synthetic resin: Class of synthetic products developed to mimic some of the physical properties of natural resin.

T

Taffeta: A fine, plain, tightly woven silk cloth, with a dry handle and crispy 'rustle'.

Tailoring: The art or craft of cutting and sewing together a garment to a high standard and incorporating a high level of labour content.

Tamponing: An even film of oil is applied to silk fabric to smooth out irregularities.

Tangüis cotton: Variety of cotton grown primarily in Peru, often organically. Some species are naturally coloured.

Tapada: One of two 'heavy wool' types of llama. See also lanuda.

Tapestry weaving: Vertical loom weaving technique, sometimes called weft-faced weaving because all the warps are hidden.

Target consumer: Marketing term implying an ideal profile customer.

Tassah moths (also tassar): *Antheraea mylitta* and *Antheraea proylei*, wild and semi-wild silk moths respectively.

Technical fabric: Manufactured to perform certain functions.

Technologist: An expert in all aspects of either garment or fabric construction, manufacturing and quality issues.

Tensile strength: Measures the stress required to pull something to its breaking point.

Tertiary colours: The colours that result when a primary and an adjacent secondary colour are mixed together.

Terylene: A trade name for a polyester fibre.

Tex: An international system of measurement used to measure the linear mass density of fibres.

Thorn proofs: Generic term for different types of strong, durable fabrics traditionally used for outdoor pursuits. Often produced from Cheviot wools or New Zealand cross-bred wools. A hard twisted yarn produces a firm-touch fabric that feels almost indestructible.

Thread count: A measure that determines the coarseness or fineness of fabric, achieved by counting the number of threads contained in one square inch of fabric, including warps and wefts.

Threader: A machine-feeding device used in the production of silk filament.

Throwing: Applying a twist to silk filament.

Thrown threads: The different types of thread produced by throwing silk.

Tie-dyeing: Process of tying, knotting or stitching a design on fabric prior to dyeing, then releasing after dyeing to reveal a pattern.

Tone: Variously describes a colour's lightness, value, brilliance, greyness and luminosity.

Top-stitching: Refers to the visible optional stitching on a garment as opposed to the functional stitching that holds the garment together.

Tow: Mass of man-made filaments without twist. In the production of linen, tow also describes one of two categories of flax fibre. Tow fibres are short, whereas the long fibres are called long-line fibres.

Trade fairs: Where manufacturers of yarn, fabric or clothing assemble together to showcase and sell new developments.

Trade name: A specific brand.

Triadic hues: Any three equidistant colours on the colour spectrum when configured as a circle of hues.

Tri-blended: Three different types of fibre blended together.

Trimmings: A generic term used to describe any number of functional components used on a garment, such as buttons and zips, as well as decorative accessories such as braids.

Tussah silk: The most common variety of **wild silk**, harvested from **tassah moths**.

Tuxing: The process of separating the outer and inner sheaths of leaves to reach the fibres that run through them.

Twill weave: A weave construction resulting in a visual diagonal line effect.

Twist: A spiral formation applied to fibres during the spinning proccess to give additional strength and which allows for different colours and fibres to be twisted together for visual and tactile effect. The term also describes the direction in which the yarn is spun ('S' or 'Z' twist).

Two-way fabric: Fabric that can be cut with the pattern pieces in either direction without compromising the end product

U

USP: Unique selling point, a marketing term.

V

Value (colour): A colour's **luminosity** and clarity.

Vat: A **dyeing** vessel.

Vat dyes: Common cotton **dyes**.

Vicuña: *Vicugna vicugna*, the smallest of the South American camelid family. Garments and fabrics made from vicuña fibres should be registered by the Peruvian government, which is the only international body recognized for the task, and assures the conservation of the animal.

Virgin Wool or **pure new wool**: The wool product has been produced from fibres that have not been previously processed.

Viscose: Generic name for regenerated natural **polymer cellulose fibre** (man-made). It cannot be dissolved naturally and therefore needs to be chemically processed, then regenerated by extrusion into a **filament** yarn. The first viscose yarn was produced from wood pulp in the early twentieth century.

Viscose bamboo: See Bamboo viscose.

Viscous: Describes a thick or sticky liquid with resistance to flow.

Visual wheel: A 16-step **partitive** and **subtractive colour wheel** created by Leonardo da Vinci, whose understanding of **complementary** colours greatly influenced Renaissance painting.

W

Wadding: Usually non-woven padded fabric used to create added insulation.

Wales: (1) Columns of loops that run along the length of the fabric. (2) Raised ridges or ribs that run vertically down corduroy, parallel to the **selvedge**. The wider the wales, the lower the numerical expression, and vice versa. The number of wales that fit into one inch (2.5 cm) is the wale count. 21-wale corduroy implies there are 21 wales per inch.

Warp: The yarns that run the length of the fabric, top to bottom.

Waterproof: Completely resistant to water penetration.

Water-repellent: Partially water-resistant.

Water-resistant: Resists but does not entirely prevent the absorption of water.

Waxing: Impregnating fabric with wax to make it shower-proof

Weaving: The process of interweaving **warp** and **weft** threads to make fabric.

Web: Single or multiple sheets of fibres partway through the **spinning process**, also known as a **batt**.

Weft: The yarns that run across the fabric, **selvedge** to selvedge.

Weighting: The application of metallic salts to silk fabric prior to dyeing and finishing. During silk processing the fibres are **de-gummed** of their natural **sericin** gum that gives the fabric a stiff and papery feel. The loss of mass that occurs during this process is restored by the application of metallic salts to add back body, lustre and physical weight.

Wet prints: Fabrics coloured by dyes (which are soluble), not pigments (which are not soluble).

White collar: Office work.

White ramie: See China grass.

Wick: The process of evaporating away moisture and perspiration.

Wild silks: These are characterized by a rough, slubby appearance that differs in colour from farmed silk. The **cocoons** are 'damaged' by the emerging moth eating its way out.

Winnowing: A method of separating the grain from the chuff sometimes used in processing **flax**.

Wool blends: A mixture of different wools and/or other fibres.

Wool classes: Classifications that grade the quality of wool fibres. Diameter of fibre, finesse, crimp, fibre length, cleanliness, colour, breed of sheep and end purpose of the wool are taken into consideration

Woollen or **Wool count**: Refers to yarns spun on the woollen system – the number of 256-yard (512m) strands to 1 pound (454g).

Woollen spun yarn: Yarn that has been **carded** and **drawn** but not **combed**.

Woolmark: A registered mark used for branding different types of Australian wool, used as a means of guaranteeing a standard of quality.

Wool sheep: The type of sheep used for wool production

Worsted count: Yarns are bought and sold by weight rather than length. The relationship between the weight of yarn and its length is expressed in terms of numbers or count, which also indicates the diameter or thickness of the yarn.
The count refers to the number of hanks each measuring 560 yards (512m) that weigh 1 pound (454g). To convert worsted count to a metric count, multiply the length by 1.129. For example, a 1/15 worsted count becomes a 1/17 metric (or Nm) count.

Worsted spun yarn: Yarn that has been **carded**, **drawn** and **combed**.

X

Xanthation: One of several processes used to make **viscose rayon** fibres from **cellulose**.

Y

Yak: *Bos grunniens*, a generally domesticated beast of burden living on the Tibetan plateaus that is also used for fibre.

Yamami silk moth: Believed to be an indigenous species to Japan.

Yarn: A continuous length of interlocked fibres with or without twist.

Yarn count: Numerical expression for size of yarn, denoting a certain length of yarn for a fixed weight. The higher the count, the finer the yarn.

Yarn dyeing: Yarn is **dyed** before being woven or knitted into a fabric.

Yolk: The grease on the fleece of an **angora** goat.

Z

Zari (or Jari or Zardozi): Gold or silver supplementary threadwork, used mainly in India and Pakistan.

Zentai: Skintight clothing that covers the entire body. The word is a portmanteau of *zenshin taitsu*, a Japanese term implying full body covering.

Cocciniglia
8038

Useful information

Index

Page numbers in *italic* refer to illustration
   captions

abacá/abaká (Manila hemp) 171, 178, *178*
acetate 183, 185, 214, 215–16
Acrilan® 10, 199, *199*
acrylic fibres 31, 64, 183, 186, 199–201
adire technique 34
agents 237, 245, 246
airtex 162, *209*
Alcantara® 188, 191
algae *167*
alpacas/alpaca fibre *13, 19, 87, 88,* 88–9, *89*
alternative plant fibres 166–83
alum 35
ambary/ambari hemp 172
angora goats *87,* 94, 96, 98
   see *also* cashmere; mohair
angora rabbits/fibre *87,* 102, 102–3, *103*
anti-soiling fabrics 43, 187, 227
anti-static fabrics 129, 152, 168, 174, *223*
antibacterial fabrics 43, 67, 77, 176, 222,
   223, 225, 233
appliqué 42, *42,* 179
aramid fibres (aromatic polyamides)
   183, 197–8
Ariaprene™ 208, *208, 209, 209*
Arnel® 214, 216
artificial fibres 10, 16, 183, 212–33
   bio-engineered fibres 182, 183, 227–33
   cellulose fibres 14, 152, 182, 183, 213–27
   defined 182, 213
   ecological considerations 152, 214, 216,
      218, 221, 224, 227, 229, 231
   fibre properties *215,* 216, 218, 222, *223,*
      224–5, *225,* 228, 231, 232
   history 214, 215–16, 217–18, 221, 228, 230
   production 215–16, 218, 221, 226, 227,
      229, 231, 232
   sustainability considerations 152, 214, 216,
      220, 221, 222, 224, 227, 229, 231
Audemars, Georges 217
Australian cashmere goats 99
Azlon fibres 227, 230

bactrian camels *87,* 92
bamboo fibre *174,* 174–7, *175, 176, 177*
bamboo kun/kuhn 174, 177
bamboo linen 176
bamboo rayon/viscose 175, 176
banana fibre 173, *173, 178, 178*
barathea 72
bashofu (banana fibre) 173
bast fibres 136, 140, 167, 168–73, 175,
   176, 178
batik 33, *33, 36*
batiste 163
Bayer, Otto 205
Beadle, Clayton 218
Bedford cord 18, 162
Bemberg™ 152, 217
bergello 41
Better Cotton Initiative 239, 240–1
Bevan, Edward 218
bias cutting 21, *75, 179*
bimli/bimlipatum jute 172

bio-engineered fibres see *under* artificial fibres
Bioceat® 214
biodegradable fabrics 10, 152, 172, 177, 208,
   223, 224, 227, 229, 244
Biophyl™ 228
biotechnology 153, 227
bleget (Shetland wool colour) 79
blended yarns 14
blowing 43 see *also* steaming
bluesign® system 193, 240–1
Bollgard® 153
Bombay hemp 172
bonding 43, 146
bouclé 14, 53, 74, *189, 190*
Boyer, Robert 230
brightening agents 43
brocade 19, *20,* 109, 110, 111, 122, *122,* 210
Brummell, George Bryan (Beau) 131
brushed fabrics 43, *74,* 165
Burberry trench coats 16, *17*
burlap 168
burn out see devore

calendering 43, 120
calico 165
Calico Printers' Association 189
Calvert, Frank 230
camelids 88–91
camels/camel hair *87, 92,* 92–3, *93*
canvas 16, 165, 170, 171
carding 13, *13*
   cotton 148, 149
   wool 63, 68, 69, 71, 85
Carothers, Wallace 186, 189, 194
casein 232
cashgora fibre 99
cashmere 22, *87, 94,* 94–6, *95,* 99, *125*
castor bean fibre 183, 233, *233*
ccara fibre (llama) 90
cebu hemp 171, 178
Celanese Corporation 214, 215, 216
CELC see Conféderation of Européenne
   du Lin et du Chanvre
cellulose acetate see acetate
cellulose fibres 14, 149, 152, *167,* 168, 176,
   177 see *also under* artificial fibres
chacu (vicuña conservation) 91
challis 74
chambray 165, *165,* 221
Chardonnet silk 217
charkhas/churkas 144, 145, *145*
Charles V, Holy Roman Emperor 96
charmeuse 125
cheesecloth 165
chemical finishes 43, 118, 146, 151, *162*
chenille 14, 162
Cheviots fabric 72
chiffon 16, *114,* 117, 124, *124*
China grass 169
Chinon® 232
chintz 164
chitin 222, *222*
chitosan 222, *223*
chromatics 45
chromotherapy 54
Chulalongkorn, king of Thailand 111

CIE (Commission Internationale de L'Eclairage) 53
ciré 164
cloqué 122, 162
closed-loop-processing 176, 208, 222, *222, 226*
Club Masters of Linen 134
CMG (Colour Marketing Group) 52
coal 10, 182, 185, 186, 195, 200, 244
coffee grounds 193, *193*
Collins, Arnold 208
Color Association of the United States (CAUS) 52
Colour Group of Great Britain 52
Colour Marketing Group see CMG
colour theory 45–8
colour-ways 23, 238
colourfast fabrics 31, 33, 34, 35, 136, 203
colour(s) 45–59
   achromatic 54
   additive system 46, 48
   analogous 46
   associations 45, 49, 51
   blue colour palette *59*
   chroma 54
   chromatic 54
   CMYK system 54
   co-primary triads 54
   colour wheels 46, *47,* 47–8, *48*
   combining 53
   complementary 46, *47,* 48
   contrast 54
   cool colours 49
   forecasting 52, 245
   green colour palette *57*
   grey colour palette 54
   ground colour 38
   half tone 38
   harmony 54
   language of 51–4
   and light 45, 48, 52–3
   luminosity 46
   matching 52, 52–3
   monochromatic 46, 54
   morphing *120*
   muted 54, 79
   neutral 54
   palettes 54, *54, 56, 57, 58, 59*
   partitive system 46, 48
   pastels 54
   perception of 49
   pink colour palette *58*
   primary 46, *47,* 48
   primary triads 54
   red colour palette *58*
   samples 238
   saturation 46, 51
   secondary 46, *47,* 48
   secondary triads 54
   shades 54
   simultaneous contrast *50,* 51
   subtractive system 46, *47,* 48
   tertiary 46, *47*
   tints 54
   tones 51, 54
   trends 51
   triadic 46
   value 46
   visible spectrum *45,* 45–6, *47*

263

warm colours 49
warm/cool 49
white colour palette 56
yellow colour palette 57
see also hue
combing 13
cashmere 96
cotton 148, 149
wool 68, 69, 71, 85
Commision Internationale de L'Eclairage
see CIE
composite materials 168
Conféderation of Européenne du Lin et
du Chanvre (CELC) 134, 135
converters 32, 113, 222, 224, 237, 245
CORDURA® 194, 196, 196
corduroy 18, 21, 53, 162
corn fibre 183, 228, 228–9
cost considerations 38, 65, 158, 189, 238,
244, 246
cotton 63, 64, 142–65
American cotton 144, 145, 146, 146, 148,
150, 151
bolls 143, 143, 147, 147, 149, 155, 213
Bt cotton 153
carding 148, 149
classification 148, 149
combing 148, 149
cotton lisle 152
Creole cotton 150
cultivation 147, 147, 148
ecological considerations 152, 153–6, 155,
159, 160
Egyptian cotton 145, 150, 151, 176
ethical considerations 153, 156, 157–8,
158, 159, 159, 160, 246
fabrics 162–5
Fairtrade 156, 158, 158–60, 160
Filo Di Scozia® cotton 152
genetically-modified (GM) 153, 154, 160
harvesting 148, 149
history and geography 143–6
lint cotton 148, 149
linters 148, 149, 152, 213, 213, 214, 216, 218
luxury types 150–2
Madras cotton 165
market 146, 182
measuring 149
mercerized 151, 152
naturally-coloured 149, 155, 155–6, 156
organic 153, 153, 154, 156, 158, 159, 160,
160, 223
Pakucho™ cotton 149, 156
Pima cotton 150, 151, 155
processing 149
production 143, 144
recycled 153
Sea Island cotton 150, 151
seed cotton 149, 149
spinning 148, 149
sustainability considerations 152, 153, 154,
158, 158, 160
Tangüis cotton 151, 155
transitional 160
see also cupro fibre; denim
cotton gins 144, 148
Cotton Incorporated 153
cotton system (spinning) 14
cottonizing 139, 171
Courtelle™ 199

Cradle to Cradle 240–1
crease-resistant fabrics 43, 97, 118, 154,
195, 200
Creora® 205
crêpe
silk 117, 118, 125
wool 74, 74
yarn 14, 117
crêpe de Chine 117, 125, 125, 217
crépon 162
Creslan® 199
crimp 14, 66, 67, 76, 187
crinkle fabric 156, 162
crocheting 16, 27, 27
Crommelin, Louis 133
Cross, Charles 218
cuprammonium process 152, 217, 218
cupro fibre 152, 153, 213, 218
curaca fibre (llama) 90
cut pile fabrics 21
Cyanamid 199

DACRON® 10, 188, 189
damask 122, 131
daveo hemp 171, 178
Dawson, Joseph 96
de-gumming 117, 118, 119, 121, 169
de-hairing 91, 93, 96, 100
deccan hemp 172
Decitex 191
denier 22, 191, 201
denim 16, 43, 132, 143, 143, 153, 160, 162,
165, 172
Denim by Première Vision fabric trade fair 247
design process 6, 8, 237, 245, 246
design product management 245, 246
Despeissis, Louis-Henri 217
devoré 38, 39, 39
dhotis 145, 145
Dickson, James Tennant 189
Dietrich, Marlene 152
distributors 246
dogtooth designs see hound's-tooth designs
Donegal tweed 72, 73
double face fabrics 19, 19
DPF (denier per filament) 22
Dralon® 199, 201
drape of fabric 16, 21, 238
Dreyfus, Camille and Henri 215
drill 165
dromedaries (camels) 92
duchesse 118, 122, 123, 123
duck 165
dupion 123
DuPont 170, 189, 192, 195, 197, 198, 199, 201,
203, 205, 208, 216
dyeing 31–5, 245
acid dyes 35
aniline dyes 35
azo/azoic dyes 35, 52
basic dyes 35
batch dyeing 35
bleeding 35
changeant technique 35, 105
chrome dyes 35
continuous dyeing 35
dip dyeing 31, 32, 33
direct dyes 35
disperse dyes 35, 216
dye lots 31, 238

ecological considerations 34, 52, 79, 137,
155, 203, 222, 224
fabric-dyeing (piece-dyeing) 31, 32, 32,
118, 119
fugitive colours 35
garment dyeing 33–4, 165
hank-dyeing 35
lab dips 31, 32, 32
matches 35
off-shades 35
ombre effect 35
over-dyeing 34, 115, 162
piece-dyeing see fabric-dyeing
reactive dyes 34, 35
resist dyeing 21, 33, 33–4, 37, 38
shading 35
space dyeing 111
strike-offs 35
stripping 34
tendering 35
tie-dyeing 21, 34, 34
vat dyes 35
yarn-dyeing 31, 118, 119
see also batik; ikat technique; mordants
Dynel 200

easy-care fabrics 43, 64, 113, 132, 188, 195,
199, 199
Eco-fi fibre 192
Ecodear® 228
ecological considerations 10, 52, 238,
240–3, 244
alternative plant fibres 168, 169, 171, 172,
173, 175, 177
artificial fibres 152, 214, 216, 218, 221, 224,
227, 229, 231
cotton 152, 153–6, 155, 159, 160
dyeing 34, 52, 79, 137, 155, 203, 222, 224
linen 137, 140
luxury animal fibres 89, 90
man-made fibres 182, 183
silk 112, 121
synthetic fibres 188, 192, 192, 197, 201,
203, 209
wool 77, 79, 84, 188
see also sustainability considerations
eesit (Shetland wool colour) 79
elastane 14, 29, 183, 189, 204, 205–7, 206, 207
elastomers/elastomeric yarns 164, 204, 204,
205, 209 see also elastane
elephant cord 18
Elizabeth I, queen of England 108, 170
embroidery 40–2, 130, 135
canvas work 41
counted-thread 41
crewel-work 40
cross stitch 41
drawn-thread work 28, 130, 135
freehand 40
jari embroidery 210
machine 42
smocking 41, 41
Zari/Zardozi embroidery 210
see also appliqué; quilting
emerized fabrics 43
Empedocles 45
emsket (Shetland wool colour) 79
environmental considerations
see ecological considerations

enzymes 43, 118, 132, 138, 140, 173, 176, 227, 231
ESPA® 205
ethical considerations 238, 244
    alternative plant fibres *171, 175*
    cotton 153, 156, 157–8, *158,* 159, *159,* 160, *246*
    silk *52,* 121
    wool *77,* 84
    see also Fairtrade
ethical trading 159, 160
European Confederation of Linen and Hemp
    see Conféderation of Européenne du Lin et du Chanvre
Expofil trade fair 247

Fabric at Magic fabric trade fair 247
fabric construction techniques 16–30, 245, 246
fabric direction 16, 18, 35, 238
face (of fabrics) 16, 18, 19, *19,* 21, 22, 24
Fairtrade standards 156, *158,* 158–60, *160, 239,* 240–1
fashion industry 236–47
felt/felting 16, *25,* 25–6, *26,* 63
fibre designation codes 228, 239
fibrefill *see* wadding
fibres 13
filaments 14, 116, 187, *187,* 190
finishing processes 43, 118, 120, 245
fire-retardant fabrics 43, 67, 118, 154
flame-resistant fabrics *see* fire retardant fabrics
flannel 16, *70,* 74, *75*
flannelette 162
flax 136, *136*
    cottonizing 139
    cultivation 131, 132, 133, 134, 136, 137, 138–9, 140
    drafting 138, 140
    hackling 138, 140
    harvesting 138, *139*
    retting 138, 140
    rippling 138, *139*
    scutching 138, *139*
    threshing 13, 138, 140
    tow 138, *139*
    see also linen
Flemish linen 130, 134
Ford, Henry 230
fossil fuels 182, 183, 186, 229, 233
    see also coal; oil; petroleum
fulling 25
Future Fabrics Expo textile fair *237*

gabardine 16, 72, 165
gamme 54
Gandhi, Mahatma 121, 145, *145*
garment technology 245, 246
gauze 117, 124, 163
gazar 124, *125*
genetically-modified (GM) plant fibres 153, 154, 160, 229, 240
geo textiles 168, 201
georgette 74, 124, *132*
gingham 165
ginning 144, 148, 149
Glen Urquhart check *72,* 73
Global Organic Textile Standard (GOTS) 225, 240–1
Global Recycle Standard 240–1
GM *see* genetically-modified plant fibres

goats/goat fibre *87,* 94–9
    see also cashmere; mohair
'golden fleeces' 87, *87*
GORE-TEX® 194, 195, *195*
grain of fabric 21
green chemistry 239, 244
Greenfil® 233, *233*
greige (undyed) 32
guanacos/guanaco fibre *87,* 91
Guanqi Li 230

habotai 117, 124, *124*
halo effect (angora) *102,* 103, *103*
handle of fabric 21, 70, 129, 238
Hanford, William 205
hanks 14, 69, 141
Harris tweed 72, *72, 73*
header cards 237, *239*
Hearst, William Randolph 170
hemp *167,* 168, *170,* 170–2, *171, 223*
henduan yaks 100
Henry IV, king of England 108
Herodotus 144
herringbone designs 16, *17, 72,* 73
hessian 168
Hikota, Dr Toyohiko 191
Himalayan mountain goat 94
Holmes, Donald 205
hopsack 73, 165
hound's-tooth designs 16, *17,* 73, *73*
Hsi-Ling, Lady 105
huacaya fibre (alpaca) *88,* 89
huarizo fibre (alpaca) 89
hue 46, 47, 48, *54*
Huguenots 108, 133
hypoallergenic fabrics 89, 152, 209, 216, *223*

ICA (International Colour Authority) 52
Idea Como fabric trade fair 247
ikat technique 21, *21,* 34, 111, *111*
importers 237
indigo 35, 165, *165*
Indigo trade fair 247
industrial hemp 170, 172
Industrial Revolution 31, 64, 108, 131, 134, 144, 155
Ingeo™ yarns 228, *229*
inlaid yarn 24
insulative fabrics 25, 42, 63, 66, 74, 95, 114, 201, 202, 209
intarsia technique 23, *23*
Intercot trade fair 247
International Colour Authority *see* ICA
International Wool Textile Organization *see* IWTO
internet 237
Interstoff fabric trade fairs 247
Intertextile fabric trade fair 247
INVISTA 195, *196,* 205
Irish linen *133,* 133–4
Irish Linen Guild *133,* 134
Italian linen 135
Itten colour wheel 47, *47*
IWTO (International Wool Textile Organization) *83,* 84, 240–1

Jacquard, Joseph 20, 108
Jacquard technique *18,* 20, *20,* 24, *24, 40,* 108, 122, *122, 133*
Jaeger, Dr Gustave 77
Japantex fabric trade fair 247

jersey 15, 24, 32, 125, *150, 175, 190*
jerseywear 22, *22*
JIT (just-in-time) production 38
jiulong yaks 100
jobbers 237
John Smedley Mill, Derbyshire *144*
Johnstons of Elgin *95,* 96
jumbo cord 18
jute 168, *169*

kapok 114
karakul (Persian lamb) 66, 81
katazome 33
kenaf 172
Kevlar® 189, 197, 198
khadi cloth 110, 145, *145*
'King Cotton' 145, 170
knitting/knitwear 16, 22–4, 245
    Aran knitwear 23, *23,* 66, *66, 103*
    Argyle (Argyll) knitwear 23, *23*
    cable knitting 24
    circular knitting 24
    course 24
    cut-and-sew knitwear 24
    double jersey 24
    Fair Isle knitwear 23, *23, 84*
    fully-fashioned knitwear 20, 22, 23
    gauge 22
    inlaid yarn 24
    intarsia technique 23, *23*
    Jacquard technique 24, *24*
    jersey 24
    lace knitting 29
    plain stitch *22,* 24
    plated knitting 24
    purl stitch *22,* 24
    single jersey 24
    stiitches *22,* 24
    tuck stitch 24
    welt 24
Kolbe, Adolph Wilhelm Hermann 185
Kwolek, Stephanie 197

lace-making 16, 28–9, *29,* 130, 131, 135
    bobbin lace 29, *29,* 130
    cutwork lace 29
    lace knitting 29
    machine-made lace 29
    needle lace 29, 130
    tatting 29
Lactron® 228
lamé 210
lamination 146, 195, 196, 209, 211
Lanatil 232
lanolin 23, 66, 67
lanuda fibre (llama) 90
laser cutting and engraving 39, *39, 211*
latex 204, 205, 208, *208, 233*
lawn 164
LEA (linen measurement) 141
LEACRIL® 199
lead times 31, 38, 238
leaf fibres 178–9
Lenpur® 232, *232*
Lenzing AG 176, 221, 222, 224, *224*
Leonardo da Vinci 48, 117
light and colour 45, 48, 52–3
lignin 168, 218, 227
linear polyamides *see* nylon
Linel® 205

linen 28, 128–41, 167
    bleaching 129, 133, 136
    ecological considerations 137, 140
    fabric properties 129
    fibre properties 136
    finishing 136
    history and geography 129–35
    lace/lace-making 28, 28, 130, 131, 135
    market 135
    measuring 136
    production 138–41
    spinning 134, 138, 141
    staple 136
    synthetic 129
    see also flax
Linen Board, Ireland 134
linseed see flax
lisle (cotton) 152
Litrax-1® bamboo 176
Living Linen Project, Ireland 134
llamas/llama fibre 14, 87, 90, 90
Loden fabric 25, 74, 74
loop-back fabrics 18, 22
loop pile fabrics 21
Louis XI, king of France 108
LUREX™ 65, 69, 210, 211
luxury animal fibres 86–103
LYCRA® 65, 164, 204, 205, 206, 207, 209
lyocell fibres 176, 177, 183, 218, 220–7
LZR Racer® swimsuit 206, 206

macramé 16, 30, 30
Made-By 240–1
'make do and mend' ethos 85
man-made fibres 182, 182–3 see also artificial
    fibres; synthetic fibres
Manila hemp 171, 178
manufacturing 245, 246
marl yarns 14, 15
mashru cloth 110
mauvine dye 31
Maxwell, James Clerk 46
Mazzucchelli, Santino 214, 215
mélange fabrics 13, 14, 15, 69, 190
melton fabric 74, 75
Mercer, John 151
mercerizing 43, 151, 152
meta-aramid fibres 197, 198
metallic yarns 14, 70, 70, 89, 122, 122, 183,
    210, 210–11, 211
metallizing 211
Metlon metallic yarns 211
microfibres 10, 188, 191, 204
micronaires (cotton measurement) 149
microns 65, 68, 76, 90, 97, 99, 136
microsuede 190
milk fibre 183
milk fibre (casein) 232, 232, 233
Milkofil® 232
Milkotton 232
Milkwood 232
mill washing 43
milling (fabric treatment) 43
mills 43, 237, 238, 245
minimums (fabric orders) 238
Moda in Tessuto e Accesori fabric trade fair 247
Modacrylic fibres 183, 200
Modal® 183, 221, 224
Modatisimo fabric trade fair 247
moget (Shetland wool colour) 79

mohair 75, 87, 96–8, 97, 98, 99, 99, 102, 103
moiré 123, 123, 215
moisture-absorbent fabric 67, 129, 143, 174,
    189, 193, 214, 216, 225, 231
moleskin 162
mommes (silk measurement) 117
moodboards 53, 237
mordants 34, 35, 118
Moroccan fabric 74
moso bamboo 174, 175
mousseline 74
mungo 81
Munsell colour wheel 48, 48
musk ox see qiviut
muslin 163

nanofibres 188, 191, 193
Nanofront® 188, 191
nap of fabric 21
napa/nappa (sheep leather) 67
Natta, Giulio 201, 203
NatureWorks® 228
needlepoint 41
neoprene 208, 208, 209, 209
nettle fibre 167, 169, 172, 172
Newton, Sir Isaac 45
Nieuwland, Julius 208
nigora goats 87, 99
noils 13, 115
Nomex® 196, 197
nylon 10, 112, 183, 185, 186, 189, 194,
    194–7, 206
nylons (stockings) 112, 112, 185, 186, 194,
    195, 197

OE standards 239, 242–3
Oeko-Tex® Standards 175, 183, 242–3
oil 10, 182, 185, 186, 189, 200, 210, 214, 244
oiled finishes 43, 146
Okamoto, Dr Miyoshi 191
olefin fibres 183, 201–3
organdie 151
Organic Content Standards (OCS) 242–3
Organic Exchange see OE standards
organic fibres 84, 153, 153, 154, 156, 158,
    159, 160, 160
organza 16, 117, 124, 200, 203
organzine 117
Orlon® 10, 199

paco vicuñas 91
Panama fabric 73
Pantone Professional System 53
para-aramid fibres 197, 198
pashmina shawls 94
pattern cutting 158, 229, 245, 246
Payen, Anselm 214
peau de soie 123
Perlon 185, 194
Persian lamb 66, 81
Peru Moda trade fair 247
PET (polyethylene terephthalate) 189, 192, 239
petit point 41
petroleum 35, 185, 188, 189, 195, 209
piece of fabric 21
pigment colour wheel 47, 47
pigments 31, 45, 47
piña cloth 178
piqué/piquette 156
Pitti Imagine Filati trade fair 247

plaids see tartans
Plastiloid® 214
ply 14, 15
polyalkene 201
polyamides 170, 183, 194–7, 207
    see also nylon
polyamides, aromatic see aramid fibres
polyester 64, 82, 154, 183, 186, 186, 188,
    188–93, 189, 200
polyethylene 183, 201, 202, 203
polymers/polymerization 183, 185, 186, 186–7,
    187, 189, 190, 197, 203
polyolefin fibres see olefin fibres
polypropylene 183, 201, 202, 203
polyurethane 183, 204–7, 205, 209
poplin 132, 163, 165
Prato Expo fabric trade fair 247
pre-shrunk fabrics 43, 112, 147
Première Vision fabric trade fair 52, 237, 247
pressing 120, 136
Prince of Wales check 72, 73
printing techniques 36–9
    devore 38, 39, 39
    digital 38, 39, 49
    discharge 38
    dry prints 37
    flock 38
    glitter 38
    hand-block 36, 36
    heat-transfer 37
    metallic 38
    mordant 38
    over-printing 38
    pigment 38
    placement 38, 38
    print runs 37, 238
    rollers 37, 38
    rotary-screen 37
    silk-screen 36, 36, 37, 37
    transfer 37, 38
    wet prints 37
Printsource trade fair 247
process colour wheel 47
ProModal® 224
PTFE (polytetrafluoroethylene) 195
puppy-tooth designs 73
pygora goats 87, 99

qiviut 101, 101
QMilch® 232
quality control (QC) 245, 246
quilting 42, 42, 114, 190

rabbits see angora rabbits
raffia 178, 178, 179
Rama V, king of Thailand 111
ramie 169, 169
rayon 112, 185, 206, 217 see also lyocell fibres;
    viscose rayon
recycling
    natural fibres 81, 85, 85, 115, 153
    synthetic fibres 191, 192, 192, 193, 195,
    197, 203, 208, 208, 209
    see also up-cycling
repeats 38
repp 165
retting 138, 140, 168, 173
reversible fabric 21, 122
rice paste 33, 33

Useful information

ripstop nylon 194, 196, *196*
Röhm, Otto 199
roketsuzome 33
Roundup Ready® 153
roves 138, 140
rovings 14, *68*, 148, 149
ruffs 130, *131*
runs of fabric 38

'S' twist 14, *15*
sales process 245, 246
samite 210
sample lengths 238
samples/sampling 31, 237, 238, 245, 246
saris 110, *110*
sateen 18, 72, 164
satin 16, 18, *20*, 53, 123, *125*, 164
S.Café® yarn 188, 193
Schweizer, Eduard 217
SCOTDIC (Standard Color of Textile Dictionnaire Internationale de la Couleur) 53
Seacell® 183, 221, 225, *225*
seasonal industrial process 245
seaweed 221, 225, *225*
seersucker 162
SEF 200
selvedges 18, 21
serge 16, 72
sericulture 105, 106–7, 109, 111, 116–20, 121
Setilithe® 214
shaela (Shetland wool colour) 79
Shanghai Tenbro® 174, 177
shantung *111*, 123
shatoosh shawls 102
sheep
    ecological/ethical considerations 84
    French merino 79
    hair sheep 67
    Icelandic 81
    Karakul 81
    merino 64, 76, *76*, 77, 82
    Rambouillet sheep 79
    shearing 68
    Shetland 79
    Wensleydale 63
    wool sheep 67
    see also wool
shibori *105*
Shinawatra, Thaksin 111
Shivers, Joseph 205
shoddy (recycled wool) 85, *85*
shot fabrics 35, *105*
shower-proofing 43
silk *13*, 104–25, 152
    Ahimsa peace silk 121
    art (artificial) silk 112, 152, 185, 217, 218
    bleaching *117*, 118
    breaking 117, 120
    calendering 120
    care 120
    de-gumming *117*, 118, 119, 121
    ecological considerations 112, *121*
    eri silk *52*, 121
    ethical considerations *52*, 121
    fabrics 122–5
    fibre properties 114
    fibrillated silk 112
    finishing 118, 120
    history and geography 105–13
    lustering 120, 122

maceration (cooking) 117, 119
market 112, 113
measuring 117
mudmee 111
muga silk 121
noils 115
peace silk 119, 121
pressing 120
production 105–11, 116–20, 121
pure dye silk 118
raw silk 106, 107, 108, 109, 112, 115, *115*, 117
recycled *115*
reeling 105, 117, 119
sand-washing 113, *113*
spider silk 115
spinning 117, 119
sueding 112
synthetic 105, 109, 112
tamponing 120
throwing 117, 119
tram 117
tussah silk *115*, 121, 123, *168*
weighting 118
wild silk 106, 114, 121, 123
The Silk Road 106–8, *107*, 109, 111, 210
silkworms/silk moths 105–6, 107, 111, 114, 116–17, 119, 121
    Bombyx mori 106, 114, 116, *116*, 119
    eri silk moths 121
    muga silk moths 121
    tassah/tassar silk moths 121
    Thai silk moths 121
    yamami silk moth 109
Singtex® 193, *193*
Sirikit, queen of Thailand 111
skeget (Shetland wool colour) 79
skeins 14
skjuret (Shetland wool colour) 79
slivers 140, *140*, 148, 149
smocking 41, *41*
Soil Association 241, 242–3
Sorona® 188, 192, 228
sourcing fabrics 237–9
soya fibre 183, *230*, 230–1, *231*
SOYSILK® 230
spandex 204
spider silk 115
spinnerets
    artificial fibre production 216, 217, 218, 227, 228, 232
    plant fibre production 152, 176
    in silkworms 116, 187
synthetic fibre production 185, 187, *187*, 190, 197, 198, 201, 203, 207
spinning 14, 245
    cotton 148, 149
    linen 134, 138, 141
    synthetic fibres 185, 187, *187*, 190, 198, 201, 207
    wool 63, 64, 68, *68*, 69–70
spinning frames *14*, 144
spinning Jenny 144
Sportswool™ 67
Standard Color of Textile Dictionnaire Internationale de la Couleur *see* SCOTDIC
standards 53, 82, *83*, *121*, *175*, *183*, 193, *225*, 239, 240–3 *see also* Fairtrade
Staudinger, Professor Dr Hermann 185
steaming 120, 136, 201

stem fibres 174, 175
stock houses 237
stockings 98, 112, *112*, 152, 185, 186, 194, 195, 197, 215
stretch fabrics 204, 205
Suncoco metallic yarns 211
Sunn hemp 172
Supima® 151, *151*, 176
suppliers 32, 237, 245, 246
supply chains 159, 240, 245
surface decoration 36–42
suri fibre (alpaca) *88*, 89
sustainability considerations 10, *237*, 238, 244
    alternative plant fibres 167, 168, 169, *169*, 172, 173, 174, 175, *175*, 177
    artificial fibres 152, 214, 216, 220, 221, 222, 224, 227, 229, 231
    cotton 152, 153, *154*, 158, *158*, 160
    man-made fibres 182
    synthetic fibres 188, 192, 197, 201, 203, 209
swatches 238
sweater-knits 22
synthetic fibres 10, 13, 183, 184–211
    defined 182, 185
    ecological considerations 188, 192, *192*, 197, 201, 203, 209
    fibre properties 187, 189, 195, 198, 200, 202, 205, *205*, 209, 211
    history 185–6, 189, 194, 197, 199, 201, 205, 208, 210
    linen 129
    market 186
    production 185, 187, 190, 197, 198, 201, 203, 207, 209, 211
    recycling *191*, 192, *192*, *193*, 195, 197, *203*, 208, *208*, 209
    silk 105, 109, 112
    spinning 185, 187, *187*, 190, 198, 201, 207
    sustainability considerations 188, 192, 197, 201, 203, 209
    wool 64, 65, 67
synthetic rubber 183, 208–9

TACTEL® 194, 195, 197
taffeta 16, 118, 123, *124*
tailoring 246
tapada fibre (llama) 90
target customers 84, 150, 238
tartans 16, 73, *73*
Tattersall check 73, *73*
technology 10, 65, 138, 174, 191, 245, 246
    see also biotechnology
Technora® 197
Teijin 191, *191*, 192, *192*
Teijinconex® 197
TENCEL® 176, 183, 221, *221*, 222, 223, 224, *224*, 226
Terylene 10, 64, 88, 189
testing *83*, *175*, *183*, 206, 238
Tex 22
Texbridge fabric trade fair 247
textile certificates 240–3
Texworld fabric trade fairs 247
thermo-regulating fabric 92, 137, *207*, 233
Thinsulate™ 201, 202
Thompson, Jim 111, *111*
Tibetan antelopes/antelope fibre 102
ticking 165
toile 165
Toray Industries Japan 191

tow 14, 190
towelling 21, 162
trade fairs 72, 237, *237, 245, 246*
Trevira PES fibres *186*
triacetate 183, 214, 216
Tricel™ 214, 216
Triexta fibres 192
tsutsugaki 33
tulle 124, *124, 141, 188*
Turkish Fashion Fabrics fabric trade fair 247
Twaron® 197
tweed *17*, 53, 69, *70*, 70–1, 72, *72, 73, 75, 162*
twill 16, *16, 17*, 72, *72, 73*, 118, 165, *165*
    cavalry twill 16, 72
    left-hand/right hand 21
twist 14, *15*, 69, 70
Tyvek® 201, 202, *202*, 203

Ultrasuede® 188, 191
union fabric 21, 134
up-cycling *17, 28, 41, 161, 188, 203, 206*
USPs (unique selling points) 84, 150
UV-resistant fabrics 168, 176, 193, 228, 231

valenki *25*
Vaucanson, Jacques de 108
velour 162
velvet 18, *19*, 21, 53, *113*, 122, 162, *179*
velveteen 162
Venetian fabric 72
Verel 200
vicuñas/vicuña fibre *87*, 91
viscose *18, 122*, 152, 154, *162, 164, 167*, 175,
    217, *217 see also* bamboo viscose;
    viscose rayon
viscose rayon 175, 183, *213*, 217–18
    see also rayon
visual colour wheel 48, *48*
voile 163

wadding 42, 143, 190
wales 16, 18
warp threads *15*, 16, *16, 18*
Washington, George 170
water-repellant/resistant fabrics 16, 43, *66, 67*,
    146, 195, *195*
wax
    as a finish 43, 146
    in resist dyeing 33, *33*, 38
    weaving/weaves *15*, 16–21, 245
    basket weave 16, *179*
    double-cloth weaving 19, *19*
    jamawar weave 110
    kasuri weaving 21
    oshima weaving 21
    pile weaving 18
    plain weave 16, *16, 20*, 165
    sateen weaves 18, 72
    satin weaves 16, 18, *20*, 164
    taffeta weaves 16
    tapestry weaving 20
weft-faced weaving 20
weft threads *15*, 16, *16, 18*
welt (knitwear) 24
Whinfield, John Rex 189
White, Jim 201
Whitney, Eli 144
wicking properties 67, 97, 174, 191, 200, 201,
    206, *207, 214*, 216
WINDSTOPPER® 195

WIO *see* IWTO
"Wonderland" exhibition, 2008 10
wood *167*, 168, 213, *213*, 214, 218, 220, *221*,
    224, 226
wool *13*, 62–85
    Botany wool 78
    carding 63, 68, 69, 71, 85
    classification 65, 68, 76
    combing 68, 69, 71
    crimp 66, *67*, 76
    drawing/finisher drawing 68, *68*, 69
    ecological/ethical considerations 77, 79,
    84, 188
    fabrics 72–5
    fibre properties 66–7, *67*
    grease-wool 68
    history 63–5
    homespun 64
    Icelandic wool 81
    karakul (Persian lamb) 66, 81
    lambswool 68, 76
    market/marketing 82–3, *182*
    measuring 65, 68, 76
    merino *25*, 64, 66, *67*, 76–9, *78*, 82, *82*, 176
    Mongolian wool *79*
    organic 84
    production 68–75
    recycled 81, 85, *85*
    resilience 67
    scouring 68
    Shetland wool *23*, 79, *80*
    spinning 63, 64, 68, *68*, 69–70
    staple 76
    synthetic 64, 65, 67
    terminology 81
    underwear 77, *77*
    woollen spun yarn 70
    Woolmark 82, *83*
    worsted 71, *71*
    worsted spun yarn 71, 74
    yarn count 69
    see also knitting; sheep
Woolmark 82, *83*
wrinkle-free fabrics *see* crease-resistant fabrics

yaks/yak hair *87*, 100, *100*
yarn count *15*, 141
Yarn Expo trade fair 247
yarns 13
yuzen 33

'Z' twist *15*
Zentai clothing 204, *204*
Zero Waste pattern-cutting *158, 229*
Ziegler, Karl 201, 203

Photo credits

Cover Courtesy Yiqing Yin, photo by Laurence Laborie; p.8 ©Amanda Johnston & Myka Baum; p.9 courtesy Somarta, Art Direction & CG by SOMA Design, photo by Misuaki Koshizuka (MOREVISION), hair by Jun Matsumoto (tsuji management), make-up by Mariko Tagayashi (M.A.C); p.11 courtesy Helen Storey, Wonderland: Disappearing Dresses, a work in progress by artist/designer Helen Storey, London College of Fashion, scientist Tony Ryan, University of Sheffield and in association with Interface, University of Ulster, 29/01/08, photograph ©Alex Maguire; p.12 ©Myka Baum; p.13 photos ©Myka Baum; p.14 (top) ©istockphoto/tankbmb, (centre) ©istockphoto/danishkhan, (bottom left and right) courtesy Doris & Walter Van Buskirk, Lightfoot Farms LLC, Kennebunk, Maine, Alpaca Breeders; p.15 courtesy Julien David, photo © Yannis Vlamos; p.16 all photos ©Myka Baum; p.17 (top left) courtesy Blow PR, design by Ashish, photograph by Ian Gillett, (top right) courtesy Derek Lam, photograph by Dan Lecca, (centre left) courtesy Linton Tweeds Ltd©, www.lintondirect.com, (centre right) ©Myka Baum, (bottom) courtesy GARYHARVEYCREATIVE, photograph by Robert Decelis, model: Tabitha Hall at Models1; p.18 all photos ©Myka Baum; p.19 (top) courtesy Ioannis Dimitrousis, photograph by catwalking.com, (centre) photograph courtesy of Gloverall, (bottom) courtesy of Gloverall, photograph by L.A. Litchfield; p.20 courtesy CELC Masters of Linen, Confédération Europénne du Lin et du Chanvre; (right) courtesy Alexander McQueen, S/S 2007, photograph by Chris Moore; p.21 courtesy Tamerlane's Daughters, photograph by Philip James; p.22 all photos ©Myka Baum; p.23 (top left) courtesy SANS, photograph by Uli Holz www.ulihoz.com, makeup and hair by Kristin Hilton www.kristin-hilton.com, model: Megi Xhidra at Fusion Models NYC, (bottom left) ©Myka Baum, (top right) Paul Harness, design by Hildigunnur Sigurdardottir, (centre right) courtesy Blow PR, design by Ashish, photograph by Ian Gillett, (bottom right) courtesy James Long, photograph by Chris Moore; p.24 courtesy Alexander McQueen, spring 2005, photograph by Chris Moore; p.25 (top) ©istockphoto/AlexKhrom, (centre and bottom) ©Myka Baum; p.26 (top and right) courtesy Ravensbourne College of Design and Communication, design by Su Pei Ho, (bottom) courtesy Anne Kyyrö Quinn©, design: Block, material 100% felt; p.27 (top) courtesy Olek, performance by Olek for "Two Continents and Beyond: Waterways", photograph by Olek and Miranda Lloyd, www.agataolek.com, (bottom) courtesy Olek; p.28 (left) courtesy Marina Shlosberg, photograph by Mike Figgis, hair and make-up by Ashliie Kuck, model: Holly (Independent), Jewellery by Pebble, London, (top right) courtesy Rachael Cassar, photograph by Jessica Cassar, (bottom) ©Myka Baum; p.29 (right) photograph by Georgina McNamara©, (left top and bottom)

courtesy Anne Wilson, Rhona Hoffman Gallery, Chicago and Paul Kotula Projects, Detroit, design by Anne Wilson© 2008 Topologies, detail 2002-08, lace, threads, insect pins, wood support; p.30 courtesy James Long, photograph by Chris Moore; p.31 courtesy Ta-ste, fashion by www.ta-ste.com - Tanja Steuer, photo by www.franziskapruetz.com - Franziska Prütz, make-up: www.juliaprimus.com - Julia Primus, model: Jenny Feuerstein; p.32 (top) ©istockphoto/DesignGeek-1, (centre) ©Myka Baum, (bottom left) ©shutterstock/paul prescott, (bottom right) ©istockphoto/mandygodbehear; p.33 (top) courtesy Kamila Gawronska-Kasperska, www.kamilagawronska.com, photo by Bartek Sejwa, http://sejwa.com, model: Victoria Evseeva(bottom left) courtesy Isabella Whitworth, (bottom right) ©shutterstock/Imagemaker; p.34 courtesy Isabella Whitworth; p.35 catwalking.com; p.36 (top left and bottom left) Pete Loud, (top) courtesy Undercover - Jun Takahashi©, (bottom) courtesy Ioannis Dimitrousis, photograph by catwalking.com; p.37 (top) courtesy Screencraft Speciality Printing, (centre and bottom) courtesy Print House Inc. www.printhouse.org, photograph by Aleta Reese; p.38 ©Myka Baum; p.39 (top) AFP/Getty Images, (bottom left) courtesy Hayley Cheal, (bottom centre) catwalking.com, (bottom right) courtesy Kamila Gawronska-Kasperska, www.kamilagawronska.com; p.40 (left) courtesy Blow PR, design by Ashish, photograph by Ian Gillett, (right) courtesy Colette Vermeulen, photo by Saty and Pratha, model: Brynja at Next, Styling: Chad Burton, Hair byTomohiro, Muramtsu, make up by Masato Inoue; p.41(top) courtesy Josep Font, Couture A/W 08/09, (left) courtesy Rachael Cassar, photograph by Jessica Cassar, (bottom) courtesy Carta e Costura, photo by Max Botticelli; p.42 (top) courtesy Vivienne Westwood, S/S 09 'Do It Yourself', (bottom) courtesy Julien David, photo by Yannis Vlamos, (right) courtesy Ichiro Suzuki, photo by Kodai; p.44 courtesy Guerra de la Paz©, Tribute, 2002-2006, mix media sculpture with assorted clothing, collection of Richard Harris; p.45 courtesy Blow PR, design by Basso & Brooke, S/S 2006, photograph by Fernada Calfat; p.46 all ©Myka Baum; p.49 courtesy Ichiro Suzuki, photo by Kodai; p.50 ©Myka Baum; p.52 courtesy Isabella Whitworth; p.53 ©Myka Baum; p.55 fashion shots clockwise from top left, courtesy Noir A/S©, photograph by Marc Hom©; courtesy Timothy Everest Bespoke Fitting; courtesy Blow PR, design by Rui Leonardes; courtesy Georgina McNamara©; all other photos ©Myka Baum; p.56 fashion shots clockwise from top left, courtesy Gudrun Sjödén, photograph by Johan Hellsröm, model: Theresa; courtesy Noir A/S©, photograph by Marc Hom©; courtesy Kris Van Assche, photograph by Etienne Tordoir; courtesy Kris Van Assche, photograph by Gaetan Bernard; courtesy John Rocha S/S 2007, London Fashion Week, photograph by catwalking.com;

(bottom right) handwoven silk scarf by Sallie Temple, photograph by Paul Crossman; all other photos ©Myka Baum; p.57 fashion shots clockwise from top left, courtesy Blow PR, design by Bora Aksu, photograph by Ian Gillett; 'green nude' photograph by Fagner Bibiano©, www.fagnerbibiano.com; 'canvas tent detail' photograph by Georgina McNamara©; all other photos ©Myka Baum; p.58 fashion shots clockwise from top left, courtesy Blow PR, design by Ashish, photograph by Ian Gillett; courtesy Blow PR, design by Manish Arora, photograph by Yannis Vlamos; courtesy Pavel Ivancic, www.muset.cz; cochineal colour eri silk scarves courtesy Sabahar Ethiopia, photograph by Sabahar Addis Ababa; all other photos ©Myka Baum; p.59 fashion shots clockwise from top left, courtesy Kostas Murkudis, photograph by Fergus Padel, styling by Jodie Barnes; courtesy Maurizio Galante, photograph by Jean-Louis Coulombel; courtesy Noir A/S©, photograph by Marc Hom©; all others ©Myka Baum; p.62 ©Myka Baum; p.63 courtesy Angelika Werth; p.64 Advertising Archives; p.65 ©Myka Baum; p.66 (left top and bottom) photos ©Myka Baum, (right) catwalking.com, design by Natalie Jacobs; p.67 (left top and bottom) courtesy Australian Wool Innovation Limited, (right) ©Myka Baum; p.68 (top) courtesy Doris & Walter Van Buskirk, Lightfoot Farms LLC, Kennebunk, Maine, Alpaca Breeders, (bottom) ©Myka Baum; p.69 V&A images, Victoria and Albert Museum; p.70 (top) courtesy Michael Angel, photo by Christopher Katke, (centre) courtesy Kostas Murkudis, photograph by Fergus Padel, styling by Jodie Barnes, (right) ©Rodin Banica; p.71 (top) courtesy Nicholas K., (bottom left) courtesy Kris Van Assche, photograph by Gaetan Bernard, (bottom right) courtesy Blow PR, design by Edward Sexton, photograph by Ian Gillett; p.72 (top) Getty Images; (bottom left and right) ©Myka Baum; p.73 (top left) courtesy Mary Binding, (top right) Catwalking.com, (bottom left) ©Myka Baum (bottom right) courtesy Linton Tweeds Ltd©, www.lintondirect.com; p.74 (left) ©Rodin Banica, (right) courtesy Femme Maison, photo by Sia Kermani; p.75 (left) courtesy Alexander McQueen, A/W 2008, photograph by Chris Moore, (right) courtesy Haider Ackermann; p.76 courtesy John Smedley; p.77 courtesy IVANAhelsinki, photography by Ivo Corda; p.78 courtesy Michael Angel, photo by Christopher Katke; p.79 courtesy Huwaida Ahmed, photograph by Stelianour; p.80 courtesy Colenimo, photograph by Mitsuaki Murata, hair by Asashi (Caren), make-up by Natsumi Watanabe (Caren), (bottom) ©Myka Baum; p.81 courtesy Haider Ackermann; p.82 courtesy The New Zealand Merino Wool Company; p.83 (bottom right) courtesy International Wool Textile Organisation©, (all others) courtesy Australian Wool Innovation Limited, The Woolmark logos are reproduced with the permission of Australian Wool Innovation Limited, owner of

269

Photo credits

The Woolmark Company; p.84 ©Myka Baum; p.85 (left and right) ©Myka Baum, (centre) ©shutterstock/Christian McCarty; p.86 ©Myka Baum; p.88 (left) courtesy Marsha Hobert at Suri Network, (top right) Mark Dodge, (bottom right) ©istockphoto/NNehring; p.89 (all) courtesy Julia Neill (designer and creator), photograph by Chris Moore; p.90 ©istockphoto/aventurus; p.92 ©Myka Baum; p.93 (top) courtesy Timothy Everest, photograph by David Goldman, styling by James Sleaford, model: Simon Blackford, (bottom) ©Myka Baum; p.94 ©shutterstock/ yansherman; p.95 (top) courtesy Johnstons of Elgin, photograph by Chris Blott, styling by Linny Oliphant, (left) courtesy Armand Basi One, photograph by Ugo Camera, (bottom) photograph by Georgina McNamara©; p.96 ©shutterstock/Kitch Bain; p.97 ©Myka Baum; p.98 catwalking.com; p.99 courtesy Timothy Everest Bespoke Fitting; p.100 ©istockphoto/ Tomo75; p. 101(all) courtesy Large Animal Research Station, University of Alaska Fairbanks; p.102 (left) ©Myka Baum, (right) ©shutterstock/ Teresa Levite; p.103 (top) courtesy Elise Kim, photo by Peter Stigter, (left) catwalking.com, (bottom right) ©Myka Baum; p.104 courtesy Karren K. Brito; p.105 courtesy Blow PR, design by Manish Arora, photograph by Yannis Vlamos; p.106 (left) courtesy Paul Smith, design Paul Smith for Gainsborough Silks, (right) Vivienne Westwood, S/S 'Do It Yourself'; p.108 Jordan Tan / Shutterstock.com; p.109 Getty Images; p.110 courtesy Lakme India Fashion Week, design by Anand Kabra; p.111 (left) courtesy Etro, (right) courtesy Jim Thompson, 'Baphoun' £90 per metre, photograph by Hans Fonk; p.112 courtesy german-hosiery-museum. de, photograph by Michael Schoedel M.A.; p.113 (left) courtesy Vivian Westwood, S/S 09 'Do It Yourself', (right) courtesy Narciso Rodriguez; p.114 (left) courtesy ANTOINE PETERS S/S 2009 'To make an elephant out of a mosquito', photograph by Peter Stigter, (right) courtesy Etro; p.115 (top) courtesy A Détacher, photo by Elizabeth Lippman; (left and bottom) ©Myka Baum; p.116 (top left) Getty Images, (top right) ©Myka Baum, (bottom left) ©istockphoto/roset (bottom right) ©istockphoto/ VickieSichau; p.117 (left) courtesy Isabella Whitworth, (right) courtesy The Gainsborough Silk Weaving Co. Ltd; p.120 (top) courtesy ANTOINE PETERS A/W 2008-2009 'Fat people are harder to kidnap.', photograph by Peter Stigter, (left) ©istockphoto/Fyletto; p.121 courtesy Noir A/S©, photograph by Marc Hom©; p.122 (top left) courtesy Armand Basi One, photograph by Ugo Camera, (bottom left) courtesy Haider Ackermann, (bottom centre) courtesy Kostas Murkudis, photograph by Fergus Padel, styling by Jodie Barnes, (bottom right) courtesy Roksanda Ilincic A/W 2008; p.123 (left) V&A Images, Victoria and Albert Museum, (right) courtesy Haider Ackermann; p.124 (top) courtesy Alexander McQueen, S/S 2007, photograph by Chris Moore, (bottom left) courtesy Yiqing Yin, photo by Laurence Laborie, (bottom right) courtesy Nicholas K.; p.125 (top) courtesy Armand Basi One, photograph by Ugo Camera, (left) photofriday / Shutterstock.com, (bottom) courtesy Yiqing Yin, photo by Shoji

Fujii; p.128 ©Myka Baum; p.129 courtesy CELC Masters of Linen, Confédération Europénne du Lin et du Chanvre; p.130 ©Myka Baum; p.131 (top) courtesy Marc Le Bihan and his team, photographer: Tarek Chergui Wallace, Editor: Charlotte Rabiller, Model: Mrikoo Des, (bottom) courtesy Blow PR, design by Rui Leonardes; p. 132 courtesy Nicholas K.; p.133 (left and middle) courtesy John Rocha S/S 2007, London Fashion Week, photograph by catwalking.com, (right) courtesy Irish Linen Guild; p.135 (left) courtesy CELC European Confederation of Flax and Hemp, (right) courtesy Corneliani; p.136 courtesy CELC European Confederation of Flax and Hemp; p.137 courtesy Icona Vera, Galaxy Dress, Ultra-Strawberry Pink Linen Satin, photograph by Christian Lartillot; p.139 courtesy CELC European Confederation of Flax and Hemp; p.140 (top left) courtesy CELC European Confederation of Flax and Hemp, (top right) ©istockphoto/dononeg, (bottom) ©Myka Baum; p.141 courtesy Yiqing Yin, photo by Shoji Fujii; p.142 ©Myka Baum; p.143 (left) ©istockphoto/AM29, (right) courtesy Kuyichi, photograph by petrovsky & ramone; p.144 (left) ©istockphoto/KarenMassier, (right) courtesy John Smedley; p.145 Time & Life Pictures/Getty Images; p.147 ©istockphoto/tonda; p.148 courtesy of ars.usda.gov, United States Department of Agriculture, National Agricultural Library; p.149 (left) ©shutterstock, (right) photograph by and courtesy of Dr. James M. Vreeland, Jr. of Peru Naturtex Partners; p.150 courtesy Ria Thomas, photograph by Matt Easton; p.151 (left) courtesy Supima Design Competition, (right) courtesy Haider Ackermann; p.152 courtesy Kostas Murkudis, photograph by Fergus Padel, styling by Jodie Barnes; p.153 courtesy G-Star RAW C.V. ©; p.154 (left) courtesy H&M, (right) graphic ©Myka Baum; p.155 (top) courtesy Stella James, (bottom) ©Kate Burrows; p.156 courtesy Ecoyarns PTY Ltd, www.ecoyarns.com.au; p.157 courtesy A Détacher, photo by Randy Brooke; p.158 courtesy Elsien Gringhuis, photo by David Joosten, hair and makeup by Maaike Beijer for M.A.C @ Angelique Hoorn management, model Leyla @ Lindamodels; p.159 courtesy Noir A/S©, photo by Marc Hom©; p.160 (top) courtesy Kuyichi, photograph by petrovsky & ramone, (bottom) courtesy COMO NO www. como-no.fr, C&M Les Petits Bonheurs SARL, Candice Augereau, Boschat Emmanuelle, Arnaud Lafontaine; p.161 courtesy Blanq, Artist and creative director: Jeffrey WANG, Photographer: Liang SU, associate Creative Director: Caroline YANG @ BLANQ, Art Director: Wawa HO & Eddie TENG @ BLANQ, Hair Stylist: Ting SHIH @ FLUX, Make-up Artist: Shu-Ling Chien, Model: Shin @ STORM MODEL, Retoucher: Chinn, Photo Assistant: Naga CHANG & Yang LIN, Styling Assistant: XiaoBao; p.162 (left) courtesy Mary Binding, (right) courtesy Maria Francesca Pepe Jewellery-Wear Design, www.mfpepe.com; p.163 (right) catwalking.com, design by Nabil El Nayal, (left) courtesy Kris Van Assche, photograph by Gaetan Bernard, (bottom) courtesy Kris Van Assche, photograph by Etienne Tordoir; p.164 (top) Nayukko Yamamoto, (bottom) courtesy

Rebecca Thorpe Knitwear, Creative Director: Rob Phillips, Photo: Hill & Aubrey, assistant: John Seyer, www.hillandaubrey.com, Beauty Director: Pace Chen, assistant: Melissa Wong, www. pacechen.com; p.165 (top) courtesy Walter Van Beirendonck, photo by Dan Lecca, (bottom) courtesy A Détacher, photo by Elizabeth Lippman; p.166 ©Myka Baum; p.167 all ©Myka Baum; p.168 courtesy Rohit Khosla Foundation, New Delhi, photograph by Prabuddha Das Gupta; p.169 (left) ©Rodin Banica, (right) courtesy Saara Lepokorpi, photo by Ville Varumo; p.170 courtesy Elsien Gringhuis, photo by David Joosten, hair and makeup by Maaike Beijer for M.A.C @ Angelique Hoorn management, model Leyla @ Lindamodels; p.171 courtesy Sanyukta Shrestha, photo by Christopher Dadey; p.172 (left) courtesy G-Star RAW C.V. ©, (right) ©Myka Baum; p.173 ©Myka Baum; p.174 ©istockphoto/clu; p.175 courtesy Wear Chemistry; p.176 ©Myka Baum; p.177 photograph by Paul Morgan, design by Ada Zanditon; p.178 (left) ©Myka Baum, (right) Getty Images; p.179 (left) catwalking.com, design by Rachel Caulfield, (right) ©Rodin Banica; p.183 courtesy Wear Chemistry; p.184 ©istockphoto;p.186 (top) ©Myka Baum, (bottom) courtesy Trevira GmbH; p.187 (left) courtesy CeramTec International, (right) R.E. Litchfield/Science Photo Library; p.188 (left) courtesy Walter Van Beirendonck, photo by Dan Lecca, (right) courtesy ehrensache; p.189 courtesy London College of Fashion, Photo by: Christopher Agius Burke; MUA: Kayoko Kishi, Model: Leontine / First Model Management London; p.190 courtesy Corneliani; p.191 (top) courtesy Henri Lloyd Ltd, (bottom) ©Myka Baum; p.192 courtesy Henri Lloyd Ltd; p.193 all ©Myka Baum; p.194 all ©Myka Baum; p.195 photo ©Myka Baum; p.196 (top) ©Myka Baum, (centre left) courtesy Invista Textiles (UK) Ltd, (centre right) courtesy Invista Textiles (UK) Ltd, (bottom) ©Amanda Johnston & Myka Baum; p.198 ©Myka Baum; p.199 Advertising Archives; p.200 courtesy 1 Granary, design by Maia Bergman; p.202 courtesy Marian Schoettle©; p.203 courtesy Hayley Grundmann; p.204 (left) ©Corbis, (right) Eye Of Science/Science Photo Library; p. 205 courtesy Terra New York, photo by Lionel Koretzky; p.206 (left) courtesy Herve Leger, (right) courtesy London College of Fashion; p.207 (left) courtesy Sweaty Betty, (others) courtesy Invista Textiles (UK) Ltd; p.208 (top left) courtesy Matmarket, (top right) courtesy HIKO-MIZUNO college of jewelry, (bottom) ©Amanda Johnston & Myka Baum; p.209 (top left) catwalking.com, (top right) courtesy Eileen Pang, (bottom left) courtesy Matmarket, p.210 Advertising Archives; p.211 catwalking.com; p.212 ©Myka Baum; p.213 (left) ©shutterstock; p.214 Eye of Science/ Science Photo Library; p.215 (left) ©Myka Baum, (right) ©kojoku / Shutterstock; p.217 courtesy A Détacher, photo by Randy Brooke; p.219 courtesy Dinu Bodiciu, Photographer: Pearly, Model: Olivia-Fayne Lamb MUA, Hair: Eimear Sweeney; p.221 (left) ©shutterstock, (right) courtesy G-Star RAW C.V. ©; p.222 ©Myka Baum; p.223 (left) courtesy

Useful information

Acknowledgements

We would like to thank the following people:

For their technical expertise and images:
Nigel and Christine Maitland of Maitland
Designs, Marie Demaegdt at Masters of Linen,
Dr. James M. Vreeland, Jr. at Peru Naturtex,
Linda F. Learn at Class Act Fabrics.

For their generosity with images and their
contribution with information:
Cheryl Benda at Wild Turkey Felt Makers,
Nell Trotter at Blow PR, Marsha Hobert at Suri
Network, Johnstons of Elgin, Australian Wool
Innovation Limited, Ursula Hudson at London
College of Fashion.

For their original images and artwork assistance:
Nicholas Vivian, Artist, Georgina McNamara,
Artist–photographer, Fagner Bibiano, Artist–
photographer.

For consultation and support:
Dilys Williams, Director of the Centre for
Sustainable Fashion at the London College of
Fashion, Jess Lertvilai, Materials and Products
Coordinator at London College of Fashion and
Central St Martins, Nina Marenzi, Director of the
Sustainable Angle.

For researching and producing the sustainable
certifications chart:
Charlotte Turner, The Sustainable Angle

Myka Baum
www.seephotography.net
Very special thanks are reserved for Myka
Baum, whose original remit was to source
the broad variety of images needed for this
publication. Myka's tenacity, professionalism
and organization deserve much credit,
but it is her acute interpretative sense and
proactive creative input that has exceeded
our original expectations of her role. She has
worked tirelessly to generate original imagery
and produced many specially commissioned
photographs, for which we are profoundly
grateful.

Lastly, we would like to thank our publisher
Laurence King and his team, especially
Helen Evans, Susie May, Sara Goldsmith
and Roger Fawcett-Tang.

This book is dedicated to
Ron Johnston 1930–2008

272